Firearms
Encyclopedia

An Outdoor Life Book

Firearms
Encyclopedia

by George C. Nonte, Jr.

OUTDOOR LIFE

HARPER & ROW
New York, Evanston, San Francisco, London

Designed by Jeff Fitschen

Contents

Introduction

The sporting use of firearms is nearly as old as firearms themselves, just as explosives were used for entertainment before ever being applied to destruction. When "gonnes" came along, man was already long accustomed to using his bow, lance, knife, sword, and other weapons for pleasure and for acquiring game to stock his larder. Old accounts are replete with references to games of skill played with tools and instruments that could also be used for war or defense. Firearms certainly didn't change this. As soon as guns could be made sufficiently portable and efficient, men used them in shooting matches and for hunting.

While the social structures of the Old World effectively prevented the average citizen from engaging in sport shooting, such wasn't the case in America. In the colonies a firearm of some sort was essential to every male able to carry and use it. Women did their share of shooting, too, when the occasion demanded.

City dwellers gradually gave up carrying guns as settlements grew, but 17th and 18th century suburbanites, farmers, trappers, post riders, coachmen, and frontiersmen kept their guns near them day and night. And with little else to entertain them, early Americans held shooting matches as often as ammunition and safety permitted. Shooting game to keep the belly filled was essential to survival, but it was also as much sport to them as were the hunting-party forays of the Indians.

With that background, long before the long-rifle, powder horn, and tomahawk ceased to be a vital daily necessity, shooting for pleasure had become an ingrained American characteristic. When a man no longer needed a gun on his plow, it was still taken down off the wall and lovingly prepared for holidays, weddings, church socials, fairs, and other occasions always livened by well-attended "shooting the mark." Beef shoots, turkey shoots, 20-rod and 40-rod guns, shooting the cross, shooting to center—all these became so much a part of the American scene that they remain today as common terms and expressions to be heard almost daily in large areas of this country. Sport shooting today covers a multitude of games from BB-guns in the basement or garage to 40-pound bench guns, triggered by remote control, which are capable of incredible accuracy.

When a gun of some sort was every man's constant companion, most people knew and used regularly most of the appropriate terms and phrases. Today, though, this is no longer true, and there is need of a single-source reference explaining and illustrating the terms generally used by the true enthusiast.

Toward that end we have prepared this book, and we hope it will serve you well.

Firearms
Encyclopedia

Abutment The shoulder in the receiver or barrel extension which supports the locking lugs in locked condition.

ACP An abbreviation for Automatic Colt Pistol, and used in the designation of cartridges developed for Colt autoloading pistols, .32 ACP, .38 ACP, .45 ACP, etc. It is marked on pistols chambered for those cartridges. It is also sometimes found on older guns and in older references as A.C.P. or C.A.P.

Action The heart of any gun, consisting of the receiver, bolt or breech block, feed mechanism, and firing mechanism. It is by far the most complex portion of any firearm, and serves as the major assembly to which barrel, magazine, sights, stock, etc., are assembled.

Typical Mauser-type turnbolt action.

1

The action is also the component which, by law, must be serial-numbered for record keeping and for payment of federal excise tax on new guns.

Generally speaking, the action contains over 90 per cent of the working parts of any firearm, and represents the bulk of the gun's cost.

There are many action types: as applied to shoulder guns, we have falling block, break open, tipping block, bolt, lever, pump, and autoloading. All are described separately elsewhere in this volume under their own headings and in some detail.

The word action is often applied synonymously with the term *lockwork* in reference to handguns.

See also BOLT ACTION, LEVER ACTION, PUMP ACTION, SEMI-AUTOMATIC.

Accurize   The process of improving the accuracy of a handgun or rifle by improving the fit and function of moving parts, refining bedding, improving trigger pull, adding better sights, etc. Particularly, in autoloading handguns and rifles, a substantial improvement in accuracy can usually be achieved.

The Win-Choke, typical of the interchangeable-tube type in which the different choke tubes are fully enclosed within the barrel, thus retaining the same appearance and weight and balance.

Adjustable Choke   A device attached to or built into the muzzle of a shotgun barrel to allow the shooter to change from one choke to another quickly. Often found installed or manufactured in conjunction with a compensator or muzzle brake.

Adjustable chokes are available in two basic forms. The oldest consists of thin-wall, threaded tubes screwed to the muzzle, or to the compensator or other installation device.

The best known of this *interchangeable-tube* type is the original Cutts Compensator, designed by Colonel Richard M. Cutts and later manufactured by Lyman Gun Sight Co. A large combination compensator and muzzle brake was firmly brazed or silver-soldered to the barrel, and interchangeable external tubes were then screwed into the muzzle of the compensator. Generally, it used short tubes for small degrees of choke and longer tubes for greater choke.

Numerous other makers have since adopted the same general configuration (containing a compensator), while others have simply modified the barrel to accept the screw-on choke tubes. Unique among the latter is the Winchester Win-Choke, in which the muzzle is counterbored to house interchangeable choke tubes completely within the barrel. Thus, changing choke tubes does not affect the external dimensions or appearance of the barrel.

The second basic type of adjustable choke may be attached

directly to the barrel, or to a compensator or muzzle brake. It is typified by the Poly-Choke, manufactured by the Poly-Choke Co. It uses the collet principle to increase or decrease the degree of choke constriction. Essentially this is accomplished by attaching to the muzzle a tube that has been split longitudinally to form several springy fingers, which are forced inward to produce choke constriction by screwing a tapered nut over them. The function is essentially that of a lathe collet or some types of drill chuck.

The collet type of choke was once considered inferior because its slender slots were exposed to shot charges and because the total degree of constriction was contained within a much shorter length of tube than that which is generally found in a solid choke. However, these have proved to be theoretical rather than practical disadvantages, and most adjustable choke users will readily agree that there are no performance differences between these two chokes.

The major practical advantage of the collet type of choke over the tube type is in that no additional tubes need be carried, and that choke adjustment may be made simply by rotating a knurled nut a fraction of a turn. To accomplish change on a tube type of choke, one must first remove the tube, select another one, and then screw it in place.

Generally speaking, it is considered practical to install adjustable-choke devices only on single-barrelled guns. Even so, special units have been designed and installed on double-barrelled guns. As far as can be determined, no such items have ever been offered commercially.

Many shooters consider the substantial bulk of some adjustable-choke devices a disadvantage since they blot out part of the target or change pitch and drop. But the Winchester Win-Choke totally eliminates those factors because it is no larger than the barrel diameter.

Generally speaking, adjustable-choke devices are still quite popular and widely used by those who by choice or necessity must use a single-barrelled shotgun for various types of shooting.

See also CHOKE, COMPENSATOR, and MUZZLE BRAKE.

The Poly-Choke, typical of collet-type adjustable chokes with compensator or muzzle brake an integral part of the design.

African Game, Cartridges for African and Asian dangerous game, elephant, rhino, buffalo, lion, etc., require massive shock and deep penetration for quick, humane kills. Consequently, a special class of cartridges for this type of hunting gradually developed in England from the 1870s onward, reaching its zenith in the monstrous .600 and .577 Nitro Express and slightly smaller (though no less powerful) cartridges of .45, .475, and .500 caliber. Such cartridges push bullets weighing 1 to 2 ounces at velocities close to 2,000 feet per second, achieving

3

great penetration by their weight and unusually strong, full-jacket construction. They were the most powerful in the world until the late 1950s, when they were surpassed by the .460 and .378 Weatherby Magnums.

These cartridges remained in wide use in typical high grade British double rifles until after World War II. Since then, though, the .458 Winchester Magnum has almost become the standard cartridge for dangerous African game, and only a very few of the older calibers remain in production. The thin-skinned and nondangerous game require no more than the typical North American big-game cartridge, though many British experts still prefer the .35 to .375 calibers.

See also AFRICAN GAME, GUNS FOR.

African Game, Guns for As most commonly used, the term African game refers to the thick-skinned, *dangerous* species found on that continent. In this context, the term "African rifle" is often used to describe rifles particularly suited for elephant, rhino, hippo, cape buffalo, (all thick-skinned), the big cats, and the few other species considered dangerous to the hunter. These animals are of great weight and size, and require massive penetration to insure quick, humane skills. The largest example of African game is the elephant, which requires a bullet that will penetrate as much as 2 feet of bone to reach the brain.

Consequently, African rifles are generally chambered for large-caliber cartridges that develop tremendous energy and achieve maximum penetration by driving unusually heavy bullets at moderate velocities. Since these cartridges generate great recoil, African rifles are relatively heavy, short-barrelled, and designed for fast handling in close quarters at very short ranges. Typical of pre-World War II African rifles is the classic side-by-side hammerless double-barrelled rifle chambered for a cartridge of .40 caliber or larger, using a bullet of 400 grains or more, driven at slightly over 2,000 feet per second.

The double-barrelled configuration gives very short length and superb handling qualities, and is the fastest of all designs for second shots. Since World War II, however, the trend has been toward modern, Mauser-type, bolt-action rifles chambered for the .458 Winchester cartridge, with the Winchester M70 African Rifle probably predominating.

In practice, the typical African rifle is intended for only a very small percentage of African game. The remaining species—the antelopes, etc., and virtually all of the plains game—are generally taken with lighter rifles and cartridges, similar to any North American big-game rifle.

See also AFRICAN GAME, CARTRIDGES FOR.

Air Gun   A form of gun using compressed air or compressed gas to launch a projectile through a conventional smooth or rifled barrel. *Not* by definition a *firearm* because of the fact that it does not utilize the process of combustion.

Air guns occur in two forms, the pneumatic type in which air is compressed by a pump and stored in that state before firing, and the spring-air type in which the air is compressed at the instant of firing by a spring-driven piston.

The earliest existing air guns date from the late 16th Century, but writings as early as 250 B. C. make reference to them. The earliest existing guns are of the spring-air type, the stock containing a cylinder and a spring-driven piston. When cocked, the spring is compressed and the piston is at the rear limit of its stroke; when the trigger is pulled, the piston is released and is driven forcibly to the end of the cylinder, compressing (and also heating) the air therein; the compressed air expands through a passage into the barrel behind the projectile and, continuing to expand, drives it out the barrel.

Another form of spring-air gun existed at about the same time and is referred to as the bellows type. Rather than a cylinder and piston, it utilized a leather bellows in the buttstock. One or both sides of the bellows was spring-driven. When the trigger was pulled, the spring(s) closed the bellows forcibly, compressing the air therein and directing it into the barrel to expel the projectile. Many bellows guns were breech loaders, the barrel tipping up to receive the ball and provided with a leather seal which prevented escape of air when firing. This was practical at the very low levels of pressure and temperature involved, while it would not have been with gunpowder.

Spring-air guns using a piston and cylinder continued to evolve and today's finest and most accurate target air guns are of the same type. Bellows guns were less efficient and disappeared from the scene in the early 19th Century.

Much more powerful were the pneumatic guns appearing in the early 17th Century. They utilized a separate pump with which a flash was charged with compressed air at high pressure. The air flask formed the buttstock of some guns; was a sphere under the barrel on others; and was often formed by a larger tube surrounding the barrel. In the first two types the flask was often removable, and could be replaced quickly in the field by a previously-charged spare flask.

In all, air was compressed by a separate pump, quite like a bicycle pump of later days. Once fully charged, the flask provided air for a number of discharges, and this prompted development of repeating air guns. Most used a simple ball magazine which caused a ball to be fed into the barrel breech as the arm was cocked, or by movement of a simple lever or catch. Thus a repeating gun could be fired as rapidly as it could be recocked and the magazine feed activated.

An example is the Girardoni (Italian) .50 caliber gun whose flask required 2,000 pump strokes for full charging. Pressing its horizontally-sliding breech block over caused a ball to be picked up from the magazine, and when released, it was forced back into alignment with the barrel by a spring, ready for firing. The Girardoni is reputed to have produced a velocity of nearly 1,000 feet per second which would have made it more powerful than many modern handguns. It was used briefly by the Austrian Army from 1780 to around 1800, issued with spare flasks which were charged from a cart-mounted pump operated by several men. Soldiers carried spare flasks and exchanged empty for charged ones in the supply area. Enemies of the Austrians considered the air gun a very unfair weapon because it gave no sound or smoke warning of its firing.

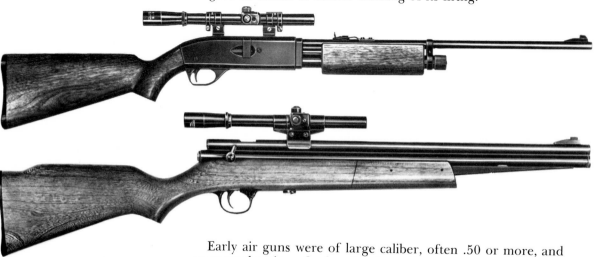

Two modern air rifles, both by Crosman. At top is the Model 622 Pell-Clip pump-action repeater. It is powered by CO_2, shoots at 450 feet-per-second velocity. Bottom gun is Model 1400 Pumpmaster, powered by pumping action, can reach velocities of over 700 feet-per-second.

Early air guns were of large caliber, often .50 or more, and were used at times for hunting large European game. Its silence made it a favorite of poachers.

By the middle-late 19th Century a unique form of spring-air gun called "Gallery Gun" was developed in the U. S. A. and remained popular for many years in shooting galleries until displaced by smokeless-powder .22 rimfire rifles.

Another uniquely American development of the spring-air gun is the "BB Gun" of the early 1900's, still immensely popular and sold by the millions each year.

In Europe the spring-air gun developed differently as a very precise and accurate target arm which is today used in Olympic and International competition. In this form the spring-air mechanism gives the most precise and consistent power impulse of all, and is thus the most accurate.

Pneumatic guns are still popular and are made in large quantities. They are generally less accurate than spring-air target guns, but are superior to smoothbored BB Guns. They allow greater air pressure to be used and are more powerful than other types, so are sometimes used for hunting small game.

The popularity of all types of air guns is greater today than ever before and will probably continue to be so because of ever-increasing restrictions on the possession and use of firearms.

See BB Gun; CO$_2$ Gun.

Airspace   The amount of empty space inside a loaded cartridge. Airspace does not always exist since it is eliminated by 100 per cent loading density in metallic cartridges. Airspace is never present in shotshell ammunition which, by its design and construction, requires the entire wad column to be seated solidly upon the powder charge.

The function and desirability of airspace changes with many cartridge variables. With high-intensity loadings of heavy bullets and slow-burning powders, airspace is eliminated as loading density reaches 100 per cent. When relatively fast-burning powders are used, charges seldom approach 100 per cent loading density, and a substantial amount of airspace exists.

Generally speaking, cartridges are designed to contain at least 10 to 15 per cent airspace when loaded to optimum velocity and pressure levels with propellants of medium-burning rate. Handloaders using slower powders may completely eliminate airspace, while faster powders will enlarge it. In either case, the change in airspace seems to have no adverse effect upon performance, providing the components and performance levels are chosen within reason. Then, too, since the bullet is held inside the case mouth, the depth to which it is seated also affects airspace.

It appears that a significant amount of airspace is more a mechanical requirement of loading machines rather than a technical requirement for proper cartridge functioning.

During the loading operation, each cartridge case is, at least for a time, charged with powder and then transferred and handled before the bullet is seated. During this brief period, it is necessary that the powder level be substantially below the case mouth, or spillage may result. Placing the powder level low enough to insure against propellant loss between charging and bullet-seating operations seems to be more responsible for airspace than any other reason.

Airspace is most evident with small charges of powder in reduced loads. Even with a kapok wad over the powder, this load still contains a great deal of airspace.

Altitude Effect   The reduction of aerodynamic drag on a bullet fired at relatively high altitudes. The higher one rises above mean sea level, the lower air density becomes, and thus air friction (and drag) on a bullet is reduced, resulting in a slightly lower rate-of-velocity loss.

The effect of altitude upon a bullet's trajectory is far less important than generally believed; in fact altitude affects a bullet's trajectory much less than typical shot-to-shot velocity variations in modern ammunition. For example, at an altitude of 10,000 feet (and a fair number of hunts take place at this and higher elevations), air density is approximately 75 per cent of sea level air density. The corresponding reduction in drag on the bullet will cause a projectile with a muzzle velocity of approximately 2,800 to 3,000 feet per second to strike, at 300 yards, approximately 1½ inches higher than it would at sea level—or ½ minute of angle or less.

Obviously, the effect of altitude is less than one might find between consecutive rounds fired under any set of conditions, and is so small that it can generally be ignored in the field. A bench rest shooter attempting to do his best at 10,000 feet might find it necessary to make a compensating sight adjustment because of altitude effect, but the hunter will not find this necessary.

In fact, the effects of altitude can frequently be beneficial to the hunter. The general tendency when hunting in the mountains is to underestimate range, and since bullet drop decreases as altitude increases, altitude effect might even be considered an automatic correction for one of our human failings.

See also MINUTE OF ANGLE.

Amateur Trapshooting Association (ATA) Official organization regulating registered trapshooting and setting the rules through its officers and directors. Its headquarters are at Vandalia, Ohio, 45377.

Trap & Field is the official monthly publication, with offices at 110 Waterway Blvd., Indianapolis, Indiana 46202.

The ATA permanent clubgrounds at Vandalia is the site of the annual Grand American Handicap. It draws more shooters than any other shotgun tournament in the world.

American Walnut More specifically American black walnut (technical name), the most commonly used gunstock wood in North America because it possesses an excellent strength-weight ratio, dense grain, and attractive coloring and figure. Quality depends greatly on location and environment; trees grown in wet river bottoms producing very plain, light, weak, and poor textured wood. Trees grown in poor soil and dry climate provide the best wood. Claro walnut from California is not a native wood, being an import from England for producing "English" walnuts commercially.

See GUNSTOCK.

Ammunition, Component Each individual item making up a complete cartridge: primer, case, bullet, powder, as well as those items peculiar to shotshells and other less common cartridges.

Angle of Departure The angle above the horizontal at which a bullet departs the muzzle of a gun. It has no relationship to line-of-sight or to angle of barrel. It actually includes the angle of the barrel, plus that portion of jump which occurs before the bullet clears the muzzle.

Angle of Elevation The angle measured between the line of sight and center line of the bore, measured in minutes of angle on small arms, but in mills on artillery, mortars, and other heavy weapons. The amount of vertical shift of the rear sight necessary to cause line of sight and trajectory to intersect at a given range.

Annealing, Case The process of making brass more malleable, less brittle and tougher by the application of heat followed by rapid cooling. During manufacture, annealing gives cartridge cases the proper hardness and springiness to hold a bullet securely and also the flexibility to expand upon firing, to seal the chamber and then to contract to permit easy extraction of the cases.

A case mouth that is too hard will split upon firing (and may well split from tension load during storage), while one too soft may allow the bullet to shift under feeding pressure, or expand too much to permit proper extraction. A balance between these two conditions is required for normal functioning of metallic cartridges, and the exact hardness will vary according to the particular cartridge or loading.

Annealing is accomplished by running otherwise-finished cases through a gas flame or induction-heating coils to bring the mouth area to a specified temperature for the required period of time. The heated areas are then quickly cooled either by blasting them with air or by quenching them in water or other liquids, which produces the required hardness, ductility, and grain structure.

In some instances, it is also necessary to anneal cases at various stages in manufacture so that they remain ductile enough for the various drawing and shaping operations.

Handloaders will note that case mouths become too hard with repeated use due to work hardening and must then be annealed. They can use a small-flame gas torch to heat the neck and shoulder of the case to the point where the brass begins changing to a blue-black color and then immediately quench the case in room-temperature water.

Traditionally, cases have been set in a tray in shallow water to reduce heat transfer to the critical head areas, however, this is not necessary if heat is applied quickly. Case heads can be held by the fingers, and case-mouth temperatures should be raised sufficiently before excessive heat reaches the head—after which the cases are simply dropped into a container of water. (If the head gets too hot to hold, you've overdone it.)

The open-flame method produces the least desirable results in that it is impossible for even an experienced operator to control the temperatures uniformly. A far more practical method consists of dipping case mouths in molten lead (about 650° degrees F) for a few seconds, then dropping them into water. Immersing case mouths first in oil or powdered graphite prevents lead from adhering to the brass. Molten lead insures that the cases will not be overheated and gives the most uniform results. Do not allow water to splash into the molten lead, however.

Annealing is necessary when (1) case necks show signs of splitting after firing; or (2) necks become so hard that excessive effort is required to pull them over an expander plug or to seat bullets therein. Annealing should also be included as either a final or intermediate operation following any extensive reforming or shortening of a cartridge case.

See also WORK HARDENING.

Anvil In a Boxer primer, that separate portion of the primer which rests against the bottom of the primer pocket and against which the firing pin crushes the priming compound. Stamped out of thin sheet metal (usually brass) in the form of a cone with the sides notched to form two or three legs, the anvil is seated friction-tight in the mouth of the primer cup, after charging and foiling.

In a Berdan-primed case, the anvil is the conical projection rising from the case metal itself. Here it serves the same function as in a Boxer primer, providing the surface against which the firing pin crushes the priming compound.

See also PRIMER, CENTERFIRE.

Aperture See METALLIC SIGHTS and PEEP SIGHTS.

Arisaka The name generally applied to Japanese military rifles originally developed by Army Colonel Nariake Arisaka, superintendent of the Tokyo Arsenal, and which were first manufactured in 6.5mm caliber in 1897 as the Type 30 infantry rifle. This model was superseded by the Improved Type 38, (also 6.5mm) which was redesigned to utilize a greatly modified

Mauser bolt. The Type 38 was produced in far greater quantities than the Type 30, and is more frequently encountered.

The Type 38 utilizes a one-piece bolt, with dual, forward-locking lugs, and its unusual safety is engaged by pushing in a cap at the rear of the bolt and rotating it ⅛ of a turn clockwise. The Type 38 also has a double-column Mauser type of box magazine holding five rounds, and is fitted with a hinged floorplate.

A typical Arisaka rifle, the 6.5mm Type 38 infantry model utilized by the Japanese army through WW II.

In its original form, the Type 38 rifle weighs 9.6 pounds and has a 31.44-inch barrel for an overall length of 50.19 inches. It is unique in having a contemporary military-style stock in which the butt is composed of *two* pieces of wood joined longitudinally.

The Type 38 was later modified to a carbine with a folding bayonet. This modified version is designated as Type 44. In 1939 an extensive redesign produced the Type 99, which has a 25.8-inch barrel and is chambered for a rimless 7.7mm cartridge.

Numerous other minor variations of the basic Arisaka design will be noticed among rifles returned to this country after World War II.

Arquebus (Harquebus) The earliest form of firearms, intended to be fired with the stock resting on the gunner's shoulder, chest, or cheek. The gun was fired by a slow match which was usually held in a serpentine or cock. The arquebus was heavy and was furnished with a forked rest upon which the barrel was laid for firing. It is believed to have been developed in the early 15th century, following the hand cannon. By the mid-16th century, the term generally meant a light firearm which could be handled *without* a rest.

Asian Game, Guns for Asian game is generally quite comparable to that of Africa, the major dangerous species being elephant, gaur, and the tiger (the latter limited as a hunting quarry because it is an endangered species). Because of their size and vitality, the first two species require the same rifle and cartridge combination used for dangerous African game. Since the beginning of breech loaders, sportsmen the world over have used African rifles on Asian game.

Other Asian game, thin-skinned and usually not dangerous to the hunter, requires no more than the typical North American big-game cartridge and rifle.

See also AFRICAN GAME, GUNS FOR.

Assault Rifle A military rifle intended purely for one-man operation and equipped to provide either semiautomatic or full-automatic fire by means of a selector switch or other fire-control device.

Today's assault rifles are typified by the Soviet AK 47 and the U.S. M16. They are chambered for an intermediate cartridge, have barrels under 20 inches, make extensive use of plastics and

Armalite AR-18 is typical of modern assault rifles, short, light, with straight-line stock and elevated line of sight, large magazine capacity, and for an intermediate cartridge; in this instance, the U.S. 5.56mm.

stampings, use gas operation and locked breeches, have magazine capacities of 20 to 30 rounds, weigh from six to ten pounds, and are quite compact. Maximum effective range in the hands of average troops is approximately 300 meters in the semiautomatic mode and somewhat less in full-automatic fire.

Some assault rifles are produced only in semiautomatic form for sale as sporting arms. They are excellent for use on a military style of target, but have little application in hunting.

Autoloading See SEMIAUTOMATIC.

Autoloading Rifle See SEMIAUTOMATIC.

Automatic Safety A mechanical safety on any firearm which is automatically engaged either by cocking or by reloading the gun. Safeties of this type are considered desirable on guns used by those with little firearms training.

Automatic safeties are generally simple in design. Opening the breech or cocking the firing mechanism acts through a push-rod to cam the safety into its fully engaged position, preventing inadvertent firing until one deliberately disengages the safety manually.

Automatic safeties are most prevalent among break-open shotgun designs, but will also be found on a few rifles, the most recent example of which is the Colt/Sharps single-shot.

Handgun grip safeties are not usually considered automatic, though, in effect, they are just that. Grip safeties prevent firing unless a deliberate effort is made to depress them by gripping the gun properly.

Automatic safeties are much more common to military small arms than generally believed. A number of present generation automatic weapons, particularly sub-machine guns, incorporate a form of grip safety. Probably the best known among these is the highly renowned Israeli Uzi 9mm Parabellum.

A number of authorities are prone to discuss other safety devices as automatic safeties when, in fact, they are not. To meet our definition of an automatic safety, the device must be one which is engaged by the mere act of cocking or loading the gun, and which must then be disengaged *manually*—requirements which are not met by internal devices such as magazine safeties, firing-pin interrupters, sear disconnectors, etc.

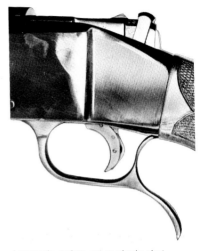

Automatic safety on a single-shot rifle (Colt/Sharps) which becomes engaged as the breech is closed and must be manually disengaged by pushing it forward before firing is possible.

Automatic Selective Ejector In any single-shot or break-open action, a device which hurls only *fired* cases clear of the breech when the action is opened. Most common is the type of ejector found in double-barrelled shotguns, in which a system of hammers, rods, and springs act upon the extractors to eject the case.

The automatic ejector is activated only by the firing of its companion lock, and thus unfired cartridges are only raised by the extractors when the breech is opened, while fired cases are hurled clear. This device is intended primarily as an aid to rapid reloading.

See also EJECTOR.

Automatic Weapon (Machine Gun; Submachine Gun) Any firearm in which a single pull and continuous pressure upon the trigger (or other firing device) will produce rapid discharge of successive shots so long as ammunition remains in the magazine or feed device—in other words, a machine gun.

Technically, any firearm, regardless of size or configuration, which will fire *more than one* shot with a single pull of the trigger. Consequently, modern military and police weapons that fire any number of shots in a single burst must be considered machine guns. In spite of this, some state laws and local ordinances define a machine gun as a weapon which fires more than five shots (California) or more than eight shots (Illinois) for a single pull of the trigger. No matter what interpretation might logically be made of such state and local laws, the federal law is pre-eminent in the field, and it is the one that you must comply with.

All of this discussion is to distinguish the term *automatic weapon* from the terms *semiautomatic* and *automatic* as they are used colloquially in reference to various autoloading guns.

See also AUTOLOADING FIREARMS, MACHINE GUN, and SEMI-AUTOMATIC FIREARM.

Aw Shucks An unusual shotgunning game devised by Remington personnel, and first installed at the Remington Farms game preserve outside of Chestertown, Maryland. It consists of an automatic trap positioned high in a tree, and five shooting stations laid out in a rough circle in a wooded area sloping downhill from the trap. At each station, after a random delay (as much as several seconds), the shooter is thrown a spaced double which, depending upon the station, may be incoming, over-the-shoulder, or crossing. Following this, again after a random delay, the shooter is thrown three targets which may be a double and a single, or three rapidly spaced singles. This is repeated at each station, with some minor variation.

Aw Shucks is the most difficult type of claybird shooting, and even the best field, skeet, and trap shooters are almost invariably reduced to wailing and gnashing of teeth by their first exposure to it. In the Remington layout, the majority of the birds must be taken through trees and branches. It is as close an approach to grouse shooting in thick cover as one could ask.

B

Back Action Lock A common gun lock during the percussion period. The mainspring and attendant gadgetry of the back action lock are located to the rear of the hammer, permitting a shorter lock plate and eliminating the forward extension found in the bar lock. It was mainly found in pistols and small-caliber rifles because of its disadvantage of substantially weakening the wrist stock where more wood was cut away to accommodate it.
See also Bar Lock.

Percussion back action lock.

Backstop Any mass of earth or other material placed behind targets to absorb bullets. The most common sort of backstop is simply a high earthen bank, sometimes faced with logs or railroad ties, and sometimes with concrete or riprap placed on the reverse slope to reduce erosion.

Back Thrust The actual rearward pressure exerted on the face of breech block or bolt by the firing of a cartridge, usually expressed simply as an absolute—for example, 6,500 pounds. It is determined by multiplying maximum chamber pressure, in pounds per square inch, by cartridge head area in square inches. Thus a 50,000 psi .270 Winchester load, with a case head area of .1728 square inch, produces a back thrust of about 8,600 pounds.

Ballistic Coefficient A number given a bullet which tells how its shape, length, weight, diameter and nose design affect its stability, velocity and range against air resistance.

Ballistics The study of the natural laws governing the performance of propellants and projectiles, and the use of these laws to predict the performance of propellants and projectiles. Ballistics is divided into two branches: interior, which relates only to what occurs from the instant of cartridge ignition until the bullet leaves the bore; and exterior, which relates to the bullet's flight from the time it leaves the muzzle until it comes to rest.

Firearms existed for many years before anyone knew about ballistics. Galileo theorized that a bullet in flight would describe a parabola, but he did not take into consideration the effect of air resistance. He was right though, in a sense, for we know now that a projectile will describe a parabola in a vacuum. Later, in 1710, Newton conducted experiments to determine the effect of air resistance on projectiles, and in 1742 Benjamin Robins stated sound ballistic theories in *New Principles of Gunnery*. But, another century passed before ballistics as we know it came under serious study.

Interior ballistics is limited to very short time periods on the order of .004 seconds or less in a modern rifle. Thus its study requires very precise measuring and calculating equipment.

Here's what happens during this brief cycle: (1) Firing pin impact crushes the priming compound and detonates the primer. (2) Priming compound burns very rapidly and throws off incandescent particles and a jet of flame, which passes through the flash hole to the propelling charge. (3) These white-hot particles and the flame raise at least a portion of the propelling charge to ignition temperature. (4) The propellant begins to burn, slowly at first, then with increasing rapidity, generating a large volume of hot gas (as high as 3,500 degrees F.). (5) The expanding gases begin to force the bullet down the barrel, resulting in increased space behind the bullet into which the gases that are being generated can expand. (6) The propellant continues to burn and generate gas, and chamber pressure rises until the bullet has moved sufficiently down the bore that volume behind it increases at a rate in excess of the ability of the propellant to maintain peak pressure in the gun barrel. (7) At this time chamber pressure and temperature start to decrease but the moving bullet has by this time acquired sufficient inertia to accelerate velocity even when the burning propellant has passed the point of maximum chamber pressure.

Generally, this point occurs when the bullet has traveled only a couple of inches or less down the bore. Internal pressure then deteriorates rapidly until the bullet completes its passage through the bore and out the muzzle. The modern high-intensity rifle cartridge's maximum chamber pressure may be around 55,000 pounds per square inch, and then drop off to less than 10,000 as the bullet exits from the muzzle. Indeed, the lowered exit pressure of the gas at the muzzle is purposely attained through propellant chemistry and geometry because of the desirability of lowered pressures, which create less upset of the bullet's flight.

Exterior ballistics starts the instant the bullet begins to decelerate, however minutely, and leaves the controlling influence of the barrel. This is when the bullet comes under the influence of gravity and begins to drop toward earth. The rate at which gravity affects it is a constant 32 feet per second per second while loss of velocity varies greatly according to air resistance, bullet shape, weight, cross-sectional area, air density, etc.

The study of exterior ballistics has progressed to the point where specific values can be established for all these factors, and can be applied mathematically to predict the performance of a given bullet with a very high degree of accuracy.

There is yet a third area of ballistics, which the layman seldom considers: terminal ballistics, or the bullet's effect and performance on striking or entering its target. A great deal of effort has been expended on hunting bullets in an effort to obtain maximum impact characteristics. Much important study in this area has been conducted by the world's military establishments; to them projectile performance against personnel, fortifications, and structures is of great importance. However, military bullets of rifle and pistol calibers are generally stereotyped in construction and design, especially because of the limitations placed on bullet design by the Hague Conventions of 1908 (i.e. bullets must not be designed to deform upon impact with personnel). Thus, the majority of military ball bullets of rifle caliber are full-jacketed, with no intentional design characteristics to insure expansion.

B.A.R.   Browning Automatic Rifle. See BROWNING, JOHN M.

Barking   The legendary practice of taking squirrels by shooting to hit the limb directly under the animal. This impact is reported to stun the animal, causing it to drop inert to the ground where it may be picked up and dispatched at leisure.

Oldtimers say this practice is invariably successful; however, shooters who have tried it report only occasional success, and that very much depends on caliber and precise bullet placement. Except with very low-velocity bullets, success is generally due to bullet and wood fragments striking the squirrel rather than concussion.

Typical barleycorn front sight (viewed from rear) on a 1930's-vintage military rifle.

Barleycorn   A form of front sight which presents to the shooter the image of a truncated triangle. This sight, in its original form, resembled an individual grain of barley, hence its name.

When used with a V-shaped-notch rear sight, it makes a reasonably practical and accurate front sight. It has not been popular on sporting arms since the turn of the century, but was generally standard on military rifles and light automatic weapons until after World War II. In fact, it is still used on some modern foreign military arms.

Bar Lock   The type of gun lock developed during the muzzle-loading period, in which the mainspring (which drives the hammer) is situated forward of the tumbler and hammer so that it, and the lock plate upon which it is seated, extend forward alongside or under the barrel.

Modern production percussion bar lock.

The bar lock is usually considered the most robust and durable of the several types, and is generally simpler to build or maintain than other gun locks. Doubtless its name is derived from the forward extension of the lock plate that supports the mainspring, which looks like a bar.

When the basic bar lock is found on relatively modern breech-loading shotguns (with or without exposed hammers), it is generally referred to as a "side lock."

See also GUN LOCK and SIDE LOCK.

Barrel Adapter   A short section of chambered barrel inserted into one of larger caliber to permit the firing of a smaller-caliber

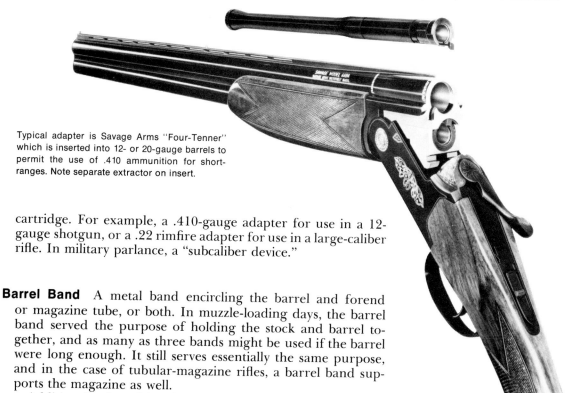

Typical adapter is Savage Arms "Four-Tenner" which is inserted into 12- or 20-gauge barrels to permit the use of .410 ammunition for short-ranges. Note separate extractor on insert.

cartridge. For example, a .410-gauge adapter for use in a 12-gauge shotgun, or a .22 rimfire adapter for use in a large-caliber rifle. In military parlance, a "subcaliber device."

Barrel Band A metal band encircling the barrel and forend or magazine tube, or both. In muzzle-loading days, the barrel band served the purpose of holding the stock and barrel together, and as many as three bands might be used if the barrel were long enough. It still serves essentially the same purpose, and in the case of tubular-magazine rifles, a barrel band supports the magazine as well.

Additionally, barrel bands may also serve as bases for either front or rear sights, or for installation of sling swivels or hooks. A military variation exists in which the band serves not only to tie stock and barrel together, but provides a solid support for the installation of a bayonet, flash hider, grenade launcher, or other muzzle attachment.

Bands on sporting rifles are generally secured by pins or screws, while those on military arms are more frequently held in place by spring-loaded catches. Bands supporting sights or sling swivels must be strongly secured and are usually soldered, keyed, or pinned in place.

Typical barrel band as found on lever-action rifles where it serves to tie magazine, stock, and barrel solidly together.

Barrel bands usually serve a purely mechanical purpose. However, in some instances, such as the Winchester Model 52 target rifles and the old Springfield Sporter rifles, they were also used to regulate bedding and thereby controlled accuracy to some degree.

Barrel Channel   The groove cut in the forward portion of any gunstock to accommodate the barrel.

Barrel Erosion   In the throat of a rifled barrel, the gradual wearing or eroding away of the surface of the metal by hot powder gases. The degree of erosion is directly dependent upon the amount of powder burned per shot and the chamber pressures generated.

Thus a medium-velocity cartridge such as the .22 Hornet, producing a velocity of approximately 2,800 feet per second from a very small charge of powder at relatively low chamber pressures, will not produce visible erosion after digesting many thousands of rounds. On the other hand, the .300 Weatherby Magnum using eight to ten times as much powder, driving a bullet 25 per cent faster, and generating chamber pressures in the 55,000 psi range may produce serious barrel erosion in less than 1,000 rounds.

Barrel erosion appears as a roughened and pitted area at the beginning of the rifling, and if allowed to develop will completely remove the rifling for as much as two or three inches (but rarely more), and produce substantial enlargement of the bore in the same area.

In addition, the eroded surface is covered with hairline cracks running at right angles to the bore, extending only a few thousandths of an inch into the surface. As these cracks develop, they enlarge the area upon which the hot powder gases impinge and thus accelerate erosion.

Barrel erosion reduces accuracy when it exists to a relatively small degree, but in a more advanced condition it may actually cause a bullet to disintegrate.

Erosion cannot be corrected once it has begun. However, the barrel may be shortened at the breech so that rechambering will remove the eroded portion.

Hard-chrome plating sometimes delays the onset and reduces the effect of erosion; however, this is often done in military automatic weapons which will be fired at high cyclic rates. Some of these are also fitted with special hard-alloy liners carrying the rifling in the first few inches of the barrel. This virtually eliminates the effect of erosion but is prohibitively expensive for commercial guns, and also produces a barrel less accurate than one made from a single piece.

Barrel Length Effect (on velocity) Assuming a standard barrel length of 22 to 24 inches chambered for a modern centerfire rifle, reducing that length will reduce the bullet's velocity, increasing the length will increase velocity. With the average modern high-intensity bottleneck cartridge, and a muzzle velocity in the 3,000 to 3,200-feet-per-second range, shortening a barrel will produce an average velocity loss of about 25 to 35 feet per second for each inch of reduction. Barrel-length increase, within the limits imposed by law and practical handling, produces essentially the opposite result.

Contrary to popular belief, it simply is not possible to ascribe a specific velocity change per unit of length in any particular gun. This is so simply because it is not barrel length *per se* that is the determining factor. Instead, the expansion ratio, which is a function of barrel length *and* chamber—or cartridge case—volume, determines velocity change. For all practical purposes, though, one may use 25 feet per second for modern centerfire rifle calibers, a figure of about 20 feet per second (based on a 20-inch barrel) in .22 rimfire calibers, and as much as 65 to 75 feet per second with magnum handgun cartridges (based on an 8³⁄₈-inch barrel) to calculate the effect of changing barrel length on a bullet's velocity.

See also EXPANSION RATIO.

Barrel Liner A thin-walled rifled tube used for relining.
See also RELINING.

Barrel Lug A protrusion on the underside of a barrel that may serve the purpose of attaching the stock to the barrel, absorbing recoil by making solid contact with a recess in the stock, or for the attachment of any accessory or other item. In most instances the lug is dovetailed or soldered to the barrel or both, though the lug is sometimes machined integrally with the barrel, especially when its primary function is to absorb heavy recoil.

Barrel Making See RIFLING.

Barrel Tenon That portion of the rear of a gun barrel which fits into the receiver. It is generally of smaller diameter than the barrel breech, and is threaded for screwing into the receiver, except in some of the cheaper rimfire rifles.

Barrel Throat, Revolver The breech end of a revolver barrel next to the cylinder which has been chambered or funneled

Portion of barrel extending rearward through frame contains the throat; funneled portion of throat can be seen.

to facilitate the entry of the bullet as it passes from the mouth of a chamber.

Because of practical manufacturing realities, the chamber mouths, in any revolver, will not be of precisely uniform diameters, nor will they be of exactly the same diameter as the barrel grooves. In addition, the individual chambers will not all be aligned precisely alike with the barrel at the instant of firing. And, as the revolver wears, all of these factors will change, particularly chamber/barrel alignment. To compensate for all this, the rear of the revolver barrel is funneled to a depth of approximately ⅓ inch and the rear of the funnel is made sufficiently large to receive and guide all bullets into the rifling as they come out of the cylinder.

Compressed paper base wad here shows how open end of body tube is plugged and held tightly inside metallic head overlay.

Base Wad   In a shotshell, the circular plug which fills the head of the case and surrounds the battery cup primer. It is common only to built-up cases made of a tubular body and separate head, whether the body be plastic, paper, or metal. One-piece drawn metal cases, or one-piece molded or compression-formed cases do not contain a base wad.

Base wads have been made variously of molded fiber, compressed paper pulp, compressed layered paper, and plastic, with or without a plastic, paper, or metal overlay.

During case manufacture, the tubular body is inserted into the thin metal head to the proper depth, and then the base wad is seated solidly inside the head. The base wad is compressed at the same time the primer pocket is punched from the outside, and this compression and piercing causes radial expansion of the wad which locks the body tightly into the metal head, which is usually knurled to provide gripping surfaces.

In this position, the wad serves as a seat for the primer, and also to absorb the rearward thrust of the powder gases when the shell is fired. Repeated firings and reloadings may loosen a base wad, or erode away parts or its upper surface. In severe cases, this may cause the base wad to be blown into the barrel during firing—perhaps even to remain there and cause damage on the next shot.

If a base wad has not become too loose, the case can be salvaged by reseating the wad with a punch (some loading tools do this automatically during the priming operation).

Battery Cup Primer   In a shotshell primer, an assembly consisting of a cap (much like a Boxer primer without anvil) and separate anvil seated in a deep, flanged supporting cup. The cup is necessary because shotshell heads are not strong enough to hold metallic primers correctly.
See also BOXER PRIMER.

BB   A term with two distinct and separate meanings, the most common being the size of air rifle barrels or air rifle spherical steel shot—.175 inch in diameter. So widely used in this respect that *BB gun* has become a generic term for all types of spring- and air-operated guns which use this type and size ammunition.

In reference to shotshells, a specific size of lead shot-.181 inch in diameter. Contrary to popular belief, BB shot size is not identical to BB ammunition size.
See also AIR GUN.

BB Cap   A very short, primed .22 rimfire case containing only a very short round-nosed lead bullet or a round lead ball. No propellant power is used; the bullet is driven solely by the priming compound.
See also CB CAP.

Bead   A form of front sight that presents to the shooter's eye the image of a round ball or disc centered atop a slender post. It is centered by the eye in an aperture or notched rear sight.

Bears, Guns and Cartridges for   The big bears of North America are among the largest and most dangerous in the world, and are certainly the most dangerous game in North America. The grizzly, the Alaskan brown, and the Arctic and sub-Arctic polar bear are quite fearless, have no natural enemies, and do not hesitate to attack man when injured or threatened, or occasionally, even without provocation. They are known to reach weights of 1,500 pounds, though few do so.

Being thin-skinned, they *can* be killed quite readily with

relatively small-caliber, high-velocity cartridges fired from any conventional rifle. However, a quick and humane kill with such cartridges depends upon very precise bullet placement and performance.

Also, all three species of bear are quite often taken at very short ranges (also in heavy cover, except for the polar) where even a fatal shot may allow the bear to maul the hunter unless the animal is simultaneously immobilized. Disabling performance requires cartridges of quite substantial power, on the order of the .375 or larger magnums.

Inasmuch as all three species, particularly the grizzly and the brown, are often hunted in dense cover and in wet weather, rifles should be relatively short, light, and handy. In addition, a scope sight should be mounted so that it may be instantly flipped out of the line of sight to permit the use of auxiliary open sights. This because rain, snow, and debris may clutter up the scope and also because the bear may be initially engaged at ranges of only a very few yards where the scope field of view is too narrow. The most practical of this type of mount is the Pachmayr low-swing, in which the thumb of the shooting hand can quickly flip the scope clear of the line of sight as the gun is mounted.

A double rifle would be ideal for big bears, but a more practical choice is a modern bolt-action carbine (20-inch or shorter barrel) chambered for the .338 Winchester or larger caliber, and fitted with both open sights and a low-magnification scope in a swing-over mount.

Beavertail Forend Most often on a shotgun, a forend of greater width than normal. It serves two purposes: a better grip for the forward hand, and to protect the hand from hot barrels during fast shooting.

Wide, curved gripping surface of beavertail forend is evident here.

Bedding In a rifle, the process of carefully mating wood and metal into intimate contact to insure the stock will absorb recoil loads without damage, and also to insure that the stock contributes all that it can to accuracy by damping vibrations and providing overall rigidity.

The ideal in bedding is achieved when all of the metal areas within the stock are in complete contact with the stock. This is achieved by coating the metal with lamp black or a similar material that will transfer to the wood on contact and then slowly and carefully scraping and carving away the surface of the wood until the metal parts have been inletted to their proper depth. This insures that the stock provides maximum support to all of the metal parts without misalignment, which would cause twisting or binding or other abnormal stresses that would reduce accuracy.

See also INLETTING.

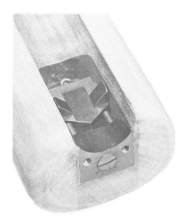

Bedding device installed in forend.

Bedding Device Seldom seen except on rimfire target rifles, bedding devices allow the shooter to vary upward or other pressure on the barrel until maximum accuracy is obtained. Such devices may be in the form of a simple V-block, or such a block containing adjustment screws, spaced from 45 to 90 degrees apart, inletted into the forend near its tip. These screws may be adjusted to put any desired pressure on the barrel.

Barrels generally respond to upward loading since, at one particular load level, they will produce maximum accuracy. A device of this sort allows that particular load level to be determined and recorded by either click adjustments or visual indicators and thus be kept constant even if stock conditions change. Some such devices utilize a weak electrical current lighting a small bulb to establish initial mechanical contact from which adjustments may be made.

Other bedding devices exist, some of which are nothing more than neoprene or similar plastic pads which are inletted into the stock to support the action. Probably the most common bedding device isn't even recognized as such—the thick, square crossbolt found in most Mauser military rifles; it provides a solid seat for the recoil lug, spreading recoil loads over a wider area of wood.

Bedding device engaging barrel.

Belted Case What we know today as the belted-case cartridge was originally developed by old line British gun makers Holland & Holland, and first introduced about 1912 as Holland's .375 Belted Rimless Magnum, (actually, the smaller belted .400/.375 dated from 1905 but received little notice). The British designers chose this form of case head because the belt functioned exactly like the substantial flange on typical rimmed cases. However, by making the rim inordinately thick and cutting a rimless type of extraction groove, the difficulties of feeding conventional rimmed cases through Mauser-type, double-column magazines were eliminated. In short, the belt was then considered nothing more than a very thick rim—thick enough so that one would not catch behind the other in the magazine.

Typical case belt at right is approximately .220″ in length and .030″ larger in diameter than the case body proper. Note extractor groove is machined in the basic belt. Conventional rimless case appears at left.

In 1920 Holland & Holland introduced a .30-caliber version of the original .375 case and called it, too, a magnum. Until after World War II, only these particular belted-case calibers saw wide commercial distribution, thus the case type became known more as a magnum than anything else, and today is associated almost exclusively with magnum calibers, and is often identified as a "magnum" case.

In theory the belted case provides the smooth feeding of a true rimless case, yet with the headspacing certainty provided by the rimmed one. As a practical matter, the belted design offers no significant headspace advantage over the rimless form. In fact, its alleged advantage in headspacing has caused a laxness in chambering rifles for it, which actually makes it less desirable. This is brought about when chambers are cut with very loose shoulder-location tolerances, allowing the case shoulder to be blown forward on firing and thus excessively stretched back near the web, weakening the case wall at that point. Rifle makers have a tendency to treat shoulder location a bit lightly, so long as headspacing is on the belt.

The belted case is often considered stronger than any other type. This is erroneous since the strength of any case design depends on the closeness of chambering and breeching, and on the thickness of the web. Assuming these other factors equal, a rimless case is equally as strong as a belted case, and vice versa.

Currently, belted cases exist in four basic diameters and numerous lengths. Largest is the Weatherby .378/.460 with a belt diameter of .603 inch, followed by the original Holland & Holland with a diameter of about .530 inch, then the Weatherby .240 with a belt diameter of .470 inch, and the .224 Weatherby with a diameter of .430 inch. Lengths range from 1.92 inches for the .224 Weatherby up to 2.91 inches for the .378 Weatherby.

Bench Rest Rifle Generally, a bench rest rifle is one that is designed purely for shooting from a permanent bench rest, and to eliminate, as much as possible, all human error.

Within the limits of weight and dimensions placed upon the various restricted classes, nothing is spared to make the guns as mechanically accurate as possible. This is particularly true in the unrestricted class where there are absolutely no limitations on the gun's size, weight, or configuration.

Bench rest rifles are usually custom-built items based on highly modified commercial bolt actions or on a few custom-built actions developed specifically for this purpose. The modifications are aimed primarily at producing maximum rigidity of action and barrel, compensation for heat produced by continuous firing, and minimum disturbance during firing.

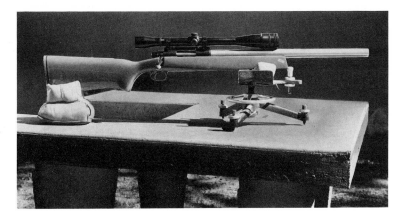

Bench rest with heavy varmint bench rest rifle.

Additionally, every effort is made to obtain optical perfection in high-magnification telescopic sights, and to insure that sight/gun relationship does not vary.

In view of the impossibility of covering here all the many details of bench rest rifle construction, it is recommended that the accompanying photos be studied carefully.

Berdan Primer A metallic primer whose anvil is formed integrally from the case in the bottom of the primer pocket. Invented by U.S. Colonel Berdan in the 1860s and used principally abroad.

Big Bore In American target-shooting parlance, this term refers to .30-caliber (usually .30/06 or .308 Winchester) rifle and cartridge used for all types of competitive shooting except benchrest.

In connection with handguns, the term is generally applied to those guns using cartridges with a greater bullet diameter than the .38 Special.

In reference to a hunting rifle, it is a rather imprecise term, and may refer to any cartridge above .30 caliber, so long as that cartridge is relatively powerful. For example, the .300 Winchester Magnum would be considered big bore, while the .30/30 Winchester would not, even though both are of the same nominal caliber.

In British African-oriented terminology, the term defines long, heavy cartridges of .40 caliber or greater, suitable for use on dangerous game.

Black Bear See BEARS, GUNS AND CARTRIDGES FOR

Black Powder The oldest small-arms ammunition propellant, consisting of a mechanical mixture of charcoal, sulfur, and saltpeter (potassium nitrate). The exact formula varies, but a common one is 15 parts charcoal, 75 parts saltpeter, and 10 parts sulfur, by weight. It would be difficult to prove that a modest percentage variation of any of the ingredients would produce a change for either better or worse.

Early black powder was a simple mechanical mixture of the various ingredients, finely ground. As such, it possessed several important disadvantages: it absorbed a great deal of atmospheric moisture and would cake solidly in casks; it was not always easily ignited; and vibration would separate it into its various components during transportation.

Artillerymen frequently had to break up the contents of casks which had caked hard in storage. Because of this, they were often furnished with the implements required to mix the previously ground raw ingredients immediately before use. Even this didn't solve all problems, for both saltpeter and sulfur still absorbed much moisture and often caked iron-hard prior to mixing up a fresh batch.

Black powder achieved its present form by mixing the ingredients wet, compressing them into cakes, and then breaking the cakes into granules of different size. As a result, ingredient separation was eliminated and caking greatly reduced. This so-called corned powder was much more powerful than the dry-mix serpentine powder. In fact, modern black powder (and it hasn't changed much except in purity since the advent of corned powder) represented as great an improvement then as smokeless powder did in the late 1880s.

So named because of its color, black powder is considered a "low explosive" and will—unlike smokeless powder—detonate if ignited unconfined. For this reason, both its manufacture and its use are generally considered hazardous.

Black powder mills are always subject to periodic blows (explosions) and, consequently, as much of the work as possible is done by remote control. In addition, mill buildings are usually "blow-away" structures, consisting of a sturdy frame loosely hung with boards. Thus, when the powder blows, the siding is shattered and blown away, but the frame remains standing and serviceable.

Once extensively used in quarrying and mining, black powder has since been displaced by a mixture of ammonium nitrate and diesel fuel or a similar sensitizor. However, this does not imply that ammonium nitrate mixtures may be used in place of black powder in firearms. Under no circumstances is it safe to make any such substitutions.

At one time there were literally scores of powder mills in this country. After World War II, only the DuPont mill survived, and in 1970 it was heavily damaged by an explosion. Only minimum production capacity was restored after the blow, and that only for military requirements. Consequently, DuPont no longer makes black powder for commercial distribution.

Black powder manufactured by the I.C.I. plant in Scotland, under the name of Curtis and Harvey, is distributed in this country under several different names.

The major use for black powder today is in modern muzzle-loading guns. It is estimated that substantially less than a half-million pounds per year are required to meet this market. Additionally, a relatively small amount is used by handloaders for obsolete-caliber ammunition, or for ammunition loaded for use in black-powder-vintage guns.

Black powder should not be treated lightly simply because it has often been stated ". . . it is impossible to produce excessive pressures by overloading." That isn't necessarily so, at least in muzzle loaders, as recent tests conducted for the Thompson-Center Arms Co. show.

With muzzle loaders, safety is easily preserved by not exceeding standard powder charges published in a variety of references for different calibers and bullet types.

With metallic ammunition, it is established that the maximum amount of powder that can be placed in the cartridge case without excessive compression will not produce excessive pressures.

Almost anyone who has attended high school chemistry class has encountered formulas for making black powder and a variety of similar mixtures, which may have been "white powder" or "yellow powder." The most authoritative advice on this subject is simply *don't!* It is extremely dangerous, and literally scores of people have been killed or maimed in the attempt to manufacture it.

Blind Magazine   A box magazine which is completely concealed within and does not protrude below the stock.

Blowback: A gun malfunction in which powder gases escape rearward and into the action. Also, a type of semiautomatic or full-automatic gun design in which there is no mechanical locking of the bolt. Instead, the breech is held closed only by the weight and inertia of the bolt, with some slight assistance from the recoil spring, until after the bullet leaves the muzzle.

Classic examples of blowback semiautomatic pistol designs are found in the Browning series of pocket-size pistols in .25, .32, and .380 calibers.

Nearly all successful submachine guns, including the very popular Uzi and the Ingram, use the blowback actions.

Blueing The typical blue-black finish applied to ferrous metals of most firearms. There are many methods of applying this finish, and even more formulas for the material to produce it.

It is not a colored coating applied to the metal, but instead a treatment which oxidizes an extremely thin layer of the metal. While a deep blue-black is the generally accepted color, a wide variety can be produced, depending upon the formula, the steel surface, and the type of oil applied in the final stages.

There are two basic methods of blueing: the traditional rust blue and the more modern one-shot hot blue (the latter is destructive to non-ferrous metals).

Traditionalists prefer the slow rust method which requires repeated applications and carding away of the rust produced, until a satisfactory finish is achieved. Under some conditions, this may require a dozen or more applications and may keep the job going for several weeks. However, this method does produce a superior finish when properly applied, and does not harm soldered joints or non-ferrous metals.

The principal advantage of the one-shot caustic method is

DO-IT-YOURSELF GUN BLUEING

1. Complete reblueing of all metal parts can be done using simple kit, which contains blueing chemicals, steel wool, abrasive fiber cloth, absorbent cotton, and gun oil. Inspect all surfaces for rust spots and pitting.

2. Remove barrel and carefully grind out any rusted or pitted spots on hard rubber wheel and wire brush.

3. Finish by polishing on buffing wheel, using graduated stages of buffing compounds until metal is bright.

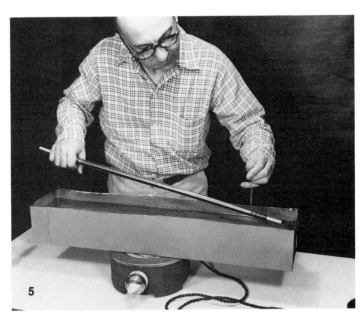

4. Metal is degreased by boiling in washing soda or borax solution. A large metal pan such as a long flower box is used, with an electric hot plate underneath.

5. Fill the barrel with oil, plug ends with cords or dowels. Lower the gun into the solution, holding it above the bottom with strings tied at both ends.

6. While metal is still hot, apply the first blueing solution, which plates the metal with a copper coating, uniformly over the entire surface. Use clean cotton wadding and rubber gloves. Apply second chemical, an acid that oxidizes the copper to bring up the blue color. Several applications may be needed to obtain the desired shade.

7. Then give barrel a coating of finishing oil from kit, using cotton wadding. Rub with fine steel wool to a bright luster.

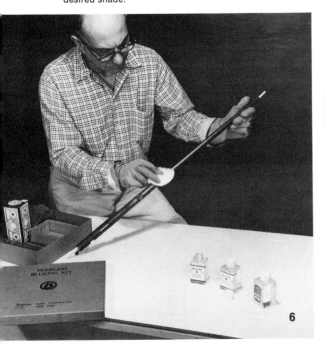

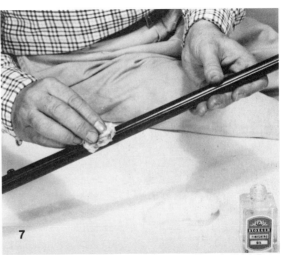

Photos by Ralph Treves

SPOT BLUEING

A. Gun metal can be touched up by spot blueing with materials in kit shown on preceding page. First, rub blemished surface with fine emery cloth or coated synthetic fiber pad (2/0 or 4/0 grit), exposing bright metal, to reduce scratches and sweat blishers. Pitted and rusted spots are gound out with hard rubber wheel on hand grinder, feathering the edges carefully to minimize gouged appearance. Clean area thoroughly with mineral solvent such as lighter fluid or naptha, using greaseless cotton wadding.

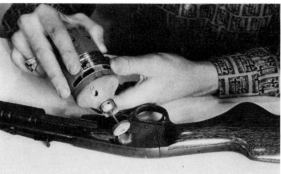

B. Use cotton swab to apply blueing solution, which plates spot with copper film. Wipe off when milky, follow with acid solution that produces the blue color. Repeat for deeper matching shade. Rather than touching up numerous small spots, it is better to restore a complete area at the same time, for a more uniform finish. Rub on gun oil to halt oxidizing process, then polish with very fine steel wool.

Bolster protrudes on right side of barrel to provide a solid seat for the percussion nipple. Here the bolster is shown as an integral part of the breech plug, and also contains the clean-out plug.

its speed and convenience.

Regardless of the method or solution used, the quality of the final finish is dependent upon two things: absolute chemical cleanliness, and a perfect polishing job.

Bolster On a muzzle-loading gun, the part protruding from the barrel into which the nipple is screwed. It may be a separate part screwed into the barrel, or it may be an integral part formed in forging the barrel, or a lump welded to the same. All are satisfactory methods if properly performed.

Bolt-Action A type of rifle action that consists of a tubular receiver into which fits a cylindrical bolt carrying locking lugs at either its front, which is the most common, or its rear. The bolt must be rotated manually into the locked position by its handle, which also unlocks and cycles the bolt fore and aft (proper feeding and ejection are usually dependent upon rapid bolt manipulation).

It was first produced successfully on a commercial scale by Peter Paul von Mauser in his model 1871 military rifle, and even more successfully in his later model 1898 military rifle (which is still in service in some parts of the world).

Bolt-action rifles are generally fitted with a Mauser or Lee type of box magazine beneath the receiver, though some very

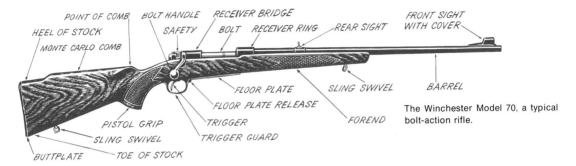

POINT OF COMB
HEEL OF STOCK
MONTE CARLO COMB
BOLT HANDLE
SAFETY
RECEIVER BRIDGE
BOLT   RECEIVER RING
REAR SIGHT
FRONT SIGHT
WITH COVER
FLOOR PLATE
FLOOR PLATE RELEASE
SLING SWIVEL
BARREL
PISTOL GRIP
SLING SWIVEL
TRIGGER
TRIGGER GUARD
FOREND
BUTTPLATE   TOE OF STOCK

The Winchester Model 70, a typical bolt-action rifle.

early centerfire rifles and many modern rimfire rifles use tubular magazines under the barrel.

With very few exceptions, all bolt-action rifles use a striker type of firing mechanism contained in the bolt which is cocked either by up and down bolt-handle movement, or by a portion of forward bolt travel.

Though associated primarily with rifle designs, the bolt-action will be found on a few single-shot pistols, and on a fair number of low-cost utility shotguns.

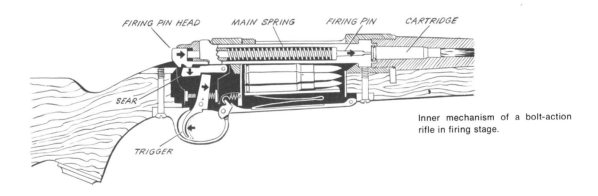

FIRING PIN HEAD   MAIN SPRING   FIRING PIN   CARTRIDGE
SEAR
TRIGGER

Inner mechanism of a bolt-action rifle in firing stage.

Bolt Guide   A rib or groove on either the bolt or the receiver to maintain alignment during bolt travel.

Bolt (Revolver)   The movable stud that rises and falls from the frame to lock the cylinder with the firing chamber in correct alignment with the bore. It is usually a pivoted lever with a stud protruding upward through the frame, activated by a protrusion on the trigger—though activated by the hammer in older single-action guns. Sometimes called cylinder stop or cylinder bolt.

Bore Diameter   The diametrical measurement across a rifled bore between the tops of opposite lands. In barrels with an uneven number (as opposed to the usual even number) of lands and grooves, it is the diameter of the circle circumscribed by the inner surfaces of all the lands. In the latter, it is exceedingly difficult to measure inside the barrel without special equipment. In the former, measurement is simply done with a conventional inside micrometer or caliper.

Most shooters, at best being equipped with a simple outside micrometer or caliper, can measure bore diameter by pushing an oversized soft-lead slug through the bore. When the slug is removed, the raised ridges on its surface represent the bottom of the grooves so must be pared away carefully with a sharp knife to expose the bottom of the grooves which represent the top of the lands in the barrel. Then, at least where equal numbers of lands and grooves are involved, measurement is simple.

If lands and grooves are unequal in number, then a special measuring fixture is required — a very close approximation may be obtained by carefully rotating the trimmed slug cleanly between the jaws of the micrometer.

While it is generally assumed that bore diameter has a fixed relationship to designated caliber, this is not necessarily so. In some instances, the bore diameter is identical with the caliber designation, such as .300-inch bore diameter in .30/06 caliber, but often this relationship does not exist. This is because there is no set system followed in caliber designation.

See CALIBER.

Bore Sight   The act of aligning the bore with the line of sight by viewing the target both through the sight and through the bore while the gun is fixed on a solid rest.

Also a device fitting the chamber or muzzle (or both) to increase the accuracy of aligning the bore on the target in the process of bore sighting. In sporting guns of relatively small caliber, no such instrument is usually necessary — but in military weapons of larger caliber, it is essential.

Boxer Primer   A metallic primer containing its own anvil pressed into the cup. Invented by the British Colonel Boxer, and used primarily in North America.

Box Lock   In a muzzle-loading gun, a gun lock in which the hammer and all other working parts are situated inside the lock plate, with the hammer protruding through a slot in the stock.

In this form, the principal advantage of the box lock is that the large flint or percussion hammer does not protrude beyond the surface of the stock.

In a modern gun (normally a shotgun), the box lock is essentially the same, but the hammer is fully enclosed and extremely compact. Its principal advantage, particularly in a double-barreled gun, is that very little wood needs to be cut away from the vital wrist portion of the stock. In addition, it makes possible—in high-grade, hand-fitted guns—the use of readily removable locks which may be drawn out of the bottom of the action (see photo).

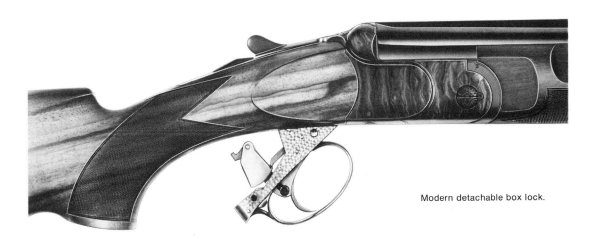

Modern detachable box lock.

The most modern type of box lock is that found in break-open, single-barrelled shotguns with either exposed or concealed hammers. A typical example is the Harrington & Richardson Topper in which the minimal working parts are assembled between the walls of the small metal receiver with the hammer protruding from a central position.

Box Magazine A box-like feed device on a rifle in which cartridges are stacked one on top of the other. It is usually removable for reloading.

Brazing A method of joining metal parts by placing copper or a copper alloy (usually brass) in the joint, and then heating the assembly so that the alloy flows and fills the joint, bending to the related parts. Brazing is commonly used to assemble barrels to ribs and lugs of double-barrelled guns, to repair firing pins and other functional parts, and, to some extent, to assemble components made up of stampings or castings.

Breech That portion of a gun which contains the action, the trigger or firing mechanism, the magazine, and the chamber portion of the barrel(s). An imprecise term generally including all the essential working parts of a gun.

Breech Block In some single-shot small arms and in artillery pieces, the non-reciprocating member that supports the cartridge case in the chamber at the instant of firing. The breech block uncovers the chamber by sliding either vertically, horizontally, or any direction more or less perpendicular to the bore axis. It may rotate in the manner of the old French 75mm gun of World War I fame, or it may tip up, down or sideways, the most common example of which is the classic British Martini-Henry.
See also BREECH BOLT and FALLING BLOCK.

Breech Bolt In any small arm, the device which supports the cartridge case in the chamber at the instant of firing and which moves fore and aft to allow all other steps in the functioning cycle to take place. The breech bolt generally contains the firing mechanism and extractor, and may contain other parts as well.
See also BREECH BLOCK.

Breech Loader Attempts at loading firearms from the breech go back almost as far as the first guns. From the very beginning it was recognized that loading from the breech offered many advantages over ramming powder and ball or shot down the muzzle. Breech-loading cannon are known to have been used shortly after 1400, but without particular success.

The most common form used a separate chamber containing powder and ball, fitted into a yoke at the rear of the barrel and wedged forward against or into the rear of the barrel. The "chamber" itself was muzzle-loaded, inserted into the gun, fired, then removed for reloading.

This design did not produce adequate sealing and great amounts of gas escaped at the barrel/chamber joint. In spite of its inefficiency and shortcomings, the system remained in limited use until the 18th century.

Another less common type had the rear portion of the barrel threaded into the balance. The breech piece could be unscrewed, loaded, screwed back into place, and fired.

Breech-loading hand weapons date later and are known from the early 16th century, apparently existing in some quantity by then. One breech-loading wheellock pistol, dated 1537, was the property of King Henry VIII and is in the Tower of London, along with trapdoor breeches that were loaded with an iron tube containing powder and ball, much like a cartridge.

In 1704 Isaac de la Chaumette devised a screw breech with a threaded plug passing vertically through the barrel at the breech. The plug was lowered by turning the trigger guard, exposing the rear of the barrel so ball and powder could be inserted. Raising the plug by turning the trigger guard then sealed the breech. The design apparently saw some service with French Dragoons.

Chaumette further improved the design with a quick-acting thread so only one turn of the guard was needed for opening and closing. By 1776 the design reached its final form in the hands of Patrick Ferguson, who armed his regiment with "Ferguson" rifles during the American Revolution. The Ferguson/Chaumette was probably the most practical of all the screw-breech designs attempted, but after the death of Ferguson, no further development took place.

Several designs appeared using tipping breeches, some of which were loaded with paper cartridges rather than loose powder and ball. Most successful was the Hall, by American John H. Hall, whose separate breech was pivoted at its rear, and raised at its front by a lever for loading. It was adopted by the U.S.A. in 1819 and remained in production until 1840.

The most significant breech-loading factor was sealing in the powder gases. This was accomplished by Pauly in 1812 with a brass-head, wrapped-paper, obturating cartridge used in a break-open breech. Not recognized for its true worth at the time, the Pauly cartridge was the basis upon which all subsequent obturating cartridges were based and which made practical breech-loading arms possible.

In 1837 Dreyse introduced the first truly successful breech-loading, bolt-action rifle utilizing a paper cartridge and a rubber breech seal. It was called the needle gun because of its slender,

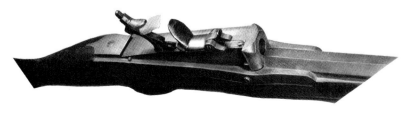

In 1811, an American, John Hall of North Yarmouth, Me., worked out the first breechloader to get serious attention from the government. A section of the rear and of the barrel lifted up to be loaded with bullet and powder. But the gun was still fired by the flintlock method.

long firing pin which penetrated through the powder charge to detonate a percussion cap placed against the base of the bullet. It was adopted by Prussia, and by the French in an improved form devised by Antoine A. Chassepot in 1866.

In 1848 Christian Sharps, an American, produced the first falling-block action using a paper or linen cartridge and percussion ignition. It used a metal gas seal which worked fairly well until worn. The breech block was actuated by the hinged trigger guard. The Sharps was successful and saw wide military use, and was readily adapted a few years later to both rim- and centerfire cartridges.

With the advent of the self-contained metallic cartridge typified by the Smith & Wesson .22 rimfire and the .44 Henry, breech-loading systems became practical and appeared in profusion, culminating in the Mauser bolt-action and the Winchester lever-action guns. All used Pauly's obturating-case principle and owed their success to his 1812 work.

The problem of gas-sealing had been solved making all manner of breech-loading systems possible, and by the late 1860s muzzle-loading systems had been almost entirely displaced throughout the world.

Breech Plug   In a muzzle loader, the plug that closes the breech end of the bore. Drilling, reaming, and rifling must be accomplished through the entire length of the barrel blank, which is then threaded to receive a plug that is screwed in to seal the breech.

The breech plug often contains an integral upper tang for securing to the stock, or some form of hook or other patent-breech system that assists in securing the entire barrel assembly to the stock.

See HOOK BREECH.

Brown Bear   see BEARS.

Brown Bess   A loose term applied to all British flintlock muskets of the 1720–1840 period. They were heavy and clumsy, but durable and reliable. Of nominal .75 caliber, four patterns were made: (1) First Pattern, 46-inch barrel, brass furniture; (2) Second Model, similar but with 42-inch barrel; (3) India Pattern, a cheaply made but similar arm; (4) New Land Musket, introduced in 1802. All patterns carried a socket bayonet with a 17-inch triangular blade.

Browning   An oldtime method of finishing gun barrels and other ferrous parts with a rich brown color by repeated treatment with a solution producing fine rust. The rust is then removed, and the metal is oiled, waxed, or varnished.

Any compound which promotes fine, even, rapid rusting will produce a brown surface in time. Special solutions for the purpose are sold by gunsmithing supply houses.

Browning, John M. North America's most prolific and famous gun designer, producer in his lifetime (1855–1926) of over fifty designs, of which over twenty were commercially produced in large quantities. Winchester produced nine of his guns, including the famous single shot, and five highly successful lever-action rifles. Colt produced ten designs, foremost of which was the famous government model M1911 pistol and its many variations.

Also three Browning machine guns, one automatic rifle, one auto pistol, and an automatic cannon were adopted by the U.S. military establishment and manufactured in great quantities through several wars. In addition, an extensive array of Browning designs, handguns, shotguns, rifles, and military weapons, were produced by Fabrique Nationale in Belgium.

Browning moved to Ogden, Utah, and opened a gunshop which resulted in his eventual production of a few hundred examples of his famous single-shot rifle, which he eventually sold to Winchester, who introduced it in 1885.

Since the successful production of his first gas-operated machine gun by Colt in 1895, Browning military weapons— principally machine guns, automatic rifles, and self-loading pistols—have been adopted as standard arms by dozens of armies. In fact, millions upon millions of these weapons are still in daily service among smaller armies throughout the world, over a half-century after their baptism of fire.

Today Browning, (formerly Browning Arms Co.) thrives in Morgan, Utah, but does not actually produce any of the many models it markets. Some of its guns are manufactured by Fabrique Nationale, while others are produced on contract by various vendors.

Brush Country Game, Cartridges for Bear, elk, moose, and deer are often as not hunted in timber or brush where limited visibility requires short-range shots, and where bullets will often encounter unseen twigs, branches, even saplings en route to the target. Such intermediate obstructions will deflect bullets significantly, often enough to cause misses. Further, lightly constructed, high-velocity bullets may disintegrate on them.

Good brush performance, then, requires strong bullets at moderate velocity, preferrably with blunt noses. These characteristics are found in calibers such as 8mm and 7mm Mauser, .30/30 and .32 Special Winchester, .35 Remington, .358 Winchester, .30/40 Krag—as well as in the obsolete .33 and .348 Winchester, .45/70, etc. High-velocity magnums may also be handloaded to lower velocities with blunt, heavy bullets for excellent performance.

Moderate velocity is no handicap for a brush rifle because most shots are taken at ranges where flatness of trajectory is not at all important.

Brush Country Game, Guns for Also called woods rifles, these guns are used for deer hunting or other medium game not larger than black bear. Since such guns are used on thin-skinned animals of relatively small size, they need not be particularly powerful, with almost anything from .30/30 to .308 Winchester being satisfactory. Shooting in brush or timber is generally at ranges under 50 yards with only a few seconds available to make the shot. Consequently, brush guns must be short, light, fast handling, and well-suited to instinctive or snap shooting. Traditionally, the short-barrelled, lightweight, lever-action carbine has been considered the ideal North American brush rifle. Recently, though, autoloading and pump-action rifles, with the lever gun's characteristics, have increased in popularity for this kind of hunting.

See also DEER, GUNS FOR.

B.S.A. Rifle Technically, any rifle produced by the British gun-making firm, Birmingham Small Arms Co. In practice, however, the term is generally applied to those lightweight sporting and heavy target B.S.A. rifles built upon variations of the Martini tipping-block action in .22 rimfire caliber.

The term is also sometimes applied to the big, heavy, .577 or .577/.450 British service rifles of the 1880s and 90s. Following the replacement of those rifles in military service, B.S.A. converted a great many to sporting rifles in many calibers from .577 downward—and they, too, are often referred to as B.S.A. rifles.

See also MARTINI RIFLE, and PEABODY RIFLE.

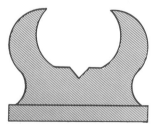
Buckhorn rear sight, shooter's view.

Buckhorn Sight A form of open, metallic rear sight in which the sides of the leaf curl upward and inward over the sighting notch, sometimes to the point of obscuring a large portion of it from the field of view.

See also METALLIC SIGHTS.

Buckshot Simply round lead shot for use in shotshells which is of abnormally large diameter compared to the sizes commonly used on birds and small game. Buckshot may range in size from 000 (.375 to .380 inch diameter) downward. Large buckshot is generally formed by swaging sections of lead wire in a "cold-header" machine. The size of the pellets prevents measuring the shot charge. Instead, pellets must be counted before being placed in the case.

Buckshot is generally reserved for use on big game such as deer (thus the name *buck* shot), and also the larger varmints. The larger-sized buckshot loads are also quite extensively used by military and police establishments throughout the world. The standard U. S. military load is the 2¾-inch 12-gauge shell loaded with nine 000 buck shot in a polyethylene granular filler; it is virtually identical to the Remington commercial load.

See also SHOT.

Bull Barrel A relative and rather imprecise term describing any handgun or rifle barrel abnormally thick and heavy for its

Typical Bull Barrel on either rifle or handgun is thick for its length as on this High-Standard .22 auto.

length. A bull barrel on a rifle will generally measure well over one inch in diameter and be cylindrical or only very slightly tapered toward the muzzle. A bull barrel on a .22 autoloading pistol may be four or five inches and about ¾ inch in diameter.

Bullet Cannelure A groove, plain or serrated, formed around the bullet, providing a recess into which the case mouth may be crimped.

Bullet Deflection   In military parlance, the term refers to windage adjustment or lateral adjustment applied to the sight to get on target. Among sporting shooters, though, it is directional deviation produced when a bullet strikes any object along its path toward the target.

A bullet striking any object may be deflected from its original path. The direction of deflection will normally be away from the center of mass of the object struck, but is unpredictable otherwise.

The amount of deflection is dependent upon the relationship of the mass of the object struck to the mass of the bullet and to the amount of damage or disturbance produced in the bullet.

Numerous variables apply, so it is generally impossible to predict the amount of deflection produced except in the case of a pure ricochet from a solid, smooth surface.

If the impact is solid and the bullet sufficiently disturbed, it may tumble or spiral from that point onward, and if heavily damaged, may fragment over a wide area and never reach its target.

Bullets least deflected by twigs, branches, etc., appear to be those of blunt shape, fairly long length, sturdy construction, traveling at moderate velocities.

See also RICOCHET.

Bullet Energy   The kinetic energy possessed by a bullet in flight (its ability to do work). Bullet energy is generally stated in foot pounds (fp), and is calculated by the simple and widely known formula for kinetic energy.

It is essential that bullet weight and velocity be known, after which one may use the following shortened and simplified method: (1) Square the velocity of the bullet in foot seconds; (2) Divide the result by 7,000; (3) Divide the quotient by twice the acceleration of gravity (64.32); (4) Multiply the quotient by the bullet weight in grains. The result will be the total striking energy of the bullet in foot pounds.

A by-product of this method is the result of step three, which is the striking energy of each grain of bullet weight at that particular velocity.

To simplify—or rather, eliminate—calculation of bullet energy for most practical purposes, you'll find a table of bullet energy per grain of weight for a wide variety of velocities in the appendices of this volume. Use of that table involves simply selecting the bullet velocity, picking the matching energy-per-grain, and then multiplying that value by the weight of the bullet in grains.

Bullet Engraving The action whereby a bullet is forced into full engagement with the rifling of a barrel at the instant of firing. Being of a diameter equal to the *groove* diameter of the barrel, the bullet is impressed by the rifling lands to their full depth. This action, and the grooves it produces on the bullet, are referred to as bullet engraving.

Grooves impressed into the surface of the bullet by the lands during its passage through the bore are clearly seen here.

Bullet, Expanding Any bullet designed to deform in a predictable manner and thereby increase its effective diameter upon entering animal tissue. The term is generally applied only to metal-jacketed types, but technically applies to solid lead types as well if they are intended to expand on impact.

Expansion increases lethality in two ways—(1) it produces a larger wound cavity, and (2) it transfers more energy to the target.

In jacketed bullets, expansion is obtained by use of a soft metal cup open at the point to expose the even softer core material (a soft-point bullet), or by use of a cavity extending down into the core (a hollow-point bullet).

The amount of expansion is determined by a combination of jacket thickness and strength, core hardness and amount of core exposed, size and extent of the hollow point's cavity, and several other variables, including striking velocity.

Nonjacketed bullets are made to expand by matching bullet hardness with impact velocity and also by the use of hollow points and specific point shapes.

See also CONTROLLED EXPANSION BULLET, HOLLOW POINT, and SOFT POINT.

Bullet, Hunting Generally, the term refers to hollow point or soft-point jacketed bullets, but the principal type of hunting bullet is the expanding variety.

Full-jacketed bullets that are used for hunting very large or dangerous game, are also used for small edible game when it is not desired to destroy edible meat.

In the final analysis, any type of bullet becomes a hunting bullet by usage.

See also BULLET, EXPANDING, CONTROLLED EXPANSION BULLET, HOLLOW POINT, and SOFT POINT.

Bullet Lubricant In its simplest form, a lubricating grease applied to a lead bullet—generally in grooves provided for this purpose—to ease the bullet's passage down the bore, prevent leading, and reduce bullet deformation. At one time lubricant was also sometimes applied to jacketed bullets, but no longer.

While any lubricant will serve the above purposes, whether it's a modern grease, a synthetic, or plain mutton tallow, more specialized lubricants are required to produce maximum accuracy. In previous times, these were generally mixtures of beeswax and petroleum jelly or similar softening agents, and finely powdered graphite in suspension. More recently, though, mixtures of Alox compound and softened beeswax have proved to be far better, and are readily available under several labels.

Lubricants may be applied to bullets in many ways. The simplest method is to smear it into the grooves by hand, though old-timers generally preferred to stand bullets on their bases in melted lubricant that would cover all their grooves. When the lubricant hardened, the bullets were cut out of this lubricant cake with a hollow punch or *cake cutter*, leaving the grooves filled with lubricant. Recently, though, lubricant has generally been applied in lubricator sizers.

See also LUBRICATOR SIZER, CAKE CUTTER.

Bullet mold, open.

Bullet Mold A device for forming bullets for small-arms ammunition from molten lead alloy. Generally, a bullet mold consists of two closely fitted iron blocks, into each of which has been formed half of a negative impression of the bullet desired. The blocks are then clamped together or held closed, and molten lead is poured in to fill the cavities. Separation of the blocks then allows the bullets to fall free.

Molds are generally fitted with pliers-type handles, for convenience in handling, closing, and opening the blocks, with alignment pins and lubrication points, and with a device known as a sprue cutter, which trims off excess lead before the blocks are opened to drop the completed bullets.

Bullet molds originally produced only a single bullet, but today molds containing two to ten cavities for either one type or assorted bullets have become popular.

See also SPRUE, SPRUE CUTTER.

Bullet Placement See SHOT PLACEMENT.

Bullet Pull That force, measured directly in pounds, necessary to extract the bullet from a loaded cartridge; it is a measure of how tightly the case neck grips the bullet. It is controlled by several factors—case-neck hardness, bullet/case dimensional relationship, case-neck thickness, area of contact with the bullet, degree of crimp, and presence and type of mouth sealer.

Generally speaking, all other factors being equal, a lighter bullet pull will result in slightly reduced pressure and velocity, while excessive bullet pull will have the opposite effect. Once a particular lot of U.S. .30 caliber match ammunition was loaded with tin-plated bullets that became soldered to their case mouths during storage, resulting in a bullet pull value of many hundreds of pounds. When this occurred, chamber pressures rose drastically to unsafe levels and wrecked several rifles. As another example, it was learned that increasing bullet pull by about 60 pounds enabled standard pressure and velocity to be obtained in a particular .45 ACP loading with ½ grain less powder.

Bullet pull values in factory ammunition may vary from as little as 30 or 40 pounds in some lead-bullet handgun cartridges to 250 pounds or more in some military-rifle loadings.

While ammunition factories have many options in controlling bullet pull, the handloader is generally restricted to the degree of crimp and to the as-sized case-neck diameter.

Handle at top allows collet inside puller to be tightened on bullet, holding it securely while case is pulled *off* by action of press.

Bullet Puller   A device that grips a bullet securely and allows the case to be pulled from the bullet. This is generally accomplished by a form of collet, which is tightened on the bullet to hold it stationary while the case is drawn off in a loading press.

Other types exist, including those using balls on a conical ramp or self-energizing flat jaws to grip the bullet. A simple, quite popular type is the inertia bullet puller, in which a loaded cartridge is secured tightly in the inverted position in a hollow hammer head. Striking the hammer causes the bullet's own inertia to pull it from the case.

See INERTIA BULLET PULLER.

Bullet Trap   A heavily constructed steel box built in such a shape that bullets entering its open side are decelerated and stopped without ricocheting or throwing fragments back toward the shooter. It usually has sloping sides and a series of deflector plates against which the bullet impacts successively until its velocity is reduced to zero. It normally has provisions for attaching a target over its working face, and is often moderately portable.

Bullet traps are available to meet all requirements from .22 rimfire on up to the most powerful sporting rifle cartridges.

Bullet trap.

Bullet, Wadcutter   See WADCUTTER BULLET.

Burning Rate   The rate at which a given powder burns. Not a precise value, just a relative position in regard to other powders.

Burp Gun   A World War II colloquialism applied today to almost any submachine gun, but originally given by American soldiers to the German MP38/40 series of weapons.

Burst Limiter   A device in a full-automatic weapon that causes a specified number of shots to be fired with a single pull of the trigger. Most common are burst limits of three or five rounds, accomplished by a ratchet or counting device.

Buttplate   Any protective plate attached to the butt to protect the wood. Since the stock is frequently placed or struck against the ground, it is highly susceptible to damage. On military arms and on early sporting arms, metal was almost universally used for buttplates. However, current practice is to use plastics almost exclusively on sporting arms.

Buttstock   The wood (usually) portion of a gun extending rearward of the breech that rests against the shooter's shoulder and provides a secure rest for the cheek and a grip or handle for See also GUNSTOCK.

Cake Cutter
A simple tubular device for removing cast lead bullets from lubricant that has been melted and allowed to harden around them and thus fill the lubricating grooves. In its most common form, the cake cutter is simply a fired cartridge case of the proper caliber with its head cut away so that as it is pressed down over successive bullets, those already cut free from the cake are pushed out through the top.

Caliber
By original definition, the diameter of the bore (land to land diameter) of any gun barrel. It does not designate bullet diameter as sometimes thought, nor does it identify a particular cartridge.

Today, though, caliber is generally used interchangeably with cartridge designation—and a designation such as .270 Winchester is generally referred to as a *caliber*.

See also CARTRIDGE DESIGNATION.

Call, Game
Any orally or mechanically produced sound which serves to attract a wild animal, or a device for producing such sounds. Generally, calls function in two different ways, the first being intended to duplicate the natural call of either a potential mate or a challenger of the same species causing the quarry to hunt for the source of sound in anticipation of either a good fight or a good mating. The second type is intended to duplicate either the natural voice, or a trouble or pain cry of a food animal, and thus attract the quarry in search of a quick and easy meal.

Lyman cake cutter.

Usually, the first type of call is used on birds, waterfowl in particular, while the second type is used almost exclusively on predators. However, the first type has also long been used to attract males of those species which generally keep harems — thus, the moose horn, deer antler rattling, elk bugle, etc.

Old-timers called many species by mouth alone, or by means of simple wood or bark horns. In addition, they used various simple mechanical calls, such as a cedar box stroked with a slate strip to call turkeys or squirrels, and rattled two dried deer horns together to attract aggressive whitetail bucks.

More recently (particularly in the last decade) electronic calls have come to the forefront, particularly for use in attracting predators. A number of manufacturers produce miniaturized tape or record players which reproduce accurately any wild call. These midget players are battery operated and are easily carried afield. The manufacturers of such electronic calls offer wide selection of calls to suit virtually any game and situation.

Primarily due to the extreme effectiveness of electronic calls — plus the fact that little or no training is required to use them — their use is for the most part restricted by law to predators. It is not, for example, permissible to use electronic calls on waterfowl or most big game animals.

While some mechanical calls are quite simple to use and require relatively little training, best results with them require not only years of careful practice, but a very high degree of knowledge of the game for which they are intended.

Calling the Shot   The action of retaining a sight picture exactly as it appeared at the instant of firing and thus determining where the shot will strike on the target. If it is apparent to the eye that the sight alignment was slightly left of the bullseye but correct vertically at the instant the gun discharged, then that shot would be called "out to the left" or, possibly, "out at nine o'clock."

Experienced shooters who call their shots regularly are often able to indicate precisely where each shot has struck without looking at the target.

Cannelure   A relatively shallow groove rolled into the surface of a bullet or a cartridge case. In the former, it serves as a seat into which the case mouth may be crimped to secure the bullet tightly. In the latter, it is generally applied to cases used in tubular magazines (though also found for the same reason in autoloading-pistol cartridges) for the purpose of providing an interior seat against which the base of the bullet rests.

For cartridges used in magazine guns (tubular or box) both types of cannelures serve to prevent bullets from being driven deeper into cases by recoil forces. Cartridges remaining in any magazine during the firing of a series of shots will be struck repeatedly on the bullets' point by either the front of a box magazine or by other cartridges in a tubular one. Unless the bullets are held quite securely, they may be driven deeply into the case. This has the effect of increasing pressures, reducing accuracy, and in some instances interfering with proper feeding.

Revolver bullets have cannelures for the opposite reason. They permit case mouths to be crimped heavily and hold bullets so that they do not move out of cases under the influence of recoil. As a revolver recoils, it carries chambered cartridges with it, and this movement tends to draw the cases off the bullet— and if the bullets are not secured tightly, they will move out of the case to protrude beyond the chamber mouth and tie up the gun.

Cannelures are also used on lead bullets to provide a reservoir for lubricant. They were also relatively common among metal jacketed bullets before the development of nonfouling alloys and some form of lubricant was desirable to prevent fouling. Cannelures are also sometimes used purely as a means of identification on both metallic cartridges and shotshells, and may also be found serving to help hold metal shotshell heads in place on the body.

Regardless of whether on case or bullet, cannelures are normally formed by rotating a smooth or lightly serrated wheel of the proper width against the item under pressure while it is supported against a pair of smooth rollers. Special tools by which the handloader may cannelure both the cases and bullet are available from both SAS and C-H Die Company.

See also CRIMP.

Cannelure in case at left serves to support bullet against rearward movement, while cannelure in bullet (center) allows case to be crimped tightly upon bullet to resist either or both rear and forward movement, also to insure tight fit of bullet/case assembly, in contrast to plain bullet shown at right.

Cant Any deviation of a gun's vertical axis from the true vertical. If a rifle or pistol shooter leans his gun slightly to the left, then it is said to be "canted left." When sights are properly aligned, canting in either direction will cause the bullet's trajectory to diverge from the line of sight in the direction of the cant, and also to strike low.

Cap Groove In a percussion revolver, a rounded guide groove in the side of the recoil shield leading to the nipple in the capping position. It aids in aligning and pressing home the fresh cap. Also a deep groove in the face of the recoil shield, running from the firing position to the capping position to provide clearance for bulged or split fired caps as the cylinder is rotated. Without this, fired caps can wedge between nipple and recoil shield and jam the cylinder immovably.

See PERCUSSION CAP.

Caplock A percussion lock; a firing mechanism for muzzle-loading guns using percussion caps.

See Percussion Cap; Percussion Lock.

Capture (Tranquilizer) Gun A single-shot gun specially designed to fire hypodermic-type darts containing tranquilizer drugs at animals. The capture gun may be of break-open design, or bolt-action type, and may utilize CO_2 as propellant, or it may be a true firearm using a special blank cartridge to fire the hypodermic dart. Capture guns are generally of large bore, ½ inch or more, and intended to launch the hypodermic dart at low velocity.

They are most widely used to subdue wild animals for capture, but occasionally used by law enforcement officers to control dangerous criminals when conventional gunfire cannot be safely used.

Carbine Simply a short rifle. A relative term, including older guns with barrels of 30 inches when rifles had barrels of 40 inches or more, and today referring to arms with 18- or 20-inch barrels when rifle barrels of 24 inches or longer are standard.

Typical carbine is shorter and lighter than its rifle counterpart, and may often be chambered for a less powerful cartridge; shown here is the U.S.A. M1 military carbine of World War II.

Cartridge, Caseless A type of cartridge which does not use a conventional metallic case and primer. A pellet or cylinder is formed by molding the propellant around the rear portion of the bullet and giving it sufficient strength to withstand normal handling and feeding loads. A consumable primer is then placed in the head of the propellant block and ignited either by percussion or by an electric current (large-caliber military weapons).

A firearm using such ammunition must have a separate sealing device to prevent propellant gases from leaking back into the action. Metallic and plastic seals have been developed specifically for the purpose.

When a caseless cartridge is fired, the primer is ignited by the firing pin, furnishing flame to ignite the main block of propellant, which then burns conventionally, completely consuming itself and the primer in the process. Only minor amounts of the propellant residue remains in the chamber.

Advantages of caseless cartridges are reduced weight and bulk, elimination of extraction and disposal of hot, fired cases, reduction of strategic materials, and lower unit costs. These factors are of vital interest to military weapons specialists, but have little appeal to the sportsman.

To date, only one form of caseless cartridge has ever been introduced to shooters. This the Daisy/Heddon V-L system developed by Jules Von Langenhoven of Belgium. A bore-diameter cylinder of whitish propellant is extruded around a small teat protruding from the base of the swaged lead bullet. Apparently the propellant is applied wet and shrinks in drying, becoming slightly smaller in diameter than the bullet.

This caseless cartridge does *not* use a primer, but is ignited by a jet of compressed air, generated by a typical air-gun mechanism, when the trigger is pressed. The gun used with this ammunition is identical to a typical spring-air rifle, except it has a more efficient seal entering the rear of the chamber, and a check valve preventing propellant gases from flowing back into the ignition-jet air cylinder.

The V-L system of rifle and ammunition has been in production since 1969, and while it performs reliably within the .22 rimfire velocity and energy range, it has not been a significant commercial success.

One other semi-commercial caseless cartridge has been tested briefly in the United States. This is the 9mm S&W caseless pistol and submachine gun cartridge. In appearance it is much the same as the V-L round consisting of the conventional jacketed bullet with a bore-diameter cylinder of propellant fixed to its base. However, it uses an electrically ignited, consumable primer seated in the head of the propellant.

Guns intended to function with it has been limited to conversions of the S&W M76 submachine gun, though there is rumor of some pistols having been similarly modified. The breech bolt of the gun includes a dependable seal which enters the rear of the chamber and electrical contacts to ignite the primer.

This system requires an electrical power source either installed in the buttstock or in a remote container. The system has existed for several years, but only in test-weapon form. No production guns or ammunition have been distributed.

U.S. postwar development in one form of cartridge for 20mm aircraft cannon. IMR-type propellant granules can be clearly seen through clear combustible binder. Round on right has base reinforcement found necessary because of forces acting on cartridges during feeding through automatic guns.

Cartridge Designation The name applied to any particular cartridge by its manufacturer or user. It is important to remember that the cartridge designation does not necessarily mean the same as the caliber. The designation normally includes an approximation of caliber but contains other information which may or may not be useful, and may even be misleading.

There are three basic systems of cartridge designation in existence: American, British, and European or metric. In their original form, developed in the late 19th century, those designations generally gave a reasonably clear picture of the cartridge to knowledgeable persons. However, since there have been so many individual variations introduced (in both the cartridges proper and designations), this is no longer true.

Originally, the American system consisted of three numerical indicators, the first of which identified the nominal bullet diameter in hundreds or thousandths of an inch, the second the weight of the black powder charge in grains, and the third the bullet by weight. In addition, a fourth designation might be present in the name of either a designer or manufacturer. Thus, the original designation of the .44/40 Winchester was .44/40/220 Winchester. Likewise the .45/70/500 U.S. indicated what we now call simply the .45/70. Some makers also added a case length designation, and separate designations for straight and bottleneck cases.

Today, though, a typical American designation may indicate nothing more than a reasonable approximation of the bullet's diameter and the maker's name, as in the .221 Remington, which actually uses a .224-inch diameter bullet.

The British system was a bit different, designating straight cases by their nominal caliber and length, as in the .577/3-inch. Then, a smaller caliber based upon that same diameter case, would be designated first .577, followed by the nominal bullet diameter, and then the case length as in .577-.500-2¾ inch.

And, like the American system, designer's or maker's names or some proprietary title might also be added to the basic designation. This system, too, has become so complicated that present British designations generally offer nothing more than a rough approximation of bullet diameter and a maker's name.

The metric system used throughout most of the rest of the world is actually the most informative of the three in its pure form, but even it's been perverted in recent times, though to a lesser degree. The basic metric system contains three, four, or five designations, depending upon the complexity of case design and special features.

A typical rimless caliber is designated, 7.92×57. The first indicator stands for the bore diameter of the barrel in millimeters while the second indicates case length. The lack of any other indicator indicates a rimless case. If the designation is written 7.92×57R, the R indicates a rimmed case. In this particular caliber, two sets of bore and bullet dimensions have been used during its lifetime; so the inclusion of a *J* immediately following the 57 would indicate the smaller (.318-inch) bullets, while the similar inclusion of an *S* would indicate the larger (.323-inch) bullets. Example: 7.92×57JR.

Thus, the metric system designates a particular cartridge by nominal bullet diameter, case length, and case type. Europeans also often add a maker's name or some flossy adjective such as *Magnum Bombe* to indicate particular high-performance load, or maker's name or any other superlative that suits their fancy.

At present, there seems to be no possibility of any general system being put into effect that would be genuinely informative. There's just one area that looks bright, and that is that as American cartridges become more popular abroad, they are being assigned straight metric designations—thus the .30/06 becomes the 7.62×63mm.

Some slight attempt has been made to use metric designations here. Examples are .358 (8.8mm) Winchester, 6mm Remington, etc. As interest in overall conversion to the metric system becomes more certain, we may expect to see wider use of it in cartridge designations, thus the .222 Remington Magnum would become 5.56×47mm.

See also Caliber.

Cartridge Trap   A covered receptacle somewhere on a gun to carry a few spare cartridges. Today they are most common on custom-built hunting rifles and on the European style of combination rifles and shotguns. However, at least one model has been supplied in the form of a pair of oversized revolver grips containing receptacles for six cartridges in the butt.

Two basic types of butt traps exist, one of which is recessed into the buttstock under the buttplate and accessible through a spring-loaded lid often referred to as a trap. This should probably be considered the American style, since it is seldom found elsewhere. The European style trap is usually located on the underside of the stock just ahead of the buttplate. Otherwise, it functions in exactly the same manner. With the exception of a few military survival guns designed to carry their complete ammunition supply in the stock, cartridge traps are most commonly made to accommodate about three rounds and never more than five.

European-style cartridge trap or magazine in underside of stock just ahead of butt plate on Colt/Sharps single-shot rifle.

Case Capacity   Usable case volume. Also that part of the case interior below the base of the bullet. Where bullet position varies, capacity is figured to the neck and shoulder junction.

Case Forming   The act of taking a cartridge case in one caliber and reshaping it into another. One of the simplest examples of this achieved wide popularity during World War II. Plentiful .30/06 fired military cases were trimmed to the correct length and full-length resized, producing perfectly acceptable and safe 8x57mm cases for reloading.

This modification was possible because .30/06 and 8mm cases used the same nominal head and chamber diameters, had the

Examples of using the .45/70 cartridge case for reforming into 8 other calibers for which cases and ammunition are no longer produced: .33WCF, .38/56, .40/60, .40/65, short .40/82, full-length .40/82, .45/90, .45/60, from R to L after .45/70.

same rimless head design, and were both designed to function in approximately the same pressure and velocity ranges. In addition, the .30/06 case was sufficiently longer than the 8mm to allow trimming to a uniform and correct length. Since that time, it has been found possible to produce quite good cases in over twenty calibers from .30/06 brass.

The most common methods of forming are simply trimming cases to length and resizing them. The majority of forming jobs include those two operations and perhaps others as well, including neck reaming, annealing, fire-forming, and neck expansion.

The purpose of case forming is to use readily available cases to form a caliber which is difficult to obtain or is too costly. There are several scores of cartridges which have been discontinued but for which tens of thousands of perfectly good firearms still exist. In most instances, a skilled and experienced handloader can place those guns back in service by forming readily available cases to suit their chambers. The table below shows most of the more common conversions of existing cases to revive obsolete chambers

See also FIRE-FORMING, NECK EXPANSION, NECK REAMING, and RESIZING.

A case gauge with cartridge case placed inside. Depth to which case enters indicates if headspace and length are correct.

Case Gauge A chamber-like cavity in a piece of metal, provided with go and no-go steps and dimensioned so that insertion of a cartridge will indicate if that cartridge is of proper size and shape.

Case Harden   A method by which steel and iron parts are given a very hard, thin, wear-resistant surface, while the interior portion of the parts retain their original properties. Parts to be treated are brought to a high heat and treated with carbon, which is absorbed by the surface of the metal. Case hardening often produces a pleasing pattern of red, blue, and gray colors— quite popular as a finish on all but barrels of older guns.

See also COLOR HARDEN.

Case Remover   Also called a case puller or case extractor or broken-case extractor or ruptured-case extractor, it is a device held by the bolt and extractor and its forward end has a hook or other engaging surfaces which will grip a ruptured case and pull it from the chamber as the action is opened.

Typical of this is the split-finger version used by most military establishments. It can be used only when the entire case head has been pulled off, leaving the body of the cartridge case stuck in the chamber. It is dropped into the chamber and the action closed upon it, causing the extractor to snap over the rim of the remover and placing the claws or hooks ahead of the broken case mouth. The action is then opened and the extractor pulls the remover out of the chamber carrying with it the remaining portion of the case. While generally a military item, case removers of this sort have been sold commercially by a number of firms, principally the old Marble Co. and E. C. Herkner.

The remover described above is of little value to the handloader stymied by a case stuck in his resizing die. Such problems usually occur when the die and case have been inadequately lubricated, or when the rim of the case is so weak that it will not withstand the pull necessary to extract it from the die. In either instance, the rim is pulled off the case by the shell holder, leaving the rest of the case, complete with solid head, wedged firmly in the die.

In this instance, the proper puller or remover is simply a threaded bolt with its head turned to fit into the shell holder or into the shell-holder seat of the loading tool. In use, the die is removed from the press and the primer pocket drilled out, then the die is replaced. The remover is slipped into the shell-holder seat, and the threaded portion is advanced into the hole drilled into the case head. Then while pressure is maintained by the tool handle, the remover is turned, screwing the threaded portion into the case and cutting its own thread as it goes. Once the remover is turned completely into the case head, sufficient force on the loading press handle will extract the case.

Case, Separated Also called a ruptured case, it is the condition of the case head's cracking away from the case body at a point just forward of the solid web. The case head is withdrawn when the action is opened, but its body remains stuck in the chamber. The case remover is the most practical tool for removing the case body. (The case body must be removed as it prevents proper chambering of subsequent rounds.)

Left, the two parts of a separated rimless case; right, a belted case showing partial separation.

Separated cases are not common today, except in reloaded ammunition whose cases have been weakened by repeated improper resizing or by excess headspace conditions within the gun.

Case separation most often results from stretching, which reduces wall thickness just ahead of the web to the point that a crack forms completely around its circumference.

Occasionally, fired cases may show a hairline crack or a brightly burnished ring part way around the case at this location, indicating an incipient separation. Even though the head remains attached, the cause should be determined and corrected before further firing is done.

See also CASE REMOVER.

Case Trimming Removing excess material from a case mouth. In a metallic case, this normally consists of rotating a cutter made specifically for use on brass against a stop which has been preset to produce the correct length.

Most modern case trimmers consist of a U-shaped frame fitted at one end with a collet type of holder that clamps the case's head, and fitted at the other end with a bearing and stop for the cutter, which is rotated by a hand crank. Power-driven versions of several trimmers are available in which the basic trimmer unit is attached to a drill-press table, and the cutter is placed in the drill chuck, and the drill stop is set to the desired finished length.

In paper or plastic shotshell cases, trimming is usually done by hand with a very simple arbor to which a razor-type cutter is attached. The case is simply slipped over the arbor, the cutter positioned at the right point, and then the case rotated against it to produce a clean cut.

Metallic cases require trimming when extensive reloading and firing has caused enough brass to flow forward in the neck to produce excessive length. Excessive length jammed into the forward portion of the chamber will, if not removed, cause elevated pressures and reduce accuracy. Plastic and paper shotshell cases do not lengthen appreciably in firing, but repeated firings sometimes cause the case mouth to become too soft to produce a solid crimp. When this happens, the weaker portion of the case mouth is cut off, and with a shortened wad column and crimping die, the case may continue in service.

CB Cap   A very low-powered .22 rimfire cartridge consisting of a shortened version of the .22 Short case loaded with a very light conical bullet, usually propelled by only the priming compound. In recent years, however, one or two manufacturers, principally CCI, have introduced a light powder charge in the CB cap.

See also BB CAP.

Centerfire   A cartridge whose primer is located in the center of the base of its case. This is distinguished from the rimfire cartridge which has primer powder in its rim. Centerfires make up the bulk of modern sporting ammunition. See also PRIMER and RIMFIRE.

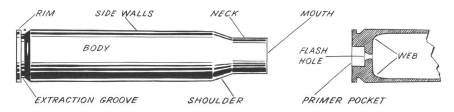

Parts of a centerfire cartridge case.

Center of Impact   The precise center of any given group of shots on target. It is located by first measuring horizontal and vertical displacement of all individual shots from reference lines, then computing the average displacements, and plotting the point from that data.

Chamber   That portion at the rear of the barrel of any gun that is enlarged to accept the loaded cartridge and support it during firing. In a revolver (and in some specialized military weapons), the recess cut into the cylinder to accept and hold each cartridge in alignment with the barrel for firing.

The chamber must be large enough in all dimensions to accept the largest standard cartridge of a given caliber, yet small enough to permit smooth operation while providing strong support to the relatively weak cartridge case.

In the United States the standard minimum-chamber/maximum-cartridge dimensions are supplied by the Small Arms and Ammunition Manufacturers Institute (SAAMI) so that manufacturers may insure interchangeability among their guns and ammunition.

See also SAAMI.

Chamber Pressure Chamber pressure makes firearms work. It is an essential part of the system and becomes dangerous only when it exceeds the limits of a particular gun/case combination.

When smokeless powder propellant is ignited, it begins to burn rapidly, generating a large quantity of hot gases which increase the pressure inside the chamber. This ever-increasing temperature and pressure increases the temperature of the still burning powder, which in turn further increases the rate at which the pressure builds.

As soon as chamber pressure reaches a sufficiently high level to overcome the inertia of the bullet and the mechanical restraint of its assembly in the case, the expanding gases force the bullet out of the case into the rifling and down the bore. During ignition gas continues to be generated, and as pressure increases the bullet accelerates until the point is reached where the bullet is generating space behind it faster than gas is being produced to fill that space—that is the point of maximum chamber pressure which begins to drop rapidly, the rate of drop decreasing as the bullet approaches the muzzle.

Peak chamber pressure is reached very early and very near the chamber in bullet travel—shortly after the bullet has first begun to move.

While chamber pressures can be controlled within relatively narrow limits in special test barrels fired under laboratory conditions, it is virtually impossible to predict pressures in individual guns with any degree of accuracy. There are simply too many variables which affect the maximum pressure. For example, bore dimension, bullet diameter, bullet length, etc. will contribute to differences in chamber pressure. Bullet construction alone can cause as much as 10,000 pounds per square inch variation in the pressures produced by a standard full-charge .30/06 load.

In modern centerfire rifles 50,000 to 55,000 pounds per square inch is generally considered the upper limit for working chamber pressures. In modern shotguns, the upper limit is usually set at around 12,500 pounds per square inch. But in the handgun, designs and characteristics vary so much that maximum pressures may be found ranging from as low as 12 000 to over 40,000 pounds per square inch!

Chamber Reamer A multi-fluted reamer used to cut the chamber in a barrel or cylinder. The chamber reamer must be dimensioned and shaped precisely to match standard specifications for the particular cartridge, and, if many chambers are to be cut, the reamer must be checked periodically to be sure that the cutting edges do not wear down where the finished chamber will be undersized.

Reamer is inserted in rear of barrel
and turned to cut chamber.

Reamers may have either straight or spiral flutes, and may be used either by hand or under power, but must be well-lubricated with a proper cutting lubricant. Great care is needed to prevent jamming of chips or cutting oversize by excessive side pressure.

Many people are familiar only with the finishing reamer commonly sold to small gunsmiths and individuals, but an industrial chamber reaming set consists of a step drill to hog out the bulk of the excess material, a roughing reamer which brings the chamber rather close to finished size, *and* the finishing reamer which removes only a small amount of metal and is intended to produce a very smooth finish.

Chamfer A slight bevel placed upon the inside or outside of a cartridge case mouth to facilitate bullet seating and crimping. Chamfering is generally accomplished with a scraping tool or tapered reamer, but may also be done with a sharp knife blade skillfully handled. Also refers to the bevelling of the inner edge of a barrel muzzle or any other hole.

Checkering A very old form of functional decoration applied to the pistol grips and forends of shoulder arms and to the grips of handguns. Modern checkering consists of fairly sharp diamond-like pointed pyramids made by cutting intersecting V-section grooves in the wood.

In contemporary form, checkering is cut by multiple-toothed cutters (like tiny files) to produce loosely spaced parallel lines that are deepened sufficiently to bring the wood left standing between them to a point. After one set of lines has been cut within the prescribed pattern, a second set is cut at approximately a 30- to 45-degree angle, thus forming uniform diamonds in full relief over the entire area.

The first set is not cut to full depth initially since the two sets are worked upon alternately until the desired depth is produced. Cutting one set of full depth first would weaken the raised remaining portion of the wood and make it more susceptible to chipping during the cutting of the second set.

The highest quality checkering is often done without any border and individual grooves are brought to an abrupt end

Checkering.

precisely at the pattern outline. However, most artisans complete the checkering by cutting a beaded or V-grooved (single or multiple) border outlining the pattern to cover up any raggedness at the end of the individual grooves.

The checkering pattern is normally laid out by tracing its overall outline and then laying out what are called master guidelines, intersecting approximately in the center of the pattern. These guidelines are deepened by a single hand tool to serve as guides for all subsequent grooves, each of which is cut by one row of teeth in a two-row tool, while the other rides in the previously cut groove. Thus each groove is cut lightly into the wood and then serves as a guide for cutting the groove next to it.

Checkering is described by the number of grooves to the inch. For example, "22-line checkering" indicates 22 grooves per inch. If the grooves are too closely spaced, generally closer than 22 to 24 lines, the diamonds are too small to provide a sufficiently rough gripping surface. Conversely, checkering that is too coarse, coarser than 16 to 18 lines, will usually be too rough and sharp for comfortable gun handling. Because the poorer grades of walnut and other woods are too porous and soft for fine checkering, they are limited to 16 to 20 lines per inch.

Not all checkering consists of complete coverage with closely spaced diamonds. The most popular variation is the skip-line or French style in which narrow intersecting bands are left uncheckered, producing small areas of true checkering interspersed uniformly with single grooves and smooth wood areas. Traditionally checkering has been cut primarily by hand, but checkering on handgun stocks has been cut successfully by special machinery. In addition, there are air and electrically driven high-speed cutting heads which are guided by hand to produce checkering generally equal to hand work.

In the early 1960s impressed checkering came into wide use by the major manufacturers. Typically this is produced by squeezing the appropriate area of a gunstock very tightly between flexible dies under relatively high heat and pressure to permanently impress a pattern that looks like conventional checkering. Much of the impressed checkering used until now has been of the *negative* type, in that where diamonds would normally rise above the wood, pyramid-shaped depressions are formed in the wood. This type of negative checkering is decorative, but it does not provide the nonslip gripping surface. Recently, though, techniques and tooling have been improved to the point that some manufacturers now produce *positive* impressed checkering that is much more functional. Even so, it still lacks the style, class, and practicality offered by genuine hand-cut checkering.

On more ornamental guns, checkering is often combined with relief carving and various inlays in an integrated pattern.

Cheek Piece For a right-handed shooter, an enlargement on the left side of the buttstock of any long gun intended to insure strong cheek to stock contact while retaining proper butt to shoulder relationship and eye/barrel alignment. In essence, the cheek piece substitutes for cast.

Choke A system of unknown origin whereby the muzzle of a shotgun barrel is constricted to control the spread of shot. Choked barrels were known before 1835, and there are indications that they may have been used as much as 100 years earlier.

Regardless of when or by whom the shotgun choke was first used, credit for its further development generally goes to Fred Kimble, of Peoria, Ill., and to W. W. Greener, noted British gunmaker, for their efforts in the 1870s.

The degree of constriction required to control shot spread is not great, and, in fact, too much constriction will actually cause the opposite effect. The form of the constriction differs substantially by manufacturer, the method used, and so forth. The degree of shot control that a given type or amount of constriction will produce is further affected by shot size, velocity, weight of shot, length of shot column, and many other variables.

While no true standardization exists, shot gunners expect the results shown in the following table from the various choke borings with medium-sized shot and standard field loads.

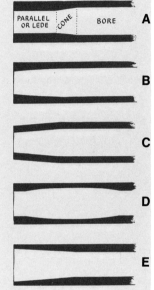

Various choke designs: (A) Standard or English choke with a simplified diagram which has a parallel portion at the end of the barrel. (B) Cone choke, also known as the American or taper choke. (C) Swaged choke, made by merely tapering the muzzle itself. (D) Recess or jug choke, usually made by hand with a rod and emery cloth. (E) Bell or reverse choke for throwing extra-wide patterns.

Choke Tube A removable tube, usually supplied in sets, screwed into the muzzle to provide a particular degree of choke. It also allows one barrel to produce a performance that varies from the other.

Chopper Lump A method of construction of barrels for double-barrelled, side-by-side shotguns in which the "lump" extending beneath the breech of the barrel is forged as an integral part of the barrel. When the barrels are assembled, the two lumps are carefully fitted on their mating surfaces and brazed solidly together into a single unit, into which locking and other functional recesses are cut.

In the days when most common doubles had their underlugs simply brazed into place as separate pieces, the chopper lump was considered far superior in strength and desirability.

Chronograph An instrument that measures the time required by a bullet to pass between two precisely measured points, converting that time measurement to velocity.

A modern, transistorized, Avtron K233 Chronograph instrument which performs all the measuring and calculating functions when connected to start and stop screens.

The more economical chronographs readily available to the average shooter simply provide a figure representing the time it takes a bullet to pass between the two points, and the operator converts the time factor to velocity by using either a conversion table or a calculator.

The more costly industrial chronographs use computers presenting a direct read-out of the average velocity in feet per second in a lighted digital display.

All modern chronographs are essentially precise electronic time-measuring devices working from a frequency generator. In use, the fired bullet passes through a conducting screen or over a sensitive photoelectric cell that starts the counting circuits, and then it passes through a second screen which stops the counting circuit, thus measuring the time required for the bullet to pass between these "start" and "stop" screens.

Portable chronographs small enough to be carried in a shooting kit are quite adequate for the handloader's needs.

Claybird Also known as the clay pigeon, clay target, blue rock, and by many other colloquialisms, it is the standard target for all shotgun shooting. It was originally made of clay but now of more modern materials providing the same frangibility.

As shown, it is a stepped, circular disc in the form of an inverted saucer, $4^5/_{16}$ inches in diameter, $1^1/_8$ inches in height, and weighing $3^1/_2$ ounces. The basic design was first patented in 1880 by George Likowsky, Queens, New York.

Prior to the adoption of the claybird, various types of glass and pitch (tar) hollow balls were utilized.

Clay Pigeon See CLAYBIRD.

Clay Target See CLAYBIRD.

Cleaning Guns Every gun, to work properly, should be disassembled and cleaned inside and out at least once each season.
Most rifles, pump shotguns, and some pistols can be disassembled and reassembled without professional experience or
tools. On guns such as double-action shotguns, disassembling is
limited to removing the barrels from the stocked action. An
important rule: always use the proper screwdriver so as not to
damage the screw head or surrounding areas.

With the gun disassembled as far as you can go, spray all parts
with a good coating of moisture-displacing rust-penetrating oil,
and leave it overnight. Next day, spray parts again and wipe off
the loosened oil, rust and grease. Use an old toothbrush to
loosen any stubborn spots. Wipe and clean all parts dry. Then
apply gun oil, very lightly covering each part, and place it on a
newspaper to allow any excess to drain off. It is important to
emphasize the use of only a slight amount of oil. Reassemble the
gun, wipe down the exterior with a lightly oiled cloth and place
the gun, muzzle down, in a safe place for a day or two to allow
any excess oil to drain. For light cleaning of a gun after each
use, see illustrated series on following pages.

Cleaning Kit, Gun Regardless of the type of gun involved, a
proper cleaning kit should contain the following items: Solid,
strong, one-piece cleaning rod; brass bristle bore brush; jag
tip and patches; tooth-brush or similar small brush for cleaning
dirt and debris out of action recesses; a bore-cleaning solvent
such as Hoppe's No. 9; a wiping cloth impregnated with a good
petroleum-base preservative or one of the more modern silicone
or synthetic preservatives; a small container of paste wax for
protecting the stock; a good synthetic lubricant such as WD-40
which remains fluid from subzero temperatures to over 100
degrees Fahrenheit; and for guns requiring any disassembly for
cleaning, a set of carefully fitted screwdrivers and pin punches.

For home use, the cleaning rod should be of solid, one-piece
construction, with a swiveling or free-rotating handle. For a kit
carried afield, a jointed rod is acceptable if care is taken to insure
that it is assembled absolutely straight so it will not scrape the
bore of the gun in use.

A cleaning kit intended primarily for use with high-grade
target rifles should also include a cleaning rod guide and stop.
The guide normally fits in the breech, centering the rod in the
bore, and the stop prevents the rod from exciting completely
from the muzzle and rubbing the bore as it is withdrawn.

Rifles which require cleaning from the muzzle, such as
Remington and Winchester autoloaders and the Savage M99

TECHNIQUE FOR CLEANING A GUN AFTER USE

1. Working from the receiver end, swab barrel with a patch moistened with nitro powder solvent.

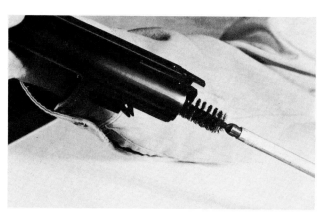

2. Run a brass bristle brush, of the proper size, back and forth several times to cut loose the powder residue.

3. Follow brush cleaning with patches moistened with solvent, swabbing the barrel until the patches emerge clean.

4. Examination should show a mirror-shiny, spotlessly clean barrel. Watch for residues of lead just ahead of the chamber, which the cleaning may not have completely removed.

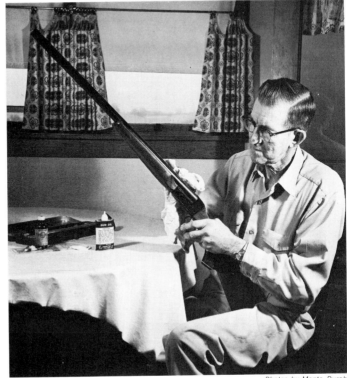

5. Last step is to reassemble gun and completely wipe outside with a soft cloth slightly moistened with gun oil. Gun should then be placed muzzle down for a while to allow oil to drain out.

Photos by Monte Burch

lever gun, will profit from the use of a cleaning rod guide on the muzzle.

For shotguns, a bore mop is more convenient for swabbing and oiling than patches—and equally so for rifles of .45 caliber or larger.

All items in the cleaning kit should be kept together to encourage prompt and thorough cleaning. Any kind of container will do for everything except the one-piece rod, but a simple canvas or leather roll with pockets for individual items seems to work best. The simplest method is to make up a kit in a roll of this sort containing a jointed rod and all other items for field use, then keep a spare one-piece rod for home use. This way the cleaning kit can always be quickly and easily tossed into the duffel bag when you're preparing for a hunting trip.

Good cleaning kits are available neatly packaged, containing all the essential items. They are packed in metal or plastic boxes which are fine for home storage, but not practical for carrying in the field.

Clean-Out Plug In a percussion gun, a threaded plug in the bolster forming a continuation of the bolster vent. Removal of the plug allows the lateral vent through the bolster to be cleaned with a pipe cleaner or similar item.

See also BOLSTER.

Clip Originally the clip was a metal device for holding a series of cartridges to permit their easy insertion into a magazine, the clip becoming a necessary functional part of the magazine. Also called a charger though the precise functions of the two differ.

The Mannlicher clip shown is typical of this type and remains in the magazine until after the last cartridge is fed into the chamber, and then either falls or is ejected through an opening in the magazine.

With the advent of the charger, the term "clip" was also applied to it in this country despite its much different function.

Lower left is a true "clip" which is an essential functioning part of the magazine; at center is a "charger" used only to fill a magazine; at right is a typical modern, staggered, double-column, large capacity *magazine* for comparison.

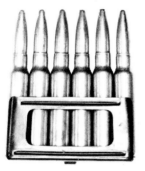
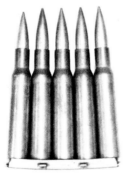

Further, as pistols and rifles were developed with detachable magazines, U.S. shooters also erroneously called them clips. Consequently, clip is also used indiscriminately to describe a detachable magazine and a charger.

Clip Lips (slot)   A recess or recesses in the top of a rifle receiver to accept and hold a cartridge clip of the stripper type so that cartridges may be pressed out of the clip into the magazine. Clips are generally provided with protrusions on their sides to seat in such recesses and hold them securely. In some rifles the empty clip must be removed manually, while in others it is ejected by the closing bolt.

See CLIP.

Clock System   A method for using a clock face as a reference for indicating wind direction and bullet strike on target. In the latter, the bullseye represents the center of the clock face and the top center of the target face becomes 12 o'clock. Thus a bullet striking directly to the right of the bull will be described as "out at 3 o'clock."

To designate wind direction, the shooter becomes the center of the clock face and the target assumes the 12 o'clock position. Thus a wind blowing from the shooter's left becomes 9 o'clock.

The clock system is also often used by varmint, big game, and bench rest shooters as well as soldiers to point out targets or to plot fields of fire.

Coarse Sight   Referring to open sights, a sight picture in which the largest amount possible of the front sight is viewed through the rear sight's notch. Also called a "coarse bead" sight.

Cock   Originally the hammer on a flintlock or percussion lock gun. Today, the act of making the firing mechanism ready for firing on any gun—consisting of compressing the spring that powers the hammer or firing pin, and retaining it in that position by the sear until such time as the trigger is pulled to release it.

See also LOCK

Cocking Indicator   Any device which the act of cocking a gun moves into a position where it may be seen or felt in order to notify the shooter that the gun is cocked.

Typical examples are the pins found on some high-grade

hammerless shotguns which protrude slightly when they are cocked, and also the exposed cocking knobs on bolt-action rifles. Exposed hammers found on some rifles and pistols are also considered cocking indicators.

A typical pistol cocking indicator is seen here in the pin that protrudes from the rear of the frame of this HK P. German autoloader.

Cocking Lever In a break-open type of action, an enclosed lever acting through cams or rods or both to force the hammers to the cocked position as the action is opened. In a few instances, a lever on the outside of a receiver, manually operated to cock or uncock an internal firing mechanism—as on the Remington-Hepburn single-shot rifle.

Collecting See GUN COLLECTING

Collimator A very precise instrument for checking alignment of optical elements for use in the assembly or repair of optical instruments, such as scope sights. As applied to guns, a small, simple optical device attached to the muzzle by means of which the sights may be brought into proper alignment with the bore.

Typical of the type is the Sweany Sight-A-Line which is fitted with an interchangeable, offset, precision-ground rod or "spud" of bore diameter. In use, the proper spud to suit the caliber is installed on the collimator and inserted into the muzzle. This action aligns the collimator parallel to the muzzle portion of the

Bushnell collimator being fitted into rifle muzzle.

bore. Then, looking through the sights on the gun at the reticle image within the collimator, the sights are adjusted until aligned precisely on the center of the reticle. This adjustment makes the line of sight parallel with the bore at the muzzle, and from that point any desired shift to compensate for drop or other effects can be made.

At present, a number of satisfactory collimators are available at prices ranging from $20 upward.

Color-Harden A form of case hardening that creates a swirling mottled pattern of reds and blues on the metal surface. It may be purely decorative, producing very little hardening, or may be of substantial depth and produce a very hard but thin surface layer while the metal beneath retains its original properties. Originally produced by applying cyanide to the heated metal, color hardening is now usually done with non-toxic substitute materials.

See also CASE-HARDEN.

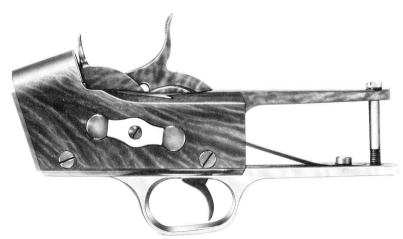

Example of modern color-hardening.

Colt, Samuel Colonel Sam Colt, the inventor of the first practical percussion-fired revolving pistols and founder of the Colt Firearm Co. of today. Though other revolving gun systems had existed for many years, Colt's efforts resulting in the Paterson model pistols of the late 1830s were the first *practical* pistols of this type.

Comb The upper surface of a buttstock which serves as a rest and alignment point for the shooter's cheek. Height of comb is varied to raise or lower shooter's eye and align it with the line of sight, and may also be shifted left or right for the same purpose.

See MONTE CARLO COMB.

Two examples of combs, the plain (top) and the Monte Carlo, showing it from underneath (center) and side.

Combination Gun Generally a break-open shotgun configuration fitted with at least one shotgun barrel and one rifle barrel. Such guns may be encountered with either two or three barrels, and less frequently with as many as four or five, and have been known to chamber for as many as four different calibers.

Probably the most practical form is the Drilling, which contains three barrels, the two upper forming a typical side-by-side shotgun with the third and rifled barrel centered beneath them.

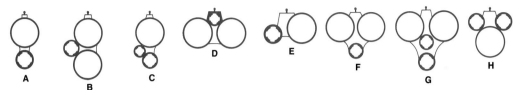

Guns of this type have long been extremely popular in Europe where hunting is often conducted simultaneously for deer, boar, other big game, and game birds as well.

See also DRILLING.

Compensator   A device fitted to the muzzle of any firearm whose function is to reduce the upward movement of the muzzle brought about by recoil forces. The earliest form of this device to see commercial application was the Cutts Compensator, marketed for many years by Lyman Gunsight Co.

A compensator fits over the muzzle and uses slots in its outer end to deflect propellant gases upward, thus providing downward thrust to counteract recoil-induced jump. Their effectiveness depends to a large extent upon the volume and the direction of the gases diverted, and other factors such as the stock design, center of gravity, etc.

See also CUTTS COMPENSATOR and MUZZLE BRAKE.

Various combination gun designs: (A) Over-and-under, shotgun on top, rifle under. (B) Over-and-under shotgun with rifle at side. (C) Shotgun on top with rifles under and at side. (D) Side-by-side shotgun with rifle on top. (E) Side-by-side rifle and shotgun. (F) Side-by-side shotgun with one rifle under. (G) Side-by-side shotgun with two rifles under. (H) Side-by-side double rifle with shotgun under.

Cutts compensator with interchangeable choke tubes (left), and adjustable choke, (right).

Compression-formed shotshell

Compensator, see Cutts Compensator.

Compression-Formed Shotshell   Abbreviated CF, shotshell design where the entire case is formed in a single piece from a slug of plastic molded under high heat and pressure. Introduced by Winchester-Western in the early 1960s, this type of construction eliminates the separate head, base wad, and body tube of earlier designs.

Though it is claimed that this construction produces a case head and rim sufficiently strong for all normal functioning, all of this type currently manufactured have a thin, sheetmetal head overlay which appears to be the same as that found on built-up cases. The properly designed and manufactured CF case is much stronger in critical areas and has a much longer reloading life than the best of the built-up plastic and paper case.

As this is written, all major U.S. manufacturers have followed Winchester's lead and offer ammunition loaded in CF-type cases in at least 12 gauge.

See also Shotshell, Metallic and Shotshell, Plastic.

Controlled-Expansion Bullet   A bullet designed to expand freely and quickly at relatively low velocities, but so strengthened that it generally will not fragment when entering animal tissue at high velocities. This allows the forward third or half of the bullet to expand normally and create a large wound channel, while its rear portion remains intact insuring deep penetration.

Such performance is usually obtained by strengthening the jacket from its midpoint rearward, or conversely by weakening the forward portion of the jacket by thinning or serrating.

Other less conventional designs are used, including the Nosler in which the bullet contains a partition separating front and rear cores, the RWS H-jacket in which the jacket is folded inward to form a reinforcing belt at midpoint, the DWM strong-jacket in which the rear portion of the jacket is made abnormally thick, the Nosler solid-base design in which the bullet's base is actually solid, and various other less practical and more costly designs.

Nosler solid-base Zipedo bullet (sectioned) shows how expansion is controlled by making the base solid and too hard to be deformed by impact and penetration, while leaving the front portion of conventional construction which will expand.

Cook-Off   The firing of a cartridge caused by the absorption of high heat from the barrel or from the chamber overheated by extensive rapid firing. Generally a cook-off occurs only in machine guns and other full-automatic weapons that fire from a closed bolt that leaves a round chambered in the hot barrel after firing. Once common among older machine guns and automatic rifles, but seldom encountered today because modern automatic weapons usually fire from an open bolt and do not chamber a cartridge until the instant of firing.

72

Copper Jacketed   A term commonly applied to bullets with gilding-metal jackets because of their copper color. However, some low-velocity bullets are made with jackets of pure copper. See also GILDING METAL.

Cordite   The term identifying an early British form of double-base smokeless powder which was extruded in thin spaghetti-like strands or "cords," thus the name. Also commonly used by journalists as "the stench of cordite" to describe almost any powder fumes or odor.

Cosmoline   A trademark registered by E. P. Houghton and Co. for a liquid rust-preventive material used to protect ferrous metal parts. This name is also often erroneously applied to a thick, black, heavy grease applied to military small arms for long-term storage protection.

CO₂   Carbon dioxide gas, which is normally supplied in sealed steel containers small enough to fit inside a gun. Used principally in air guns and in special "capture" or "tranquilizer" guns.

CO₂ Gun   A form of air gun in which a sealed steel container of CO_2 gas under pressure substitutes as an energy source for compressed air.

Crack, Season   See SEASON CRACK.

Crane   In a modern solid-frame, swing-out revolver, the U-shaped yoke on which the cylinder rotates, and which holds the cylinder in the frame.

Colt revolver crane opened about halfway to show how it carries the cylinder in and out of the frame.

Crazy Quail A shotgun game using standard clay targets in which birds are thrown from an underground trap at random throughout 360 degrees. The shooter is placed in a partially enclosed booth that limits his field of fire.

In this manner, the shooter is provided with targets flying in many directions, coming straight in, heading straight out, crossing at right angles to either right or left, all at varying ranges, and requiring that the shot be fired within the length of time that the target remains within the restricted field of fire. A well-named sport.

Creasing The fabled act of stunning an animal (or person) by gunshot in order to capture it (or him) alive and relatively unharmed. As legend would have us believe, this was accomplished by firing a shot to just barely nick the top of the neck or some portion of the skull, rendering the animal temporarily unconscious by the impact on the brain or spinal column.

There may have been people and guns accurate enough to do this, but there are no records to prove that any individual ever accomplished this act deliberately and predictably. Modern high-velocity bullets would most likely cause death from massive shock and secondary projectiles (bone and tissue fragments) under those conditions.

Creep In a trigger pull, excessive motion between full finger pressure and sear release usually caused by either excessive sear engagement, rough engaging surfaces, or both.

Crimp A turning-in of the case mouth against or into the bullet, to create a strong mechanical assembly and to control the bullet.

Crimp Die The die which finishes the crimp folds, then radiuses the edges, and recesses the center of the crimp.

Crooked Stock A buttstock, usually on a shotgun, bent or shaped into an S-curve so that the gun may be fired off the right shoulder with the barrels aligned with the left eye or vice versa. Such stocks are used by visually impaired shooters. It is also called an offset stock.

Cross Bolt In a stock, a bolt or pin passing laterally through the stock directly behind the recoil lug. It strengthens this area,

Heavy, square bolt through Mauser stock directly behind recoil lug (only bolt head shows) adds strength.

transfers recoil loads over a wider area of the stock, and is most commonly found in the massive square bolt installed in virtually all military bolt-action Mauser rifles.

Cross-eye Stock   A buttstock bent or formed to allow the gun to be mounted to one shoulder of the shooter while his opposite eye views the sights. Also at times called a "bent" or "goose neck" stock.

Crowning   The rounding or chamfering normally done to a barrel muzzle to insure that the mouth of the bore is square with the bore axis and that the edge is countersunk below the surface to protect it from impact damage.

Traditionally, crowning was accomplished by spinning an abrasive-coated brass ball against the muzzle while moving it in a figure-eight pattern until the abrasive had cut away any irregularities and produced a uniform and square mouth.

Left barrel has traditional form of muzzle crowning; right is counterbore used on modern target barrels.

Today, though, muzzles are generally crowned in a lathe using a formed cutting tool, an operation requiring only a small fraction of the time needed formerly.

Alternatively, crowning is sometimes accomplished simply by running a 45-degree countersink or other cutter into the muzzle to produce an angular bevel which serves the purpose fully as well, though it is not as attractive as a smooth radius. Another method is to counterbore the muzzle, but this sort of crowning is usually found only on large-diameter barrels.

Regardless of the method used, the outer edges of the muzzle are usually radiused slightly and polished smooth.

Often, older guns incur slight muzzle damage wherein a nick or burr breaks over into the bore. This frequently affects accuracy adversely, and a simple recrowning job will remove the defect and restore accuracy.

Cut Shell   A shotshell which has been cut partially through forward of the head in hope of reducing shot dispersion. A dangerous practice, to be avoided.

Cutts Compensator   The earliest commercially successful recoil-reducing device applied to firearms. It was developed by Col. Richard M. Cutts, (USMC, Ret.) as a device for reducing muzzle climb of the Browning Automatic Rifle and the Thompson Submachine Gun.

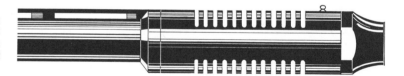

Cutts Compensator gives killing shot patterns for all game at all ranges. It offers maximum recoil reduction, uniform patterns even at extreme short or long range.

Manufacturing rights were acquired in 1929 by the Lyman Gunsight Co., which has continuously marketed this item in various forms. Intended solely for shotgun use, it incorporates interchangeable or adjustable-choke tubes of one sort or another.

See also ADJUSTABLE CHOKE.

Cyclic Rate   The rate at which any full-automatic weapon will fire in rounds per minute. Some designs do not achieve full cyclic rate until several rounds have been fired, thus the true cyclic rate is seldom achieved except in unusually long bursts. Hardly any automatic weapon is capable of actually firing the number of rounds indicated in a single minute. Continuous fire for sixty seconds would overheat the gun almost to the point of failure, even if sufficient ammunition were contained in the feed system.

Cylinder A cylindrical carrier in a revolver containing chambers for several cartridges (usually six) and rotated about its longitudinal axis to bring cartridges successively into alignment with the barrel for firing. At the instant of firing, the cylinder becomes a part of the barrel, functioning as the chamber; at all other times it combines the functions of magazine and feed system. The cylinder is rotated into position by a pawl or hand, and locked there during firing by a bolt or stop.

See REVOLVER.

Cylinder Gap In a revolver, the gap between the cylinder and the barrel breech when the cylinder is held forward by cartridges placed in its chambers.

This gap is properly measured by placing standard cartridges in the chambers (alternatively a headspace gauge) and then using thin feeler gauges to determine the gap thickness.

Individual manufacturer's tolerances vary, but a new revolver of good quality will generally have a cylinder gap of no more than .006 to .008 inch. The gap cannot be eliminated, and a

Some cylinder gap is normal, and the .008″ shown by this feeler gauge is not unusual for a new gun and may be considered excellent in a used gun.

minimum of .003 inch is required for free and easy rotation of the cylinder under all normal conditions. The gap allows some gas to escape, thus reducing velocity, though the loss is generally much less than believed.

Attempts have been made to eliminate cylinder gap by extending the cartridge case forward beyond the face of the cylinder and, through a cam arrangement, forcing the cylinder forward, placing the case mouth inside the barrel breech at the instant of firing.

This particular system was designed by Nagent, and is most often found on Soviet 7.62mm service revolvers and, more recently, on a very finely made target revolver manufactured in Czechoslovakia for use in Olympic shooting events by Soviet bloc marksmen.

Other systems have involved counterboring the face of the cylinder to accept the rear of the barrel breech when the cylinder is cammed forward. None of these systems are generally considered practical solutions except when very carefully hand-fitted at substantial increase in cost.

Damascus Barrel A form of barrel construction once considered superior to all others, particularly for thin-walled shotgun tubes.

At a time when the cheapest barrels were formed by welding a strip of flat metal longitudinally around a mandrel, Damascus barrels were made by twisting and welding small pieces or rods (sometimes alternating iron and steel) into larger ones, which were then coiled around a mandrel and forge-welded in a spiral.

The literally thousands of individual welds and the variations in material produced pleasing patterns of light and dark finish which, as late as the 1890s, were considered the hallmark of fine barrels. These patterns were, in fact, so regarded as a sign of superior quality, that more than a few unscrupulous makers of plain welded barrels devised means of applying the Damascus patterns to secure higher prices.

The main problem with Damascus barrels is that in forge-welding the multitude of seams by hand, it is inevitable that slag and other inclusions weaken the structure, and that some of the welds are poorly done, even by the finest craftsmen.

Well-made Damascus barrels with adequate wall thickness were satisfactory for black-powder ammunition. However, it has been proved that even when in perfect condition such barrels are not generally considered safe for use with modern smokeless powders, even the lightest field and target loads.

Certainly many old Damascus-barreled guns are still in almost daily use with modern ammunition; however, there is a mass of data existing regarding hundreds, perhaps thousands, of identical guns which have failed under this load. A typical failure with smokeless-powder ammunition causes the barrel to open up slightly ahead of the chamber, sending barrel and for-end fragments to mangle one's off-hand or forearm. There are numerous shooters with crippled arms who will attest to this fact.

It has often been wrongly rumored that one can test the safety of Damascus barrels by hanging them from a wire, striking them with a mallet, then listening to the tone produced. True, a flat tone will indicate an obvious flaw in the tubes, but a bell-like ring does not necessarily indicate adequate strength for smoke-less-powder loads.

Typical decoy of today.

Decoy   A likeness of a bird that is used to entice others of its species within gun range. Though most often associated with waterfowl, decoys are successfully used to attract doves, crows, and a variety of other game and varmints.

Depending upon the species and conditions of their use, decoys may range from precisely detailed life-sized replicas in natural color to nothing more than a lump of mud with a paper head stuck on it, a cardboard silhouette, or, of all things, simply a white tablecloth crumpled up on the ground. The latter is quite successful in attracting geese in the broad rice fields of the Texas Gulf Coast.

In a few instances, the decoy is in the form of an enemy of the species hunted—as when an owl decoy is used to attract crows, which love nothing better than to attack and dismember an owl.

Originally, decoys were either carved from wood in the classic American manner, or, in earliest times made from bundles of grasses or reeds. At one time, some purists even went so far as to stretch carefully tanned skins and plumage over their wood or grass decoys. Today, this type of detail and life-like-ness is unnecessary, and most modern decoys are cast or molded in a rubber-like, relatively low cost plastic. Generally, they are used with game calls.

Once live decoys were widely used. However, Federal Migratory Bird Regulations have prohibited their use for many years.

Deer, Guns for   Deer, mainly whitetail, is by far the most popular and the most often hunted big game in the United States. Consequently, the term "deer rifle" has become an integral part of the American hunter's language.

Whitetail deer are relatively small, seldom over 200 pounds, highly nervous and evasive, and relatively easy to kill. A hit in the principal vital areas, such as the brain or spine, will produce an instant kill with any cartridge possessing enough power to penetrate those areas. Hits in heart and lung areas will usually produce certain kills, even with low-power cartridges of the rimfire and handgun class; however, the animal is quite likely to run several hundred yards before collapsing, and could easily be lost.

To be reasonably sporting and certain of not losing game with moderately well-placed hits, cartridges providing a minimum of 1,200 foot-pounds of energy are required for deer hunting. In the smaller bullet diameters, this should be accompanied by a good amount of bullet expansion to insure destruction of vital organs and provide a good blood trail in the event the animal does not go down immediately.

Since the average deer is killed at a range of much less than 100 yards, and usually in brushy or timbered country, high velocity and flatness of trajectory are not especially important. This is the reason the .30/30, .35 Remington, and the old .38/55 built such excellent deer-killing reputations.

Much more important is light weight, compactness, and fast handling. A good deer rifle must come up like a good upland shotgun, fast and right on target. Traditionally the lever-action carbine has provided this, but modern, short-barrelled pumps and autoloaders do as well, and the bolt-action carbine is gaining much favor.

Mule deer present a different problem in that they are often hunted where long, across-canyon shots are the rule. This requires a flat-shooting, accurate, long-range rifle, yet one not so specialized it won't be handy hunting up brushy draws and creek bottoms. This dictates a rifle of medium weight and barrel length, fitted with a 4x or medium-range variable scope.

Mule deer cartridges should shoot flat enough to allow hitting to 300 yards without excessive holdover. The .30/06 and .270 are excellent choices—the larger bores not shooting flat enough and the smaller ones lacking brush-bucking ability.

De-Loader (Unloader) In the muzzle-loading field, a device which fits over the nipple (or into the nipple-seat after its removal) and injects a burst of carbon dioxide to force the powder charge and projectile out of the barrel without igniting the powder. This device normally uses a standard CO_2 cartridge of the type sold for use in CO_2 guns.

Unloading a muzzle-loader in this fashion is quite practical when a misfire has occurred or when powder has become damp, and is also useful to remove the load when firing is not desirable. However, much care must be taken when using this device because it can expel a projectile and powder charge with enough velocity to cause injury. In effect, it converts the muzzle-loader into an air gun. Most common of the type is the Root Muzzle Unloader.

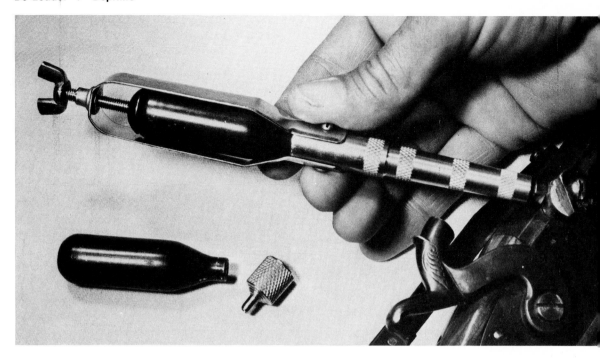

CO₂-actuated deloader.

There is also a little known form of de-loader applied to breech-loading cartridge arms. It is a device that is inserted into the loading port or mouth of a magazine and causes cartridges to be ejected by the magazine spring, completely emptying the magazine in a single operation. One type of de-loader consists of a bag attached to a plastic device containing spring fingers, which are inserted into the loading port of Winchester M94 and similar tubular magazine rifles, causing all the cartridges to be forcibly ejected into the bag.

Other de-loaders have been made for use with different magazine systems, but are seldom encountered. One such type, made only for the military, rapidly strips cartridges from box magazines by means of a toothed wheel, and another extracts cartridges from loaded machine gun belts by means of a notched bar.

Some guns contain a built-in release that is pressed to release cartridges from the magazine. The U.S. M1 Garand and Austrian Mannlicher-Schoenauer rifles have such devices.

Deplating An electrolytic process for removing chrome, nickel, or other electroplated finishes from guns or other plated objects.

Deprime (Decap) To punch out the fired primer.

Deringer The generic term applied to a wide variety of very small, large-caliber, single- or double-barrelled pistols which may be of either muzzle- or breech-loading construction. Also spelled "Derringer."

See also DERINGER, HENRY.

Deringer, Henry (1786–1868) An American gunsmith and manufacturer, made famous by the short, single-shot percussion pistol he first made in 1825.

Dewat An acronym for "DEactivated WAr Trophy." Generally used in reference to machine guns or submachine guns (or other full-automatic weapons) made unserviceable by cutting and welding.

Such deactivations have been variously specified by governmental directives up to the enactment of the Gun Control Act of 1968, which greatly restricted the general ownership of such guns, classifying them with functional automatic weapons. Generally, the deactivation consisted of grinding off the firing pin, welding the barrel to the receiver (preventing its ready replacement), and welding a hardened steel plug into the chamber end of the barrel.

See also GUN CONTROL ACT OF 1968.

Percussion Deringer of the mid-1800s from which the name derived.

Director of Civilian Marksmanship (DCM) A position established under the National Defense Act in June 1916, along with the National Board for the Promotion of Rifle Practice, to promote rifle marksmanship among civilians. At the same time, funds and facilities to support civilian marksmanship were made available, and military ranges were opened to civilian shooters.

The DCM, a field-grade Army officer, controlled the issue of both expendable and nonexpendable items (targets and ammunition, rifles and equipment) to NRA-affiliated clubs. The DCM also regulated the sale (at relatively low prices) of limited quantities of rifles, pistols, ammunition, and related items to NRA members. These practices continued until recent years, at which time the anti-gun and disarmament interests generated sufficient political pressure to weaken the function of this office, eliminate individual sales, and drastically reduce the supply of all items to gun clubs.

From its conception and through the middle 1960s, the DCM and its companion, the National Board for the Promotion of Rifle Practice, were invaluable in training civilian riflemen who were called to service during the three wars of that period.

The disconnector of this Star pistol is forced down by the slide at all times except when the slide is fully forward in the locked position and, thus, forces the trigger bar out of engagement with the sear. This prevents firing the gun by trigger pressure at any time except when it is fully locked.

Disconnector That part of any gun design which disengages the trigger from the sear so that as the action closes after a shot while the trigger is still pressed, the gun will not fire. In some designs the disconnector also prevents firing until the breech is fully locked.

Doll's Head A form of auxiliary locking device on a double-barrelled shotgun wherein an extension of the rib or barrel breech is shaped like a ball on a post, and seats into a recess in the standing breech. It is of little real value in strengthening the action unless absolutely perfectly fitted, and even then useful only when the main locking system begins to wear.

Double Action In a revolver or autoloading pistol, the capability of cocking and dropping the hammer to fire the gun by a single

The gun on the left represents a typical double-action revolver (Colt Police Positive Special); at the right is a typical double-action auto-loading pistol (S&W M39).

84

pull of the trigger. Most of these actions also provide a capability for single-action fire. In autoloading pistols, double action normally applies only to the first shot of any series, the hammer being cocked by the slide for subsequent shots.

Double-Barrelled Gun Any gun consisting of two barrels joined along their length, either side-by-side or one over the other.

The term "double" when used alone usually indicates the former, while the latter is designated "over/under" or "superposed."

With very rare exceptions, all double-barrelled guns are of the break-open type. Both barrels may be chambered for shotshells, or both for rifle cartridges, or chambered for one of each.

Double-barrelled guns are generally more costly than their repeating or single-shot counterparts because they require two separate, independent firing mechanisms, and very carefully brazing or soldering of the barrels with intervening spaces or ribs in precise alignment so both barrels will shoot to the same point of impact.

This process of barrel alignment is called regulating, and is a particularly painstaking process in the case of rifles in which the slight differences in points of impact acceptable in shotguns cannot be tolerated. A top-quality double rifle may require many trips to the range for targeting and subsequent resoldering until the barrels are properly regulated.

See also COMBINATION GUN.

Typical modern side-by-side double-barrelled gun, top, is represented by this Savage/Stevens/Fox with ventilated rib. Typical over-under or superposed double Savage Model 440, bottom.

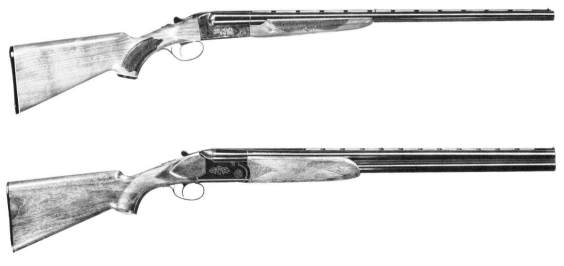

Double Base Powder   Any smokeless propellant powder ammunition that contains nitroglycerin in addition to the basic nitrocellulose ingredient.

Double Pull   A form of trigger pull commonly found in military rifles where the trigger moves some distance with relatively little pressure, then requires considerably increased pressure for the very short amount of travel remaining before the sear is released. It is considered an essential safety feature for military arms used under conditions of stress.

Double Rifle   See Double-Barrelled Gun.

Double-Set Trigger   A mechanism containing two triggers, one for cocking the mechanism, which requires substantial effort, and the other for firing. The latter is generally adjustable to an extremely light pull (perhaps an ounce or less).

Such a light pull may be obtained with safety by using the firing trigger to release a secondary hammer, which is cocked by pressure on the set, or cocking, trigger. Pressing the firing trigger releases a hammer which strikes a pivoted sear releasing the main hammer or firing pin.

It is often thought that most double-set trigger mechanisms provide faster lock time than a conventional single trigger; however, this complicated mechanism often results in a slower lock time.

See also Lock Time, Single-Set Trigger.

Pulling rear trigger until it engages allows gun to be fired by front trigger with very light pull.

Downhill Shooting Many people believe that when shooting downhill, the bullet will strike substantially above point of aim; others believe that the reverse is true, that the bullet will strike much lower than intended. Actually, any bullet fired above or below the horizontal will be affected *less* by gravity, and the greater the angle from horizontal, the less the effect of gravity will be (which is reduced to zero if the shot is fired vertically).

Horizontal gun/target range is the key factor, and the effect of gravity will remain the same for *any* horizontal range, no matter how steep the angle of the shot. Visualize a right triangle with yourself at its foot and your target at its vertex. The length of the hypotenuse is the *slant* range to the target, and the length of the base is the *horizontal* range. If your rifle is zeroed for the horizontal range, it will also be zeroed for the slant range. Thus, when you attempt a shot at a ram appearing to be 350 yards away (slant range) at an upward angle of 30°, the horizontal range will be just a hair over 300 yards—so, if your rifle is zeroed for 300 yards, you should hit the ram where you aim.

This is easily calculated if time and inclination permit, and if you can determine slant range with any degree of accuracy. The horizontal range will vary from the slant range as the cosine of the angle of elevation. In the aforementioned example, the cosine of 30° is .87—which multipled by 350 yards slant range give us a horizontal range of 304 yards.

All of the foregoing applies whether the angled shot is taken above or below the horizontal, consequently, your rifle will shoot high—but only slightly—when shooting uphill or downhill.

Draw-File A method of smoothing gun barrels in which a very large file is drawn the full length of the barrel. Commonly used in refinishing badly pitted surfaces of rough military barrels.

See also STRIKING.

Dreyse, Johann Nikolas, 1787–1867 The father of the bolt-action rifle, Dreyse spent over fifty years in gunsmithing, invention, and manufacture. In 1809 he worked with Pauly. Though at first a producer of muzzle-loading guns, Dreyse eventually developed the so-called Prussian Needle Gun and cartridge breech-loading system. Tested as early as 1841, the Dreyse breech-loader was adopted by Prussia in 1848 with much secrecy—the first successful breech-loading military rifle produced in quantity.

The needle gun brought much fame to Dreyse, but it appears to be the main achievement of his career.

See BOLT ACTION; NEEDLE GUN.

Drift The lateral bullet displacement from the center line of the bore produced by its rotation. Drift is probably best described as sideward motion of the bullet in the direction of twist, as if the bullet were rolling on a cushion of air in that direction. The effect of drift is slight, so little, in fact, that it is unnoticed at conventional hunting ranges.

With the 150-grain M2 military load in the .30/06 cartridge, fired in a 24-inch barrel, with one-in-ten twist, the total effect of drift is only 6.7 inches at 1,000 yards. And, since drift is proportional to the velocity-loss rate, the bulk of that 6.7 inches of drift occurs during the last few hundred yards of the bullet's flight. Some long-range rear sights, notably that of the M1903 Springfield rifle, have a drift correction built in.

Also, a cylindrical tool, usually brass, used as a punch to remove (or used for the final seating of) pins, sights, or other friction-tight parts.

Drilling The German designation for a three-barreled combination gun based upon the German word *drei*, for numeral three. Generally, a drilling contains two smoothbore barrels and one barrel centered beneath them chambered for a rifle cartridge. However, there is no set rule, and any combination of borings and calibers might be encountered.

Drillings have long been quite popular in Europe where the highly controlled hunting conditions often offer both big game and small game, as well as some species of birds. The rifle barrel takes care of big game and the shot barrels allow an immediate switch to the others. For the same reason, drillings have become moderately popular for some types of hunting in this country.

Generally speaking, a drilling is a rather expensive piece of ordnance. It has all the complexities of a high-grade double-barrelled rifle or shotgun, plus a third barrel and firing mechanism and auxiliary sights.

See also COMBINATION GUN.

Drop, Stock The measurement of the slope of the top of the buttstock from the line of sight of any gun, though generally applied more to shotguns than to rifles. Drop is generally measured at the front of the comb and also at the heel of the butt—though if a Monte Carlo comb or rollover cheekpiece in-

Arrows indicate stock drop.

corporating a raised comb is present, it may also be measured at other points.

The simplest method of measuring drop is to invert the gun and place it on its sights on a table top and then measure from that surface to the proper points on the stock. However, when aperture sights or scope sights are involved, the line of sight must be established by a string or wire stretched above the stock at the proper point, and measurements taken from that reference line.

Drop is necessary in any gun to bring the sights up to eye level when the butt is against the shooter's shoulder. This is less important in rifles where a precise aim is taken than in shotguns where pointing often replaces aiming and the shot is frequently taken quickly.

Duck Gun   A long, powerful, heavy shotgun intended primarily for use on waterfowl at long ranges. Waterfowlers generally use the most powerful loads available in a given gauge, thus a duck gun is made heavier than usual to soften recoil, and the barrel is made longer to extract the maximum ballistic performance from the ammunition and for smoother swinging on long pass shots. Also, it takes the most powerful loads.

Where a typical 12-gauge upland gun may weigh 7–7½ pounds, be chambered for the 2¾-inch shell, and have 26–28-inch barrels, its companion duck gun will weigh 8–8½ pounds, be chambered for the 3-inch Magnum, and be fitted with a 30-inch or longer barrel.

Dud   In sporting parlance, a misfired cartridge — in military language, an artillery shell or other explosive projectile, grenade, explosive charge, etc., which did not detonate as intended.

Dum Dum Bullet   Originally a rudimentary form of soft-point jacketed bullet manufactured at the British arsenal in Dum Dum, India, during the 1890s. Made in .303 British caliber early in that cartridge's history, the dum dum bullet was probably an attempt to duplicate the wounding power of the earlier large-caliber lead service bullets while retaining the long range and high velocity of the new smokeless-powder small bores. This is reasoned conjecture, since there are no records which indicate exactly why production of this bullet was undertaken.

Regardless of the fact that grenade and artillery shell fragments produced much more terrible wounds, a great hue and cry arose against military usage of expanding bullets. The result was the prohibition of such bullets in "civilized warfare" by the Hague Convention of 1908.

At times, various armies were reported to have issued orders for the summary execution of any enemy soldier found either using or possessing expanding-bullet small arms ammunition. In fact, rumors of this sort circulate even today. Because of the publicity originally received by the dum dum, journalists generally refer to any expanding bullet by that name.

Dummy Cartridge An inert cartridge used in testing gun actions for proper functioning. Normally they consist of a standard cartridge case and bullet, with an uncharged primer seated in the pocket, and sometimes a length of dowel inside the case to support the bullet.

Normally one or more holes are drilled into the case to make it clearly identifiable, or the case is blackened, and the inert primer may also be drilled with a small hole. Military dummies may carry various grooves, or coloring for identification.

Duplex Loads Today a method of loading a metallic cartridge with more than one type of powder (of different burning rates) to obtain maximum performance. Generally this results in a heavily compressed, layered propellant charge, and maximum ignition efficiency may be sought by the use of a flash tube extending from the primer. Duplex loading sometimes produces a slight gain in velocity, but this has seldom proved worth the additional cost and complexity of loading. Consequently, no factory- or arsenal-loaded ammunition uses this method.

However, a number of handloaders have advocated duplex loading for maximum performance, one of the most prominent being Elmer Keith, noted hunting and gun expert and writer. More recently Richard Cassull has offered his special wildcat .454 Magnum cartridge for use in special-built single-action revolvers. As loaded by Cassull, this cartridge uses three different powders and produces in excess of 2,000 feet per second with a 250-grain bullet—albeit, at chamber pressures generally considered dangerous in factory-made guns.

During the transition from black to smokeless powders, another form of duplex loading was widely used, and survives yet to this day in the use of breech-loading black-powder match rifles. It consists of placing a very small charge of quick-burning smokeless powder in the case first, next to the flash hole, and then filling the case with black powder to the base of the bullet. Such loads were noted for extreme accuracy, and were generally credited with improved ignition of the main powder charge and greatly reduced black-powder fouling.

In the past few years, the term "duplex load" has also been applied to a limited number of special-purpose military cartridges which contain more than one bullet fired simultaneously.

Ear Protectors Products designed to protect shooters' ears from permanent damage now known to result from even modest exposure to gun reports. They are available in several forms, from simple rubber plugs through pressure-sensitive ear-fitting valves, to acoustical muffs which completely cover the ear.
See also HEARING.

Eject The act of throwing the empty cartridge case clear of the action after it has been extracted. Except in revolvers and non-ejector guns, generally accomplished either by a spring-loaded plunger in the bolt face, or by a fixed member over which the bolt draws the case.

Ejector The device that hurls the empty cartridge case clear of the breech after it has been withdrawn from the chamber by the extractor. In early reciprocating, bolt designs of the ejector a fixed or loosely pivoted member was permanently positioned in the receiver so that when the bolt moved back over it, the case was struck and hurled clear. A more recent, more economical, and simpler design has achieved great popularity—a spring-loaded plunger in the face of the breech bolt which maintains constant heavy pressure against the cartridge head at all times and thus hurls the case from the breech just a quickly as the case clears the confinement of the receiver.
See also AUTOMATIC SELECTIVE EJECTOR and EXTRACTOR.

Ejector rod on big-frame Colt New Service DA revolver.

Ejector Rod In a revolver with a swing-out cylinder, it is the rod extending forward from the center of the cylinder which is pushed rearward to extract and eject all fired cases simultaneously. In a single-action revolver, it is the spring-loaded plunger housed under the barrel and used to punch fired cases out of the chambers individually.

See also REVOLVER.

Elevation The vertical adjustment made within or upon a metallic rear sight or a telescopic sight to compensate for bullet drop at various ranges. The proper amount of elevation will angle the line of sight downward so that it intersects the bullet's flight at the desired point.

Elevation is generally measured or indicated in "clicks," which are fractions of one minute of angle, usually ¼ or ½, though much smaller increments are used in very precise target sighting equipment.

Also a specific sight setting, i.e., "14 minutes."

See also MINUTE OF ANGLE.

Elk, Guns for Elk and moose are the largest antlered game hunted in North America and weights of well over 1,000 pounds are not uncommon. In addition to their substantial size, these animals have very heavy bone and muscle structures. Quick, humane kills depend upon relatively powerful cartridges capable of both deep penetration and substantial bullet expansion. While under ideal conditions a typical deer rifle and cartridge will produce a quick elk kill with good bullet placement, such conditions do not often exist. As often as not, a big elk will present only a raking shot from front or rear where as much as 3 to 4 feet of the body must be penetrated in order to reach the vital organs.

Elmer Keith, prominent big game hunter, states that he has been presented with more quartering rear shots on elk than anything else, and thus does not consider suitable any cartridge which will not drive its bullet through from rump to chest cavity. That means penetration of 3 to 4 feet of muscle, bone, and paunch contents. Another criterion described by several authorities is the ability of the cartridge to penetrate sufficiently to break both shoulders of an elk on a broadside shot. Considering the heavy bone structure involved, this amounts to about the same requirement levied by Keith.

While many elk have been killed with lesser cartridges, the .30/06 with 180-grain bullets is generally considered minimum, though the 7mm Remington Magnum with comparably heavy bullets would seem to do as well. With heavily constructed bullets driven at velocities in the range of 2,600 to 3,000 feet per second, both of these calibers will generally reach the vitals of an elk at almost any angle except directly astern. However, this is possible only with bullets that will hold together well for maximum penetration. Naturally, the more powerful calibers such as the .300 Winchester Magnum, .338, .375, etc. will do the job even better and are preferred by many hunters.

The heavy recoil of proper elk cartridges requires a rifle of at least moderate weight for comfortable shooting. A fair amount of weight is also essential for steady offhand shooting and rapid recoil recovery. Since elk are taken at long ranges as well as short, good rifle and cartridge accuracy is essential. Many elk are killed within rock-throwing distance in timber, but many are also taken across canyons at ranges up to 300 yards or so, requiring a high degree of accuracy for proper bullet placement.

Enfield Originally used as the official name of the British government arsenal located at Enfield Lock in England. Soldiers, however, have the habit of identifying their individual arms by the name of the maker inscribed thereon, thus British soldiers have referred to the various weapons manufactured by the En-

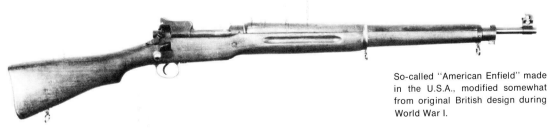

So-called "American Enfield" made in the U.S.A., modified somewhat from original British design during World War I.

93

field Arsenal as simply "Enfields," regardless of what they might be. This applies equally to muzzle-loading rifled muskets of the 1860s, later breech-loading Lee-Enfields, and, even certain revolvers manufactured there.

An exception to the above is the popular identification as "Enfield" in the United States of the U.S. Rifle caliber .30 M1917. This rifle was manufactured by three different plants — Remington Arms at Bridgeport, Connecticut, Remington Arms at Eddystone, Pennsylvania, and Winchester at New Haven, Connecticut during 1917 and 1918. However, because this rifle was simply a slightly modified version of the P-14 .303 British service rifle, it was given the common name of "U.S. Enfield" or "M1917 Enfield."

Hundreds of thousands of both United States and British Enfield rifles have been sold as surplus and so they are quite common today.

See also LEE-ENFIELD.

Engine Turning   An overlapping pattern of circular spots produced by spinning the end of an abrasive-coated rod against a metal surface. Generally applied to the bolts of rifles and shotguns and often incorrectly termed damascening.

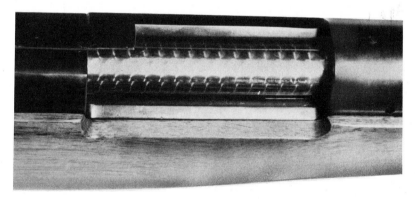

Engine-turned pattern formed on bolt surface spinning abrasive rod.

English Stock   A form of shotgun stock common to British field guns with a straight grip, slender wrist, and relatively straight and high comb.

Erosion   The melting, burning, or wearing away of metal from the inner surface of the barrel by heat, pressure, and velocity of expanding powder gases. This usually occurs directly ahead of the chamber and progresses gradually several inches up the bore. Erosion destroys accuracy, reduces velocity in advanced stages, and can actually produce substantial enlargement of the bore.

Etching A method of decorating metal gun parts. An acid-resistant coating is laid over the surface and then cut away to form the desired pattern. Acid is poured over the coated area and allowed to eat away metal to a predetermined depth only in those areas where the protective material has been removed.

Carefully done, etching can produce very attractive results. More often it is poorly done and the results are ruinous. Etching reaches its highest level when combined with engraving or when cleaned up by the use of gravers.

Exit Pupil The clear aperture in the ocular or eyepiece lens of a telescopic sight or a binocular. It is measured, usually in millimeters, by holding the instrument at arms length, and aligning it so that the aperture can be seen, then laying a scale over it.

The amount of light transmitted to the eye is directly proportional to the size of this aperture. However, the eye is limited in the size exit pupil it can utilize to about 7mm.

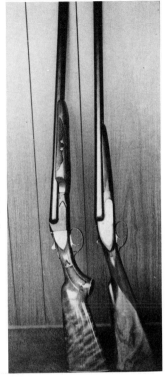

Typical American shotgun stock (left) has pistol grip; English stock (right) has straight grip.

Expansion Ratio The ratio of the volume of the bore, measured from the base of the seated bullet to the muzzle, to the volume of the cartridge case. An expansion ratio of 9:1 means the bore volume is nine times the case volume.

While it is generally believed that barrel length has a great effect on velocity, expansion ratio is actually the more important factor. Barrel length affects velocity only in that expansion ratio is directly dependent upon it. A .38 Special revolver with a 6-inch barrel actually has a greater expansion ratio than many rifles with 20-inch barrels.

There is also a maximum expansion ratio at which any given cartridge load combination will produce maximum velocity—unfortunately, in virtually all modern, high-intensity, bottleneck calibers, this ratio cannot be obtained with a barrel of manageable length. For example, the .243 Winchester requires a barrel of nearly 30 inches to produce an optimum expansion ratio and velocity—yet commercial rifles in this caliber are generally fitted with 22- to 24-inch barrels, and occasionally a few at 26 inches. Many modern high-intensity cartridges would require barrels 30 to 40 inches long to achieve the expansion ratio and the efficiency of a .30/30 carbine.

Express Cartridge A class of cartridges not often used today, which used abnormally light bullets for their caliber, fired at unusually high velocities. Named after the "Express Train Cartridge" developed in England in the middle 1880s.

Express Rifle A black-powder rifle intended specifically for use with Express Cartridges.

Extract To remove the fired case from the chamber as the action is opened. In repeating guns, this is accomplished by a hook on the reciprocating member on the breech that engages a rim or groove on the case head. Not to be confused with eject.
See also EJECT.

Extractor That member which withdraws a fired cartridge case from the chamber as the action is opened. In reciprocating bolt design, the extractor is normally attached at the front of the breech bolt and engages the rim of the cartridge as chambering is completed, and retains its grip until the ejector functions.

In nonreciprocating actions, the extractor may take a number of forms, the most common of which is the spring-loaded plunger of the typical break-open shotgun, which is actuated by cams inside the action as the breech is opened.
See also EJECTOR.

Eye Relief In a telescopic sight, the optimum distance from ocular lens to the viewing eye at which the full field of view may be seen through the scope. Short eye relief is acceptable for use on guns of light recoil, but where heavy recoil is involved, it may endanger the shooter when the eyepiece is driven backward in recoil. Not a precise value, eye relief in a particular scope may vary from 2 to 4 inches, and be described as 3 inches. Eye relief may be designed to practically zero in some target scopes, to as much as 18 inches for certain applications. Generally, field of view varies inversely with eye relief.

While eye relief is a precise value from an optical design viewpoint, it is not as a practical matter. It may be defined as the distance from the surface of the ocular lens to the eye at which the maximum field of view may be seen. However, first the overhang of the eyepiece over the lens, then the overhang of the brow over the eye must be subtracted to obtain a useable value. Then, internal diaphragming of the scope cuts off the outer limits of the field view. Thus, when overhangs are subtracted, a scope with technically 4 inches of eye relief is reduced to 2¾ inches—then internal diaphragming results in the full *useable* field being visible from any point within 1 inch either side of the 2¾-inch point. Relief may then be described as 1¾ to 3¾ inches.
See also FIELD OF VIEW, TELESCOPIC SIGHT.

Falling Block   A form of single-shot action where the breech block travels vertically in a mortise in the receiver and is supported by abutments in the receiver against the forces developed during firing.

See also BREECH BLOCK, SHARPS RIFLE.

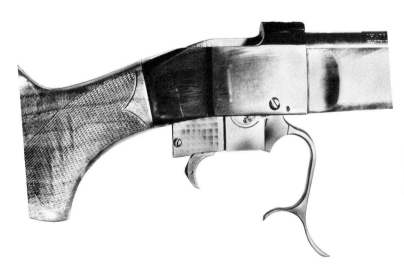

Typical of falling block rifles, the block in this Sharps/Colt is lowered through an opening in the bottom of the receiver by a finger lever.

False Muzzle   Most often associated with high-grade target guns of the late muzzle-loading and early breech-loading period. The false muzzle is a removable extension of the barrel, and is sometimes made by fitting a separate block of steel to the barrel, and then drilling, rifling, and reaming both it and the barrel to insure that the rifling in each is identical and properly aligned.

The false muzzle is held in alignment by dowel pins and is sometimes secured in place by a clamp. Used *only* for loading through the muzzle, it *must* be removed before firing.

False muzzle in use is attached to barrel muzzle in perfect alignment, then serves to position patches and allow bullet to be inserted into bore in perfect concentricity.

At its upper end, the rifling of a false muzzle is relieved to permit easy entry of the base of a paper-patch bullet. Thus, when the bullet is thrust through the false muzzle into the bore proper, a minimum of distortion is produced.

The false muzzle may be fitted to accept multiple-strip paper patches or bullets already patched by wrapping. In addition, some false muzzles are fitted with their own lever-operated bullet-seating mechanism used in lieu of a manual bullet starter.

Though used primarily on muzzle-loading match rifles of the slug-gun type, false muzzles are also used on breech-loading target rifles whose bullets are loaded through the muzzle in search of maximum accuracy.

Fanning   A method of rapidly firing a single action revolver. The gun is held rigidly in one hand, while the heel of the other is swept rapidly and repeatedly over the hammer carrying it to the cocked position while the trigger is held back allowing it to drop and fire the gun. Double-action revolvers cannot be fanned.

An expert shooter fans a Colt single-action revolver.

Farquharson Rifle A falling-block, single-shot rifle action patented in 1872 by John Farquharson, and originally manufactured by George Gibbs of Bristol, England. Later manufactured in numerous variations by Webley, Bland, Westley Richards, of England, and various European firms.

The Farquharson is considered by many to be the epitome of traditional single-shot rifle development. With its detented under-lever wrapping around the trigger guard and its massive breech block heavily supported in a substantial receiver it has great strength. It utilizes an enclosed-hammer firing mechanism seared directly off the trigger nose and driving a firing pin angled steeply upward.

Though occasionally encountered in small calibers, the Farquharson was used mainly for big-bore British "Express" cartridges intended for large game. Typically it was fitted with a 28-inch or longer barrel (perhaps half-octagon and half-round), high ramp front sight with interchangeable insert, a British multiple-leaf Express rear sight, a slender forend, and a pistol-grip buttstock of typical British shotgun style. The Gibbs Farquharson is by far the most common, and even it exists in several variations. Even today with the Farquharson-like Ruger and Colt/Sharps modern single-shot action available, the Gibbs and other better Farquharson variations are still highly sought after for building custom rifles.

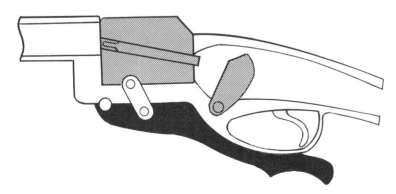

Schematic showing basic parts of Farquharson rifle action.

Fast Draw Generally, the sport of drawing a single-action revolver and firing blank cartridges in the fastest time possible.

Fast-draw competition is conducted under strict rules, and precise electronic timing devices are used to measure speed. Two methods of timing are used. The first includes the shooters reaction time. The draw is initiated (and the timer started)

Lady fast-draw fan working against the electronic timer.

when the shooter sees a signal light flash. The timer is then stopped by a triggering device activated by the sound of the shot. In the second method, the timer is started when the shooter releases a pushbutton switch at the beginning of the draw, and is stopped by the shot. The first method is most common now, and championship times run as low as 0.2 second.

Feed The process of transferring a cartridge from the magazine to the chamber. Or, the system and method employed for this process in a particular gun, i.e., magazine feed, belt feed, gravity feed, etc.

Feed Ramp   That part in the breech of any gun (except a re-volver) which funnels a cartridge from the magazine and into the chamber. It is generally in the form of a sloped and slightly concave surface leading from the upper front of the magazine toward the chamber. It functions by catching the bullet of the incoming cartridge and deflecting it upward into the mouth of the chamber as it is driven forward by the bolt.

Ferguson, Major Patrick (1744–1780)   A British officer and firearms enthusiast of Scottish descent who was killed in the American Revolutionary War.

In 1776 he developed and patented an improved breech-loading rifle which became the first practical breech-loaded rifle used by British forces.

Ferguson Rifle   The first practical military breech-loading rifle designed and patented by Major Patrick Ferguson, a British Army man. Major Ferguson had rifles of his design made at his own expense and equipped his regiment serving in the American Revolution. Unfortunately, Major Ferguson was killed in the battle of Kings Mountain, and without his immediate and active support, the rifle disappeared from the scene in spite of its obvious advantages over the smoothbore flintlock musket of the era.

The Ferguson action was quite simple, consisting of a round breech plug passing through a matching hole at the rear of the barrel and caused to travel vertically by means of a multiple, high-pitch thread. One complete revolution of the attached

Feed ramp, typical of those found in many repeating rifles and autoloading pistols, is found here on the barrel of a Smith & Wesson M39 pistol.

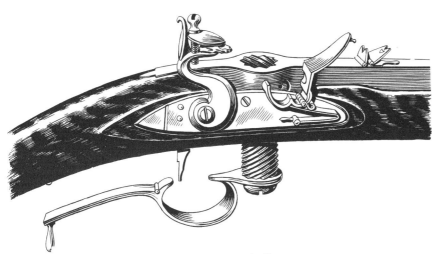

Ferguson breech-loading flintlock rifle.

trigger guard caused the breech plug to move downward flush with the bottom of the bore. Another full turn clockwise closed the breech completely. In use, the action was opened, a round lead ball dropped into the bore, followed by the proper powder charge, the action was closed, the flash pan of the flintlock action primed, and the gun was ready to fire. The design was such that if paper cartridges were lacking, simply pouring loose powder into the barrel chamber would suffice, the rising breech block forcing excess powder from the action.

While the threads in the breech and breech plug were likely to gather considerable fouling and cause difficult operation after the firing of a few rounds, the Ferguson rifle was far superior for military use to any other gun in use at that time. It was, in fact, far ahead of its time.

Extremely few original Ferguson rifles survive today, and they are among the rarest items in collections devoted to arms of that period.

Field of View   In a telescopic sight, the area which may be seen through the scope at optimum eye relief, generally circular in shape and measured by its diameter or horizontal spread in feet at a distance of 100 yards.

Fine Sight   Referring to open sights, a sight picture in which the tip of the front sight is held to be just barely visible at the bottom of the rear sight's notch. Also called a "fine bead" sight.

Fire-Forming   Expanding a case to fit a larger or differently shaped chamber by firing it therein, usually with a reduced powder charge.

Firing pin protrusion on a typical bolt-action rifle. Measurement is from bolt face to tip of pin.

Firing Pin   That part of any gun which directly strikes the primer to fire the cartridge. It may be a fixed protrusion on a striking rod, a fixed or pivoted member on a rotating hammer, and it may be driven by its own spring, or by another member propelled by either a spring or camming device. In submachine guns, usually only a teat integral with the bolt face.

Firing Pin Protrusion   The amount a firing pin protrudes beyond the face of the breech at the instant of firing or maximum forward travel. Dependent somewhat upon the amount of energy imparted to the firing pin by the firing mechanism,

Firing pins are generally concealed and not easily seen or examined. Here is an exposed revolver hammer (Smith & Wesson M1917) with firing pin at upper left and the pitting that results from much use.

there is a certain minimum and maximum protrusion required for efficient and uniform primer ignition. Less than minimum will produce either erratic ignition or misfires — while excess protrusion may pierce the primer cup and allow gas to escape back into the action.

In some designs, excessive protrusion will result in the nose of the firing pin protruding beyond the breech face even when cocked, and thus interfering with proper feeding, and possibly causing a premature firing as the cartridge is chambered.

Typical firing pin protrusion in a modern bolt-action Mauser-type rifle is .055 inch minimum, .065 inch maximum.

Fit and Finish Terms describing overall workmanship in guns. Generally, a gun containing close but smooth-fitting metal parts, a very smooth polish and blue on metal surfaces, good quality inletting and very close fitting of wood to metal, etc. would be regarded as having good fit and finish.

Flanged The British terminology for a rimmed cartridge case; thus any rimmed cartridge of British origin may be found labeled as ".450/3¼ Flanged."

Flash Hider A device attached to the muzzle of any gun for the purpose of concealing (not reducing) the flash or flame gen-

erated by the burning propellant and by the ignition of expanding gases as they contact the oxygen-rich atmosphere. Usually a large conical or tubular extension clamped to the muzzle.

See also FLASH SUPPRESSOR.

Flash Suppressor   A device attached to the muzzle of a firearm that serves to disrupt, or reduce the amount of flame produced upon firing. The most common type consists of tuning-fork-like fingers which extend beyond the muzzle and vibrate under the impulse of firing to disrupt and reduce flash.

See also FLASH HIDER.

Flinch   An involuntary movement occurring either at the instant of firing or in anticipation thereof, which deflects the gun off target before the bullet exists the muzzle. Flinching is generally caused by some fear—either real or subconscious—of the discharge, or by attempting to compensate for recoil before it actually occurs.

Flint   The angular piece of flint or similar stone or mineral deposit used in a flintlock to strike sparks from the frizzen. The

Modern prong-type supressor as supplied on the Finnish M.62, 7.62mm assault rifle.

Conventional flint in proper position for firing in flintlock.

flint was once made only by hand from natural flint nodes, but is now sometimes cut from agate, certain forms of Arkansas stone, and other sparking material. It is also called "gunflint."

Flintlock A form of ignition system which dominated firearms from the early 1600s until displaced by the percussion lock in the middle 1800s. Essentially, the flintlock provided a hammer or cock in whose jaws was clamped a shaped piece of flint. The spring-powered movement of the hammer striking the flint against an upright steel frizzen or battery showers sparks into a small charge of priming powder whose flash ignites the main charge through a vent into the barrel.

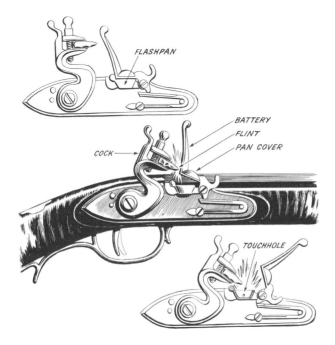

Flintlock mechanism. Trigger pull releases the cock holding the flint, which snaps down and strikes the battery, forcing it back and sending sparks into flashpan.

Additionally, the flintlock contained a vertically operating sear as well as a half-cock or safety notch. The flintlock is principally distinguished from its snaphance predecessor by the pan covering being incorporated into the frizzen and being actuated automatically by flint impact upon the frizzen.

See also PERCUSSION LOCK, GUN LOCK, and SNAPHANCE

Floating Barrel A barrel that is bedded so that it does not touch the stock at any point, even during firing vibrations.

Floor Plate In a gun with a fixed box magazine, the metal or plastic piece which closes the bottom of the magazine body and supports the follower spring. In a detachable box magazine, whether for rifle, pistol, or other gun, the bottom of the magazine that is sometimes then called a "bottom piece," or "base."

Typical hinged floor plate on a Mauser-type action.

On long guns with fixed magazines, the floor plate may be immovable, detachable, or hinged at one end. In detachable magazines, fixed floor plates are the rule. However, some are removable, to allow easy cleaning, especially those found on military rifles and the more modern autoloading pistols.

Flush-Seating Seating a wadcutter bullet completely within the case, its nose flush with the case mouth.

Fluted Chamber A form of chambering for bottleneck cartridges generally used only in automatic or semiautomatic military weapons in which a conventional chamber has shallow, thin, longitudinal grooves cut into its interior surface. The grooves generally taper in depth, being their deepest at the neck, becoming shallower to the rear, until they disappear completely about a quarter or a third of the chamber length forward of its mouth.

These grooves or flutes are generally numerous, eight to sixteen being closely spaced, and may be made with a cutting tool or impressed by a male die.

The purpose of chamber flutes is to permit propellant gases to bleed back between the case and chamber walls and thus reduce case adhesion, and reducing the force required for extraction. Ideally, the forward portion of the case actually floats on a layer of high-pressure gas during firing rather than gripping chamber walls.

Marks of chamber flutes show clearly on the 20mm fired case at left; unfired round at right.

Though not currently used in true sporting arms, fluted chambers are found in Soviet M38 and M40 Tokarev rifles, the Spanish CETME, the German G1, the SIG Assault rifle, and a wide variety of higher-powered automatic weapons.

Folding Gun Usually a shotgun, a lightweight, utility gun of small bore that folds upon itself at the hinge pin for ease of packing or carrying. Found both in single- and double-barrelled

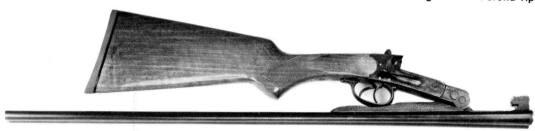

Spanish-made folding .410 double shotgun with side-lever action.

versions, the one illustrated is of Spanish origin and currently manufactured by Sarasqueta in .410 gauge.

Follower The platform against which the last cartridge or cartridges in a magazine rest, and the means by which the magazine spring forces an entire column of cartridges successively into position for feeding.

In a tubular magazine, the follower is simply a round plunger riding over the end of a magazine spring; in a Mauser-type or box magazine, it is a more carefully shaped platform sometimes provided with ribs or grooves to assist in aligning the cartridges correctly with the feed lips for feeding.

Forcing Cone That portion of a shotgun barrel directly ahead of the chamber, where the relatively large diameter of the chamber is reduced to bore diameter. It is, in effect, a short cone segment.

As a shotshell is fired, and as the shot charge and wads exit the case, they expand radially to fill the mouth of the forcing cone, and are then squeezed down to bore diameter as they pass through the cone.

At one time, the shape, internal finish, and condition of the forcing cone were considered quite important. Any roughness at this point would increase the deformation of pellets in the outer layers of the shot charge, and those pellets would tend to fly wide of the denser portion of the pattern. However, plastic shot-protectors greatly reduce this effect, and thus minor differences in forcing cones are not now quite as important.

Forend Latch A spring-loaded mechanical fastener on a shotgun which retains the forend on the barrels, yet allows easy removal without tools.

Forend Tip A device of wood or metal attached to the front of the stock forend. Originally, a forend tip (sometimes called a forend cap or nose cap) strengthened the stock mechanically, provided a seat for a ramrod, and sometimes also aided in holding a stock and barrel together. In some modern pump, autoloading, or lever action guns, it still serves most of those same purposes. Insofar as the average sporting rifle is concerned, however, it has become a purely decorative device, usually of contrasting-colored wood.

In military weapons a forend tip is usually incorporated into a barrel band, bayonet support, gas cylinder, or other functional components.

Forsyth, Alexander J., 1768–1843 A minister and ardent hunter, chemist, and mechanic, Forsyth was displeased with flint ignition. In 1807 he produced his Scent-Bottle percussion ignition system in which detonating powder (fulminate) was fed out of a magazine, then detonated by a hammer to ignite the main charge. Forsyth patented his system and set up as Alexander Forsyth & Co. (London) to produce guns to utilize it. Forsyth's patents were sufficiently inclusive that other forms of percussion ignition were stalled until the patent expired. He brought suit against several gunmakers who designed other (and sometimes better) percussion systems.

See Percussion Lock.

Fouling Shot A shot fired after a gun barrel has been cleaned and oiled to establish a uniform condition for all subsequent shots. Varmint and target shooters often fire one or two fouling shots to avoid the slight differences in center of impact that exist between a clean, oiled bore and a fouled one.

Fowling Piece (Fowler) Originally a smoothbore muzzle-loading gun intended to fire a charge of small shot at winged game. Called a fowling piece because it was shot at fowl, it featured a barrel often longer and thinner walled than barrels intended for ball. It existed in one form or another nearly from the beginning of firearms and was the ancient counterpart of today's shotgun. The term remained in common use into the 19th century but is seldom encountered now, having been replaced by shotgun.

Frankford Arsenal (FA) The U.S. Army manufacturing and experimental arsenal at Philadelphia, Pennsylvania, and the site of the majority of all military small arms ammunition development.

At one time, it was the major production facility for U.S. military small arms ammunition.

Ammunition bearing "FA" as part of its head stamp was manufactured at Frankford Arsenal.

Freebore A portion of the barrel ahead of the normal bullet seat or throat in which the rifling has been cut away, leaving the bore smooth and untapered.

Its purpose is to delay the resistance encountered when the bullet first engages the rifling, thus allowing a bit more time for the propellant to burn and build up gas pressure before the bullet is momentarily retarded by its entrance in the rifling. It will usually increase velocity without increasing chamber pressure, but at the expense of burning a larger powder charge.

There are no standards for freebore and it is sometimes difficult to distinguish between a slightly longer than normal throat and deliberate freebore. For all practical purposes, freebore is seldom more than ½ inch in length.

See also LEADE and THROAT.

Free Rifle A rifle designed specifically for international-type shooting. The rimfire "free rifle" is fired at the range of 50 meters only, and the centerfire "free rifle" is fired at 300 meters only in

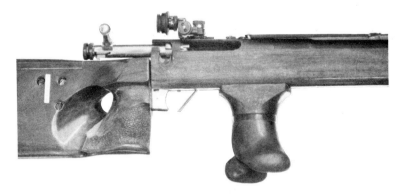

Side detail of a specially built free rifle used by a member of the Soviet team in the World Championship matches at Phoenix, Arizona, in 1970. Note plam rest, finely adjustable set trigger, adjustable sights, adjustable buttstock, and other sophisticated refinements usually found in a free rifle.

international competition. These rifles are used in the prone, kneeling, and standing positions and are designed to give optimum performance in each of these positions. Aside from the weight limitation of eight kilograms (17.6 pounds) there are no other restrictions upon the gun proper other than safe operations with functional reliability.

A free rifle is generally very carefully stocked to fit the individual fitted with an adjustable hook buttplate, a finely adjustable set trigger, extremely precise metallic sights and perhaps even a mirage shield stretched over the barrel. Sights are often hooded or shielded and may be offset or inclined to compensate for individual idiosyncrasies or physical characteristics.

Freshing Out   The act of recutting the rifling of a barrel (usually a muzzle-loader) to remove roughness or pitting and restore its serviceability. Only a small amount of metal is removed from the bottoms of the grooves and from the tops of the lands, retaining original rifling twist, depth, and width, increasing only bore and groove diameter. It is generally accomplished by running single-tooth cutters directly on the original surfaces, deepening the grooves first, and then cutting down the lands.
See also REBORING.

Front Sight   The forward aiming point, near the muzzle, of any metallic sighting system.
See SIGHTS, IRON and SIGHTS, TELESCOPIC.

Full Charge   Any cartridge loaded to factory or SAAMI-standard, full-power specifications—as opposed to handloads of lesser power, or special target loads of less velocity and energy.
See also MID-RANGE LOAD.

Functioning Cycle   The basic operations that must take place in any firearm using self-contained ammunition, whether it be a simple break-open shotgun or the most complex selective-fire assault rifle.
Beginning with the gun loaded and cocked, the eight steps of the functioning cycle are: (1) ignition, (2) unlock, (3) extract, (4) eject, (5) cock, (6) feed, (7) chamber, and (8) lock. This is the most common sequence, however, there is not only a great deal of overlap, but some of the operations happen simultaneously.
Individual gun design and degree of complexity may also cause the sequence to be changed—as in a break-open, exposed-hammer shotgun in which the cycle for a given shot begins with manual cocking of the hammer.
The various steps may occur automatically as in an autoloading gun, or they may be performed manually as in the case of the break-open shotgun when ejection is accomplished by plucking the fired case from the chamber.
Regardless of the gun design, all of the above operations must take place in any functional firearm.

Gain Twist A form of rifling, not generally found in modern sporting guns, where the rate of twist increases from breech to muzzle. Still occasionally used in muzzle-loaders and some large-caliber, high-rate-of-fire military automatic weapons, but at one time quite common in muzzle-loading arms of all sorts.

Garand, John C. (1888–   ) A Canadian-born arms designer who came to the United States as a child, and subsequently designed and perfected the M1 .30 caliber semiautomatic rifle popularly called the Garand. It was adopted by the U.S. Army in 1936 and used until the early 1960s.

Gas Check A shallow brass or copper cup affixed to the bullet base to reduce leading and improve accuracy.

Gas-Cutting The escape of propellant gas between a bullet and the bore early in the sequence of firing, usually at the time the bullet is first entering the rifling. Given a properly dimensioned chamber, case, barrel, and bullet, no significant amount of gas will escape. However, with an oversize bore, an undersize bullet, or defective chamber or case, the bullet will not seal the bore as it begins to move forward and gas will escape around it. The larger the gap, the more gas will escape and the greater the bullet's velocity will be.

The effect of gas-cutting is generally considered limited to the bullet itself, however, it also accelerates barrel throat erosion to a much lesser degree. As gas escapes, it burns or melts away portions of the bullet's surface—the amount depending upon bullet material, amount of pressure and velocity of the gas.

A lead bullet at high gas pressure may be partially melted or vaporized and distorted beyond recognition by excessive gas-cutting, so much so that accuracy is completely destroyed and barrel leading is promoted. On the other hand, a heavily jacketed bullet may withstand the same conditions with only minor scoring or pitting.

Gas Operation A system of semiautomatic or full-automatic firearms operation in which a portion of the propellant gases is vented out of the bore through a small port. The venting of the gases drives the piston rearward to provide the power for unlocking and opening the action and compressing a return or recoil spring, which in turn provides powers for closing the action and completing the functioning cycle.

For all practical purposes, we may consider the modern gas-operated sporting rifle to be nothing more than a pump-action rifle in which a gas-driven piston substitutes for the shooter's arm and muscle. This is most clearly seen in the Remington M760 pump rifle compared to the same firm's M740 42 semi-automatic. All internal action parts are nearly identical in both guns, the only substantial difference is in the gas piston and cylinder under the barrel, which provides the motive power. Essentially the same situation will be found in pump and auto shotguns by various makers.

Prior to World War II, gas operation was considered inferior to recoil operation for semiautomatic and full-automatic firearms. However, the success of the U. S. M1 Garand rifle and M1 Winchester carbine proved that gas operation was superior in reliability, durability, and adverse-condition functioning. In the past score of years, the vast field of light and heavy machine guns—once almost exclusively recoil-operated—has been taken over by modern gas-operated designs.

Gas Port In autoloading or automatic weapons, a hole drilled into the barrel through which gas is vented to act against a piston and provide power for operation of the mechanism. In a sporting rifle, a hole through the receiver located near the junction of bolt face and case head. Its purpose is to provide an escape route for high-pressure gases should a case or primer rupture upon firing, greatly reducing the amount of gas that might otherwise be directed back through the action and possibly into the shooter's face.

See also GAS OPERATION and VENT.

Gauge The term identifying bore diameter of a shotgun. It originated in firearms antiquity when all guns used a spherical lead ball, and represents actually the number of balls suitable for a given bore that could be cased from one pound of lead.

It was originally applied to rifled as well as smoothbore arms, and many old writings will be found referring to a rifle or smoothbore as "carrying 20 balls to the pound." The term has long since been dropped from rifle usage, but remains as a matter of convenience applied to shotguns.

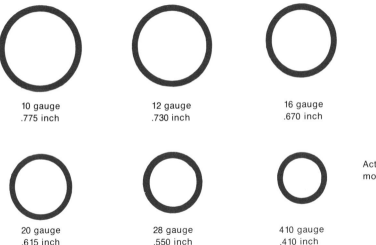

10 gauge
.775 inch

12 gauge
.730 inch

16 gauge
.670 inch

20 gauge
.615 inch

28 gauge
.550 inch

410 gauge
.410 inch

Actual bore sizes of the six gauges most commonly used.

However, the bore diameter of 12 lead balls to the pound is not identical to the nominal diameter of a modern 12-gauge barrel. The same applies to all other gauges. At the time the gauge system developed, it was essential that a fair amount of "windage" exist between ball and bore to insure ease of loading and to compensate for dimensional variations. Consequently though the 12-gauge barrel measured .729 inch in diameter, the 12-gauge ball of the day measured substantially less. This same situation exists to some degree today, though over the years minor dimensional changes have been made in the barrels in the interest of improving performance and standardization.

The following table gives the actual barrel bore diameter of various gauges.

See also WINDAGE.

BORE DIAMETERS OF VARIOUS GAUGES

Gauge	Bore Diameter (inches)	Gauge	Bore Diameter (inches)	Gauge	Bore Diameter (inches)
1	1.669	13	.700	25	.571
2	1.325	14	.693	26	.563
3	1.157	15	.677	27	.556
4	1.052	16	.662	28	.550
5	.976	17	.650	29	.543
6	.919	18	.637	30	.537
7	.873	19	.626	31	.531
8	.835	20	.615	32	.526
9	.802	21	.605	33	.520
10	.775	22	.596	34	.515
11	.751	23	.587	35	.510
12	.729	24	.579	36	.506

Gilding Metal A cupronickel alloy used almost universally for bullet jackets, though replaced to some degree by mild steel in a few European countries. Formulas vary considerably, depending upon the manufacturer, the bullet and its use. The proportions may vary from 60 per cent copper and 40 per cent nickel to 87 per cent copper and 13 per cent nickel, plus minute amounts of other materials.

Gilding metal is ideal for bullet jackets because of its unique property of being self-lubricating, allowing it to be used in steel barrels at high velocities without being rubbed off and deposited in the bore to accumulate as metal fouling. Reference is sometimes made to this property in trade names, such as Winchester's "Lubaloy" and Dynamit Nobel's "Nobeloy."

In addition, gilding metal is easily and economically worked, reasonably low in cost, and yet possesses sufficient strength for virtually any sporting ammunition requirement.

During wartime and other periods of copper shortage, mild steel thinly coated with copper or an alloy with similar properties is often substituted for gilding metal in bullet jackets. Bullets so jacketed cannot be visually identified, but a magnet will attract them.

Glass Bedding Generally, reinforcing a wooden gunstock with a reinforced fiberglass-epoxy compound to (1) increase local strength, (2) spread concentrated stresses over wider areas (such as around the recoil lugs) (3) obtain intimate stock/action and wood/metal pressure relationships necessary for maximum accuracy and, (4) reduce or eliminate warping tendencies of portions of the stock by sealing out moisture permanently.

Best results are normally obtained when the metal is first inletted intimately into the wood, after which wood is uniformly removed in desired areas to allow space for the bedding compound, taking care to leave key areas of wood untouched so that they will support the metal parts in proper relationship to the stock.

The metal is coated with a release compound, often plain paste wax; the recesses in the wood are filled with a pasty mixture of epoxy compound and finely chopped glass fibers. The metal parts are placed in the stock and drawn down into their proper position by the stock screws, while the bedding compound sets up. When a sufficient amount of bedding compound is used, the excess will all be squeezed out, eliminating any voids. The excess bedding compound is best rough-trimmed, when set to a stiff rubbery consistency, and then allowed to cure completely before final trimming.

When carefully and properly done, glass bedding is not a stop-gap measure or a cover up for poor inletting—it not only strengthens the stock, but also improves accuracy and consistency.

Revolver grip adapter.

Grease Gun A World War II colloquialism for the U.S. M3 and M31 .45 caliber submachine gun.

Greener Safety A form of manual safety generally found on double-barrelled lead shotguns, situated on the left side of the buttstock just below the top lever. Introduced by W. W. Greener, an English gunmaker, on guns of his manufacture during the middle 1870s.

Grip Adapter A simple hard rubber or plastic (or sometimes metal) filler piece that fits on a revolver between the rear of the trigger guard and the front of the grip frame to provide better support for the hand.

Grip Safety A separate mechanical safety, spring-loaded and protruding from the grip or stock, usually found in an autoloading handgun but occasionally on submachine guns and machine guns, rarely on revolvers. When at rest, a grip safety prevents firing by trigger movement, but allows firing when depressed. It is located and constructed so that it is easily depressed without conscious effort when a normal firing grip is taken on the gun.

Grizzly Bear, See BEARS, GUNS and CARTRIDGES for

Groove Diameter The diametrical measurement of a rifled bore to the bottom of opposite grooves, or the diametrical measurement of the circle circumscribed by the bottoms of the rifling grooves in the event grooves are not opposed.

With barrels having an equal number of grooves, groove diameter can be determined quite easily by first pushing an oversized, soft lead slug through or into the bore, then measuring it with a standard micrometer across the raised ridges engraved by the rifling grooves.

When an uneven number of grooves exist, there are no directly opposed ridges over which to take an accurate measurement — thus it is only possible to approximate its diameter by carefully rotating the slug in a micrometer. A precise measurement can be obtained only with the use of a V-block and wires by the method used by machinists.

It is sometimes thought that groove diameter is the same as caliber but this is not necessarily so. As a practical matter, many cartridges are given a caliber designation vastly different from that of either barrel groove or bore diameter.

It is standard practice, however, and generally considered necessary for proper functioning and accuracy, that the bullet be at least equal to groove diameter.

Group A general term describing a cluster of shots on target generally used as an indication of gun and ammunition accuracy. The standard method of measurement is from center to center between the widest-spaced holes. To conserve ammunition and time, many individuals use five-shot groups for informal testing and evaluation, but ten shots are normally required in competition or where a truly accurate evaluation is required. Several groups must be fired to constitute a valid accuracy test.

The establishment of bullet-hole centers to permit accurate measurement can be quite difficult. Where shot holes are widely separated, bullet-diameter plugs may be placed in the widest holes, after which the outside distance between those plugs is measured, and one-bullet-diameter is subtracted from that dimension to obtain the center-to-center distance.

When shot holes are very closely grouped and overlapping, this method is not practical, and an optical measuring device is used. While it might not seem easy to measure those ragged-edge holes precisely, those who score bench-rest targets use highly specialized optical instruments capable of measuring to .0001 inch.

Guard Screw   A screw that secures the action and trigger guard
to a stock. Also called a stock screw. In a Mauser-type bolt-
action rifle, the screws which hold the trigger guard/magazine
unit to the receiver, sandwiching the stock in between.

Gun Collecting   Man has collected firearms since their beginning, just as he has collected art objects. Further there are only
two *basic* reasons for collecting guns—one is monetary, the other
personal.

A fine gun collection is an excellent hedge against inflation,
inasmuch as choice items always appreciate in value much
more rapidly than dollar values decrease. In short, a rare and
valuable gun that would have been worth the price of a new
Chevrolet in 1934 might well be worth a couple of Cadillacs
today!

The second basic reason for collecting guns is by no means
as easy to understand. Most men simply *like* guns and when
their opportunities and economic situations permit, they will
acquire a few specimens simply for the pride of possession.
However, this doesn't represent true collecting, but merely
acquisition. Acquisition becomes collecting whenever a fairly
large number of guns are involved, or when the choice is
narrowed down to a particular field, type, or historical relationship to individuals or events.

A collection need not be large—for example, a complete
collection of U.S. martial cartridge handguns can be housed
in a desk drawer. On the other hand, a complete collection
of Mauser military rifles, if it could even be assembled, would
include hundreds of specimens and fill a large room.

Quite often, the collector's choice of arms will be closely
related to his vocation. For example, a professor of military
history might well collect and study military small arms because
they would be, to some degree, essential to a complete understanding of his academic specialty. Conversely, a supermarket
manager might collect percussion revolvers, there being
absolutely no connection whatever between them and his vocation, but simply because he likes them.

In starting a collection one should determine a particular
field within which his acquisitions will be made. Simply buying
appealing guns at attractive prices generally produces a con-
glomeration of unrelated items which have no particular value
or purpose, and which will probably not increase in value
sufficiently to enable the purchase of prize pieces.

Once the field has been chosen, a reference library should
be acquired and studied assiduously—intelligent buying only
is possible with ample knowledge. The new collector should
list basic pieces around which his collection will be made and
those pieces should be acquired first, and in the best individual

condition possible. A common mistake at this point is to acquire as many pieces as possible, with the result being that only the most-common and lowest-priced items are bought.

At the same time, more desirable items are increasing rapidly in price.

A far better method is to acquire at least one choice and more costly gun for each two or three common ones. In other words, if you're collecting percussion Colts, as soon as you've picked up a decent .44 Army and .36 Navy, go shopping for a Dragoon. This will require more money for single purchases, but it will result in a much more valuable collection at less cost in the long run.

Once a collection has been started, retention or growth of its value can be assured by acquiring items only in the best condition and by taking all practical means to insure that the condition does not deteriorate. Even the cheapest piece in your collection will appreciate considerably if it is in top condition and if that condition is maintained. The same item in mediocre condition, if allowed to deteriorate over the years by handling and neglect, may even decrease in value.

Friends and relatives are the collector's worst enemies. There are many people who will pick up and snap a $50,000 wheel-lock and think nothing of it!

Gun Control Act of 1968   The Gun Control of 1968, a federal law enacted as part of the overall Omnibus Crime Control and Safe Streets Act of 1968.

The basic provisions of GCA '68 became effective December 13, 1968. Shooters should at least know what they are NOT PROHIBITED from doing under the provisions of the Act, and these points are best summarized by the National Rifle Association:

The Gun Control Act of 1968 DOES NOT:

Prohibit the purchase of ammunition over-the-counter in another state.

Prevent a person from transporting firearms and ammunition to another state for the purpose of hunting or competition, or attending gun shows. (Sales or other transfers of firearms by or to nonresidents at gun shows are prohibited.)

Require the registration of firearms or firearms owners. (Registration is required for fully automatic firearms.)

Include antique firearms or muzzle-loading cannon.

Require a manufacturer's license for the handloading of ammunition for one's own use.

Prohibit the loan or rental of a firearm to a nonresident for temporary use for lawful sporting purposes.

Prohibit the sale or delivery of a rifle or shotgun to a person who is participating in organized rifle or shotgun competition, or engaged in hunting, and whose rifle has been lost, stolen, or inoperative. (The buyer must submit to the seller a sworn statement that firearm was lost or stolen or inoperative, and identifying chief local law enforcement officer of residence of buyer.)

Prohibit the sale or delivery of a federal firearms licensee of a rifle or shotgun to a resident of a contiguous state which authorizes such sale. (A sworn statement, notification to the chief local law enforcement officer of the buyer's place of residence and a seven-day waiting period are required prior to delivery to the buyer.)

Include shotgun shot or unprimed nonmetallic shotgun cases or hulls, black powder or blank cartridges in the definition of ammunition.

Prohibit the importation by a licensee of sporting firearms from foreign countries. (A permit is required from the Secretary of the Treasury.)

Prohibit the shipment by nonlicensees of firearms to a licensed manufacturer, importer or dealer for "repair or customizing" and the return of such firearm, or a firearm of the same kind and type, to the sender.

Prohibit the transportation, shipment or receipt of ammunition-loading equipment.

Apply to air or CO_2 shoulder arms or handguns.

Prohibit the shipment, sale or other transfer of a firearm by a nonlicensee to a licensee resident in another state.

Prohibit a nonlicensee from selling or otherwise transferring a firearm to another nonlicensee who resides in the same state.

Prohibit a nonlicensee from shipping a firearm owned by him to himself at an alternate residence in another state, provided that the carrier is informed in writing.

Prohibit the shipment of a person's firearms by a commercial mover to a new residence in another state.

Prohibit a nonlicensee who does not appear in person from purchasing a firearm from a licensee in the same state. (A sworn statement, notification to the chief local law enforcement officer of the buyer's place of residence and a seven-day waiting period are required prior to delivery to the buyer.)

Guncotton   A very early form of nitrocellulose explosive in which cotton was treated by nitric acid. It is often erroneously thought to have been used as a smokeless propellant in the early days, but instead was used as a base from which certain smokeless powders, including Cordite, were manufactured.

See also CORDITE.

Gun Metal   A bronze alloy used during muzzle-loading days for making cannons. Generally dark gray in color and containing about 90 per cent copper and 10 per cent tin, with small percentages of lead, iron, and zinc included. It is not used in modern guns. The term is sometimes used to describe the bluish-black color of the alloy.

Gunning The sport of shooting at game with any firearm, but most commonly used in reference to hunting with a shotgun.

Gunpowder The term generally applied to black powder, but also commonly and erroneously applied to smokeless propellant powders and thus responsible for a great deal of the confusion that currently exists regarding the properties of each.
See also BLACK POWDER.

Gut-Shot A hit through the abdominal cavity and an all-too-common error in bullet placement occurring most often on broadside shots at running game. Many hunters underlead running deer, with the result that bullets strike far back in the paunch.
A gut-shot animal may show very little visible evidence of being hit, and run out of sight to die a lingering death. Even if the animal is eventually found, a gut-shot releases all sorts of intestinal and stomach contents, and acids which may ruin the meat. Far better a clean miss or poor placement farther forward than the inevitably fatal but wasteful gut-shot.

Standard factory stock (top), custom stock (center), and target stock.

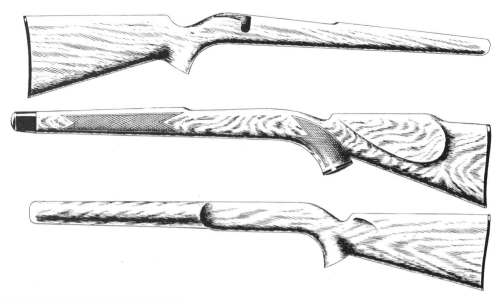

Gun Stock The rear member of a shoulder arm which attaches to the breech or barrel and is used to hold the weapon to the shoulder. It is usually made of wood or, in some modern guns, plastic material.

See RIFLE STOCK, SHOTGUN STOCK.

Gyro-Jet The trade name of a unique rocket-propelled projectile designed and produced in limited quantity by MBA Associates for use in a plastic smoothbore handgun of the same name. The Gyro-Jet loaded cartridge consisted of an unusually long steel projectile, hollowed at its rear to accept a small solid-fuel rocket motor containing angled exhaust nozzles for the propellant gases and also a central pocket to accept a standard Boxer-type primer.

When the primer is struck by the gun's firing pin, it ignites the rocket motor, whose gases are then exhausted through the angled nozzles, thrusting the projectile forward, and at the same time giving it sufficient rotational velocity for stablization.

The Gyro-Jet and ammunition offer high downrange energy potential, but initial projectile acceleration is quite slow, and thus short range energy is quite deficient. The principal advantages of the system are practically nonexistent recoil energy and very cheap and simple gun construction.

Only limited quantities of the Gyro-Jet handgun were produced, and they are generally collector's items today, as are the individual rocket cartridges.

The Gyro-Jet was not commercially successful in either rifle or pistol form and relatively few were made. Today they are generally considered collectors guns.

The guns were cheaply made from plastic moldings and unlovely to look at. They resembled plastic toy guns more than real firearms and so did not appeal. Despite this, they were priced at $200 to $300 each. Ammunition was quite costly and not widely distributed or available in quantity.

Due to low acceleration produced by the miniature rocket motor, projectiles required several yards to build up velocity. This destroyed any value as a close-in weapon for military, police, or defensive use. One writer claimed the projectiles could be caught in the hand as they exited slowly from the muzzle. The spin-stabilization employed did not produce sufficient accuracy for conventional use at significant ranges.

Military use was never seriously considered because of bulk and weight of ammunition and low short-range penetration.

Half Cock A position of the hammer in a hammer-actuated firing mechanism that serves as a manual safety. In most instances, as typified by the M94 Winchester, the half-cock notch in the hammer is cut deeply so that the sear's nose cannot be forced out of it by pressure on the trigger. Also, the sear supports the hammer and prevents it from striking the firing pin under any reasonable impact.

Generally, the sear can be disengaged from the half-cock notch only by drawing the hammer back toward the full-cock position. If it is desired to lower the hammer to the rest position from half-cock, it is necessary to first draw it back to free the sear from the notch, while depressing the trigger which moves the sear out of the hammer's path.

Half-cock systems are found on virtually all exposed-hammer rifles and shotguns and are also common to all single-action revolvers.

One other form of half-cock safety systems will be encountered on Lee Enfield rifles, and on some other older bolt-action rifles. It consists of a secondary notch in the cocking piece which will engage the sear and function exactly as described above. Its purpose in the Lee Enfield is not a safety, but to allow the mainspring to be unloaded and thus subject to less strain when the rifle is left with a round chambered for a prolonged period of time. Other systems of unloading the mainspring under such circumstances have been applied to the Italian Mannlicher-Carcano, as well as others. In all instances, a separate manual safety is furnished.

So-called half-cock positions exist on many self-loading pistols, but do *not* function as a manual safety. Instead, they are really *intercept* positions to prevent firing if one's thumb slips during manual cocking and allows the hammer to fall.

Half-Jacketed A form of bullet design in which a soft lead core is swaged to final shape and dimension inside a thin copper jacket or cup that extends only partially up the length of the bearing surface.

Half-jacketed bullets have the advantage of producing violent expansion at velocities practical in handguns, and are also quite simple and economical to produce. However, they have a distinct disadvantage since a portion of the naked lead-bearing surface contacts the bore directly, and since initial acceleration loads upset the soft unjacketed portion of the bullet into greater contact with the bore which produces excessive leading and more often than not reduces accuracy.

Half-jacketed bullets achieved wide popularity in the early 1960s because of their relatively low cost and because they could easily be made at home in low-cost swaging dies and presses, principally the Swag-O-Matic manufactured by the C-H Die Company.

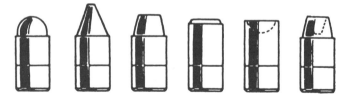

Typical half-jacket designs in which the bullet jacket comes only partly up the bearing surface, leaving bare lead to contact the bore.

Hall, Colonel John H. (1778–1841) The inventor of the Hall rifle. Born of a distinguished professional family and involved in privateering during the War of 1812, he joined the army and became interested in improving the existing firearms. His breech-loading flintlock rifle was patented in 1811, and in 1813 he received his first order from the U.S. Government for 100 pieces. In 1818 he was assigned to Harper's Ferry Armory to supervise production of 1,000 Hall rifles, which were completed by 1824, with all parts interchangeable, a previously unheard of feat. Hall continued at Harper's Ferry to produce and improve the basic design until 1840, and died only a year later. Hall's achievement of complete parts interchangeability was far greater and more important than the design of the rifle, which was never entirely satisfactory. It was Hall who first achieved firearms parts interchangeability, not Eli Whitney to whom the credit is often given.

Hall Rifle An early American breech-loading flintlock rifle invented and manufactured by John Hall, and for a time a standard U.S. martial rifle. The Hall was manufactured privately from 1813 and at Harper's Ferry Armory from 1819 to 1824, and by North until the 1840s.

The Hall used a rectangular breech block, bored from the front with a chamber to accept the round ball and powder charge. Hinged at the rear, the breech block was pivoted upward by a finger lever beneath the gun, exposing the mouth of the chamber for loading with either loose powder and ball, or paper cartridges of the day. The breech block was then lowered into proper alignment with the bore by the finger lever, after which it was fired in typical flintlock fashion.

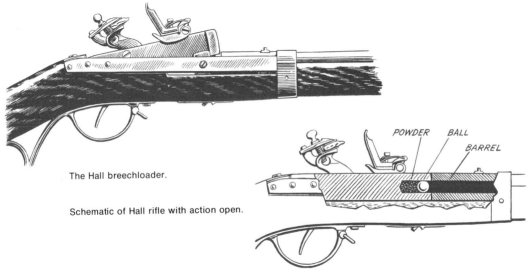

The Hall breechloader.

Schematic of Hall rifle with action open.

A great many Hall rifles were converted to percussion (and production from 1833 was percussion) in spite of much opposition to this great improvement by hidebound U.S. Army Ordnance officers.

Though the design was no longer standard at the time of the Civil War, a fair number of Halls did see use during the conflict. The Hall action was quite advanced in design for its day, but the technology to make it genuinely functional and reliable did not exist.

Even when carefully fitted selectively by hand, the Hall allowed considerable gas to escape at the barrel and breech block junction, and extensive firing increased this to the point where it not only greatly reduced the power of the gun, but also created hazards to the shooter. For this reason its service life was short.

A fair number of Hall rifles and carbines survive today and they are very desirable collector's items.

Hammer In any gun, a pivoted, spring-driven member which rotates with force to strike and drive forward the firing pin to fire the cartridge. The hammer is normally rotated rearward by the breech bolt, compressing the hammer spring (mainspring), and is caught and held cocked by a sear. Trigger pressure then disengages the sear, allowing the hammer to be driven against the firing pin by its spring. Hammers usually have an extension spur manual cocking.

Hammerless Any gun not fitted with an exposed hammer. Such guns are divided into two classes: those with the hammer enclosed by other parts of the gun; and those in which a reciprocating striker is used in lieu of a hammer. The majority of so-called hammerless guns actually do contain a concealed, pivoted hammer.

Hand Cannon The earliest known form of small firearm, consisting simply of an iron (bronze or copper) tube closed at one end and fitted to a pole similar to a pike pole. Provided with touch-hole or vent at the rear of the tube, it was fired by a slow-match or hot wire pressed manually to powder in the touch-hole. The pole extending rearward was held under the gunner's arm to direct his fire with one hand while the other applied the match. This precluded any precise aiming for the act of ignition required the gunner's full attention. Loading was from the muzzle.

The earliest hand cannon is known as the Tannenberg Buchse, after the Tannenberg castle in whose ruins it was discovered. The castle was destroyed in 1399, so this specimen is known to date from before that time. Some contemporary accounts describe hand cannon in existence prior to 1399, but it is not known precisely when the type came into use. Inaccurate and inefficient, due to its clumsy construction and the poor powder available, it is doubtful that the hand cannon had any significance in battle other than the fear it might have put into ignorant and superstitious troops encountering it for the first time.

Handgun Any firearm designed and intended to be fired with one hand. The definition includes single-shot designs, autoloaders, and revolvers.

Handgun Cleaning With the exception of revolvers, handgun cleaning does not differ from that of any other gun. Because of its construction—its chambers are separated from its barrel which allows gases to escape — the revolver is subject to a buildup of powder fouling, lead deposits, and carbonized lubricants and preservatives at this gap.

The most common problem occurs when these materials become solidly packed into the narrow space between the top of the barrel breech and the underside of the topstrap. If neglected, this mixture becomes quite hard and extremely difficult to remove. Once it reaches that state, small scrapers filed from pieces of brass or aluminum must be used to laboriously dig this residue out, though solvents are of some help. If a stiff bristle brush and a good solvent are used after each shooting session, this area can easily be kept clean.

Revolvers are also subject to more leading than other types of guns, especially in the tapered forcing cone at the barrel breech. Loads that normally would not cause leading in a solid barrel will often do so here because of the expansion/swaging action that takes place as bullets pass from the chamber mouth and into the forcing cone. Lead deposits accumulated in the cone are quite difficult to remove. Often it is necessary to use a wad of steel wool twisted into the bristles of a bore brush or, better yet, a device called the Lewis Lead Remover which uses a piece of copper gauze to abrade away the lead in the tapered area.

Because handguns generally contain smaller working and lighter recoiling parts, they are more susceptible to malfunction caused by accumulated dirt and debris; consequently, meticulous cleaning is vital.

A typical handgun cleaning kit should contain all of the items found in any cleaning kit, including a one-piece rod. In addition, it should contain short lengths of spring wire or brass rod shaped to chisel points and a small stiff-bristle brush that can be used for removing debris from minute recesses.

Probably the most familiar of all handguns in the U.S.A. is this single-action Colt Frontier Model.

Wood hand guard covers upper rear of barrel.

Hand Guard   Generally on a military rifle, a wood, metal, or plastic cover over the barrel to allow it to be grasped without injury when the barrel becomes quite heated from sustained rapid fire.

Handloading (Reloading)   The process of charging fired center-fire cartridge cases with fresh powder, primer, and bullet for further firing. Basically this consists of: (1) resizing the fired case by forcing it into a die which returns it to its original dimensions; (2) forcing out the fired primer; (3) expanding the case neck to a uniform inside diameter; (4) seating a fresh primer; (5) placing a fresh charge of powder in the case; (6) seating a new bullet in the case neck.

This is possible because the cartridge case is not destroyed by firing, as are the other components. The case represents nearly one-half the total cost of any cartridge; by reusing it, handloaded cartridges can be produced for significantly less cost than factory-loaded ammunition.

So long as they are in good condition, cases of brass, plastic, or paper in rifle, handgun, or shotshell types may be hand-loaded.

Basic equipment for handloading consists of: a press or tool which provides the power; dies for resizing, expanding, and bullet seating which are screwed into the press; a depriming punch (normally a component of the resizing or expanding die); a repriming punch (usually a part of the press); a shell holder for gripping the case for the various operations; and/or a powder scale or powder measure.

Handloading serves not only to reduce shooting costs, but

also to obtain special-purpose ammunition and to improve accuracy. Many handbooks and references on the subject are available from producers of tools, components, and equipment, and also from book publishers.

Hangfire The condition whereby the primer does not ignite at the instant of the firing-pin blow but is delayed by several milliseconds. Technically, a hangfire can take place and never be noticed by the shooter. It has been determined that the average individual with normal hearing and perception can usually identify a hangfire if there is more than a 10- or 12-millisecond delay between firing pin impact and primer ignition. Anything less will usually go unnoticed, though experienced ammunition testers have been known to perceive hangfires with as little as 3- to 6-millisecond's delay. A perceptible hangfire occurs when the shooter hears two distinct sounds—"click-bang," the click is the impact of the firing mechanism, and the bang is the report of the gun.

There have been many stories told and published about hangfires in which the cartridge fired as much as 30 to 60 seconds after firing pin impact. Ammunition technicians advise that such a hangfire is technically impossible and that such reports stem from other causes, such as delayed firing pin impact, or "cook-off" in a hot barrel.

Generally, unless the ammunition has been abused, hangfires are a result of a too light firing-pin blow. The major contributor to ammunition-caused hangfires is generally that primers have become wet or have had oil infiltrate and contaminate the compound.

See Cook-Off.

Harpers Ferry A small arms manufacturing facility established in 1796 at Harpers Ferry, Virginia (now West Virginia), at the meeting of the Shenandoah and Potomac rivers. Construction was begun in 1796, the first arms (243 muskets patterned after the French Model 1763) production occurred in 1801. Production rose until at its peak 10,000 rifles and muskets were produced annually, including the Hall breech loader.

Harpers Ferry Armory also served as a storage depot for as many as 75,000 stands of arms.

Threatened with capture by the Confederate Army, the commander fired Harpers Ferry on April 18, 1861, destroying much equipment and 20,000 stands of arms before retreating. Destruction was not complete, though, and some machinery, arms, and parts were salvaged by the Confederates.

Today the site of the old armory is a national park of considerable interest and historical significance.

Headspace In a gun, the distance from the breech face or bolt face to that portion of the chamber or barrel that supports the cartridge.

In a cartridge, that distance between the rear face of the case head and the forward face of the surface which arrests its movement into the chamber.

On rimless cases, headspace is measured from the rear of the head to a datum point (usually standardized upon a specific diameter circle) on the case shoulder or cone. In the gun it is measured from the breech face to a similar datum point on the chamber cone. Two other types of cases share this method of measurement: the rebated-head (rim of less diameter than the case), such as the .284 Winchester, and the semi-rimmed type such as the .225 Winchester—though the latter also shares the headspacing method of the rimmed case.

Rimmed cases were once the most common, and, in fact, are responsible for today's headspacing standards and tolerances. In them, headspace is simply the distance from rear of case

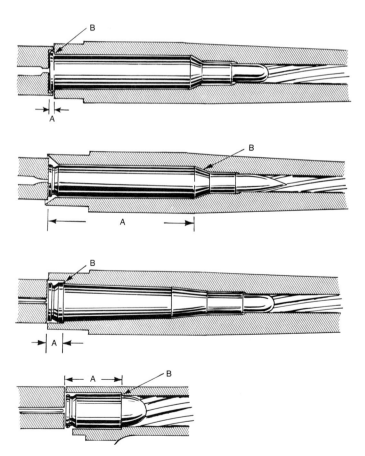

Rimmed Cartridge. Headspace **(A)** is measured from bolt face to front edge of rim. Rim **(B)** holds cartridge in place and stops the travel of the case into the chamber.

Rimless Cartridge. Headspace **(A)**, the distance between the bolt face and case head, is determined by the case shoulder. On rimless cartridges, the shoulder of the case **(B)** stops travel of the cartridge into the chamber.

Belted Cartridge. Headspace **(A)** is measured from bolt face to front edge of belt. The belt on the case **(B)** seats against a shoulder in the chamber and stops travel of the cartridge into the chamber.

Rimless Pistol. Headspace **(A)** for rimless pistol cartridges is measured from bolt face to edge of case mouth **(B)**, which seats against shoulder in the chamber and stops travel of the cartridge into the chamber.

head to front face of rim. In the gun it is measured from the breech face to the rear face of the barrel against which the rim seats. Surprisingly, the most modern belted case uses the same method, with only the exception that a shallow counterbore or recess is cut in the barrel breech to accommodate the belt. Measurement is from the head to front edge of belt in the case, and from breech face to the bottom of the counterbore in the gun.

The third method of measurement is used only on straight rimless cases and is the distance from the rear of the case head to the front surface of the mouth. In the gun it is the distance from the breech face to the shoulder at the front of the chamber. The .30 carbine and .45 ACP cartridges are typical examples.

Generally speaking, a tolerance of .006 inch is allowed in gun headspace, and cartridge cases are compatible within the varying production policies of the individual manufacturers.

Excess headspace is generally considered dangerous—though in a gun in good mechanical condition this is not necessarily so unless there is an inordinate amount of headspace. If the headspace is excessive, the cartridge case will rupture or separate upon firing; however, danger to the shooter is minimal because the separated head portion of the cartridge case usually expands to fill the chamber and prevent hot gases from escaping rearward.

Correction of excess headspace in the gun generally requires removing the barrel, shortening it at the breech, and rechambering to the correct depth. Minor degrees may be corrected by building up the locking surfaces on the breech or bolt.

Correction of excess headspace in rimless cases generally consists of fire-forming to move the shoulder forward so that it contacts the chamber shoulder properly. Correction in rimmed or belted cases requires peening or otherwise moving the front surface of the belt or rim forward.

Hearing, Shooting Damage In years gone by it was considered effeminate to protect one's ears while shooting. Artillery men were well aware that the tremendous blast of big guns could produce loss of hearing, but small-arms shooters chose to ignore the possibility.

It is known now that even only a moderate amount of shooting with virtually any rifle, handgun, or shotgun will produce some hearing loss.

Shooting noises are described as "explosive sounds" and create abnormally high pressures transmitted to the inner ear. These high pressures generate excessive movement of the inner ear fluid, causing damage to the delicate microscopic hair cells, and thus deterioration of one's hearing.

In their extreme, shooting noises can produce physical pain

in the ears, as well as a ringing after-effect, and headaches. Even when no pain is produced, a ringing or buzzing sensation known as tinnitis may follow noise exposure, and this is a sure sign that excessive pressures have effected the inner ear. Any such sensation should be regarded as an urgent warning that the ears are being abused—and steps should be taken to reduce or eliminate the exposure before further damage occurs. Even though the ringing and buzzing disappears in a few hours or days, the damage to the inner ear remains. It is not a temporary condition that will cure itself.

Loss of hearing due to shooting noise may not be apparent at first since it is most likely to occur in the frequency range above that of normal speech. If deterioration continues, it will encroach upon the upper limits of speech range (500–3000 cycles per second)—and will become noticeable. First indications are difficulty in hearing telephone conversations and in picking up normal speech against high background noise.

It will sometimes be noted that a slight loss in hearing occurs after shooting, but that recovery *appears* to take place in three or four days. This is only partial recovery, and a portion of the damage is irreparable. Continued exposure to shooting noises will increase damage, bringing serious hearing impairment.

Ear muffs (left), covering entire ear, provide maximum protection to preserve normal hearing.

A refinement of the ear plug is the noise filter (right), which protects ears against harmful noises, yet has a canal that allows normal conversation and air circulation.

Ear protectors of one sort or another are the only defense against shooting-induced hearing loss. Most of the commercial types available provide 20 to 40 decibels of noise reduction as perceived by the ear, and this is sufficient to preserve normal hearing under extensive exposure to the noisiest small arms.

Generally speaking, ear muffs provide more protection than simple ear plugs, though some of the more recent individually fitted, ear-canal plugs approach the efficiency of muffs. The latter are usually more costly than muffs and must be professionally fitted to individual ears, the right and left not normally being identical. Such plugs are also the most difficult to insert and remove, which means that they may not always be used. In the end, muffs are the most practical, providing maximum protection with acceptable cost and convenience.

Shooting noises become most damaging when firing is indoors or in a range enclosure or near walls which tend to amplify and reflect pressure waves. Firing outdoors under a roof and over a paved firing point also intensifies the effect in one's ears. Protection should especially be worn under those conditions.

High-intensity magnum cartridges and short barrels produce the most severe effects because they generate greater pressures. The effect of a .300 Magnum is greater than that of a .30/30. The use of muzzle brakes and compensators also increases noise damage.

Ear protection should be worn by observers as well as shooters. In fact, in some instances the observer is subject to more damage than the shooter. The shooter is directly behind the gun muzzle, while the greatest sound pressure is directed generally forward and outward in a wide cone. Thus an observer standing alongside the gun will be subjected to greater sound pressure than the shooter.

In an emergency, any form of ear plug that can be removed can be used. Common are rolled-up cleaning patches, cotton, and even cartridges. There is hazard in stuffing *anything* into the ear, though, so great care should be exercised. *None* of these methods is nearly as effective as properly designed ear plugs or muffs.

If you are especially sensitive to noises, a combination of fitted plugs *and* a set of good, close-fitting muffs will provide maximum protection.

Should any ringing or buzzing or temporary hearing loss be noted after shooting or observing shooting, visit your otologist immediately and request an audiogram to determine how much damage has occured.

Henry, Tyler The inventor of the Henry rifle and its .44 rimfire cartridge—the rifle being later improved into the Winchester M1866, and then further improved into the M1873, and the cartridge developed into the .44/40 Winchester centerfire.

Though other designers had used the toggle-link breech system without success, it was Henry who devised a practical system and a practical cartridge without which the earlier efforts would not have succeeded. For many years Winchester rimfire cartridges carried the initial "H" imprinted on their heads in honor of Tyler Henry.

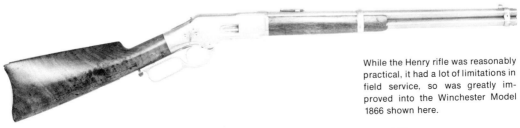

While the Henry rifle was reasonably practical, it had a lot of limitations in field service, so was greatly improved into the Winchester Model 1866 shown here.

133

High Base A shotshell with a thick head or base wad, limiting capacity to relatively small amounts of shot, wads, and powder. Generally used for light target loads and combined with a "low brass" head overlay.

High Brass The name applied to a shotshell whose metal head, which may be brass or plated steel, extends roughly one-fourth to one-third of the unfired shell length forward from the brass. High brass cases are used for higher powered field and magnum loads and are of *low base* construction. The long metal head thus fully encloses the relatively weak area where the walls meet the base wad.
See also HIGH BASE, LOW BASE and LOW BRASS.

Hip Shooting A form of shooting where the gun is held generally at waist level and pointed instinctively without reference to the sights. Most commonly used with handguns, but equally applicable to shoulder arms.

The cavity in this minie bullet base is easily seen and is typical of that in all hollow-base bullets.

Hollow Base A bullet design containing a cavity in the base. Most commonly encountered in swaged lead wadcutter bullets in .38/357 caliber in which it shifts the bullet's center of gravity forward to increase stability. It is occasionally found in jacketed handgun bullets of relatively light weight, where the cavity serves primarily to lengthen the bullet's bearing surface and overall length to provide sufficient loaded-cartridge length for reliable functioning.

Hollow Point A bullet design that expands dramatically on impact due to a cavity in its point. Found in both lead and jacketed bullets, probably the most common being the high-velocity, .22 Long Rifle rimfire cartridges used primarily for small game hunting. In jacketed bullets, generally used in

Large cavity in nose of this handgun bullet is easily seen left and center. In rifle bullets intended for higher velocities, cavity is smaller and jacket is carried more toward nose. At right is another form of hollow base, quite shallow, in a jacketed bullet.

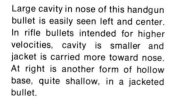

closed-base designs, with the cavity formed by not quite closing the mouth of the jacket in forming the bullet ogive.

The cavity may vary from a needlelike hole in small-caliber, high-velocity bullets, to massive deep holes one-half to three-fourths of the bullet's diameter in low-velocity lead bullets.

Typical hooded sight with tubular hood and replaceable inserts.

Hooded Sight A front sight with any conventional aiming element that is covered by a hood or tube which serves to protect it from damage and from being worn bright, and which also eliminates glare and insures more uniform illumination by excluding direct light. Sometimes fitted with adjustable or interchangeable aiming points.

Hook Buttplate A butt attachment that provides a long extension at the toe of the stock to fit under the shooter's arm preventing the butt of the rifle from rising out of position. Often a shorter spur extends from the heel of the butt over the shooter's shoulder to further immobilize the butt.

A hook buttplate is generally adjustable, at least vertically, and often in all directions. It is generally used only in international-type offhand rifle shooting.

Hunting Bag A carry-over from the earliest days of firearms when a great many implements and supplies were required to reload and service a muzzle-loading gun. Essentially it was a simple flap-top leather bag carried on a shoulder strap and containing grease, caps, balls, patches, nipple prick, nipple wrench, spare flints, patch knife, worm, and any other item that the hunter or traveler might require over many months on the frontier to keep his arms in operation.

Modern guns require no such extensive logistical support; however, some hunters use modern variations of the old hunting bag in which to carry a knife, compass, ammunition, matches, lunch, and other items for their comfort and convenience, along with a few critical spare parts or tools for their guns.

The modern day target shooter's version of the hunting bag is a sophisticated wood or metal case, usually called a "shooting box," which contains all the paraphernalia and ammunition likely to be needed on the range.

Hypervelocity A military term generally applied to all firearms ammunition producing a muzzle velocity in excess of 5,000 feet per second. Some hypervelocity ammunition has achieved velocities in excess of 9,000 feet per second.

Ignition   That part of the functioning cycle where the priming compound is detonated by firing-pin impact, and the resulting flame and incandescent particles pass through the flash hole to ignite the propellant powder.

Incendiary Bullet   A type of military small-arms bullet that contains a small amount of incendiary material that ignites upon impact. They are normally color-coded for identification, the U.S. marking being blue-painted bullet tip. Such rounds are definitely *not* to be used for hunting or other sport shooting because of the fire hazard.

Inertia Bullet Puller   See BULLET PULLER.

Inertia Firing Pin   A form of firing pin most commonly found in the Colt-Browning Government Model pistol in which the pin is slightly shorter than the recess in which it moves. When the hammer is at rest against the pin, the latter's nose does not protrude from the breech face to contact the primer of a chambered round. In this respect it serves as a valuable safety device when a firearm is carried with a round chambered and the hammer in the fully down position.

Inletting That portion of a stock which is cut away to accept the metal parts of a gun; in effect, a negative impression of the metal parts carved into the wood to permit a close, tight assembly. Inletting should conform as closely as possible to the contour of metal parts, particularly in load-bearing areas. Generally, inletting has a significant effect on rifle accuracy.

Instrumental Velocity The velocity of a bullet as it is computed with a chronograph. The chronograph screens are set up at a distance from the muzzle, and computed velocity of the bullet passing between those screens is actually the *instrumental* velocity at a point exactly midway between them.

If velocity of a given load is determined to be 2,850 feet per second with the first chronograph screen 10 feet from the muzzle and the second 20 feet from the muzzle, then the velocity is 2,850 feet per second "instrumental at 15 feet."

Velocities quoted at the muzzle are actually corrected from instrumental values.

See also CHRONOGRAPH.

Center is the full-power 7.62mm NATO rifle and machine gun cartridge, flanked left by the Soviet 7.62x39mm M43 and right by 5.56mm U.S. cartridge.

Intermediate Cartridge A military cartridge generally used in selective-fire assault rifles and light machine guns whose velocity and power falls roughly midway between submachine gun and pistol cartridge of the 9mm Parabellum class and the World War II type of rifle and machine gun cartridges of the 7.92 mm German and .30 U.S. class. Only three intermediate cartridges are currently in wide use, the World War II vintage .30 U.S. carbine, 5.56mm (.223) U.S., and the Soviet 7.62x39mm M43. One other saw substantial use during World War II, the German 7.92x33mm Kurz.

International Shooting Union (ISU) An organization founded in 1921 to promote and develop international shooting sports, organize world championships, supervise Olympic shooting competition, and develop rules governing all such activities.

The ISU succeeded the original *l'Union Internationale des Federation et Association Nationales de Tir*, which was established in 1907 and disbanded in 1915.

ISU headquarters has no single fixed location, generally being moved after each election of officers to the city and country of the new president. In the United States. the ISU is represented by the National Rifle Association.

See also NATIONAL RIFLE ASSOCIATION.

Investment Casting A method of casting relatively small and intricate parts that may be made satisfactorily from sophisticated alloy steels of great strength. Further, the investment process permits casting in many instances to exact final finish and dimensions which eliminates the need for much expensive machining.

Investment casting was at one time often referred to as the "lost wax" process and is reported to have been used extensively in ancient Egypt.

Today, investment castings may be found in all kinds of guns, including those of high quality, and used for bolts, receivers, sears, hammers, triggers, and many other parts subject to high stresses.

Following the first sizable use of investment-cast parts in guns, there was substantial sales resistance to them for quite a few years because of a lack of understanding of the differences in quality between them and the traditional sand-cast or permanent-mold cast parts associated with cheap, flimsy goods. Now there is no longer any stigma attached to investment-cast gun parts and they are used by all of the major manufacturers in varying degrees.

A modern investment casting is produced by first forming a precise wax or plastic pattern of the part desired. This pattern is then successively coated with a ceramic slurry which builds up into a relatively thick shell, reproducing it to the finest details and dimensions. The coated pattern is first dried and then fired at a high temperature, fusing the ceramic coating into a one-piece shell mold, and at the same time melting and entirely vaporizing the wax pattern.

Later, molten metal is poured into the mold. Once the metal has hardened, the ceramic shell mold is removed by cracking, chipping, or sand-blasting and a precise metal duplicate of the wax pattern emerges, which often requires only cleaning and removal of the sprue. Some parts are ready for use as they come from the mold. while others are designed specifically for some finish machining operation before use.

Again, shooters who have an aversion to cheap castings should not transfer that feeling to modern investment-cast parts. They are, in fact, frequently superior to identical machined parts.

Iron Sights   See SIGHTS, IRON

Jacketed Bullet One in which the soft lead core is surrounded by a jacket or envelope of thin gilding metal, or other suitable material. Aside from the variations mentioned under "expanding bullet," there are two basic jacket forms: the closed base in which the jacket is drawn from the point and is closed over the base, leaving the point exposed for forming into a soft point or hollow point, and the closed-point design in which the jacket is drawn from the base and is closed over the point, leaving the base exposed.

Three jacketed bullets of Winchester design (from left), 175 Power Point (soft point) for 7MM Magnum, 150 Silver Tip (high velocity) and 150 Spitzer soft point.

Assuming good design and manufacture, each type is accurate, and choice depends upon the performance required. Generally speaking, closed-base jackets are used on sporting bullets, and open-base types on military projectiles.

See also EXPANDING BULLET and GILDING METAL.

Jag A cleaning-rod tip that contains ridges or grooves which grip a cleaning patch or other swabbing material wrapped around it.

Jorgensen, Erik   Chief armorer at Norway's Konsberg Armory in the 1880s, and co-designer with Ole Krag of the Krag-Jorgensen rifle.

See KRAG, OLE; KRAG RIFLE.

Keeper A metal, plastic, or leather ring, loop or clamp used on a shooting sling to retain adjustments and prevent slipping.

    See also SLING.

Kentucky Pistol A muzzle-loading, single-shot pistol contemporary with the Kentucky rifle and sharing its style and characteristics. Generally fitted with a full-length stock, and a steeply curved, rounded butt, the former with a brass or cast-metal tip and the latter without any protective metal. They were usually rifled, but not always.

    Kentucky pistols were evidently produced in far smaller quantity than the rifles. Few survive today and they are much sought after by collectors.

    See also KENTUCKY RIFLE.

Kentucky pistol.

Kentucky Rifle Strictly an American development of the flint-lock period, generally conceded to have evolved from the short, heavy Jaeger rifles brought to North America first by German colonists and, later, by German mercenary troops employed by the British during the American Revolutionary War. The term "Kentucky" developed because of the area in which the rifle was widely used, not because it was manufactured there. Development was seated principally in Pennsylvania.

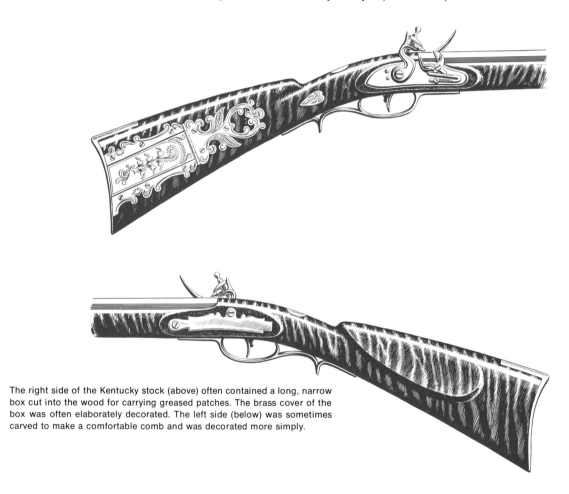

The right side of the Kentucky stock (above) often contained a long, narrow box cut into the wood for carrying greased patches. The brass cover of the box was often elaborately decorated. The left side (below) was sometimes carved to make a comfortable comb and was decorated more simply.

As finally developed, the typical Kentucky rifle used a quite long but light barrel of medium caliber and was generally stocked to the muzzle (though half-stock versions were not uncommon). Stocks were usually very slender and appeared to be delicate in construction. They had a great deal of drop, a deep crescent buttplate, and usually contained brass patch-boxes on the right side.

Kentucky rifles were never mass produced, invariably being the individual creations of small shops or individual gunsmiths, and they naturally appear in countless variations. Strangely, many Kentucky "rifles" are now believed to have been originally made with smoothbore, rather than rifled barrels.

Kentucky rifles are one of the purest forms of 18th Century Americana and are much sought after by collectors.

See also KENTUCKY PISTOL.

Keyhole The elongated hole in a target caused by a bullet which strikes more or less sideways, rather than point on. It results from either a serious imbalance in the bullet, insufficient rotational velocity to stabilize it, or deflection by some object.

Killing Power A very imprecise term applying to the ability of a particular bullet or load to produce a quick, one-shot kill on game, providing there is reasonably accurate bullet placement. Killing power cannot be measured in precise terms. While a certain degree of energy is required, killing power cannot be directly equated with energy. It is more dependent upon the bullet's ability to penetrate deeply, destroy bone and muscle, create massive hemorrhage, and produce heavy shock to an animal's nervous system.

The killing power of any caliber is increased by using a bullet which expands as it penetrates tissue. Killing power may also be increased by increasing velocity, which produces more severe wounds by transferring greater energy to the target and by creating secondary missiles of flesh, muscle, and bone fragments within the target. This type of performance causes more of a bullet's energy to be transferred to the target, rather than be expended in further travel after complete target penetration.

Kleanbore A trademark applied to Remington's first non-corrosively primed .22 rimfire ammunition. Ammunition so labeled was first sold in late 1926.

Knockout Rod A close-fitting rod used with a mallet to drive cases or bullets through or out of sizing dies or swages.

Krag, Ole H., 1837–1912 Best known for the Krag-Jorgensen rifle, developed with Konsberg chief armorer Erik Jorgensen. It was adopted by Denmark in 1889, by the U.S.A. in 1892, and by Norway in 1895.

Commissioned at twenty in the Norwegian Army, he progressed from artillery to small-arms work, and by 1870 was assigned as a captain to the Konsberg Arms Factory. His first rifle was developed there with Swedish engineer Axel Peterson. It was adopted by the Swedish Navy in 1877.

Retired in 1902, Krag remained active, producing a self-loading pistol in 1912. He designed a number of other arms, but only the Krag-Jorgensen saw wide acceptance.

Krag Rifle   The Krag-Jorgensen rifle design originating in Norway and covered by the patents of Ole H. Krag and Eric Jorgensen in the 1880s.

The basic Krag rifle was adopted by the U.S. military in 1892 and by Denmark in 1889 in slightly different forms. In 1894, the same basic design, with variations, was adopted by Norway.

U.S. Krags were manufactured at the National Armory at Springfield, Massachusetts until their replacement by the M1903 Springfield rifle.

The Krag in all its forms has a particular reputation for smooth and easy bolt manipulation. This is partly because of its design, and partly because of the hard, smooth, case-hardened skin on the bolt and receiver, as well as the excellent quality of workmanship.

U.S. Krag rifle, M1892.

The Krag action is characterized by a single locking lug on the right side of the bolt head, a long extractor on top of the bolt that also serves as a bolt guide and a bolt retainer, and a deep cut in the receiver wall where the root of the bolt handle seats to function as a safety locking lug.

The most obvious characteristic, though, is the exposed box magazine formed integrally on the right side of the receiver and refilled with loose cartridges through a hinged cover which opens forward in the foreign version, and downward in the domestic.

The majority of the U.S. Krag rifles which survived military service were sold at low cost to NRA members or issued to American Legion posts in this country, and the type remains quite common today. It is still popular as a hunting rifle, and many fine custom-built rifles have been based on the Krag.

Cartridges for the Krag are still manufactured today as .30/40, and in bullet weights of 150, 180, and 220 grains.

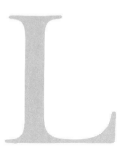

Laminated Stock Any gunstock that has been made up of many layers of similar or dissimilar wood, glued or boned together under great pressure, normally with a weatherproof or water-resistant adhesive.

While laminated stocks use less costly and attractive wood, they involve greater fabrication costs—these disadvantages are offset by their almost complete resistance to warping or moisture absorption, both of which cause shifts in center of impact and the degree of accuracy. Laminated stocks are also generally heavier than one-piece types, and the hard glue lines dull cutting tools more quickly.

Land In a rifled barrel the raised spiral rib left standing between the grooves.

See Rifling.

Lapping A method of polishing the interior of a gun barrel (or other metal surface), by passing a tight-fitting, soft-metal plug coated with very fine abrasive powder and oil through it.

Leade (Lede) Also known as the "throat," the origin of the rifling in a rifled barrel. It is that portion of the bore immediately ahead of the case mouth in which the rifling lands have been cut away to allow entry of the bullet. Lands are normally cut away completely for a short distance, and then rise at a very shallow angle which permits the bullet to be more easily engaged by the rifling as it progresses from the case.

Generally, the leade begins slightly beyond the bullet ogive, and its function is twofold: to permit the bullet to move freely during the early stages of ignition and propellant combustion, and to aid in centering the bullet in the rifling.

Leading An accumulation of lead in a bore caused by lead bullets being abraded by, and the lead adhering to, the barrel's lands and grooves. A leaded barrel has a significant and visible amount of lead deposited in the lands and grooves at some point. This condition is generally brought about by inadequate bullet lubrication, or by driving such bullets too rapidly for their soft, weak construction.

Leading is further brought about or accelerated by a rough bore finish, which is why the annular reamer marks frequently left in the leade of a rifle barrel, or the throat of a revolver barrel, often stimulate leading. Once it has begun at those points, it will continue forward and thicken as firing progresses. Rusted, pitted, or eroded barrels are also more susceptible to leading. Generally, the softer the lead-bullet alloy, the more likely leading is to develop.

Once lead has accumulated in the bore, it can usually be removed by vigorous application of a tight-fitting bronze or brass (not iron or steel) bore brush. Failing this, there are mild abrasive compounds which may be applied with a tight-fitting patch to scour away the lead, or mercury may be poured into the plugged bore where it will amalgamate with and soften the lead so that it may be wiped out freely.

See also LEADE.

Lee, James P., 1831–1904 Best known for development of the straight-pull Winchester-Lee 6mm military rifle, adopted by the U.S. Navy in 1895. Born in Scotland, Lee emigrated to Canada and then to Wisconsin where he formed the Lee Firearms Co. in Milwaukee in the early 1860s. There he produced a side-opening, single-shot, rimfire carbine which was rejected to Union Ordnance. In 1874 Springfield Armory produced a few (145) of Lee's falling-block, single-shot rifle but it was not adopted. His invention of the detachable box magazine under the receiver was used on his M1879 rifle and shortly copied throughout the world. The M1879 rifle was developed into the Remington-Lee, which was sold both commercially and in the military market. He was also prominent in development of the British Lee-Enfield service rifle, which contained features of the M1879 and others.

Lee Straight-Pull Rifle A unique rifle designed by James P. Lee and manufactured by Winchester for both commercial and military sales. It was a bolt action in which the bolt handle was merely pulled back and thrust forward to unlock and lock. This was accomplished by a cam on the bolt handle operating against a surface in the receiver to raise and lower the rear end of the bolt where it engaged a locking abutment in the receiver.

The Lee Straight-Pull rifle was adopted in 6mm caliber by the U.S. Navy as the M1895, and 10,000 were purchased. This constituted the bulk of production, only about 1,700 being made as sporters by Winchester.

Lever Action An American arms development stemming from pre-Civil War days. Typically these lever-action rifles consist of a massive receiver containing a reciprocating bolt which is actuated by a large lever forming the trigger guard. The breech is opened and closed by pulling the lever down and forward to the limit of its travel, then swinging it back to the stowed position. Most older lever-action guns use tubular magazines forward under the barrel, and have separate buttstock and forend.

Traditional-form lever-action rifle with tubular magazine and side receiver. Marlin M1895.

The first genuinely practical lever-action rifle was the Henry, patented by D. Tyler Henry in 1860. Other designs existed shortly before it, but did not combine all functions of the action so that they could be performed by a single manipulation of the lever. Others of the period required additional operations, at least that of cocking the hammer.

Probably the most important lever-action rifle was the Winchester M1866, a derivation and improvement upon the Henry, followed by the Model 1873, again a much improved development of the Henry patent.

The most popular and successful lever-action rifle is the Winchester Model 1894, designed by John M. Browning, and manufactured continuously since 1894, with production today exceeding three million pieces.

Though the lever-action has today been somewhat superseded by more modern systems, it is still immensely popular, And while many other firms produced lever-action rifles ex-

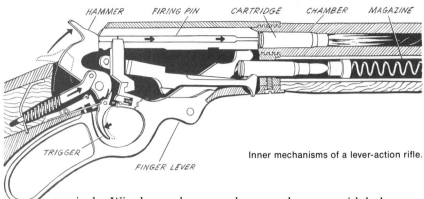

HAMMER   FIRING PIN   CARTRIDGE   CHAMBER   MAGAZINE

TRIGGER

FINGER LEVER

Inner mechanisms of a lever-action rifle.

tensively, Winchester long ago became the most widely known, and today Winchester is synonymous with lever-action rifles in many parts of the world.

Winchester, Savage, Marlin, and Sako produce modern lever-action rifles, and several foreign companies make copies of obsolete models.

Loading Density   The relationship of the volume of a propellant charge to the volume of the chamber in which it is fired. In this respect, chamber volume is actually the volume of the case, to the base of the bullet, when the case is fire-formed.

If the powder charge fills 75 per cent of the available space, then the loading density may be said to be 75 per cent—while if the space is completely filled (without compressing the charge), loading density is 100 per cent.

In other words, the more the propellant charge is confined, the greater the loading density, and the greater the loading density, generally the greater the pressure that will be generated.

With a given case and powder charge, loading density is affected directly by the depth to which the bullet is seated—so when working with high-density loads, it is important that seating depth not be appreciably changed.

Further, any increases in loading density—other factors remaining equal—produces some increase in burning rate, and this rate increases as density approaches 100 per cent.

Loading density, as it applies here, is not a precise value, for it does not take into consideration the additional unoccupied space between individual powder granules. Instead, it is an approximation based upon the power charges being well settled in the case to reduce that space to a minimum.

Loading Gate   In a revolver, a hinged portion of the recoil shield that may be swung out to provide access to the cylinder for loading fresh rounds and extracting fired cases. In some rifles, a spring-loaded door or panel in the receiver or magazine tube through which cartridges are pressed into the magazine.

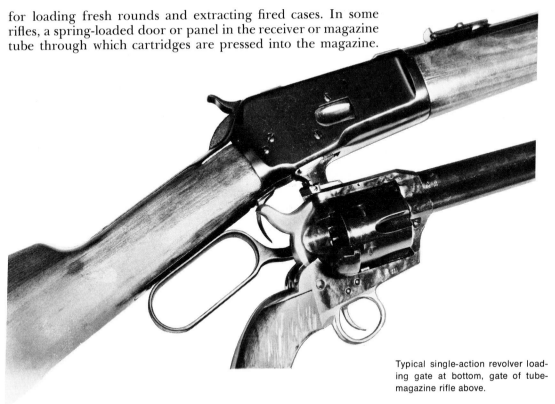

Typical single-action revolver loading gate at bottom, gate of tube-magazine rifle above.

Loading Press   Any tool which provides a seat for a die, a movable ram or shell holder, and a means for forcing cases into and out of dies.

Lock   Originally the complete firing mechanism of a muzzle-loader consisting of the hammer and the complete mechanism necessary for cocking it and driving it forward to fire the gun. Today, a more general term referring to virtually any type of firing mechanism.

A typical percussion lock in the style of the 1840s.

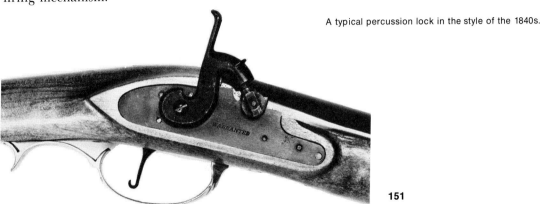

151

Lock Time The period of time between sear release and firing-pin impact upon the primer. Though this period is exceedingly short and can be measured only with sophisticated timing equipment, serious competitive shooters consider it to be of vital importance. They feel rightly that the longer the time between sear release and firing-pin impact, the greater will be the possibility of their aim being disturbed by outside influences or from trigger pressure.

As an example of typical lock time, the unaltered U.S. M1903 rifle consumes .0057 second from sear release to firing-pin impact. The same gun modified to "speed lock" form for international match shooting reduces this period of time to .0022 second.

While the above may make lock time appear to be quite important, only the very finest marksman with the most accurate guns will be able to actually see any difference on target.

Lockwork A term loosely applied to all of the moving parts of any enclosed firing mechanism, and used primarily to differentiate from the basic lock as found on breakopen shotguns and muzzle-loading arms.

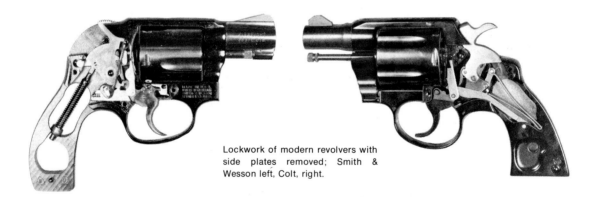

Lockwork of modern revolvers with side plates removed; Smith & Wesson left, Colt, right.

Lot (Lot number) In ammunition, a numerical or alphabetical identification code applied to individual production lots for control purposes. Applied to all packaging, it allows tracing of any particular lot or purchase back to time and place of manufacture, even to specific machines and operators, raw materials, etc. Essential in investigating defective ammunition.

Low Base In a shotshell, a case that has a relatively low or thin base wad. Low base cases are generally used for heavy and magnum loads where maximum space is needed for large charges of both shot and powder—as opposed to target loads requiring space for both, and therefore much thicker base wads.

See also HIGH BASE.

Low Brass A shotshell with a very short metal head which does not extend past the base wad. Generally used on "high base" cases.

Lubricator-Sizer A tool for bringing cast lead bullets to proper roundness and diameter while simultaneously forcing lubricant into the lubricating grooves. A bullet is pressed into a sizing die by a lever-operated ram, and while it remains stationary in the die, lubricant is forced through passages in the die and into the lubricating grooves by either a cam-operated pump or spring pressure.

Most hand-operated lubricator-sizers first press the bullet full depth into the die, inject the lubricant, then lift the bullet back out of the top of the die—though the Star and Phelps tool ejects bullets downward, on through the die, each being pushed out by the next.

Luger, George, 1848–1922 Designer of the Luger pistol, he was born in Steinach, Austria, and served in the Austrian Army. After leaving the army, he worked with Von Mannlicher in converting the Werndl rifle to magazine feed, and on an experimental self-loading rifle. In 1891 he became associated with Ludwig Loewe (which became DWM) in Berlin. When Borchardt brought his self-loading pistol to Loewe for production, Luger redesigned the gun extensively. The first redesigned guns were tested in 1898, and in 1900 it was adopted by Switzerland. Further development by Luger and the DWM firm resulted in finalization of the design in 1908. Luger apparently did nothing noteworthy after that, but the Luger pistol placed his name high in the annals of gun making.

See LUGER PISTOL.

Lyman #450 Lubricator-sizer, the oldest and simplest type still made.

Luger (Parabellum) Pistol A unique self-loading, recoil-operated pistol devised by George Luger from the clumsy Borchardt of 1893. It utilizes a toggle-joint breech which breaks vertically as barrel and barrel extension move rearward in recoil upon the frame. Cartridges were fed from an 8-round, single-column magazine housed in the grip. It was adopted in 1900 in 7.65mm caliber by Switzerland, and in 1904 in 9mm caliber by the German Navy, and in 1908 by the German Army.

It was manufactured for commercial sale from 1902 on. Many nations adopted the design, but it was tested and rejected by the United States.

Many variations of the basic Luger exist, with the 4-inch barrel, M1908, 9mm the most common. Barrel lenghts range from 3⅝ inches to rifle lengths fitted to the carbine version. Not made after 1937, the Luger, under the name Parabellum, was again placed in production by Mauserwerke in 1971. See LUGER, GEORGE.

M

Machine Gun A relatively heavy, full-automatic weapon chambered for cartridges ranging from standard military rifle sizes up to .55 or .60 caliber. Generally, the term "cannon" is applied to guns and ammunition with projectile larger than 20mm, so anything under that is generally classified as a machine gun. It usually requires a crew of two or more for sustained operation, as opposed to assault rifles and automatic or machine rifles which are generally handled by one man.

See also Assault Rifle and Submachine Gun.

Typical machine gun design of pre-1960 is this Browning .30-caliber flexible aircraft design used by many nations during World War II. Ground guns are virtually identical but heavier.

Machine Rest A mechanical rest and clamping system, usually of the return-to-battery type, in which a rifle or pistol is secured solidly and fired to test its accuracy by isolating the gun from human influences.

Machine rests are generally quite heavy, not only to aid in absorbing recoil, but to insure rigidity and smooth travel of all working parts. They must be very solidly installed on massive, reinforced concrete bases extending into the earth below the frost line, or be equally well supported by some structure. The purpose of any machine rest is to reduce to zero the possibility of any human or mechanical error or influence except those produced by the barrel/ammunition combination.

While a machine rest is generally used to test guns, a special type is used solely to test ammunition. In its most typical form, it is known as a Mann rest, and uses a special heavy barrel with a special modified action. The barrel is supported upon two accurately ground ways or in a V-block by concentric rings clamped around it, and this ringed barrel and action recoils freely with each shot (fired by remote control to avoid disturbance), and must then be pushed forward into the firing position.

See also BENCH REST.

Magazine   In whatever form, the container carrying cartridges that are forced under spring pressure into position to be fed into a gun's chamber.

The most typical form for centerfire rifles is a simple sheet metal box containing two staggered rows of cartridges in a vertical stack. The cartridges are forced upward against shaped feed lips by a heavy spring acting beneath a follower shaped to fit the bottom most cartridges and to position them properly against the lips for feeding.

Typical modern magazines—top is traditional tubular form normally housed under the barrel; left is staggered double-column detachable type; right is single-column removable autoloading pistol type.

This type of magazine may be detachable and therefore intended for recharging when removed from the gun, or it may be an integral part of the gun charged through the open action by either inserting individual cartridges or by using chargers or clips. In the latter form it is generally considered to be of the Mauser-type, and in the former, of the Lee-type.

Similar magazines that contain a single, vertical row of cartridges are common to some rifles and to most autoloading pistols. So-called box magazines of this type are generally positioned vertically under the action, but may also be found positioned horizontally to either side, angularly to either side, or vertically above, particularly in military automatic weapons.

The second most common type of magazine is the tubular form originated on American lever-action rifles. It generally consists of a tube beneath and parallel to the barrel, into which are placed a number of cartridges in line, bullet-to-primer, and which are then forced rearward for feeding by a heavy spring and follower.

A rotary form of magazine is also used but is less common. Originated by Mannlicher, it consists of a spool-like spindle carrying individual cartridges in lengthwise grooves in its outer surface. The spindle is spring-loaded and rotates to bring cartridges successively against the feed lips for subsequent chambering.

See also CHARGER and CLIP.

Magnum A gun chambered for a magnum cartridge, generally heavier and more robust than a "standard" model. Also, an action specifically designed to handle larger-than-ordinary cartridges. Applicable to handguns, rifles, and shotguns alike.

Magnum Cartridge In rifle calibers, a designation generally referring to a belted case loaded to higher-than-normal pressure, velocity and energy levels for the particular bullet diameter. At present, there is but one domestic exception: the .222 Remington Magnum, which is based on the *rimless* .222 Remington case somewhat lengthened and thus really only a "magnum" in relation to its predecessor.

In a handgun cartridge, simply one loaded to unusually high levels of power and velocity compared to others quite similar— for example, the .44 Special with its relatively modest performance, and the .44 Magnum based on the same case, slightly lengthened, but loaded to triple the pressure and energy. While magnum cartridges are legion in the rifle field, there are currently only three used in handguns: the .357, the .41, and the .44 Magnums, all originally developed for Smith & Wesson revolvers.

Left is .30/06 "standard" compared with belted .300 Weatherby Magnum (second from left) both much longer than the less powerful .44 Special.

Mannlicher, Ferdinand Ritter Von Austrian small arms designer of principally military rifles and light automatic weapons, most of which were manufactured by the massive Steyr plant.

Though Mannlicher died in 1903, he left behind a legacy of over 150 different repeating, automatic, and semiautomatic firearms designs, of which nearly one-third saw serious production, and of those, several models became arms of over a score of nations.

The rifle most often associated by sportsmen with Mannlicher is this short M1903 military carbine in 6.5mm caliber, and the sleek sporting rifles based upon it.

Among his other accomplishments, Mannlicher pioneered the en bloc-type cartridge clip later used to great success in the U.S. M1 Garand rifle; rotary magazine; short-recoil automatic operation; straight-pull locking systems such as later used by Ross; short-stroke gas piston; and many other principles of modern firearms design, which were not necessarily practical at the time of their invention because of technological and metallurgical shortcomings. He is probably best known to sportsmen because of the fine, light, full-stock hunting rifle exported in quantity to this country under his name—and also for the term "Mannlicher stock" which refers to a slender and graceful sporting rifle stock whose forend extends to the muzzle of a short barrel.

Mannlicher Rifle In this country, the light, slender sporting carbine based on the M1903 Greek service rifle designed by Mannlicher. Fitted with spool magazine and stocked to the muzzle, it was considered for nearly half a century to be the epitome of light, fast-handling, bolt-action hunting rifles. Generally chambered for the rimless 6.5x54mm cartridge, it could also be had in 7mm, 8mm, 9mm, and 9.5mm calibers. After World War II, it was also offered in the more popular American cartridges. Manufacture was discontinued about 1970.

Mannlicher stock with typical foreend extending to the muzzle.

Mannlicher Stock On a breech-loading rifle, a stock with a slender forend extending fully to the muzzle. It was so named because it was popularized on the M1903/05 Mannlicher-Schoenauer short sporting carbine, even though it was common before that on military rifles and muzzle-loading guns.

Martini-Henry Rifle The Peabody action as modified by Martini to contain an internal, self-cocking striker firing mechanism combined with a barrel of Alexander Henry's design. The action was patented in 1868 by Friedrich Von Martini and adopted by the British government in 1871, fitted with Henry's barrel in caliber .577/.450. It was displaced in 1891 by the Lee-Metford rifle, but continued in limited service through World War I.

See PEABODY RIFLE.

Matchlock The first mechanical system for firing a gun—all previous methods required that the shooter manually apply a red-hot coal or other slow-burning material to the breech. A matchlock consists of a trigger—a simple lever system—connected to a hammer-like "serpentine" which holds a burning slow-match

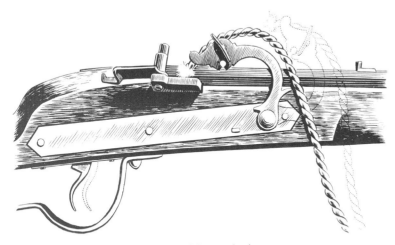

Matchlock firing mechanism.

Pressure on the trigger acts through the linkage to rotate the serpentine about it pivot point, and lower the glowing end of the slow-match into priming powder held in a pan or recess on the barrel, which ignites the propellant charge. In its most primitive form, the matchlock is believed to date from as early as 1475, and remained in wide use well into the late 17th and 18th centuries. Actually, it remained common in many Asiatic countries until quite recent times because of its simplicity and their lack of ability to produce the more sophisticated flint and percussion locks.

Mauser, Peter Paul   Born June 27, 1838, the son of an armorer at the Royal Württemberg Arms Factory, he died on May 29, 1914, after establishing in 1873 what is now known as the famed Mauser Werke at Oberndorf am Neckear, Germany and beginning what is probably the world's best-known small arms manufacturing dynasty.

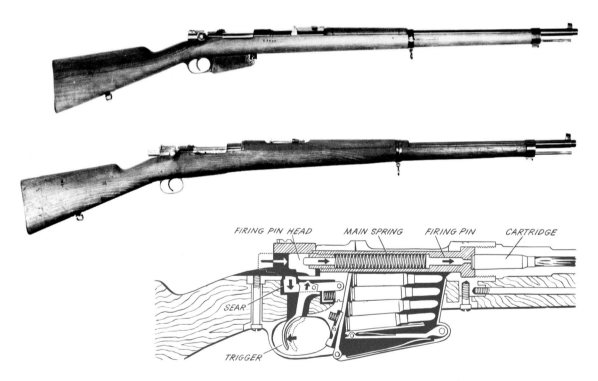

Typical Mauser bolt-action rifles (from top): Model 1891, Model 1895, and inner mechanism.

Mauser's first success came in 1871 with the Prussian Army's adoption of his single-shot, bolt-action M1871 rifle, which soon after became the standard infantry weapon of all the German states, and was purchased and manufactured widely abroad. With this success as a base, Mauser went on to develop his tubular magazine, a repeating version of the same basic gun, and then the more modern bolt-action rifles of 1889 and the early 1890s, capped by his principal achievement, the Model 1898 turn-bolt rifle which armed literally millions of soldiers of many nations during the massive wars of 1914–18 and 1939–45.

The M1898 Mauser rifle stood the test of time and service so well that it continued to be manufactured well into the 1950s for military use, and is still produced for sporting purposes in only slightly modified form. Until the 1960s, virtually all bolt-action sporting rifles were based upon the very sound M1898 design.

Maynard, Dr. Edward (1813–1891) An American dentist and inventor who in 1845 patented the tape primer that was adopted in 1855 for official United States military weapons. In 1851 he invented an improvement in breech-loading rifles, and this improvement was incorporated into what came to be known as the Maynard rifles and carbines and the special cartridges for them.

See also MAYNARD RIFLE.

Maynard Rifle A form of tip-up, single-shot rifle design originating during the Civil War period. Also the type of cartridge originated for Maynard rifles, in which a tubular brass case was fitted with a very wide or thick rim for extraction and a flash hole centrally located in the head. Ignition was provided by a conventional percussion cap on a nipple placed so it would flash through the flash hole in the case head to ignite the powder charge.

Maynard Tape Primer A form of percussion ignition invented by Dr. Edward Maynard and intended to replace the metallic percussion cap. Essentially Dr. Maynard's primer consisted of thin wafers of percussion compound (the same as found in percussion caps) cemented between two narrow strips of paper, equally spaced, and varnished for waterproofing.

This long strip of primers was then wound into a roll and fitted into a recess in the Maynard lock plate ahead of the

The Maynard tapelock was the action used on this U.S. Army rifle Model 1855. The Army paid Dr. Maynard $75,000 for the military rights to his lock.

161

percussion hammer. An internal ratchet mechanism then advanced the paper strip one segment each time the hammer was cocked. When the hammer was brought to full cock, a single pellet of priming compound was positioned directly over the nipple. When released, the hammer fell and crushed the prim-

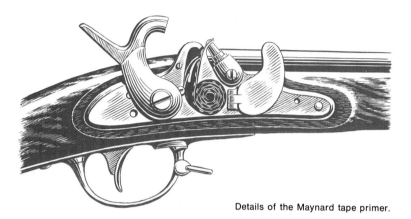

Details of the Maynard tape primer.

ing pellet against the top of the nipple igniting it, and simultaneously a sharp knife edge on the rear of the hammer face sheared off that segment of the strip. In this form, the Maynard tape primer closely resembles today's paper roll caps for cap pistols.

The U.S. Army adopted the Maynard tape primer in 1855, but in field service it was not as superior to the common percussion cap as it had appeared it would be. Consequently, it was phased out during the Civil War period.

Maynard primed arms and the paper rolls are much sought after by collectors today.

Mean Radius A method of measuring gun and ammunition accuracy and generally used only by military establishments. Mean radius is determined first by identifying the precise center of impact of a group of shots, then by averaging the distance individual shots have struck from that point.

See also CENTER OF IMPACT.

Metallic Sights The two-element, nonoptical-glass sighting systems found on rifles, handguns, and shotguns, also called "iron sights." The most common form consists of a simple metal post set vertically at the muzzle, with a rear element attached near the breech and containing a U-, square-, or V-shaped notch.

In use, one simply looks through the rear element and positions the front element in its notch, then positions that composite image directly on the target.

Such sights are referred to as "open sights," because of the open and uncovered rear element.

Metallic sights also include the aperture type in which the rear element consists of a disc with a tiny hole in its center; this element is placed as near as possible to the shooter's eye. A much higher degree of accuracy is obtained with the aperture sight.

One other type of metallic sight exists, and that is the single-element variety typified by the Seventrees "Guttersnipe," which is seldom encountered. It uses a relatively short single element containing a shaped groove or channel through which the target is sighted.

See also RECEIVER SIGHTS.

Micrometer.

Micrometer The basic measuring instrument used by machinists and an essential gauge to the handloader and gunsmith. A micrometer consists essentially of a C-shaped housing with a fixed anvil at one side of the open mouth, and a movable spindle at the other which may be turned in and out toward the anvil.

Very accurate adjustment scales are placed on the outside of the stem and barrel of the micrometer and may be read directly in thousandths or ten-thousandths of an inch to precisely measure bullets, cases, action parts, etc.

Micrometer Adjustment In reference to sights, vertical and horizontal adjustments are produced by plungers attached to finely threaded and fitted spindles, as in a conventional micrometer. This type of adjustment mechanism is also used in powder and shot measures, headspace gauges, and other tools related to gunsmithing and maintenance.

Micrometer adjustment on Redfield Olympic rear sight.

Micro-Sight A common term for adjustable handgun sights derived from the name of the Micro Sight Company. At one time Micro was the only manufacturer of precisely adjustable, target-type rear sights for handguns in quantity. Thus, handgun shooters have come to refer to any adjustable target-type sight as a "Micro Sight."

Mid-Range Load Any centerfire cartridge loading producing substantially less than full-charge-load velocity and recoil. The term is most commonly applied to .38 Special and .45 ACP handgun match ammunition loaded to fire wadcutter and semi-wadcutter bullets at reduced velocity. It also applies to rifle ammunition loaded for ranges up to 300 meters, though no such factory loads are currently available.

See also FULL CHARGE LOAD.

Mid-Range Trajectory Height (MRT) The point at which a bullet's trajectory reaches its highest point above the line-of-sight. This height will vary according to the height of line-of-sight above bore's centerline, so the only precise reference is a line from muzzle center to target. However, factory-published ballistic tables generally list trajectory height from one of several sight heights. Comparison between tables is thus not always practical.

Because of external ballistic realities, no bullet reaches its maximum height at exactly midpoint in muzzle-to-target range; instead, its highest point is approximately 55 per cent of the distance from the muzzle to the target, measured from the muzzle. However, shooters accept the MRT as given in published data as being at the midrange point.

Knowing the MRT for a given gun and ammunition combination is useful in determining how much, if any, one needs to "hold low" in shooting at a target at a closer range than at one for which the gun is sighted. It is also helpful in initial targeting or zeroing of a gun in that one may shoot at half-range, and simply adjust the sight to place the bullet impact above the point of aim at a distance equal to the MRT—thus insuring that the bullet will strike quite close to point of aim at its full range.

Mil An angular unit of measure generally used with military weapons except individual small arms for adjustment of sights and accuracy determination. One mil is the angle subtended by 1 unit of distance at 1,000 units of that distance. Put another way, 1 mil is the angle subtended by 1 inch at 1,000 inches, 1 yard at 1000 yards, and 1 meter at 1000 meters, etc. To do this precisely, the mil must equal 1/6283 of a circle; however, most military establishments have standardized upon the mil as 1/6400 of a circle. This has the advantage of having a denominator capable of division into whole numbers. For all practical purposes, it does represent the mil as originally defined. The mil is not used by civilian shooters, nor is it used in military small arms work except in producing indirect fire.

See also MINUTE OF ANGLE.

Minimum Cartridge Generally speaking, a performance or a dimensional level established by a game-control agency to insure that hunters use a gun and ammunition combination of adequate power to insure clean kills.

Some agencies specify the minimum cartridge by bullet energy at the muzzle—others simply by caliber, or by caliber, velocity and bullet weight. Regardless of the method by which the minimum cartridge is defined, the pertinent regulations then prohibit any lesser cartridge from being used on the species hunted.

Minute of Angle (MOA)   The angular unit of measure generally used to describe the accuracy capability of ammunition and guns. It equals ¹⁄₆₀ of a degree, making 21,600 minutes in circle. One minute of angle subtends 1.047 inches at 100 yards, twice that amount (2.094 inches) at 200 yards, and so on. For all practical purposes, 1 minute of angle is considered to be 1 inch at 100 yards, 2 inches at 200 yards, 3 at 300, etc.

Sight adjustments are generally established and regulated in minutes of angle or fractions thereof. A sight described as having ¼-minute click or adjustment is one in which 1 click or graduation of movement will shift the line of sight—in relation to bullet impact—¼ inch at 100 yards.

See also MIL.

Miquelet Lock   A form of flintlock dating from the early 17th century and native to Spain. It is characterized by frizzen and pan cover combined as a unit; by an externally mounted mainspring; and a sear acting horizontally through a hole in the lock plate. The gun has a large, angular cock, or hammer, with a ring-headed thumbscrew, for tightening the flint vise.

Many miquelet variations and evolutionary phases exist and it was not entirely replaced in the sphere of Spanish influence until the early 19th century.

Misfire   The failure of a cartridge to ignite and function normally no matter what the cause. Generally speaking, the cartridge itself is usually blamed, though the fault more often may be the gun or the conditions under which the cartridge has been stored or handled.

Any failure, no matter the cause, of the primer to detonate will cause a misfire. However, a misfire may occur even when the primer ignites, but the condition of the propellant is such that the primer flash does not ignite it. Wet or chemically deteriorated powder is generally the cause of such misfires, but a blocked flash hole may cause misfires too.

Misfires are best avoided by first insuring that ammunition is not exposed to excessive temperature, humidity, or other conditions which might affect the reliability of primers and propellants.

In addition, it is essential that the gun be kept in proper mechanical condition, with particular attention paid to correct firing-pin protrusion, correct headspace, and adequate main-spring strength.

Monobloc A form of construction and assembly for double-barrelled shotguns wherein the breeching and locking surfaces are cut into a single separate housing or "bloc" into which the breeches of the barrels are brazed or threaded. In theory the monobloc design is stronger than chopper lump or traditional design where underlugs are simply brazed to the breeches of the barrels.

See also CHOPPER LUMP.

Monte Carlo Comb An elevated comb which rises above the normal comb line (comb nose to heel of butt) in a step ahead of the butt. This comb permits a high line-of-sight while keeping the buttplate down at shoulder level.

Moose, Guns for A good elk rifle and cartridge combination will normally do quite well on moose, which are sometimes larger than elk, but are generally taken at shorter ranges. However, because of their habits, they will be encountered with heavy matting of mud on their coats which functions almost like armor plate and causes expanding bullets to open up prematurely. Consequently, the need for heavily constructed bullets and their ability to penetrate deeply is particularly important.

If your rifle is adequate for elk, then it's all you'll need for moose.

See also ELK, GUNS FOR.

Mountain Hunting, Guns for The requirements for a mountain rifle are a paradox. A fellow clambering up 3 miles of granite tumbled on end to sneak within range of a trophy sheep or goat, wants as light rifle on his back as possible. On the other hand, that trophy may never by any closer than 300 yards, and the split-second for shooting may come when you're thoroughly winded from a long climb and shaky as a bamboo ladder.

If you could carry it, the ideal gun for mountain hunting would be a 14-pound varmint rifle capable of half-minute-of-angle accuracy and chambered for the flattest-shooting cartridge available in 6mm or greater. However, that isn't practical, so a medium-weight sporter of maximum accuracy is your best bet.

If the rifle is too light, it may be a joy to carry but it won't settle down quickly when you're huffing and puffing, and it may not be as consistently accurate as you'd like. A rifle weighing 8 to 8½ pounds with scope and sling is about right.

Flat-shooting cartridges are essential, with good long-range performance and wind-bucking ability. The 6mm's with 100-grain bullets at 3,000 feet per second may be considered minimum, with the 7mm–.30 belted magnums being the practical maximum.

Multi-Groove   See POLLY-GROOVE and RIFLING.

Muzzle Bell   Simply a funneling or flaring of the bore at the muzzle, usually produced by over-zealous use of a bent or rough cleaning rod to the extent that the tops of the lands, and perhaps a bit of the grooves as well, are worn away. Belling is probably more common among rifles whose design requires cleaning from the muzzle, and which by nature of their use, are cleaned almost daily with sectional rods not noted for their straightness.

Belling reduces accuracy, the degree dependent upon the amount of belling, and whether it is concentric with the bore. The only practical cure for inaccuracy caused by this condition is amputation of the belled portion, and recrowning at the cutoff point.

Belling can be prevented by: (1) using only straight, clean, and smooth cleaning rods, (2) a cleaning rod guide over the muzzle, (3) cleaning only from the breech, and (4) cleaning no more vigorously or frequently than absolutely necessary.

If one wants to retain original external dimensions and contours of a barrel, belling can be corrected by counterboring precisely concentric with the bore, and to a diameter which will not reduce barrel walls more than 50 per cent from their original thickness.

Muzzle Brake   A device attached to the muzzle to reduce recoil and, to some extent, muzzle jump. Regardless of the vast array of sizes, shapes, and internal configurations, all brakes function by momentarily trapping propellant gases as they emerge from the muzzle and by diverting them at right angles to the bore's centerline, or slightly rearward.

When gases are diverted in sufficient quantities, they reduce rearward thrust, and if deflected rearward, exert forward thrust and thus tend to counterbalance a portion of recoil. Generally speaking, the greater the percentage of gases diverted and the more nearly they approach 180 degrees change in direction, the greater the amount of recoil reduction produced.

Practical limitations generally prevent achieving more than about 40 per cent recoil reduction with even the best and most efficient muzzle brakes. It is not possible to divert gas directly rearward because of its effect on the shooter, and even approaching rearward diversion can produce shock-wave effects on bystanders and also greatly increases the intensity of the muzzle blast.

The disadvantages of size and bulk, interference with line of sight, increased muzzle blast and discomfort, and cost have generally limited the use of muzzle brakes on conventional sporting guns. On the other hand, they have become very widely used on military arms, and are almost universally used on weapons over .50 caliber.

See also CUTTS COMPENSATOR.

Muzzle-Loader Any gun with a solid breech which must be loaded through the muzzle by first pouring in a charge of *black powder*, followed by a projectile (or projectiles), sometimes with a wad or wads placed both beneath and over the projectile(s). In their most common original form, muzzle-loaders use either the flintlock or percussion lock for ignition—though some specialized versions now use a conventional Boxer-type primer enclosed in a special device.

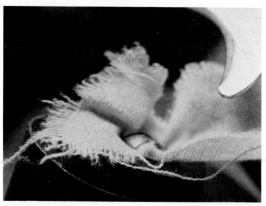

Loading and firing the muzzle-loader

First, black powder is poured into the muzzle from the powder horn (far left). Patch is placed over muzzle and ball is pressed with thumb of short ball seater into barrel. Excess patch is then cut off with sharp knife, then ball is pressed into muzzle far enough to permit easy entry of ramrod (near left). Then charge is rammed home. Cap is placed on nipple of percussion lock, (lower left, this page) and muzzle-loader is ready for firing.

Photos by Leonard Lee Rue III and George Nonte

Muzzle-Loader

Typical American muzzle loader is this reproduction of a Kentucky rifle currently manufactured by Navy Arms.

Since the late 1950s, numerous firms have placed muzzle-loading guns back into production, and today hundreds of thousands of these guns are sold annually. Such shooting has become a very popular facet of shooting sports in general, and is often closely associated with a detailed study of history of the period of the particular gun chosen—even to the extent of taking on full period costume, accessories, life styles, etc.

See also FLINTLOCK and PERCUSSION LOCK.

National Match Ammunition Ammunition of superior accuracy generally manufactured by or for the U.S. Government particularly for use in the National Rifle and Pistol Matches. At present, there are three standard National Match loadings. Cartridge, Match, Caliber .30 M72; Cartridge, Match, Caliber 7.62mm M118; and Cartridge, Ball, Match Grade, Caliber .45 M1911. Such ammunition is loaded to the highest practical standards of accuracy.

This ammunition is issued by government authorities only for National Matches, certain other matches, and for training of authorized competitive teams.

When loaded specifically for National Match use, the headstamp includes the letters NM. When selected from existing stocks, the label is simply stamped "Match Grade" or "For National Matches."

National Match Course (NMC) The standard course of fire for both rifle and pistol competition as established by the National Rifle Association, the governing body of national shooting events.

The National Match course for pistol consists of ten rounds timed fire, ten rounds rapid fire, and ten rounds slow fire. In the latter, the ten rounds are fired at 50 yards in a 10-minute time limit. Timed fire consists of two strings of five shots, with a 20-second time limit for each string, at a range of 25 yards. Rapid fire is the same, except that the time limit per string is 10 seconds.

Thus, the basic National Match Course consists of thirty rounds fired in three stages with a single gun with a possible score of 300. A *full* aggregate National Match Course consists of firing the same thirty-shot course with each of three guns, .22 rimfire, any centerfire caliber, and .45.

The National Match Course for rifle consists of ten rounds of slow fire at 200 yards from the standing position, ten rounds of rapid fire at 200 yards from the standing to kneeling or sitting position, ten rounds of rapid fire at 300 yards from the standing to prone position, and twenty rounds of slow fire at 600 yards from the prone position.

During slow fire the time limit is 1 minute per shot at ranges up to 600 yards and 1½ minutes at ranges beyond 600 yards.

During rapid fire the clock starts when the shooter is in the standing position and following the command "commence firing." Then, the shooter drops to the kneeling or sitting position and has 60 seconds to fire his ten shots if he is using a manually operated rifle, or 50 seconds if he is using a semi-automatic. The same basic rules apply to the prone position: The shooter drops from standing to prone position at the command but his time limits are 70 and 60 seconds respectively.

If the match is open to both manually operated and semi-automatic rifles, the time limits are those used for the manually operated guns unless otherwise stated by match officials.

As far as the NMC is concerned, a "centerfire" pistol is any revolver or autoloader firing a cartridge of .32 caliber or greater. In order to keep the number of guns to a minimum, many competitive shooters use the same .45 caliber autoloader for both .45 and centerfire stages.

National Match Rifle and Pistol A military gun specifically manufactured, or remanufactured, to precise standards of accuracy and function, specifically for use in the U.S. National Rifle and Pistol matches, and for issue to military and civilian shooters judged competent to use them in various other official competitions.

Since the early 1900s, there have been National Match versions of the M1903 rifle, M1 rifle, the M14 rifle, and not the M16 rifle.

National Match handguns have been built since 1957 and only on the .45 caliber M1911 pistol.

In most instances, National Match guns have been built up at Springfield Armory or one of the other national arsenals on an annual basis and in limited quantities. From time to time, a few of these guns have been offered for sale to qualified competitive shooters and National Rifle Association members.

Whether of new manufacture or rebuilt from guns in inventory, National Match guns carry a separate federal stock number (from the standard models) and are marked in various places with the letters "NM" stamped into the metal.

Standards and procedures for production of National Match guns change continuously, the experience of one year's National Matches being employed in the guns made up for the following year, and so on.

Colt's also once designated certain commercial target auto-loading pistol models as "National Match."

National Muzzle-Loading Rifle Association (NMLRA) An organization formed for the promotion of the shooting of muzzle-loading guns, and which governs all registered competition.

The NMLRA operates from its headquarters at Friendship, Indiana, adjacent to its famous Walter Cline range. This range includes facilities for every type of muzzle-loading shooting, including bench-rest, slug guns, buffalo, trap, quail walk, primitive field matches, and all the activities related to shooting muzzle-loaders. There are extensive campground areas where typical (and technically correct) primitive camps are set up.

The facilities are extensive enough for major national matches to draw 1,500 or more shooters, and many thousands of spectators, not to mention hundreds of exhibitors and sellers of muzzle-loading goods and services.

The NMLRA conducts two major matches annually, the "Beef Shoot" in the spring and the "Nationals" during Labor Day week in the fall. At this time there is no more picturesque sight than the primitive campground areas with their teepees and period-costume participants, and the firing line where authentic guns and costumes are the order of the day.

The NMLRA is made up of hundreds of affiliated clubs throughout the country (and even some in foreign countries) and conducts an extensive series of local, sectional, and regional matches throughout the year.

The association also publishes *Muzzle Blasts*, a magazine devoted to muzzle-loading guns and shooting, which is distributed to all association members as well as to other interested subscribers.

National Rifle Association (NRA) The principal organization (and largest with nearly 1,500,000 members) representing the interests of gun enthusiasts and the shooting sports.

Formed in 1871 under a charter granted by the state of New York, the NRA had as its goal "To promote rifle practice, and for this purpose to provide suitable range or ranges in the vicinity of New York, and a suitable place for the meetings of the association in the city itself, and to promote the introduction of a system of aiming drill target firing among the National Guard of New York and militia of other states."

The first NRA president was Major General Ambrose E. Burnside, inventor of the Burnside carbine of Civil War vintage, and a veteran of that war. For many years, the NRA's main effort was directed at promoting military-style shooting with whatever rifle was the U.S. standard at the time.

In those early days, it ignored shotgun and pistol shooting. Except for its occasional activities in long-range or international shooting, its entire competitive program was built around the development of a substantial pool of civilian riflemen trained with military weapons and in military fashion which could be drawn upon to bolster the national defense.

This did, in fact, occur during the Spanish-American War and also World War I. When it became obvious that the United States would be drawn into the trenches of France, the NRA launched a small-arms firing school program, and in 1916 the National Defense Act incorporated many NRA ideas and earmarked $300,000 to promote civilian marksmanship training. It also authorized the war department to distribute appropriate arms and ammunition to organized rifle clubs, under rules established under the National Board for the Promotion of Rifle Practice. It also authorized the issue of arms, ammunition, and related supplies and equipment to NRA clubs for the purpose of training civilians in the use of the standard service rifle.

Eventually NRA clubs and individuals were to train many thousands of soldiers who eventually fought during World War I. In many instances, the NRA-conducted training was the *only* marksmanship training received by soldiers drafted and sent overseas almost immediately thereafter. And, during World War II, a similar and even more extensive NRA program provided marksmanship training for countless thousands of potential soldiers before they were actually drafted into service.

Today the National Rifle Association is active in many fields, including all aspects of shooting. It publishes its magazine, *The American Rifleman,* regulates domestic competitive rifle and pistol shooting, conducts the national matches, and most recently hosted and conducted the World Championships in 1970, and generally looks after the interest of shooters and gun enthusiasts throughout the nation.

Its headquarters in Washington, D.C., contains extensive reference material and a very fine small arms museum.

National Shooting Sports Foundation (NSSF) Active and energetic, the foundation is the only national organization devoting most of its efforts to the cause of hunting.

Chartered in 1961, for the purpose of "arousing in the minds of the American public a better understanding and a more active appreciation of the shooting sports," the NSSF operates out of offices in Riverside, Connecticut, informing the public about the rewards and pleasures of shooting and hunting as recreation.

The membership of the NSSF includes 114 companies representing not only the sporting arms and ammunition industry, but the makers of hunting clothes, accessories, publishers, and others as well. In addition, the foundation has more than 1,000 associate dealer and distributor members.

With this broad base of support, the NSSF conducts a continuing campaign geared to educating the public and informing interested sportsmen. Each year over a million pages of newspaper and magazine publicity are devoted to firearms safety, field ethics, basic conservation, and the contributions of hunters to wildlife management. Over five million pieces of literature are circulated annually from a varied list of publications, many of them being used by schools and by fish and game commissions. The print order on one item alone totalled 1,700,000 copies in 1972.

Public service messages on hunting and conservation are mailed to radio stations across the country. The foundation speaks for the entire sporting arms industry at congressional hearings and the like, though it avoids lobbying. The NSSF also provides financial support for outdoor education, college shooting programs, and Young Hunter Safety Clinics. Advertising valued at more than $200,000 is annualy placed in various pro-hunting publications.

In 1972, the foundation was primarily responsible for President Nixon's proclaiming September 23 as the first "National Hunting and Fishing Day." The NSSF then carried most of the burden of promoting this nationwide event and encouraging the public as well as the 55 million sportsmen to participate.

National Skeet Shooting Association (NSSA) The NSSA, 212 Linwood Building, 2608 Inwood Road, Dallas, Texas 75235, established rules through its officers and Board of Directors and is the record keeper of registered skeet shooting. It publishes the official monthly magazine, *Skeet Shooting Review*, and an annual record of averages for each registered shooter. The Association was formed in 1935, reorganized in 1946.

Neck Expansion Pulling the reduced case neck over an expander to produce uniform and correct inside diameter without regard to wall thickness.

Neck Resizing   Resizing in a die which reduces only the neck of the case.

Neck Split (Crack)   A longitudinal crack in the neck of a cartridge case, due often to work-hardening or the case being too heavily stressed by the bullet.

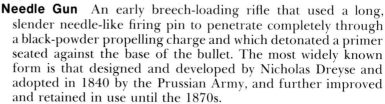

Needle Gun   An early breech-loading rifle that used a long, slender needle-like firing pin to penetrate completely through a black-powder propelling charge and which detonated a primer seated against the base of the bullet. The most widely known form is that designed and developed by Nicholas Dreyse and adopted in 1840 by the Prussian Army, and further improved and retained in use until the 1870s.

Also a last-century frontier colloquialism for the U.S. Trapdoor Springfield rifle with its hinged breech block and long, slender firing pin.

Schematic of needle-gun cartridge at instant of firing with needle-like firing pin penetrating base wad and powder to strike cap.

Nipple Charger   A piston and cylinder device operating much like a hypodermic syringe and used to force finely granulated black powder into a percussion gun's nipple.

In normal loading procedures, no powder is placed in the nipple vents—however, when a misfire occurs, filling the vents with fine-granulation powder and firing again with a fresh cap will often produce proper ignition. The additional powder packed into the nipple vent generates enough force to blow out whatever obstruction there might have been and to ignite the propelling charge.

Brass nipple charger supplied by Navy Arms.

Nipple (Percussion)   Often referred to as "cone," it is the seat upon which a percussion cap is placed and detonated by the hammer of a muzzle-loading gun.

The nipple is pierced through its length—very narrow at its midpoint and wider at both ends—which allows the cap's flame to flash through and ignite the powder charge.

While in a precisely regulated lock, whether rifle, pistol, or shotgun, the hammer face is not intended to actually strike the top of the nipple, it often does so and thus the nipple must be made of high-quality materials and very carefully hardened and tempered. It must not be too hard or it will shatter when struck by the hammer; it must not be too soft or it will be easily deformed by such a blow. It is generally threaded and screwed into the bolster or breech where the fit here must be tight to prevent escape of gas.

Typical percussion nipple on modern muzzle-loading reproduction.

Older percussion caps deposited highly corrosive residues in nipples, which were nearly impossible to clean thoroughly, and they soon became hopelessly rusted and corroded. Thus, gunwise shooters always carried spare nipples and a nipple wrench for field replacement.

Though nipples are generally made of fine tool steel, many shooters generally consider the Ampco (made from a beryllium-copper alloy with a brassy appearance) the best available today.

Nipple Wrench A small, compact wrench, most often of T-handle shape, made specifically to remove and reseat percussion nipples. Nipple wrenches are usually of socket-type design and are made of hardened and tempered fine steel.

Nitro Solvent A term once widely used to describe various cleaning solutions that were credited with the ability to remove powder residues once considered harmful to bores. Although numerous compounds were sold under dozens of names, the one most widely known today is Hoppe's #9.

The importance of so-called nitro solvent has greatly decreased with the discovery that it was primer residue and not powder residue that caused severe rusting, and that modern primers and powders leave no corrosive residue whatever.

Nobel, Alfred B., 1833–1896 The inventor of dynamite and smokeless propellants used in firearms. Born in Sweden, Nobel moved to St. Petersburg with his father who manufactured munitions, as well as agricultural implements, for the Russian

Government. In 1850 he visited the United States, and on returning to Russia, began to experiment with nitroglycerine. To reduce its hazards he experimentally produced dynamite in 1863, and blasting gelatin in 1876, followed by gelatin dynamites. By 1887–88 he had patented nitrocellulose and a basic smokeless propellant. His many patents and developments in explosives earned him a fortune which was used after his death to establish the series of Nobel Prizes for services to mankind.

Non-Ejector Guns Normally a break-open shotgun or rifle in which the extractor only frees empty cases from the chamber and raises them sufficiently to be plucked out by the fingers. The term could technically be applied to those bench-rest and varmint rifles from which the ejectors have been removed to simplify recovery of cases for reloading.

North-South Skirmish Association This is an organization devoted primarily to the preservation of the shooting and military skills of the American Civil War period. A national organization headquartered in Pennsauken, New Jersey, it contains many chapters throughout the country, all of which are fully equipped with muzzle-loading arms of the Civil War period, and which are accoutered and uniformed in the fashion appropriate to the original organization from whom they have taken their title.

For example, recently a Confederate unit was formed in Illinois, headquartered in Peoria, designated Co. B. 15th Tennessee Infantry. The unit that originally bore this designation was formed in southern Illinois by Southern sympathizers who fled to fight with the Confederacy. Thus, this outfit is armed with Enfield and Mississippi rifled muskets and is uniformed and equipped in the Confederate style.

North-South Skirmish clubs and organizations meet for competitive shooting with their standard military arms only, and also to re-enact particular Civil War battles and in general participate in festive occasions. In addition to the units equipped with small arms, there are some cavalry units, and a few companies of artillery which actually put on firing demonstrations (with both blank and inert ball ammunition).

Obturation The sealing of the propellant gases inside the chamber and bore of a gun, preventing any escape rearward into the action. In all sporting firearms (except those using caseless cartridges) this is accomplished by the cartridge case itself. Under pressure of expanding powder gases the ductile case is forced tightly against the chamber wall, preventing rearward escape of gas.

Artillery pieces using separate-loading ammunition achieve obturation by means of asbestos pads, plastic seals, or expanding metal seals.

A cartridge case lacking ductility to expand fully against chamber walls, or a case that cracks, splits, or ruptures, or chamber pressure too low to expand the case properly will prevent adequate obturation and allow gas to flow back outside the case walls and into the action.

See also CARTRIDGE, CASELESS.

Offset Sights Sights offset from the gun barrel to allow use of the left eye while shooting off the right shoulder or *vice versa.* Usually they are simply attached to horizontal bars or brackets screwed securely to the receiver and barrel of the gun. May also apply to scope sights.

Ogive The curved, rounded, or pointed forward portion of a bullet. All of the bullet forward of the bearing surface, regardless of shape.

Oil Dent Surface dents in a resized cartridge case, usually appearing at some point on the shoulder. They are caused by excess lubricant flowing to a specific point and being trapped there between the case and die. The lubricant, being incompressible, causes the *case,* under resizing pressure, to flow around the dollop of grease and thus become dented.

Unless oil dents are of such magnitude that they split or perforate the case, they cause no harm, and will disappear upon firing.

If oil dents persist, reduce lubrication to the absolute minimum.

One-Shot Hunt A type of big-game hunt wherein each hunter is registered, his gun and ammunition inspected, and then he is issued only one round of ammunition. If that shot misses, he must withdraw from the hunt. If an animal is wounded by the single allowable shot, the hunter is usually not permitted to fire the coup de grâce — it is done by one of the guides or hunt officials.

Probably the best known event of this type in the United States is the big "Wyoming One-Shot Antelope Hunt," which is by invitation only and functions more as a gala social event than as a hunt as the term is generally used.

Various European game preserves also administer one-shot hunts for some of their more desirable big-game species. In some instances, the hunter must use a single-shot rifle, a requirement not made on the Wyoming hunt.

Open Sight A rear sight whose aiming element consists of an open-top notch of some kind.

See SIGHTS, IRON.

Operating Lever In a lever-action gun, the part that opens and closes the action. Also called a finger lever.

Operating Slide The rod, arm or other structure of a shoulder arm connecting the bolt-operating mechanism to either a gas piston or forearms handle.

Over-and-Under Gun A double-barrelled gun on which the barrels are stacked vertically, one atop the other.

P

Paine Sight A form of revolver sight used by Chevalier Ira Paine, a famous competition and exhibition shooter of the 1880s whose feats with his Smith & Wesson .44 caliber revolvers became legendary. Essentially, the sight consists of a U-shaped notch in the rear and a round bead on a very thin stem up front.

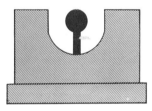

Paine sight.

Palm Rest A fully adjustable auxiliary hand grip, often shaped in the form of a ball. It is attached to the underside of a target rifle at approximately its balance point, and grasped by the off hand with the elbow resting on the hip bone or other portion of the torso, which allows the shooter to steady his rifle. It is authorized for use only in certain matches in international rifle competition.

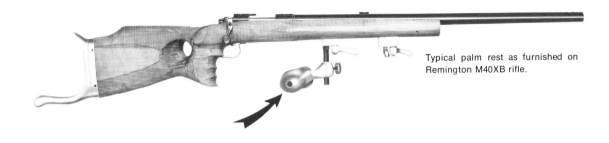

Typical palm rest as furnished on Remington M40XB rifle.

Paper Patch Bullet See PATCH.

Parkerizing A rust-resistant surface finish applied to military small arms which converts the metal surface to a layer of crystalline iron phosphate. The resulting finish has an etched or matted surface which holds oil and preservatives well. It usually is light gray or gray-green in color, turning dark with application of oil. Also called simply a phosphate finish.

Partition Bullet A trade name used by Nosler Bullet Co. for its unique controlled-expansion hunting bullet intended to give optimum expansion combined with maximum penetratration.

Instead of being formed in the conventional manner, open at the nose and closed at the base, the Nosler jacket is formed by swaging a partition approximately midway in a length of copper tubing. This partition is in effect solid, though it has a very small hole in its center. Then, a lead core is inserted into the nose and shaped to a typical soft-point configuration; a separate core is inserted in the other end and formed into a base.

Thus, when this bullet enters a target, the front portion expands in conventional fashion, while the rear portion in effect remains a full-jacketed wadcutter bullet and continues its penetration.

This design avoids bullet disintegration and failure to penetrate at high velocities, while at the same time ensuring adequate expansion at long ranges where velocity has dropped off.

Partition bullets are considered by many to be the best form of big-game bullets available.

See also EXPANDING BULLET.

Partition bullet is partitioned by ring swaged into jacket.

Patch Cloth or paper applied around an unlubricated lead bullet used to prevent leading, to ease loading (when used with muzzle-loaders), and to improve rifling engraving. Cloth patches are generally reserved for round balls, while paper is used only on cylindrical bullets.

Cloth patching may be any smooth, hard, tightly woven cloth washed free of sizing. Most often it is lubricated by rubbing into it a mixture of beeswax and tallow, or Vaseline, or similar grease. Today the most common patch material is plain, striped pillow ticking, well laundered, and of a thickness to match both bore and ball diameter so that the patched ball may be rammed easily, yet not be cut by rifling or burned through by the powder gases.

Round balls are generally patched by laying the lubricated patch over the muzzle, then seating the ball flush with the muzzle mouth, then trimming the excess patch material off with a sharp knife.

Patch thickness, material, and lubricant may require variation in order to achieve maximum accuracy with a particular barrel and ball combination.

Cloth patch is cut off after ball is seated flush with muzzle.

Paper patches are most commonly used in wraparound form, being carefully rolled wet onto the bullet's bearing surface with a small amount of overlap at the base, which is then folded over or twisted onto itself. The entire assembly is then allowed to dry, shrinking the patch tightly around the bullet. Patch blanks must be cut and measured carefully to fit a particular bullet, allowing two complete layers without overlap on the bearing surface.

Less commonly used is the strip patch, which may be two or three narrow strips laid across the muzzle so that they intersect its center, then folded up over the bullet bearing surfaces as it is seated in the barrel.

Regardless of the type, paper patches require the use of a carefully fitted false muzzle to prevent tearing or cutting of the patch as it enters the muzzle.

Paper patches of the wraparound type are also used on bullets to be either breech-seated or loaded in cases for many of the older black-powder, breech-loading guns of large caliber, such as the .40/90 Sharps and .44/77 Remington.

Paper patches are most often made from high-quality, high-rag-content bond cut so that the grain is perpendicular to the bullet's flight in the case of a wraparound patch, or occasionally parallel to it in the case of strip patches.

Generally, wraparound patches are loaded and shot dry, while strip patches may often be lightly lubricated with sperm oil.

See also BALL SEATER and FALSE MUZZLE.

Patridge sight.

Patridge Sight A form of revolver or rifle sight developed during the 1880s by E. E. Patridge, an exhibition shooter. It is the sight form most widely used today, consisting of simply a square notch at the rear, and a properly proportioned square-faced flat-topped blade at the front.

Prior to the advent of the Patridge and Paine sights, typical revolvers and single-shot pistols used nothing more than a V-shaped or other irregular groove or notch at the rear, and a tapered or rounded blade at the front, sometimes replaced by a round bead or a cone.

The Paine and Patridge sights, as simple as they may seem, offered tremendous aiming advantages over their predecessors.

Pattern Distribution of the shot in a shotgun charge. This is measured at a standard distance of 40 yards and in a 30-inch circle. For example, a full-chock charge is supposed to throw a pattern of at least 70 per cent of the shot into a 30-inch circle at a distance of 40 yards.

Pauly, Johannes S., 1766–c1820 Swiss inventor credited with the development of the first successful centerfire guns using an obturating (sealing) metallic-head cartridge. In spite of highly successful demonstrations of his gun/cartridge combinations in the early 1800s, Pauly and his developments were generally ignored. Had they not been, practical metallic cartridges and arms to use them might have come forty years earlier.

Pauly also patented a system which used a jet of heated, compressed air to ignite the powder charge—a method reintroduced in 1964 by Daisy/Heddon in its VL caseless cartridge guns. He also patented balloon features that proved successful, along with several other firearms patents and designs which failed.

Pauly was apparently unknown before his 1812 patents and was nearly so again at the time of his death. Perhaps his developments were too advanced for his time.

Peabody, Henry O. The inventor of the Peabody that later was developed into the Martini rifle. Little is known of his early years except that he was an expert mechanic with an interest in firearms. His first successful rifle patent was in 1862 for a tipping-block, single-shot, breech-loading action for metallic cartridges. Peabody never attempted to produce this design or his later improvements. All production was by the Providence Tool Co., and sales were through M.F. Benton of New York. Peabody continued to make significant improvements in his basic action through 1873.

See also MARTINI RIFLES AND PEABODY RIFLE.

Peabody Rifle A form of breech-loading single-shot rifle patented by Henry O. Peabody in 1862 and manufactured by the Providence Tool Company, Providence, Rhode Island, in the middle 1860s.

The Peabody consisted of a massive receiver hollowed out to contain a relatively long, solid breech block that was pivoted at its rear, with its front being lowered to open the breech and expose the chamber, then raised to close and lock the action by a finger lever that formed the trigger guard.

With the action closed, the pivot at the rear of the breech block supported it solidly against the backthrust of the firing cartridge.

In its basic form, the Peabody rifle contained a massive external hammer reminiscent of percussion days, acting through a long firing pin that pierced the breech block lengthwise.

Though never an official U.S. Army rifle, the Peabody was purchased by the Connecticut State Militia in .45/70 caliber. It

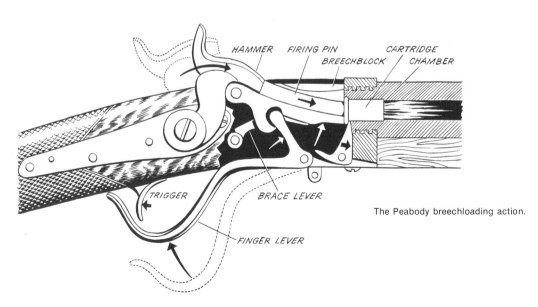

The Peabody breechloading action.

was exported extensively, the largest single buyer probably being Turkey, whose troops were armed with it during the third Russo-Turkish War which culminated in the Battle of Pleven, Bulgaria, in 1877.

Curiously enough, during that battle, the Russian assault forces were first taken under fire at long range with the Peabody rifle, then when the advancing waves came within a couple hundred yards, the Turks cast aside the big single shots and picked up their Winchester M1866 lever-action rifles and decimated the Russian forces. However, the Turks were eventually forced to yield under siege.

The life of the Peabody rifle was relatively short. It achieved its greatest development as the Peabody-Martini, later shortened to simply Martini, where it was fitted with a hammerless, internal, automatic-cocking firing mechanism, and became, in .577/.450 caliber, the standard rifle of British troops throughout the world. It was the standard rifle from 1871 to 1888, being replaced by the .303 Lee-Metford. It remained in colonial service for many years, and large quantities turned up as surplus from India and Africa after World War II.

Pedersen Device A semiautomatic designed by J. D. Pedersen to convert the U.S. M1903 rifle into a fast-firing assault weapon. Developed in 1917, it was produced secretly as the "U.S. Pistol, caliber .30, M1918" in hopes of surprising the enemy with it in the anticipated 1919 Spring offensive of World War I. The war ended and the contracts were cancelled after 65,000 units had been manufactured.

It was essentially a blowback, self-loading pistol mechanism which could replace the bolt in specially altered M1903 rifles. Rifles so modified were stamped "Mark I." Placed in the rifle, the device fired 80-grain bullets at 1,300 feet per second through the M1903 barrel from a 40-shot magazine inserted from the upper right. Examples are also known to have been made for the Russian M1891 rifle and the U.S. Rifle, Cal. 30, M1917 (U.S. Enfield), but apparently neither reached production status.

After World War I, all stocks of the Pedersen Device were ordered destroyed. Apparently not all were destroyed, since numerous specimens have turned up in recent years.

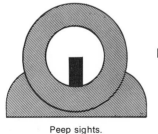

Peep sights.

Peep Sights A form of rear sight mounted on a rifle receiver as close as possible to the shooter's eye and containing a very small aperture through which the front sight is viewed.

The principal advantage of the peep sight is that in looking through (rather than *at* a conventional, open rear-sight element) the eye does not focus on the rear sight element but on the front sight and target. As an additional advantage, the eye tends to center automatically the front sight in the aperture without conscious effort on the shooter's part. Consequently, one may actually ignore the rear sight completely, eliminating the need for focusing on the rear element.

Peep sights are generally classified as "receiver" sights since they are mounted at the rear of the receiver, as close to the eye as recoil of the particular rifle will permit. Ideally, the sight should be immediately in front of the eye—and it is on rifles of light recoil. However, on conventional hunting rifles, rearward recoil movement requires the sight to be placed 2 or 3 inches away from the eye.

See also METALLIC SIGHTS.

Pennsylvania Rifle A purely American development of the flintlock period emanating primarily from Pennsylvania during the 18th and early 19th centuries. It is popularly referred to as the Kentucky rifle, probably because of its extensive use in that territory.

Purists differentiate between Kentucky and Pennsylvania rifles in subtle differences in style and detail, but both are essentially the same.

See also KENTUCKY RIFLE.

Pepperbox An early form of revolving repeating pistol in which a number of barrels were bored in a circle in a single piece of metal resembling the cylinder of a modern revolver. Functioning was the same as a revolver, the entire cylinder being revolved to bring successive barrels under the hammer for firing. Though occurring as far back as the 16th century, the pepperbox did not become practical until the advent of the percussion cap in the early 1800s. Pepperboxes were made in a wide variety of sizes and styles, and reached their popularity peak during the percussion period. Few were made after the advent of practical metallic cartridges. Both single- and double-action pepperboxes were made.

Single-barrelled revolvers after the 1840s were more accurate and easier to handle and soon displaced the rather clumsy and muzzle-heavy pepperbox.

Percussion Cap An external ignition device patented by Joshua Shaw in the early 1800s and in wide use by the 1830s, eventually displacing flint ignition almost entirely by the 1850s. It consists of a thin, soft copper cup containing in its closed end a disc or pellet of (originally) fulminate of mercury. The cap is placed over a cone or nipple containing a vent leading into the powder charge. When the cap is then struck by a hammer, the fulminate detonates and a jet of flame passes through the vent to ignite the powder charge.

See CAPLOCK; NIPPLE; PERCUSSION LOCK.

Percussion ignition caps are thin copper cups containing a thin pellet of detonating compound.

Percussion Ignition The form of ignition for muzzle-loading guns using the percussion cap developed by Joshua Shaw in the early 1800s and achieving wide distribution by the 1830s because of its great advantages over the flintlock. (Technically, modern rimfire and centerfire ammunition is also "percussion ignited.")

The key to percussion ignition is Shaw's percussion cap which in its definitive form consists of a small cup drawn from thin sheet copper into which was pressed a thin pellet of detonating compound and then waterproofed by application of a disc of paper or foil and a drop of lacquer or varnish.

The percussion cap is placed over a nipple and is struck by the hammer which crushes the detonating compound against the nipple, igniting it, and causing a jet of flame, and incandescent particles to ignite the main powder charges. This jet of flame passes through a vent drilled centrally through the nipple which opens, usually, through another, larger vent leading directly into the powder chamber.

Nipple passage of percussion ignition system connects to powder charge, allowing passage of cap flame.

Originally percussion caps were charged with a detonating compound based upon fulminate of mercury. However, in later years, other less hazardous and less ruinous (to the gun) compounds were utilized, and until very recent times chlorate detonating mixes were most common. All produced highly hygroscopic residues which attracted moisture from the atmosphere and promoted rapid rusting of the gun surfaces exposed to them.

Modern percussion caps, still available from several domestic and foreign manufacturers, use noncorrosive detonating compounds.

The percussion cap offered the first truly waterproof method of firing guns and 100 per cent reliability. Despite its tremendous advantages, the percussion-cap system had a very short life. The technology that made it possible also produced the metallic cartridge. For all practical purposes, this system endured from the 1820s to the 1860s, the shortest life span of any ignition system.

See also LOCK, NIPPLE, and PERCUSSION CAP.

Piece A vernacular term for any firearm, apparently with its origin in early artillery terminology, i.e., "field piece."

Pin Hole In a paper shotshell, a small hole burned through the case wall just forward of the head overlay.

Pistol A term originally applied to all handguns, but now more or less limited to single-shot and autoloading designs. A firearm made or designed to be fired with one hand. Any small, concealable, short-barreled hand firearm. Reportedly derived from Pistoia, an early Italian gunmaking center.
See HANDGUN.

Pitch The distance vertically from the muzzle of a shotgun to a line drawn at right angles to the butt and tangent to the standing breech. It is best seen in the accompanying drawing, and usually measured by placing the butt flat on a floor, with the breech touching the wall, and measuring the distance from the wall to the edge of the muzzle.

Pitch, in combination with pull and drop, determines the angle of the barrel when the gun is properly mounted.

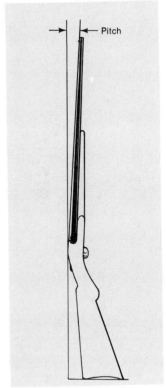

You can determine the pitch of a shotgun in the following way: Stand the butt on a floor with the action touching a wall. Measurement from the muzzle to the wall is the pitch.

Pittman-Robertson Act The common name for the Federal Aid to Wildlife Restoration Act, enacted in 1937, which provides for the distribution of the 10 per cent federal excise taxes collected on arms and ammunition to the states on a matching-fund basis. The states providing 25 per cent to be used specifically for game conservation activities, including acquisition and improvement of habitat, species studies, staffing of departments, research, and surveys.

The entire U.S. wildlife conservation system as it exists today originated with the availability of Pittman-Robertson funds, and would probably never have developed without them.

Plastic Shotshell A type of shotshell case first introduced in quantity on the commercial market in 1962 by Remington Arms Co.
See also SHOTSHELL.

Plinker A rifle or handgun, usually of small caliber and low power (most often .22 rimfire), generally light in weight, simple in design, and moderate in cost and accuracy. It is used

principally for casual fun shooting and taking small game.
The term also is applied to one who "plinks," or shoots casually.

Poly-Groove   A form of rifling that has found periodic popularity but has never gained lasting acceptance. It generally consists of an uncommonly high number of grooves that are both narrower and shallower than conventional grooves.

Poly-groove rifling reduces bullet deformation which theoretically should result in greater accuracy. Use of high-intensity loads, however, results in rapid erosion of the fragile lands, reducing barrel life and nullifying the other advantages. Its most practical application is in rimfire calibers using lubricated lead bullets.

See also EROSION and RIFLING.

Position, Shooting   See SHOOTING POSITION.

Possible   A term used to describe a perfect numerical score in target shooting (i.e., the highest score possible). This is without regard to the tie-breaking X- and V-rings.

See also V-RING and X-RING.

Powder Efficiency   The efficiency of any fuel (and powder is a fuel) is measured as its "thermal efficiency," its capacity to produce heat energy per unit of weight. While this method of measurement suffices for the engineer, it is of little value to the handloading shooter. The handloader is interested in powder efficiency from two other angles—maximum performance from the minimum amount (and therefore cost) of powder, and maximum velocity and energy from minimum chamber pressure.

The first measure of efficiency is relatively easy to obtain, requiring only that one check published loading data. Use a reliable loading manual listing the cartridge and bullet weight desired and compare the amounts required of the different powders to produce a specific velocity at a particular load level.

Generally it is simplest to use the maximum listed loads. Since all the published maximum loads for a given caliber or bullet weight will be producing essentially the same pressure, the smallest amount of powder that produces a particular velocity level is the most efficient—at least insofar as conversion of powder to velocity is concerned under that particular set of conditions. And this may or may not relate to the technical thermal efficiency of the powder used.

The second measure of efficiency may be determined in

much the same way, *providing* both chamber pressures and velocities are listed.

In this instance a comparison is made of the pressure level developed in producing a specific velocity by the various powders. A simple visual comparison will be sufficient in some instances; however, a more accurate appraisal can be made by calculating the velocity produced per grain of powder.

These two measures of efficiency are quite different—the first will generally indicate a rather fast-burning powder is most efficient, while the latter will often indicate a slow burning powder. For example, in the .30/06 with 180-grain bullets, IMR 3031 and powders of similar burning rate are by far the most economically efficient, while the much slower powders such as IMR 4350 and H4831 are the most efficient from the pressure: velocity ratio viewpoint.

Powder Flask   A container for black powder to be used with muzzle-loading arms. Generally of copper or other non-sparking metal, fitted with a spout which meters predetermined charges of black powder by volume. It serves both as a container and as a device for measuring the proper powder charges.

See also POWDER HORN.

Powder Horn   A container for carrying, but not measuring black powder, generally made from a cow's horn that has been cleaned, scraped thin, plugged at the wide end, and stopped at the other. It is sometimes made of other types of horn, and occasionally from sections of antlers or ivory.

Typical percussion-period powder flasks of various sizes.

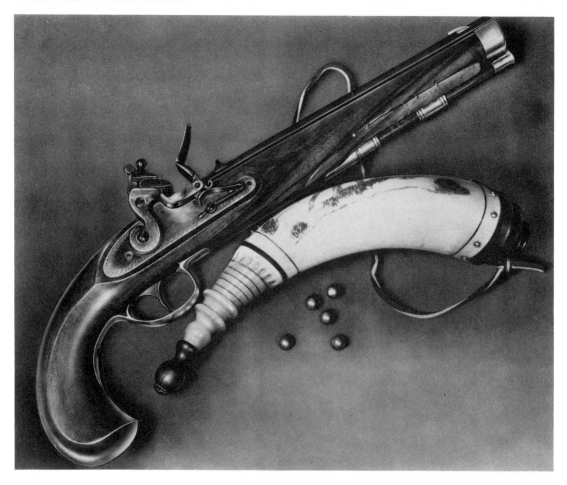

Finely decorated powder horn with flintlock pistol and balls.

Horn developed as the major material because of its resistance to moisture, ready availability, ease of working, existing shape, and non-sparking characteristics.

See also POWDER FLASK.

Powder Measure A volumetric measure, usually adjustable, with which correct, uniform powder charges are metered into cases.

Powder Residue All forms of propellant powders leave residues in the cartridge case, in the chamber, and in the barrel. This is true whether the gun is a muzzle-loader, a rifle, a shotgun, or a handgun.

Black powder, of course, leaves copious amounts of solid

residue, which amounts to as much as 40 per cent of the original charge! Black powder residue is not particularly tenacious and is easily removed by cleaning with water or any good solvent— providing it has not been allowed to harden. It is chemically basic and strongly hygroscopic, that is, absorbing and retaining moisture which can cause rapid rusting of affected metal parts under conditions of relatively high humidity.

Smokeless powder residue is acidic and constitutes a minute portion of the total charge. In addition, it can also be highly tenacious and difficult to remove. Some of the so-called ball powders produce particularly tenacious fouling which has been known to build up heavily and reduce accuracy, to the extent that severe abrasive cleaning is required to remove it.

Powder Trickler A small device which will feed very minute quantities of powder as a knob is turned.

Practice Shooting Marksmanship ability cannot be obtained from books or films, it must come from regular practice. Essentially, practice for a given type of shooting or hunting is most productive if conducted under identical conditions. For example, plinking with a lever-action carbine and squib loads cannot produce a long-range marksmanship with a heavy-barrelled, bolt-action varmint rifle. Ideally, practice should be conducted with the same gun and ammunition that will be used for record. However, in the interest of economy and reduced space, worthwhile practice can be conducted with reduced-load ammunition and the same, or similar, gun. Of lesser value, but still worthwhile, is dry-firing (snapping on an empty chamber) the appropraite gun at realistic targets placed only a few yards away. Air or CO_2 guns also provide worthwhile practice indoors.

Simple plinking at tin cans in the city dump cannot be considered good practice. During practice, maximum concentration should be applied to sight alignment, trigger squeeze, and position.

Practice for stationary targets may be conducted on paper bullseye targets, but unless bullseye targets are the ultimate goal, a center-hold sight picture should be employed. If, for example, the ultimate goal is woodchucks, then a picture of the 'chuck is better than a bullseye. Paper targets printed with a likeness of many species of game are readily available, both full-sized and reduced.

Practice for any form of hunting should be conducted at various ranges—from as close as 40 yards, out to the maximum range you'll expect to shoot game. Practice should also be conducted from the firing positions that will be encountered in the field. Shooting prone from a rest won't help much when the

Simulate running deer (above) by setting up an outdoor range with heavy clothesline strung on pulleys between trees and then at angle to a third tree holding a bicycle wheel minus tire. The deer target, cut out of cardboard, is pulled rapidly across field of view by man turning wheel. Also practice shooting running game (below) by placing a cardboard target in a tire and having a partner roll it down hill. Bouncing tire simulates bounding game.

only shot likely to be had at a deer will require standing to see over brush.

Shooting running game is the most difficult, and is the most difficult to simulate in practice. Ideally one should practice by shooting running varmints or small game in preparation for big game. Lacking that, a hoop covered with paper, or a simple plywood disc, can be rolled down an incline and shot at as it speeds away. For indoor moving-target practice, an air rifle may be used in conjunction with a pendulum target hung on a string from the ceiling. It is a fair representation of a moving target as it swings. Also, a shooting gallery, with its moving, cast-iron ducks and bunnies, provides excellent practice.

See HOLDOVER; SHOOTING RUNNING GAME..

Pressure Gun   A special laboratory device used for measuring chamber pressures. The most common type diverts a portion of the powder gases into an orifice drilled at right angles to the chamber and against the face of a closely fitted piston that rests against a short round cylinder of soft copper.

When the pressure gun is fired, gas rushes into the chamber and against the piston, compressing the "copper crusher." The crusher is then removed and its length is measured. The amount it has been shortened by the firing of the test load is used to calculate chamber pressure, based on careful tests conducted during the manufacture of that lot of crushers.

This type of pressure gun is known simply as a "copper crusher," and is the most commonly encountered. Other types exist which use strain gauges and piezo-electric crystals to determine pressures.

Pressure guns are generally constructed to readily accept a wide variety of test barrels which can be interchanged quickly. Normally they are found only in ballistic laboratories and are quite costly. Their principal use is in testing and development of ammunition—in development of new loads and in the continuous testing necessary to insure that quality standards are met.

Primer   The small cap fitted in the pocket in the head of a centerfire cartridge case or enclosed in the folded rim of a rimfire case. The primer contains a sensitive explosive compound which, when struck by the firing pin, ignites the powder charge. There are two basic types of centerfire primers: the Boxer, which is most generally used in the United States, and the Berdan, which is used in Europe.

See also BOXER PRIMER and BERDAN PRIMER.

Primer, Corrosive   See PRIMER, NONCORROSIVE and PRIMER, CENTERFIRE.

Primer Crimp   Metal of the case head turned over the primer radius to hold the primer in place. Common only in military ammunition intended for full-automatic weapons.

Primer Indent The imprint of the firing pin visible on a fired primer.

Primer Leak Gas escape around a primer at the case head, evidenced by powder smoke smudges on the case head.

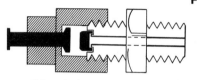

Primer lock screws into nipple seat, replaces nipple.

Primer Lock A modern form of percussion lock which uses a Boxer-type primer instead of percussion cap. In place of the original percussion nipple, the primer lock carries a fitting into which a regular primer is placed and then is topped by a second fitting containing a short firing pin that is struck by the hammer. Design and construction are such that even with the heaviest black-powder charges gas cannot escape rearward through the flashhole as it can when percussion caps are used.

Primer locks have additional advantages of ready availability of primers and more uniform ignition.

See also PERCUSSION LOCK and PRIMER, CENTERFIRE.

Priming Tool A separate hand or bench tool for seating new primers in cases.

Primitive Hunting Hunting large and small game with muzzle-loading guns. Many states now authorize special primitive hunting seasons for deer, turkey, and other game during which time modern guns may not be used. Consequently, the special seasons allow the charcoal burner (and sometimes archers) to have a reasonable chance of taking game.

More and more primitive hunters are duplicating frontier conditions and equipment; it is not at all unusual to encounter hunters using authentic replicas of a Hawken or Kentucky rifle, dressed like 18th century frontiersman, using hunting methods and carrying provisions that were common to the American frontier in the 1780s. They represent the ultimate in sport hunting.

The magazine *Muzzle Blasts*, published by the National Muzzle Loading Rifle Association, offers a good deal of information on primitive hunting.

Primitive Shooting A term referring to all forms of muzzle-loader shooting, but more specifically to that shooting which is done with either original or reproduction black-powder guns under simulated frontier conditions and in period costume.

The most outstanding example of organized, controlled

SCENES OF PRIMITIVE SHOOTING

Lining up for the Seneca Run, primitive garb abounding and flintlock rifles at the ready.

Leveling off and firing away, great clouds of smoke rolling up in the face of the shooter.

Running, always running, to the next shooting position with gun in hand.

The teeth are used to pull the powder horn plug as the first step in reloading.

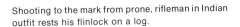

Squeezing off at a semiconcealed target in woods. Tri-cornered hat and other Colonial garments are popular in primitive shooting.

Shooting to the mark from prone, rifleman in Indian outfit rests his flintlock on a log.

Photos by Jim Carmichel

primitive shooting is "Running the Seneca," a match regularly conducted as part of the National Muzzle Loading Rifle championship held annually at the Walter Cline range in Friendship, Indiana. This match requires all contestants to be dressed in full period costume which may be anything from Indian breech clout and moccasins—to swallowtail coat and beaver hat, the rifle a flintlock Kentucky. Contestants *run* a twisting creek bed for some 300 yards, correctly identifying and firing at at least five semiconcealed targets *en route,* stopping and loading as required.

Pronghorn Antelope, Guns for   The pronghorn is a relatively small, lightly built, highly nervous animal that is relatively easy to kill. Any cartridge powerful enough for whitetail deer is quite adequate. However, due to their habitat, they are generally shot at quite long ranges. It is not impossible to stalk an antelope to within 100 yards, but the average hunter is more inclined to take him at 200 to 300 yards (or even more), and perhaps on the run.

Pronghorns require a precisely accurate rifle using extremely flat-shooting cartridges; those of the .243 Winchester and 6mm Remington class are ideal, though more powerful numbers such as the .270 and some of the smallbore magnums do quite well, despite their excess power. Flatness of trajectory and high velocity are of paramount importance.

Pronghorns require a rifle of medium to long barrel length and sufficient weight to handle well for off-hand use and running shots. Any modern bolt-action rifle that is properly stocked and tuned will generally deliver adequate accuracy. Current-production Remington, Winchester, and Mauser-type guns chambered for 6mm are probably the best all-around choice.

Ideally, the pronghorn rifle should be fitted with fixed-power scope of 4X, or a 2½–7X variable. Neither open nor aperture sights are adequate for the longer shots that pronghorn will offer.

Proof Fire   To test fire a gun with a cartridge developing more than standard chamber pressure.

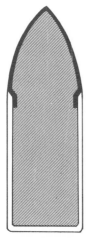

In protected-point bullet, a thin cap covers part of core projected beyond jacket.

Protected-Point Bullet   A form of expanding bullet identical to the soft point, except that a thin metal cap covers the otherwise exposed portion of the core at its point. This cap is generally a very thin, soft copper alloy barely hard enough to resist deformation from handling and gun functioning, but sufficiently soft to promote expansion on target.

Probably the best-known bullet of this type is the Winchester-

Western "Silvertip," in which a soft, metal cap is placed over the point of the bullet core and both are inserted into the jacket and swaged to final shape. The protective cap extends down inside the jacket proper and is locked securely in place.

Another form of protected point is the Remington Bronze Point. In this design, the core does not extend beyond the mouth of the jacket, but is replaced by a conical bronze or brass point with a wedge-shaped base that extends down into a cavity central in the nose of the core. Upon impact, the Bronze Point decelerates much more rapidly than the core (because of its lighter weight and lesser momentum) and thus acts as a wedge causing the core to begin expanding.

See also EXPANDING BULLET.

Protruding Primer A primer not fully seated in its pocket and therefore protruding beyond the case head. A dangerous condition that can cause premature firing as the cartridge is chambered, especially in autoloading guns.

Public Range A shooting facility in which range facilities, targets, and the necessary services are supplied—and often guns as well—where the individual can shoot under closely-controlled conditions. Most public ranges are operated by private enterprise for profit, and a fee is charged, either based on the length of time a shooter will use the facilities, or the number of shots he will fire.

Public ranges may vary from a small single-field trap-shooting layout with hardly any facilities—to multi-million dollar complexes containing ranges for rifle, pistol, shotgun, and often archery as well. Some are fully outdoors while others are fully enclosed to permit their operation in the midst of heavily populated areas. Typical of the latter is the Bullet Hole of Shawnee Mission, Kansas, operated by B. E. Hodgdon, Incorporated. It contains over forty firing positions for handgun, rifle, and archery, including underground tunnels for longer ranges, and is combined with a well-equipped retail store.

Probably the most common public range in the United States is the small-to-medium-sized gun club which opens its range to the public. Generally such a club possesses only shotgun facilities, and will usually have at most two skeet and two trap fields in conjunction with a moderate sized clubhouse.

Pump Action A form of action in which the mechanism is operated by reciprocating the forend. Also sometimes called a "trombone" action.

At one time pump-action rifles were quite common in the various rimfire calibers but constitute a small portion now. Pumps have been produced in large quantity for centerfire cartridges only by Remington. Colt and the now defunct Standard Arms Company produced relatively small quantities of centerfire pump-action rifles, but only for a short time, over a half-century ago.

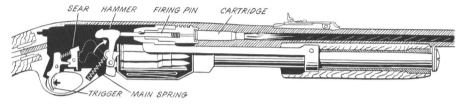

Inner mechanism of a pump-action rifle.

The older pump action designs were relatively weak in that they used non-rotating locking systems of various types and had very little camming power for seating cartridges, and were not particularly strong on extraction. However, the current Remington design utilizes a rotating bolt with front locking lugs which offer as much strength as comparable bolt-action rifles and also quite adequate seating and extraction power.

Pump actions are more common among shotguns, with nearly a dozen companies producing them today. Since the middle 1890s, more pump shotguns than any other type except single-barrels have been produced domestically. Classics of the type are the Winchester M1897 and M12.

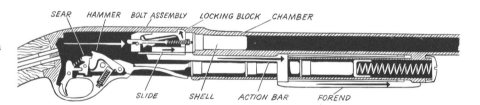

Inner mechanism of a pump shotgun.

R

Ramp Sight   A front sight for handgun or rifle in which the aiming element is relatively low and is situated upon—or is an integral part of—a relatively wide base which slopes upward from rear to front and is attached solidly to the barrel.

The ramp reinforces an otherwise rather weak aiming element and simplifies installation on the barrel by providing a much greater joining surface.

Ramps and ramp sights come in a variety of forms, some being simply screwed in place, some soldered, or screwed *and* soldered, some fitted in dovetails or pinned in keyways on the barrel or rib, and others an integral part of a ring which encircles the barrel and is pinned or soldered in place—once favored for rifles, but no longer.

Ramp front sight.

The most common type is the separate ramp screwed or soldered in place, into which the aiming element is dovetailed.

In handguns, the ramp may be formed integrally with the barrel, or to the rib attached to the barrel, and the sight element may be an integral element, or be dovetailed and pinned, or keyed, into place.

Rangefinder Reticle   A reticle or aiming point in a telescopic sight that allows target range to be estimated. In its simplest form, it consists simply of an additional fixed crosswire in the reticle, parallel to the main horizontal crosswire, and spaced so that the gap subtends a particular distance, often 18 inches at 100 yards.

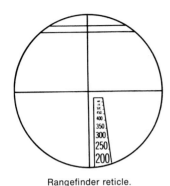

Rangefinder reticle.

In use, the two parallel crosswires are placed over the target animal, allowing an estimate of range to be made by comparing target image size with the space between the wires. For example, in the reticle with an 18-inch gap, an average adult whitetail deer would be expected to fill the gap, from breast to back, over the shoulders, at a range of 100 yards. If the deer only half filled the gap, it would be presumed to be approximately 200 yards.

A second form of reticle is typified by the Redfield Variable Accu-Range. In this instance, magnification is varied through an external manual control until the target image fills the gap between the wires. The movable element is linked to a range scale visible inside the field of view so that the range may be read directly without the shooter taking his eye from the scope.

A variation of the second type is found in the Auto-Range reticle and *mount* system developed by Realist, Inc. However, the external control used for varying magnification is connected directly to an external cam which raises and lowers the rear of the *scope* within the mount to automatically compensate for target range. This elevation cam must be shaped specifically for each individual cartridge and load, to match that load's trajectory.

Such mechanisms produce only a very rough approximation of actual range, and are totally dependent upon the size of the target animal for their accuracy. Any of the three types will produce reasonably accurate results if the size of the target matches the design gap between the range-finding wires. However, in the case of an 18-inch spacing, a deer whose body measurement is 2 inches less than that dimension in height will automatically throw in roughly a 10 per cent error—and far greater variations will be found among typical game animals of all species.

Rebore Drilling and reaming out the rifling of any barrel and then rerifling it to a larger caliber or different specifications. One of the most common reboring operations is taking rusted or shot-out Winchester M1886 barrels of .33, .38, and .40 caliber and drilling, reaming, rerifling and rechambering them to take the .45/70 cartridge, thus restoring such guns to service with like-new barrels.

Reboring is almost always practical to some extent. Old-time guns were generally rebored only sufficiently to clean up a ruined bore, but today standardization of calibers and bore diameters allows reboring from one standard caliber up to the next, for example, .270 Winchester up to .30/06, the .30/06 to .338, etc. Generally, barrel walls are sufficiently thick to allow this much increase in calibers. However, barrel quality must be considered, and soft-steeled rimfire or oldtime barrels cannot be rebored to use modern high-intensity cartridges producing much higher pressures.

Chamber dimensions must also be considered. The rebored caliber should use a case and chamber slightly larger in all dimensions than the original that allows recutting of the chamber to minimum tolerances for best performance, but it is not uncommon to use a nearly identical chamber—such as the .270 to .30/06.

Assuming quality of workmanship to be comparable, a restored barrel will shoot fully as well as it did when new and in its original caliber.

Reboring was once considered more economical than rebarrelling, and in a few instances that is still true, however, modern mass production of replacement barrels has brought the cost down to where there is no great economic advantage to reboring for standard rifles. In many instances, though, it is particularly desirable to retain the gun's original, unaltered external condition and appearance. Reboring allows this, even if it might be more costly than a replacement barrel.

Rebounding Hammer A gun in which the hammer or firing pin automatically draws back after striking the primer and is held in the retracted position.

Rechamber The reaming of an original chamber to either larger or different dimensions. It is generally done in conjunction with reboring or relining or to produce an "improved" version of the caliber for which the gun was originally chambered.

It is also possible to rechamber for a larger and more powerful cartridge using the same diameter bullets as the original caliber. An example of this would be rechambering a .30/06 to .300 Winchester Magnum.

Relatively little metal is removed in the rechambering process, and for this reason, use of both the "rougher" and "finisher" chambering reamers is not necessary, often just the single finishing reamer is adequate.

Recoil The rearward thrust produced against one's shoulder or hand when a gun is fired. This can be calculated in foot-pounds of energy as an absolute value under standard conditions, but the recoil energy value thus obtained isn't necessarily a true indication of how recoil will *feel* to the shooter. *Apparent* recoil, the "kick" you actually feel, is influenced by many variables. Excessive stock drop will *increase* apparent recoil; increased butt face area will *decrease* it; abnormally heavy muzzle

203

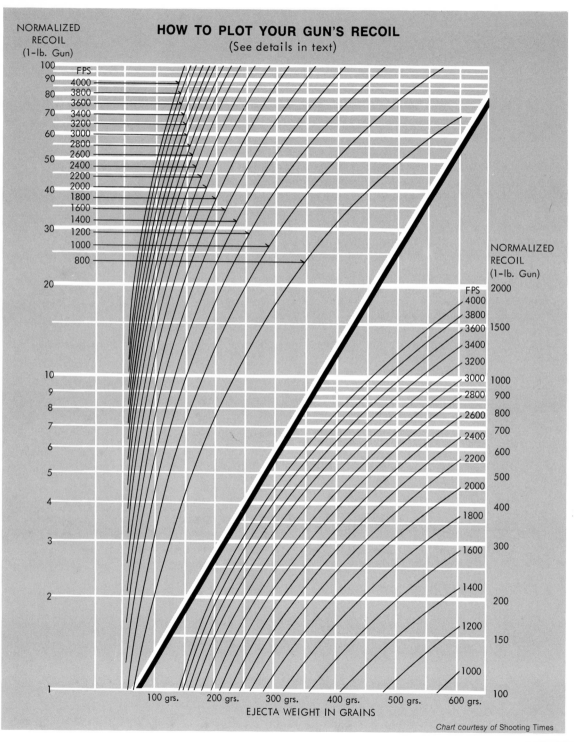

HOW TO PLOT YOUR GUN'S RECOIL
(See details in text)

NORMALIZED RECOIL (1-lb. Gun)

NORMALIZED RECOIL (1-lb. Gun)

EJECTA WEIGHT IN GRAINS

Chart courtesy of Shooting Times

blast and flash will *increase* it. All these effects are there, even though the gun weight, caliber, and load remain the same, thus producing the same absolute recoil energy.

Further, individual tolerance for recoil varies greatly. Some big men *feel* more recoil from a .30/06 than is felt by a 98-pound woman. Twelve-year-old boys have been known to shoot a 12-gauge magnum with far less discomfort than their adult fathers. These differences can't be predicted or measured, yet they exist.

Recoil energy can be calculated for any gun and load if gun weight, muzzle velocity and weight of the ejecta are known. The first two are easy and can be taken from catalogs. The ejecta weight must be calculated, and is the weight of the bullet plus 1½ times the weight of the powder charge.

Since calculation is bothersome, we reproduce here a normalized recoil chart constructed by Paul Jaeger and published in the April 1973 edition of *Shooting Times* magazine. From it you can determine the recoil energy of any gun falling within the velocity (800–4,000 fps) and ejecta weight (100–600 grains) range of the chart.

To use the chart, move across the bottom until you come to the ejecta weight (bullet weight plus 1½ times powder weight) of your load—say the .30/06 150-grain load whose ejecta weight is 225 grains. Then go vertically from that point until you intersect the curved line representing the muzzle velocity—in this case, 2,900 feet per second. Then move right to the recoil scale and read the figure there—135 in our example. This 135 represents the normalized recoil of a 1-pound gun in foot-pounds. As a last step, divide by the weight of your particular gun in pounds, (8) and the result is the recoil (16⅞) of your rifle with that load.

Cartridge	Bullet Weight (Grains)	Average Powder Weight (Grains)	Ejecta Mass
.222 Rem.	50	21	82
.22/250	50	38	107
.243 Win.	80	47	151
.270 Win.	130	55	213
7mm Rem. Mag.	175	67	276
.30/30 Win.	150	35	203
.308 Win.	180	44	246
.30/06	180	50	255
8 x 57 Mauser	165	82	243
.357 Mag.	158	12	176
.38 Spl.	158	5	166
.44 Mag.	240	21	272
.45 ACP	230	5	238

Repeat the process using 7 pounds and 9 pounds for gun weights and you'll see readily that a lighter gun kicks harder, a heavier one lighter.

This procedure may be used with handguns and shotguns as well as rifles. A table of ejecta weights of common calibers and loads is also shown, but if you step outside that abbreviated list, it will be necessary to break down a cartridge and weigh the powder charge. With shotshells, it will be necessary to add the weight of all wads to the shot charge, *then* add 1½ times the powder charge weight to obtain total ejecta weight. Aside from that, the procedure is the same as for rifle or handgun.

The chart allows you to quickly determine absolute recoil energy—but as has already been pointed out, variations in gun stocking and design, and in individual recoil tolerance, are the final determining factors in just how much recoil is actually *felt* by the shooter.

Recoil-Absorbing System A mechanical system attached to, or a part of, the buttstock which absorbs recoil energy by compression of springs or other devices between the buttplate and the stock.

Such devices are seldom encountered in sporting guns, and the only commercially manufactured example is the Hydro-Coil which was first produced independently on a small scale, and briefly offered as an option on some Winchester shotguns and rifles.

In view of the cost and complexity of such devices, as well as their limiting effect on stock styles and materials, they have met with very little favor, and the conventional recoil pad is generally preferred.

At least one gentleman is known to have had his moustache and beard caught tightly and most painfully between the telescoping members of a Hydro-Coil unit.

Recoil Buffer A device often found in military automatic weapons that reduces the impact of recoiling parts upon the receiver or major other components of the gun. In its most common current form (as found in the M16, 5.56mm rifle) the recoil buffer consists of a series of washers and springs which are stacked in a tubular column and struck by the bolt as it nears the limits of its rearward travel, compressing to absorb the bolt energy. It serves not only to reduce secondary recoil forces acting upon the shooter, but also the possibility of damage to recoiling parts by cumulative impacts.

In larger caliber weapons recoil buffers often consist of

hydraulic and compressed-gas mechanisms much more sophisticated in design and function.

Recoil Lug   Generally that surface on the receiver of a rifle or shotgun that transfers the bulk of the recoil forces to the stock. The most common form is found in the Mauser-type, bolt-action design and consists of an integral flange extending downward from the recoil ring directly under the chamber. Its wide, flat surface is closely inletted so that when the gun is fired it transfers all recoil forces to the stock, either directly or through a reinforcement in the wood. The latter may be a bolt, plastic insert, or glass bedding compound.

Recoil lug (arrow) on barrel of Mauser M660 rifle.

Recoil lugs take many forms. In the Krag rifle of 1892–98, the rear surface of its integral box magazine functions as a recoil lug. In single-shot rifles and modern repeating shotguns, the rear face of the receiver acts as the recoil lug. In the modern Remington M700 series of rifles, a separate steel plate clamped between the face of the receiver and the barrel functions as the recoil lug. And, in magnum rifles producing abnormally high recoil, it is fairly common practice to attach a secondary recoil lug of large dimensions on the underside of the barrel well forward of the receiver.

In any event, without an effective means of transferring recoil energy to the stock, it would be impossible to maintain a tight assembly of the wood and metal components under recoil forces sometimes as high as 800 Gs.

Recoil Operation   A gun mechanism in which recoil energy is absorbed and stored in springs and then utilized to cycle the action in a semiautomatic or full automatic mode. The most typical sporting application in long guns is the well-known

Browning "hump-back" autoloading shotgun in which the barrel and bolt, securely locked together during firing, recoil some distance before cams unlock the two and hold the bolt to the rear while the barrel reverses and is forced forward into battery. At that point, the bolt is released to be driven forward by its spring to feed, chamber, and lock—readying the gun for the next firing.

In handguns, probably the most familiar system is found in Colt/Browning M1911 .45 caliber autoloading pistol. Its barrel and slide are locked securely together at the moment of firing, but during the first part of their combined recoil travel, the barrel is pulled downward and unlocked from the slide which then continues rearward of its own momentum, compressing the recoil spring and cocking the hammer. The slide is then driven forward to feed and chamber a fresh round and then pick up the barrel and relock to it and move into battery, ready for firing.

The Browning system is known as long recoil, wherein the barrel recoils more than the cartridge length (several inches); the Colt/Browning system is called short recoil, wherein the barrel recoils only a fraction of an inch.

See also BLOWBACK and GAS OPERATION.

Recoil pad with lattice-work cushion.

Recoil Pad Any nonmechanical device attached to a rifle or shotgun butt to cushion the rearward force of recoil. They are generally made of natural or synthetic rubber which compresses easily.

Functionally, such pads come in two types—those which appear to be solid and contain a layer of spongy material which provides the cushioning, and those of open design in which the cushioning is provided by an open lattice work of narrow rubber strips which collapse under impact. Pads also differ in methods of attachment. The most common type is attached permanently to the butt of the gun by long wood screws. Another type is the slip-on design in which the basic pad is provided with an extended cuff that is slipped over the gun butt to grip it tightly and hold the pad in place.

Regulating The process of adjusting the relationship of the barrels in a double rifle so that both will place their bullets at the same point of impact. It consists mostly of trial shooting interspersed with shifting and resoldering the ribs and wedges between the barrels—a very difficult and time-consuming operation requiring long experience.

It is also performed to a much lesser degree with double-barrelled shotguns in order to place the patterns of both barrels together.

Regulating can be avoided only by fitting separate sets of sights on each barrel—a practice resorted to on turn-barrel muzzle-loaders.

Release Trigger A highly specialized trigger mechanism used on some trap shotguns. It *reverses* normal trigger function in that the trigger must be held rearward as the gun is loaded and cocked, and the gun is fired only when the trigger is *released* and forced forward by the trigger spring.

The release trigger was once widely favored by trap shooters because of alleged advantages of control, ease of firing, reduced possibility of inadvertent firing, etc., but it is seldom seen today.

Reloading Press The device into which assorted dies, priming devices, shell holders, and other accessories are assembled for reloading cartridges. The most common type is the C-frame press which is installed on a bench. It consists of a large casting shaped like the letter "C" at the top, with a mounting flange beneath that, and a massive housing extending below. The top arm of the "C" is threaded to accept dies for case resizing and bullet seating, while the long housing at the bottom holds a large-diameter ram which slides vertically in it and in alignment with the die hole at the top of the press.

O-Type reloading press.

The top of the ram is fitted with a seat for interchangeable shell holders into which a case is placed so it can be primed and loaded by forcing into and out of whatever dies are screwed into the top of the press.

Most presses contain a priming device near the bottom of the C-frame—usually a swinging arm containing a fixed punch and an alignment collar at its upper end to accept a fresh primer. The priming device is pressed forward into a slot in the ram which aligns the primer and punch with the case's primer pocket. Moving the ram downward pulls the case over the primer, seating the latter. The priming arm is usually spring-loaded so that after priming it pops back out of the ram.

Operation of such a press involves first screwing the proper die in position, placing the right shell holder in the top of the ram, and inserting the correct diameter punch and collar in the priming arm. A clean, lubricated case is then placed in the shell holder and the tool handle is moved downward through its full travel, forcing the case fully into the resizing die that contains a punch that drives out the fired primer. The handle is raised to partially extract the case from the die and seat the new primer, then lowered, allowing the priming arm to fly clear of the ram. The handle is then raised through its full travel, lowering the ram and completely withdrawing the case from the die.

C-type press.

H-type reloading press.

When bullet-seating or case-expanding dies are used, a case is simply placed in the shell holder, and then run directly in and out of the dies by movement of the tool handle.

Several other types of reloading presses perform the same operation, using different designs. One is the O-type press, virtually identical to the C-frame, but with the open side of the "C" closed for greater strength and rigidity. Second is the H-type in which the closed "C" or "O" is simply squared off, rotated slightly, and provided with a different form of ram and handle linkage. Less common is the post-type press in which dies are placed in an offset arm attached to a large-diameter vertical column. The foot of the column is fitted with a large base containing a shaft to which the handle and ram linkage are attached. A ram is a close-fitting sliding member surrounding the post

Innumerable variations on the four basic designs exist, but the C-type is by far the most common and generally the most economical, and, in the more massive models, suitable for any reloading operation.

Remington Arms Company The American gun manufacturer established by Eliphalet Remington in 1816 as a manufacturer of rifle barrels and flintlock sporting guns. Today, Remington produces a variety of shotguns and rifles, as well as a complete

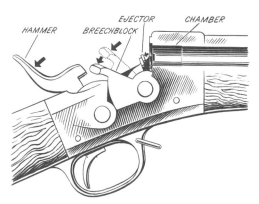

The Remington rolling block action.

line of sporting and military ammunition. It operates its gun plant at Ilion, New York, an old ammunition plant at Bridgeport, Connecticut (where administrative officers are also situated), and a new ammunition plant at Lone Oak, Arkansas. From time to time the company operates government-owned small arms ammunition plants throughout the country.

The Remington .40/90 breechloader was a favorite among professional buffalo hunters.

Since the American Civil War, Remington (under any one of its several names used during the period) has been a principal supplier of sporting and military arms and ammunition. In more recent years, particularly since World War II, it has become probably the most progressive of the old-line arms manufacturers.

Today Remington Arms is a division of the great DuPont industrial complex.

Remington, Eliphalet (1793–1861)   The founder of Remington Arms Company.

Repeater   A manually operated shotgun or rifle (once often applied to handguns, but no longer) containing a supply of extra cartridges which may be quickly and easily loaded into the chamber for fast repeat shots. By manipulation of bolt, lever, or sliding forend, the breech is unlocked and opened, the empty case extracted and ejected, the firing mechanism cocked, the next cartridge in the magazine fed and chambered, and the breech closed and locked. Normally all this is done by two movements of the operating handle, lever, or slide.

Reprime (Recap)   To seat a fresh primer.

Revolver   A handgun in which the cartridges are contained in separate chambers of a cylinder behind the barrel. Cocking the revolver (either by withdrawing the hammer or pulling the trigger) rotates the cylinder and aligns that cartridge and chamber precisely with the barrel, locking the cylinder securely in place for firing. Trigger pressure releases the hammer to fire the cartridge.

Some gap must exist between the forward face of the cylinder and the barrel breech allowing a small percentage of the propelling gases to escape while the bullet is passing through the barrel. A gap of .003 inch is generally required for proper functioning, and as much as .008 to .010 inch is common, though most new, quality revolvers do not exceed .006 inch.

211

Typical single-action revolver.

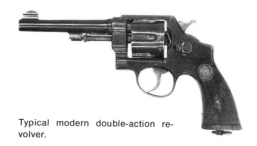

Typical modern double-action revolver.

Limitations in revolver design prevent its use with sharply bottlenecked cartridges operating at relatively high pressures. It is most suitable for straight-walled cartridges, whose lengths must be relatively modest, (no more than 1¾ inches if gun size is to remain manageable). In standard sizes and calibers, revolvers are generally limited to chamber pressures not exceeding 20,000 pounds per square inch. However, in the large magnum calibers, pressures of 40,000- to 45,000 pounds per square inch have been considered acceptable when careful attention is given to selection and heat treatment of cylinder, frame, and barrel.

Single-action revolvers are the oldest form and are mechanically the simplest. They require the hammer to be manually cocked for firing, and are generally of solid-frame construction with the cylinder fixed in place. Fired cases are extracted individually by a rod held under the barrel.

Double-action revolvers *may* be cocked manually but are generally fired by simply pulling the trigger through. This raises the hammer, rotates the cylinder, and then releases the hammer to fire the cartridge.

A basic mechanical difference is that single-action revolvers rotate the cylinder through a hand or pawl connected to the foot of the hammer, while double-action designs do it through a hand or pawl attached to the rear of the trigger.

See SINGLE ACTION; DOUBLE ACTION.

Revolver, Colt Though revolving-cylinder, muzzle-loading arms had been made in small quantities by Collier and others for many years, it remained for Samuel Colt to invent a mechanism that would, combined with the percussion cap, make practical revolvers possible. Colt obtained his first English revolver patent in 1835, and an American one in 1836. Colt's first guns were the various models of "Paterson" revolvers produced at the Paterson, N.J. plant. These were unnecessarily complicated and fragile in design and the company failed in only a short time. Both revolving pistols and shoulder arms were produced.

Colt resumed production in 1847 with an improved, simpler, and much larger gun now called the Walker model and made for the U.S. Dragoons. Though still far from perfect, this model was acceptable and formed the basis for all future Colt percussion arms. The success of the 1847 model made Colt solvent again and further dragoon models (three in all) were developed from the 1847.

In 1849 Colt introduced his Pocket Model, which was the same design scaled down to .31 caliber, and in 1851 his .36 Navy revolver, not quite so small. Later he was able to adapt the Pocket Model to .36 caliber by relatively modest modification and offered it as the Pocket Model of Navy Caliber.

In 1860, the epitome of Colt percussion revolvers was reached in the .44 Model 1860 Army with its creeping lever and graceful streamlining. A similar version was produced in the Navy size. The basic Colt revolver continued unchanged from this point until supplanted by the Model P single-action cartridge revolver in 1873.

Beginning with the Model P, Colt continued to maintain the status it had achieved with percussion guns, in spite of Sam Colt's death in 1862. Improvements in Colt revolers continue to be introduced regularly today, and since 1900 Colt has been the principal American manufacturer of autoloading pistols as well.

Rib A raised portion on top of the barrel which may serve as a sight base, or simply be decorative.

Rifle Stock The rear member of a rifle, usually of wood, sometimes plastic, which attaches to the breech or barrel assembly and provides a means for holding the gun to the shoulder. Basically, there are four parts of the stock that affect fit and feel to the shooter—the comb, cheeckpiece, pistol grip, and forend. See illustration below.

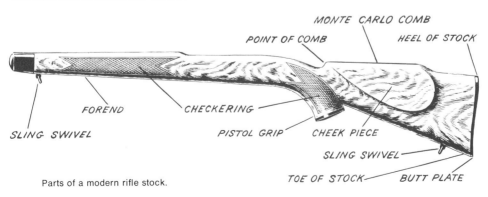

Parts of a modern rifle stock.

Rifling The spiral grooves in a barrel which impart spin or rotation to the bullet to stabilize it in flight.

Rifling may take many forms, but in general the diameter of the grooves at their deepest point is approximately equal to the diameter of the bullets to use, and thus the raised lands between the grooves actually cut into the bullet, and force it to rotate as it passes down the barrel. Any number of grooves may be used, the fewest commonly encountered being the two-groove rifling of some replacement Springfield rifle barrels used during World War II—and the most is twenty or more found in some forms of multigroove rifling. In conventional sporting guns over .22 caliber, grooves are generally nominally .004 inch deep.

Typical 8-groove rifling viewed down the bore.

Rifling may be formed in several manners. Traditionally, each groove is cut by a hook-type cutting tool carried through the bore on the end of a rod—with numerous passes required to cut each groove to proper depth. A modern variation of this method uses a broach that contains a row of several successively higher cutting edges for each groove and which cuts all grooves to proper depth and twist in a single pass through the barrel.

Two other rifling methods do not require any metal to be cut away, one of which is commonly called "button rifling," and is accomplished by forcing a very hard (usually tungsten carbide) "button" through the bore. The surface of the button contains a negative impression of the rifling and displaces (rather than cuts) metal to form the grooves. The other, and most recent, is "hammer-forged" rifling in which a short pierced billet of barrel steel is placed over a mandrel (rod) containing a negative impression of the rifling—and then forged down over the rifling and formed to proper length and profile.

When properly and carefully done, all four methods produce extremely accurate bores.

See also REBORING.

Rimfire A cartridge which has its primer sealed in and around the rim of its case. The firing pin of a gun striking any part of the rim will ignite the primer charge. Popular examples of rimfire cartridges are the .22 short, .22 long, .22 long rifle, .22 Magnum, and 5mm Remington Rimfire Magnum.

See also CENTERFIRE and PRIMER.

Rolling Block A common type of early single-shot, breech-loading action, generally for a rifle. Both breech block and hammer are pivoted below the level of the barrel, and when the breech is closed and the hammer down, a portion of the hammer rides under and supports a locking shoulder on the rear of the breech block. The simplest full-strength single-shot action ever devised, the rolling block was manufactured in tremendous quantity for world-wide sale by Remington from 1865 to the 1930s under patents by Leonard Geiger (1863) and Joseph Rider (1864).

See REMINGTON ARMS COMPANY.

Round A single, complete loaded cartridge.

Ruger The name by which the firm of Sturm, Ruger & Company, Southport, Connecticut, and also Newport, New Hampshire, is generally known. This company entered the firearms industry in 1949 by introducing a very simple but reliable blowback .22 rimfire autoloading pistol, which is still in production today.

Production followed with frontier-style, single-action revolvers (first in rimfire and later in centerfire) bolt-action and single-shot rifles, double-action magnum revolvers, and shotguns.

The driving force behind Sturm, Ruger & Company, has been William Ruger, well-known in the arms industry. Ruger was personally responsible for most of the design work on the earlier models, and still maintains very close personal control over the company and all its activities.

Sturm, Ruger has been the most successful of any *new* firearms manufacturer in this country since the 1870s.

Running Game, Shooting   There are many theories for shooting fast-moving game such as deer, antelope, or jack rabbits, but all amount to "shoot where he *will* be, not where he *is*."

For a given situation in which game speed, angle of travel, range, and bullet velocity are known, a precise lead can be calculated—but this isn't possible in the field. In actual practice, the shooter simply establishes the amount of lead that *looks* right to him and fires. Apparently, not two people see lead quite the same. On identical shots, one man may claim a 15-foot lead, while another will insist he "held right on." The former is generally true when a sustained lead is established, the rifle swung steadily ahead of the target then fired. The latter is true where the gun is "swung through" the animal from behind, then fired as it passes over the target point on the animal. In this instance, the lead is still present, but not so apparent to the shooter.

Regardless of what the shooter might *think* he sees at the instant of firing, the bullet must be directed at a point in space ahead of the moving target.

Ruptured (Separated) Case   A case pulled into two parts just forward of the head; normally caused by excess headspace or repeated incorrect resizing.

S

Safety   Any device activated manually or automatically which prevents accidental or inadvertent firing of any gun. Normally refers to a manually operated lever or button which, when engaged, mechanically blocks sear, hammer, or firing pin, or any combination thereof.

See Grip Safety.

Safety Lever   Sometimes called a safety block or transfer bar. In a modern revolver, a movable bar which prevents the hammer from striking the firing pin unless the trigger is deliberately pulled. Some function by mechanically blocking hammer movement, others by providing a mechanical link between hammer face and firing pin.

Scabbard   A leather sheath into which a rifle is placed for carrying on horseback.

Scatter Load   A shotshell load designed to produce a wider and less dense pattern than a standard load. Scatter loads are used by hunters going after small or upland game in thick cover and at very close ranges, and with a gun that is not necessarily bored specifically for this type of shooting. This type of hunting requires an abnormally broad pattern. Where a conventional load in a modified-choke barrel might produce an 18-inch pattern at 15 yards, a scatter load will be double that pattern. This greatly reduced pattern density also reduces occurrences of mangled game.

Several approaches have been used to produce scatter loads: One consists of dividing the shot into several segments by thin cardboard strips or discs, another uses a post protruding up into the shot charge from the wad column. All seem equally successful in widening the radial dispersion of the shot charge as it leaves the muzzle.

Schnabel   On a rifle or shotgun, a flaring of the forend tip to form a sculptured knob. Purely decorative, it was developed in Central Europe.
See FOREND.

Scope Mount   Any mechanical device for attaching a telescopic sight to any gun, usually a rifle. Mounts generally consist of a base (or bases) attached permanently by screws to the gun's receiver and machined to accept rings or clamps which attach to the tubular body of the telescope. Mounts are then generally classified as to fixed or quick-detachable, allowing easy removal of scope; swing-over, permitting scope to be pivoted aside; top or side design, according to location on receiver; fixed or adjustable for windage and/or elevation; fully adjustable (for nonadjustable scopes); and also often by height.

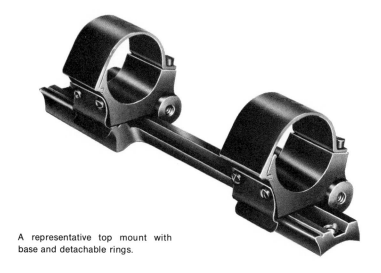

A representative top mount with base and detachable rings.

The most common type is the thick top mount with opposed-screw adjustment for windage only, using two rings to secure the scope, and the scope and rings may be readily removed with only a coin or screwdriver to make auxiliary sights available.

Sear The part or device which serves to engage the hammer, striker, or other firing device and hold it in the cocked position until firing is desired. A sear must be of good design and material since loads imposed on it are quite high. The sear is disengaged to cause firing by trigger movement.

Season Crack A longitudinal crack or split in a cartridge case, usually in the neck directly over the seated bullet. It generally results from the case neck being held in an excessive state of tension by the bullet inside it. The maximum amount of tension that can be tolerated is dependent directly upon the ductility and hardness of the case. A case neck which is abnormally hard has little tolerance for tension and is therefore most likely to crack. A softer case will withstand such stresses almost indefinitely.

Season cracks are seldom found in modern factory and arsenal-loaded ammunition because of the high degree of quality control. However, repeated reloading work hardens the brass at the neck until it reaches the point where cracks may occur only a few days or weeks after the bullet has been seated. This problem can be eliminated by periodic annealing of case necks.

See also ANNEALING CASE, CARTRIDGE CASE, METALLIC.

Sectional Density A mathematical factor, generally expressed as a three-place decimal figure, representing the ratio of bullet weight (mass) to its cross-sectional area. Major independent manufacturers list the sectional density for each of their bullets, but it is easily calculated. It is simply the weight of the bullet in pounds, divided by the area of the bullet base in square inches.

Sectional density has no relation to bullet shape or length. All .30 caliber (.308-inch diameter) bullets weighing 200 grains will have a sectional density of .301, even though one may be very blunt and relatively short while the other is needle-pointed and 20 per cent longer.

The greater a bullet's sectional density, the lesser will be its rate of velocity loss due to drag, and the deeper will be its penetration in a target. Consequently, bullets having relatively high sectional density for their caliber are preferred for long-range shooting (high velocity retention) and for use on large, dangerous game (increased penetration). However, the greater the sectional density, the greater the chamber pressure produced, hence the lower will be the velocity due to safety limitations. As a result, unusually long, heavy bullets (in the medium-caliber range—.270-.32—with sectional densities above .300) are seldom used, only those with sectional densities in the vicinity of .225-.275 are common.

Sectional density also plays an important part in determining the proper burning rate of powder and amount that may be used in a given cartridge.

Sensitivity   Referring to a primer, a measure of its ability to be ignited by a certain amount of firing pin energy.

Set Trigger   A trigger firing mechanism which does not engage the sear, hammer, or firing pin directly—instead, a separate, miniature hammer-type firing mechanism is interposed between the trigger and the main firing mechanism.

Pressure on a separate lever or forward pressure on the main trigger cocks this mechanism, so that when the main trigger is moved, the set mechanism "fires" and its hammer or lever strikes the sear or other linkage to cause the main firing mechanism to act.

The set trigger mechanism reduces the weight of pull on the main trigger to much less than can be obtained *safely* with direct trigger engagement.

In addition, some set triggers function in less time than is required for a direct linkage. This is not universally true, but is so in best-quality triggers.

See also DOUBLE-SET TRIGGER, LOCK TIME, and SINGLE-SET TRIGGER.

Sharps, Christian (1811–1874)   Designer of several successful firearms, principally the big side-hammer percussion, breechloading carbine of Civil War vintage which used a linen cartridge—later refined to handle conventional rimfire centerfire cartridges.

During the 1870s, heavy Sharps rifles became the most sought-after of the so-called "buffalo rifles." Sharps eventually produced what is considered to be the epitome of American

The famous .45/120/550 "Buffalo" Sharps rifle.

single-shot rifles—the hammerless model of 1878, commonly called the Sharps-Borchardt.

Today, few Sharps rifles survive, and all models are considered valuable collector's items.

See also BORCHARDT, HUGO, "SHARPS-BORCHARDT RIFLE," and SHARPS RIFLE.

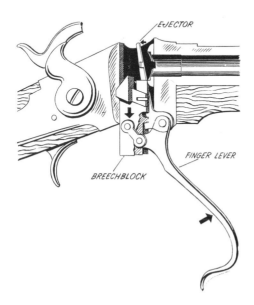

The Sharps falling-block action.

Sheep, Big Horn, Guns For   See MOUNTAIN HUNTING, GUNS FOR.

Shooting Preserve
Whether for private or public use, the preserve consists essentially of a sizable parcel of land upon which game of properly chosen species is raised and periodically released. When shooting preserves are properly designed, stocked, and managed, they produce an extremely close approximation of "natural" hunting.

Unfortunately, not all preserves are operated properly, and the so-called "put-and-take" practice used by some preserves amounts to little more than game being placed directly in front of shooters' guns, subjecting shooting preserves to some criticism.

Why preserves? They are simply the logical outgrowth of the decreasing amount of publicly owned lands available for hunting. Free access to public and private land and natural replenishment of wild game can no longer support the number of hunters in existence today.

There are many hundreds of excellent shooting preserves in this country. Those wishing to learn their names and locations may obtain a directory from the National Shooting Sports Foundation, 1075 Post Road, Riverside, Connecticut 06878.

Shooting Stake A rest for rifle shooting in the field, generally a pointed stake with an adjustable shelf on which the forend is rested.

Short Action In a rifle, one whose bolt and receiver are designed for shorter-than-standard cartridges. In a revolver, a modification to reduce hammer and trigger travel to the minimum, thus reducing lock time and cocking time.

Shot In the earliest days of firearms, shot referred to virtually any projectile, regardless of size and without differentiation as to number of projectiles fired simultaneously. With the advent of rifling, the term "bullet" replaced shot in reference to single projectiles fired through a rifled barrel.

Today the term shot is applied to single-projectile ammunition only in reference to large-caliber military weapons intended for piercing armor, for example, "shot, APC (armor-piercing capped)," or "shot, APDS (armor-piercing, discarding sabot)."

In sporting arms, the word shot applies to the spherical lead pellets loaded into shotgun shells.

Shot has always been made and formed into those neat little balls by pouring molten lead through a perforated plate and allowing it to fall quite some distance during which time individual droplets are formed into spheres by surface tension. The balls, still relatively soft, fall into water and are cooled and hardened.

Early shot was of pure, soft lead and was superseded by lead hardened by adding a small percentage of antimony. With the coming of the hardened shot, pure lead shot became known as "drop" shot and the harder variety became identified as "chilled" shot.

Chilled shot resists deformation in the barrel, and also in game, thus it generally produces better patterns and is considered best for use on large furred or feathered game. When preventing shot deformation becomes particularly important, plating the individual pellets with copper or nickel is common, despite its considerably higher cost.

Shot comes in a variety of sizes from number 12 to 000 buck. Up to the small buckshot sizes, the method of manufacture already described is normally used. In the larger sizes, individual pellets are formed between two cup-shaped dies in what is known as a cold-heading machine; it clips short sections of lead wire and squeezes them to shape.

In recent years there has been much controversy over the death of migratory waterfowl from ingesting expended lead shot which has accumulated in their feeding grounds. Ingestion of such shot during feeding produces a form of lead poisoning which eventually causes death. Today, there is much activity directed at developing a suitable substitute for lead shot which will not produce the same effects on game.

Soft steel shot appears to be the most acceptable; it eliminates the lead-poisoning problem and produces reasonably good ballistic and killing results. However, it is much more costly and does some damage to gun barrels. Eventually steel shot may become an acceptable replacement for lead shot.

Shotgun Cleaning Cleaning procedures for shotguns are no different than those for rifles and other firearms. The one additional problem that does occur is occasional heavy leading of the bore—usually in the forcing cone or at the beginning of the choke—when loads not containing a shot protector are fired.

Dozens of methods have been described in various publications for removing such an accumulation of lead. If lead deposits have accumulated over a long period, and are perhaps partially bonded to the bore with rust in between, complete

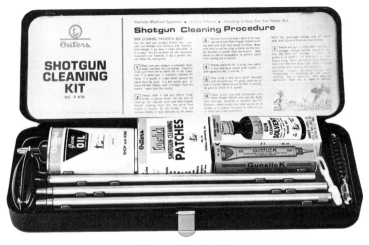

Shotgun cleaning kit.

removal is quite difficult whatever the means. However, if the gun is checked visually after each shooting session, lead accumulations are easily removed by using a tight fitting, brass-bristle bore brush. In particularly stubborn cases, a few strands of fine steel wool wrapped around the brush and rubbed vigorously (and only over the lead deposits) will remove them.

It is probably more important in a shotgun than with any other type to avoid excessive amounts of oil and lubricants in the bore and action which can easily penetrate a paper shotshell or an often-reloaded plastic shell causing misfires or substandard performance. Metallic cartridges are not quite as susceptible.

It is especially important that waterfowling guns are thoroughly cleaned after each use even to the extent of complete disassembly, because of their abnormally high exposure to moisture.

See also Gun Cleaning.

Shotgun, Double See Double-Barrelled Guns.

Shotgun Shooting Ideally, somewhat different guns are required for various types of shooting. A gun for upland game is fitted with a fairly short stock with moderate to large drop, a short (not over 26-inch) barrel bored rather open. On the other hand a waterfowling gun will have a straighter and longer stock, a longer (30-inch) and more tightly choked barrel, and will be heavier to absorb the recoil of powerful, long-range loads.

A trap gun will be stocked quite straight and long, with a long (over 30 inches) and very tightly choked barrel. A skeet gun is just the opposite. It has a short stock with plenty of drop, and a short, loosely choked barrel.

With a shotgun, one engages in area shooting rather than point shooting. The object is to place a relatively large pattern, or blanket, of many shot over the entire target. Rifled arms require placing a single projectile at a precise point on the target.

See Duck Gun; Skeet; Trap.

Shotgun Stock Since shotguns are pointed rather than aimed, and used for area rather than point shooting, and that shooting is done very quickly, stock dimensions and fit to the individual are important. Most shotgunners see only the barrel or front sight in relationship to the target, thus the eye itself becomes the rear sight, and its position relative to the centerline(s) of the barrels becomes very important.

If the eye is too high, the gun will shoot high, and vice versa. If the eye is too far left, the gun will shoot left, and vice versa.

The top line of the comb against which the shooters cheek rests controls the position of the eye in relation to the barrels. Thus the height and angle of the comb are critical, as is its deviation right or left of center. Since the dimensions and shape

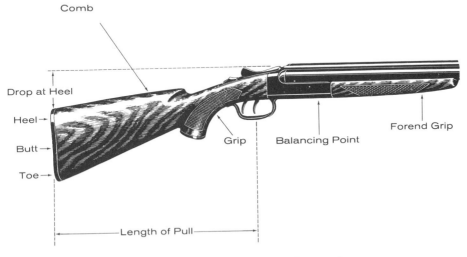

Comb

Drop at Heel

Heel →

Butt →

Toe →

Grip

Balancing Point

Forend Grip

Length of Pull

of every shooter's face and neck are different, the comb must be shaped and positioned accordingly to align the eye correctly.

Pitch and pull also affect shooting accuracy and require individual adjustments.

Some autoloading guns place part of the mechanism in the stock, and this limits the shape and dimensions to some extent.

See CAST; COMB; DROP; MONTE CARLO COMB; PITCH; PULL.

Shot Pattern The dispersion made by all of the individual shot pellets of a shotshell fired generally at the center of a large sheet of paper, or, in some instances, at a metal plate coated lightly with white lead.

When the metal plate is used, pellets simply strike and drop off, leaving their impact points marked by smears of lead and the white coating knocked off of the plate. While not as portable, the plate system is by far the simplest and quickest to use. In either case, the resulting pattern of marks or holes presents the entire shot charge as if it were in a single plane, which it is not.

Examination of shot patterns serves several useful purposes. First, it enables one to determine whether the center of the pattern is aligned with the center of aim. Then, corrections can be made, or at least one can hold off sufficiently to center the pattern on the target. Contrary to popular belief, many

Patterns of Various Shotshells

Size No.	Diameter (inches)	Pellets in 1 ounce	Size No.	Diameter (inches)	Pellets in 1 ounce
12	.05	2385			
11	.06	1380	Air Rifle	.175	55
10	.07	868	*BB	.18	50
*9	.08	585	BBB	.19	42
*8	.09	409	T	.20	40
*7½	.095	345	TT	.21	35
7	.10	299	TTT (or F)	.22	30
*6	.11	223	TTTT (or FF)	.23	27
5	.12	172	4 Buck	.24	21
*4	.13	136	3 Buck	.26	18½
3	.14	109	2 Buck	.27	15
*2	.15	88	1 Buck	.30	11
1	.16	73	0 Buck	.32	9
B	.17	59	00 Buck	.33	8½

shotguns may place the centers of their patterns a foot or more away from the point of aim.

Second, examination determines the pattern percentage delivered by a particular gun/choke/load combination. This is done by shooting the pattern at 40 yards (standard for all except skeet guns) and then placing a 30-inch circle (made from wire or inscribed upon plastic sheet) over the densest portion of the pattern, counting the number of pellets that fall within the ring, and then calculating what percentage they are of the total charge.

It is also possible to superimpose a silhouette of game or target over a shot pattern and determine whether the pattern is dense enough to insure clean kills.

Pattern shape and density are affected by many factors, among them choke type and degree of constriction, forcing cone dimensions, individual loads, shot size, wad type and material, velocity, interior bore finish, and numerous unidentified variables.

It is impossible to predict what pattern will be produced by a particular load in any gun, and identical guns may produce substantially different patterns with identical loads. Consequently, the only way to determine what a given combination will produce in the field is to shoot and evaluate a large number of shot patterns.

See CHOKE and SHOT STRING.

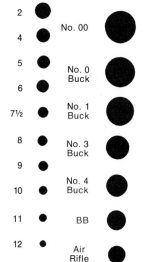

Shot Placement Placing one's bullet in the most desired portion of the target. When hunting big game or edible small game, proper shot placement consists of causing the bullet to strike in a vital area without producing excessive tissue destruction.

In the case of edible small game, this almost invariably means striking the brain or spine. In large game, where retention of an undamaged trophy is often of paramount interest, the head or brain shot is not acceptable and other vital areas must be chosen.

On relatively easily killed species of medium-sized game, the areas most often chosen are the neck and heart/lungs region. The neck shot is only for experts, because the bullet must strike or sever the spinal column and that target is quite small. A precise knowledge of the anatomy and bone structure of a particular species is required for correct placement of a neck shot. This leaves the average hunter with only the heart/ lungs area as his target. It is relatively large, even in the smaller species, and easily located on a broadside or head-on view of the animal.

In the larger, particularly dangerous species, the same vital areas are involved, but the animal's possible behavior sometimes dictates that a nonfatal area be struck first to immobilize the animal. Generally speaking, the breaking of one or both shoulders is considered the best immobilizing shot, with breaking down the rear quarters a fair second choice.

Both shots require cartridges capable of quite deep penetration. While these vital areas are easily located on broadside or frontal views of the animal, such opportunities are few. When the shot must be taken at any other angle—and that's most of the time—it is essential that the hunter know the location of the animal's vital organs and then to visualize the proper point within the animal's body and aim at that point, rather than any point outside.

Most four-footed animals have the heart/lung region centered roughly one-third of the distance up from the belly line and on a line with the rear edges of the forelegs or shoulders at that point. No matter what angle the animal might be viewed from, this imaginary point, low between the forelegs, must be the aiming point. Even if an animal is headed directly away from the gun, this is still the point which should be struck for a quick, clean kill.

The same approach must be taken toward an immobilizing shot. The major bones and joints which must be broken to immobilize the animal must be the internal point of aim, without regard to the body surface.

Shot placement may be considered the most important single aspect of hunting marksmanship. Poorly placed bullets will sometimes produce quick kills, but will more likely produce a crippled animal which escapes either to die a lingering death from the wound itself, or to become disabled and eventually die of starvation and exposure. Unless the hunter is lost and starving, there is no acceptable excuse for improper shot placement. If the circumstances at a given time preclude *proper* shot placement, then the shot simply should not be taken.

Shot Selection See SHOT.

Shot String The elongation (along the line of flight) of a shot charge in flight. Shot charge behavior is most commonly visualized in the form of a disc, perpendicular to the line of flight, as it travels through the air. Instead, the shot charge is dispersed much more longitudinally than it is laterally. It assumes the shape of an elongated egg as it travels through the air. The length of the charge may be as much as 15 or 16 *feet!*

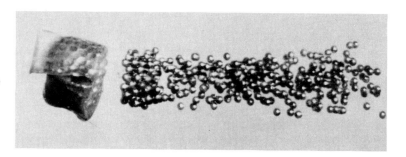

Shot string beginning to elongate shortly after leaving muzzle.

Theoretically, a long shot string compensates somewhat for errors in leading a moving target, but at the same time it causes fewer shot pellets to strike the target — while a very short shot string places the maximum number of pellets on target, it makes more precise aiming and leading necessary.

Side Lever An unlocking lever located on the side of the receiver, found only on older guns and recent low-cost single-barrelled guns.

Side Lock A form of firing mechanism used primarily in side-by-side, double-barrelled shotguns, but found occasionally in other types, including combination guns, multiple-barrelled guns, and double-barrelled rifles.

Essentially the side lock is simply a modernized and refined version of the traditional bar lock but with the hammer transferred to the *inside* of the lock plate. Thus, all moving parts of the lock are located on the inside of the lock plate, working in recesses in the stock, completely enclosed, and with the entire outer surface of the lock plate exposed.

Traditionally the side lock utilizes integral firing pins formed upon the hammers, though some modern versions use striking hammers with separate, short firing pins situated in the standing breech.

A modern side-lock double; lock plates extend well back into stock.

The advantages of the side lock are ease of care and cleaning. Typically they may be lifted out in their entirety after removal of one or more retaining screws. Some more costly versions may be held in place by concealed lips and catches, dispensing with the lock screws.

The side lock's main disadvantage is that it requires a great amount of wood to be cut away at the weakest part of the stock, thus making the stock even weaker and more susceptible to breakage. Also, the inletting for a side lock (when done properly) is much more costly and time consuming than for other types; the side lock unit itself is more costly to produce than an equally satisfactory box lock or some other type of firing mechanism.

The most modern shotgun side lock represents the highest degree of refinement of the traditional bar lock dating back to the early days of the flintlock period.

During the transition from muzzle- to breech-loading and into the early 20th century side locks appeared with external hammer, but the hammers were gradually dispensed with and today are used only in certain specialty items.

The most modern shotgun side lock represents the highest degree of refinement of the traditional bar lock dating back to the early days of the flintlock period.

See also Bar Lock.

Sighting In   The basic process of aligning the rifle sight—whether metallic or telescopic—so that the line of sight intersects the trajectory of the bullet at the chosen range. When done properly, the bullet will strike precisely on the point of aim, at least within the accuracy capability of the gun and cartridge.

See also Bore Sight and Zeroing.

Sighting In

SIGHTING IN A BOLT-ACTION RIFLE

1. Place target at 25 yards. Rest rifle solidly on a rolled tent or other support and remove bolt. Look through bore and align bull's-eye in center of bore. Then look through scope and adjust windage and elevation crosshairs so they also center on bull's-eye.

2. Replace bolt, and fire three test shots.

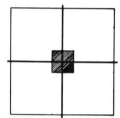

3. Draw lines between the three bullet holes and mark center of the group. Then adjust elevation knob so horizontal crosshair bisects the center of the group.

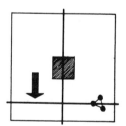

4. Adjust windage knob on the scope so the vertical crosshair bisects the center of the group. With cartridge of approximately 3,000-foot-seconds velocity, the rifle is now sighted in at just over 200 yards.

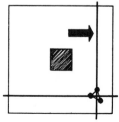

Sight Insert   An interchangeable blade or element used in a target-type, hooded front rifle sight. Such a sight is provided with a circular seat which will accept a metal or plastic ring into which is placed a wide variety of shapes and sizes of sighting elements, allowing the shooter to choose the one best suited to the range, target, and lighting conditions encountered.

Typical target front sight with various inserts.

A few open-type front sights have also been offered with interchangeable inserts or sighting elements, but none have ever become popular or achieved wide distribution.

Sight Radius   The distance between the front and rear elements of a metallic sight system. It is measured from the rear face of the front sight to the rear face of the rear sight. Generally speaking, the greater the sighting radius, the more accurately the sights may be aligned, and the less human error will exist.

Sights, Iron   Metallic sighting instruments, both open as well as aperture-type receiver sights. Basically there are four types of iron rear sights. One is the notch, either in the form of a V or a U. The second type employs a flat unnotched bar with the center located by a white line or diamond (relatively rare). The third is a hole, or "peep." Fourth is the Patridge type of open rear sight, which uses a square cut to be employed with a square-blade front sight.

See also PATRIDGE SIGHT and APERTURE SIGHT.

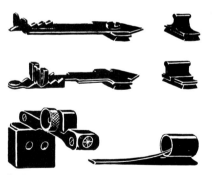

(1) The standard iron rear sight combined with a bead front sight. (2) An improved rear sight with adjustable V notch and removable bead front sight. (3) Peep-type rear sight with hooded front sight.

Sights, Telescopic   A magnifying telescope mounted on a rifle (also occasionally a shotgun or pistol) in alignment with the centerline of the bore and fitted with an aiming point (reticle). When the aiming point is placed on the target the bullet will strike the point of aim.

231

The telescopic sight offers several advantages over even the best of metallic sights. Its magnification makes it possible to identify and aim accurately at small targets at long ranges and under poor light conditions. Moreover, the eye need not continuously shuttle back and forth between two elements as in aperture sights or three as in open metallic sights. The telescope presents the target and the reticle (aiming-point) image in essentially the same optical plane, allowing the eye to focus only at that one point to obtain a clear, sharp sight picture.

The telescopic sight improves the hitting ability of the shooter with perfect vision, but in the case of an individual with poor eyesight, it makes accurate aiming possible where iron sights could not be used at all.

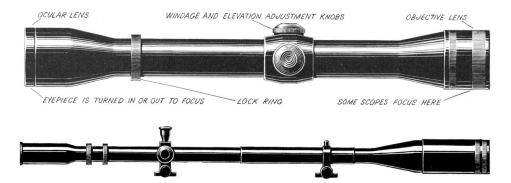

Hunting scope sight (above), and varmint and target scope.

Telescopic sights are precisely adjustable for alignment and zeroing. In a few target and hunting sights, adjustments for windage and elevation are accomplished in their mounts. The typical scope, however, contains a very precise click adjustment which moves the reticle cell by means of finely threaded internal stems attached to knobs fitted to the outside of the scope body. Adjustments as precise as ¼ or ⅛ MOA (minute of angle) are common, and the more costly target and varmint scopes often have 1/12 or finer increments of adjustment.

Two types of scopes are currently in wide use—the fixed-magnification and the variable. Fixed-power scopes may be found in many magnifications from as little as 1½X up through 30X; variable-power types are most common in the ranges 2½X–7X and 3X–9X, with a few available in 4X–12X range. In the fixed variety, the 4X and 6X are by far the most popular, with 3X–9X being the most common among the variables.

Eye relief is particularly important in installing a telescopic sight on a rifle or heavy recoil. If eye relief is too short, the eyepiece might strike the shooter's face during recoil. Generally, the lower the magnification, the greater the eye relief possible.

Telescopic sights must be strongly built to withstand repeated recoil loads as high as 800G. In addition, they must be tightly sealed to prevent entry of atmospheric moisture and dirt. Most modern scopes are also purged of air and filled with an inert dry gas (mainly nitrogen) under slight positive pressure.

See also EYE RELIEF, RETICLE, and SCOPE MOUNT.

Single Action   A revolver design which requires the hammer to be cocked manually for each shot. Also an autoloading pistol design which requires manual cocking of the hammer for the first shot with cocking for subsequent shots in any given series being accomplished by slide motion.

See also REVOLVER.

Single-Base Powder   Smokeless small arms propellant powder composed primarily of nitrocellulose and not containing nitroglycerin.

Single-Set Trigger   A trigger system wherein one fingerpiece protrudes into the guard and the gun may be fired by a single, relatively heavy, rearward pressure, or alternatively, the fingerpiece may be pushed forward thereby cocking an internal hammer, after which very light rearward pressure on the same

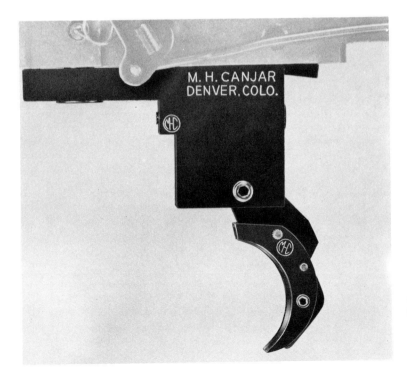

Canjar single-set trigger. Fingerpiece is pushed forward to set.

233

fingerpiece will release the internal hammer to strike and disengage the sear.

The primary function is to permit an unusually light trigger pull (as low as an ounce or two) with safety.

See also DOUBLE-SET TRIGGER.

Single-Stage Trigger   A trigger whose movement is limited and whose resistance increases smoothly until firing results, as opposed to a double-stage trigger where resistance and movement are in two distinctly different stages.

Single Trigger   In a double-barrelled shotgun, a firing mechanism consisting of one trigger which, with successive pulls, will fire first one barrel, then the other. There are two types, selective and non-selective. The former is fitted with a selector button or lever (which may actually be the thumb safety button) that in one position causes the right barrel (or lower barrel in an over-under gun) to be fired first, and in the other position causes the left (or upper) barrel to be fired first.

The non-selective single trigger functions in a set sequence which cannot be changed, and generally fires the right (or lower) barrel first.

Single triggers are of two basic design types: The purely mechanical one uses a cam or ratchet-operated system for engaging the sear of the second barrel after the first is fired; the inertia type uses a floating block moved by recoil to re-engage the second sear. The inertia type is the least reliable, inasmuch as it is dependent upon a certain minimum recoil influence which may not always be achieved with light loads or when the gun is lightly held.

If the type is not known, it can be determined simply by opening the barrels and cocking the gun, and pulling the trigger. If *only* one firing pin is released by two consecutive trigger pulls, the design is activated by an inertia block; if *both* firing pins are released by two consecutive pulls of the trigger, it is a mechanical design.

Sizing (Case) Lubricant   A high-film-strength lubricant applied sparingly to cases to ease passage through resizing dies.

Skeet Stock   A shotgun buttstock with considerable drop and short pull designed specifically for skeet shooting.

Sling A strap usually attached to a rifle, though sometimes found on shotguns as well, which may be purely a carrying aid, or used to aid in target shooting, or a combination of the two.

A carrying sling need only be a leather or cloth strip attached near the butt end and to the underside of the forend near its tip, or in European fashion, to a small stud soldered to the barrel ahead of the forend tip. So long as the carrying sling has sufficient slack or "belly" to comfortably go over the hunter's shoulder while the rifle dangles against his back, no system of adjustment is required.

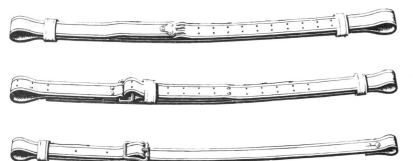

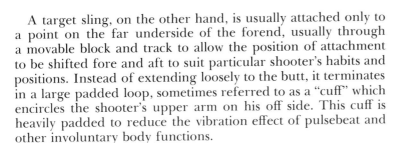

Whalen sling (top), military (center) and carrying strap.

A target sling, on the other hand, is usually attached only to a point on the far underside of the forend, usually through a movable block and track to allow the position of attachment to be shifted fore and aft to suit particular shooter's habits and positions. Instead of extending loosely to the butt, it terminates in a large padded loop, sometimes referred to as a "cuff" which encircles the shooter's upper arm on his off side. This cuff is heavily padded to reduce the vibration effect of pulsebeat and other involuntary body functions.

The target sling is fitted with minute adjustments in the form of peg or friction locks and keepers so that the cuff-to-attachment distance may be carefully regulated to suit the individuals physical dimensions and the shooting position involved.

The combination sling—suitable both for carrying and as an aid to accuracy—is probably best typified by the U.S. military variety. In its current form, it consists of an adjustable loop of heavy leather or flexible cloth webbing which is attached to the forend. Attached to the rear of this loop through a square metal ring is a single strap which passes also through the rear sling swivel or attachment point on the butt and is then attached back to itself through a buckle which provides some further adjustment in overall length. To make ready for carrying, the upper loop is simply lengthened by its adjustment device to provide sufficient slack to reach around the carrier's shoulder.

To prepare for target use, the rear section is either disengaged completely, or all its slack is let out, then the rear portion of the forward loop is placed around the upper and off arm and the sling is adjusted to the proper length—after which the adjustment device or a separate keeper is moved back against the arm to prevent the sling from sliding.

Most shooters today consider a carrying-type sling almost indispensable for big-game hunting. As an aid to accuracy, the properly adjusted shooting sling is far more effective than many believe. A first-class competitive shooter with a top-flight gun and ammunition will often be able to shoot groups from a prone position with a sling as close as he can with the same equipment and ammunition from a bench rest.

Two swivels above are plain types, two below are detachable.

Sling Swivel   The name given to the loops of metal rod through which slings are attached to guns. Actually, "swivel" is a misnomer, since none of these devices are actually capable of swiveling. At most, some pivot on two axes, while many move in only one.

Two basic types exist, identified by the ease by which they may be removed from the gun: the fixed types, which are permanently attached to their bases or attaching screws, and the quick-detachable types in which the loops are connected to separate bases by a quick-release mechanism, allowing the sling and loops to be removed while the bases remain permanently installed.

Small Bore   In general target-shooting parlance, a term indicating the .22 rimfire cartridge and guns chambered for it. In traditional British terminology, small bore may mean a centerfire hunting rifle/cartridge of any size under the .375 Magnum Holland & Holland, because small-bore rifles were considered suitable only for the taking of light and medium game in Africa and India, and the term big bore was applied only to those massive cartridges considered suitable for elephant, rhino, buffalo, etc.

See also BIG BORE.

Smith, Horace (1808–1893)   One of the two original founders of the Smith and Wesson Revolver Company in 1854. Born in Cheshire, Mass., an expert machinist and inventor, he was employed in the late 1840s by Allen, Brown, and Luther where he met D. B. Wesson. In 1851 Smith patented a breech-loading mechanism which was combined with B. Tyler Henry's patent to produce a lever-action repeating pistol in partnership with D. B. Wesson. In 1855 they formed the Volcanic Repeating

Arms Co. to attract capital for continued production of the same guns. In 1856 Smith left Volcanic to work as a gunsmith, and then in 1857 renewed the partnership with Wesson to produce a small .22 rimfire revolver and improved cartridge. This gun, and the Rollin White patents on which it was based, gave Smith & Wesson a monopoly on cartridge revolvers until 1869 when the patents expired. Smith retired in 1873. The company formed by him and D. B. Wesson survives today, one of the world's largest handgun producers.

See HENRY, B. TYLER; WESSON, D. B.

Smokeless Powder   The modern propellant for all small arms ammunition, invented in the middle 1880s and first used widely in this country in the early 1890s, beginning with the U.S. .30/40 service rifle cartridge in 1892.

Smokeless powder is a fuel which burns efficiently without external oxygen—as opposed to gasoline, a fuel which requires addition of atmospheric oxygen for proper combustion.

Single-base powder is composed basically of nitrated cellulose—the source of the cellulose being either cotton linters or a particular form of wood pulp. This material is mixed with nitric acid and solvent and converted to a stiff dough to which is added very small amounts of other compounds to provide particular performance characteristics, after which the dough is extruded into cylindrical kernels of IMR-type powders, then dried and coated with graphite and whatever deterrent is required for a particular performance.

Double-base powders, however, require the addition of varying degrees of nitroglycerin, which is done after nitrating and before extrusion.

Burning rates are controlled by the size of granulation (individual kernel size), relationship of perforation size to kernel size, and by the use of various types and amounts of deterrent coating. In reality, a fast-burning pistol or shotgun powder may not defer chemically from a slow-burning rifle powder such as H4831.

There is considerable danger throughout the manufacture of this extruded form of smokeless powder, whether single base or double base—though the incorporation of nitroglycerine in the latter certainly increases the hazard.

Before powder is ready for packaging, all traces of solvents and acids must be removed before it is dried to a specific moisture content. Following that, individual lots of powder must be blended and tested extensively until specific performance levels are met. This applies principally to those powders sold commercially for handloading, where each lot must closely duplicate the performance of another lot of that same powder manufactured several years earlier. Powder sold to industrial loading plants need not be so closely controlled inasmuch as each plant determines specific loading data for each lot of powder received.

More recently, so-called "ball powder" has become popular. Its manufacture is much simpler, converting nitrated cellulose into an emulsion of which the individual droplets are hardened. The droplets, roughly spherical in shape, are then separated, dried, coated, and blended as with IMR types. However, a number of ball powders are passed between rollers while the droplets are still fairly plastic, reducing all to a standard thickness and thus providing closer control over burning rates. The same result could be accomplished by very careful screening and grading of the different-sized droplets, but this procedure would be vastly more expensive.

Smokestack An autoloading pistol malfunction in which the fired case is extracted and rotated outward, but not hurled clear of the action. It is then caught between slide face and barrel breech as the action closes, open mouth up, thus the "smokestack" appelation. In this position the case prevents chambering locking, and firing the next round.

Snaphance (Snaphaunce) An early form of flintlock in which the steel or frizzen and the pan cover are separate parts rather than a single part as in later arms. Some variations required the pan cover to be opened manually before firing; in others it was driven clear as the cock fell. The snaphance is also distinguished by its lack of a safety or half-cock notch. Inadvertent firing was accomplished by moving the steel forward out of the flint's path.

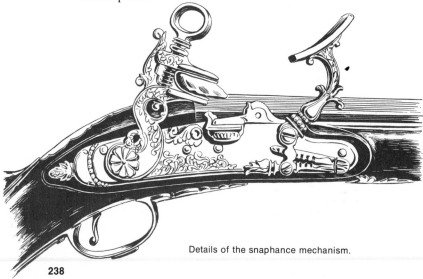

Details of the snaphance mechanism.

There are many minor variations, the Dutch (introduced before 1550) being the most common. The name is believed to also be Dutch in origin, deriving from the similarity of the cock's action to that of a pecking rooster. Originally, *Schnapp-hahn*, it was eventually corrupted to *Snaphance*. The type had been all but replaced by the true flintlock by the mid-17th century, though made in Africa in small quantities as late as the mid-19th century.

See FLINTLOCK.

An Italian (Brescian) snaphance smoothbore with a folding butt, made in the 17th century.

Snubnose An imprecise term describing all short-barreled revolvers. Generally it refers to guns of medium and small-size frames with barrels no longer than 2 inches which are easily concealed on one's person.

Soft-Point Bullet A form of jacketed expanding bullet in which the jacket is closed at the base, open at the point, and a portion of the lead core is exposed for the purpose of upsetting and initiating expansion upon initial impact with the target.

See also EXPANDING BULLET.

Spencer, Christopher Minor (1833–1922) Inventor of the Spencer repeating rifle first offered in 1860 and used by Union forces in the American Civil War after 1862.

Spencer Rifle An exposed-hammer, tubular-magazine, lever-action rifle invented by Christopher Spencer and introduced in 1860. Beginning in 1862, it was purchased by Union ordnance for use in the American Civil War. Its principal use was as a carbine by Union cavalry, but 12,000 to 13,000 infantry rifles with their much longer barrels were also procured during the war.

The Spencer used a large .56 caliber copper-cased rimfire cartridge of very short length. Its seven-shot magazine was located in the center of the stock and could be charged through preloaded metal tubes carried in a box slung over the soldier's shoulder.

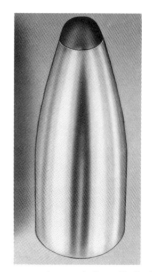

Typical soft-point bullet with lead core exposed at point.

The Spencer action was unlike any other, before or since. Its breech block pivoted at its lower front edge and was locked into the receiver by a block rising out of the upper surface of the breech block to engage an abutment in the receiver. In opening the action, the finger-lever first retracted the locking block into a recess in the breech block, then pivoted the breech block around a pin at its lower forward edge.

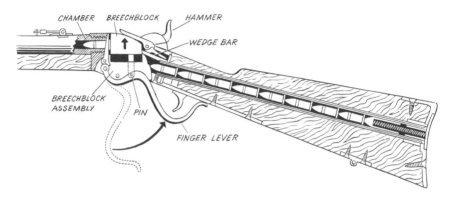

Inner mechanism of the Spencer rifle action.

As the breech block reached a limit of its downward travel, a cartridge was released from the buttstock magazine and forced forward. When the breech block rotated back into its closed position, its upper forward edge engaged the cartridge rim and forced the cartridge through an arc, over a guide, and into the chamber. This unusual over-the-top feed has not been successfully employed in any other action except the Browning/Remington .22 autoloading rifle.

A conventional firing pin angled through the breech block was struck by an exposed, percussion-type hammer mounted on the gun's right side and driven by a typical back-action lock inletted in the wrist of the stock.

While the gun's lever action allowed the shooter to reload quickly, he had to pull the hammer back to full cock before firing each shot. This separate-cocking was inferior to the automatic cocking of the Henry rifle already on the scene, and undoubtedly contributed much to the Spencer's early demise, as did the limitation imposed on cartridge length by the action. Reciprocating-bolt actions could be lengthened for any cartridge, the Spencer could not.

The Spencer carbine remained in service with the U.S. Cavalry well into the 1870s and saw considerable action during the Indian wars. Because of financial difficulties, the Spencer company ceased operation in 1869. Certainly the improvement of the Henry into the Winchester M1866 hastened its demise.

Sporterizing Modifying a surplus military rifle, (though technically any firearm) for any specific purpose.

In a bare-bones sporterizing job, of say, a U.S. Springfield M1903 rifle, the bayonet band, middle band, handguard, and other surplus metal parts would be removed, and the original forend would be cut to a convenient length. The wood might then be refinished and the metal reblued.

To carry the job further, the military sights would be replaced by commercial metallic sights, or possibly a telescopic sight and mount which would require alteration of the bolt handle and the original safety. To go further still, sporterizing might include the addition of a new machine-made stock, or the owner

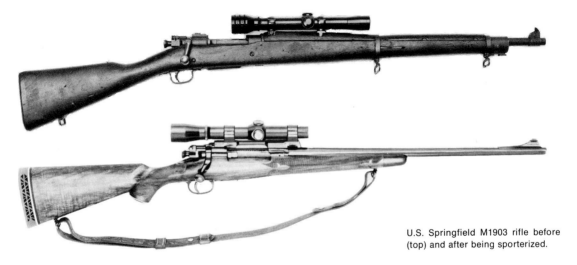

U.S. Springfield M1903 rifle before (top) and after being sporterized.

might fit and finish a semi-completed stock, or if money was no object, he might engage the services of a first-class stockmaker to do a custom job from the start. In addition, the barrel might be shortened or reduced in diameter or both, and minor alterations might be made to improve efficiency or appearance or its adaptation to sporting taste.

While a bare-bones job of sporterizing can be done with little cost, a full-house sporterizing job will cost two or three times more than a comparable new sporting rifle in field grade.

Springfield Armory From 1778 until the late 1960s, the principal U.S. government-owned and -operated small arms manufacturing facility. It was established in Springfield, Mass. by an act of Congress in April of 1778 as an ammunition laboratory, and in 1795 it began the manufacture of smoothbore flintlock muskets for the U.S. armed forces. From that point on it was the primary maker of military small arms except during wartime when civilian industry production of specific items exceeded its capabilities.

Until recently the armory was also the site of virtually all U.S. military small arms research and development, including extensive evaluation and testing of foreign as well as domestic developments.

The armory was phased out as a so-called "economy move" in the late 1960s, thus eliminating the traditional seat of domestic small arms expertise and manufacturing skills. All that remains of it today is the Springfield Armory Museum of small arms and related items, operated as a separate non-profit corporation from original Armory land and buildings donated by the U.S. Government to the city of Springfield.

The famous "Springfield Rifle," the U.S. M1903, received its name from the Springfield Armory marking on its receiver ring.

Sprue The small amount of excess lead attached to a cast bullet or ball at point where the molten metal was poured into the mold. Also, the hole through which molten lead is poured into the mould in the process of casting a bullet.

Sprue Cutter The pivoted plate on a bullet mold which is rotated to shear off the sprue from a cast bullet before it is dropped from the mold.

Squeeze Bore A barrel that begins at a fairly large caliber immediately ahead of the chamber and then tapers, either gradually and consistently or in steps, to a smaller caliber at the muzzle.

A projectile used in a squeeze-bore barrel has a basic body equal to the muzzle diameter, but it is fitted with bands or flanges equal to the breech diameter. When fired, the projectile's bands are continuously compressed to exert greater resistance against the bore which effectively seals and maintains elevated chamber pressures for a much longer period than usual, thus producing substantially higher velocity.

The world's various military establishments have experimented with squeeze-bore systems to obtain ultra-high velocities from conventional firearms. One name commonly linked with such experiments is Harold Gerlich, who designed several squeeze-bore systems and ammunition for both the German and United States governments prior to World War II. Only in Germany did Gerlich's designs actually reach production and field service in the form of the 28/20mm anti-tank gun which was used to a very limited extent early in the war.

The production of this long tapered bore and its rifling is extremely difficult and costly. Further, unusually high barrel stresses are involved, and bore life is often measured in only scores of rounds. As far as present day technology is concerned, the squeeze-bore is not practical. Nevertheless, we continue to hear rumors of a modern squeeze-bore system which may see production within the next few years.

Star Crimp   The most common form of shotshell-mouth closure found today. It consists of folding over the case mouth in neat V-shaped segments to form a flattened, and slightly depressed, self-locking seal over the shot charge.

Two forms of star crimp—Winchester left, Remington right.

It is known as the star crimp because of the appearance, and sometimes as the folded crimp because of the action taken to form it. Such crimps are found in 6- and 8-segment forms.

Unlike the old-style roll crimp which required an over-shot wad or card, the star crimp opens cleanly with nothing to disrupt the shot charge and interfere with its uniformly dense pattern. In addition, the star crimp is both simpler and more economical to manufacture.

The star crimp cannot be used over rifled slugs, or over large-size buckshot loads which haven't enough "give" to allow the folds to form.

Starlight Scope   An observation or weapon-aiming telescope designed around a highly sophisticated light amplification system and generally available only to military and law-enforcement agencies. It is so efficient that on clear, moonless nights U.S. Army snipers have achieved one-shot kills of the enemy at ranges as great as 600 meters. Such units are quite costly, ranging from around $3,000 to a great deal more.

Steel Jacketed   Referring to a bullet assembled in steel jacket which may or may not be covered with some other metal. The term is seldom used, except by uniformed journalists who commonly refer to any full-jacketed military bullet as "steel jacketed."

Jackets made only of steel are very seldom used except during wartime shortages of more desirable alloys. In Europe considerable use is made of steel jackets with a thin layer of non-ferrous alloy bonded to the outer, or even both, surfaces. Coated steel is often used for jackets in military ammunition, even though

243

in some instances the coating is very thin and may even be nothing more than a flash coating of copper plating.

See also JACKETED BULLET.

Stocks, Care of Wood, even the highest quality walnut found in top-grade custom gunstocks, is a very perishable material. It is easily gouged and dented—though breakage isn't too common—and it can be damaged by absorbing moisture in damp weather and drying out when humidity is quite low.

The best way to insure longevity of a stock (or any other piece of wood in its original form) is to apply an impervious finish over *all* its surfaces. For this reason, better factory stocks and all custom stocks are well sealed on all internal cuts and all end grain cuts followed by careful filling of the grain to produce a smooth finish (on the outside), after which a waterproof coating is applied. Today, that coating is most likely to be a synthetic, such as Remington's RKW (which is sprayed on).

The finish must be kept as clean and as dry as possible—usually by simply wiping it off periodically with a damp cloth. Care should be taken to insure that excess oils and lubricants applied to metal parts are not allowed to soak into the stock through inletting cuts or breaks in the finish. Any breaks in the finish—nicks, dents, or scratches, etc.—should be immediately sealed with a touch of lacquer or the original finish material. Any new stock on which the checkering or other ornamentation has been cut through the original finish should have those areas thoroughly sealed by a deep-penetrating material.

Excessive wear of the original finish can be prevented by thick well-rubbed coats of top-grade hard paste wax. Straight carnauba wax is often recommended, but Johnson's yellow paste floor wax performs quite well and is more readily available. It should be applied in several light coats, each well buffed and polished. A stock waxed in this fashion will last forever if not abused.

If the finish does wear through or becomes damaged over a wide area, modern epoxy-type finishes may be sprayed directly over the original coating so long as it is completely grease free.

Regardless of the finish or its condition, any gunstock exposed to excessive moisture will swell and warp, perhaps even split, as a result. Consequently, guns should be protected from rain or snow and should be wiped dry at every opportunity. Particular care should be taken to prevent water from soaking into the spaces between wood and metal, which can be prevented by carefully working wax into all exposed gaps.

Wood can lose too much water as well as absorb it. A stock exposed to excessive dryness will give up its moisture, producing cracks, splits, and warping. The finer and more varied the figure in the grain, the more likely splits and cracks will occur as the stock dries out. A hunting trip in the desert won't cause any problems so long as the gun is not deliberately exposed to sun's rays for long periods. It is long-term exposure to abnormally low humidity that causes stock trouble—such as in well-heated homes lacking humidifiers to maintain relative humidity at comfortable levels. If your house feels uncomfortably dry in the winter, the air is too dry for your gunstocks.

Striker The firing pin in some bolt-action guns.

Stripping Failure of the bullet to initially follow the rifling, visible as scrape marks or skid marks at the front of the ogive where it first enters the rifling.

Submachine Gun A very loose term describing short, compact, individual, full-automatic weapons chambered for cartridges in the handgun class. Generally of very simple, low-cost mate-

Submachine gun in the American image, M1921 Thompson, cal. .45.

rials and construction, and of blowback design, and fitted with only rudimentary sights and stocks. Submachine guns generally weigh from 6 to 10 pounds, have magazine capacities of thirty rounds or thereabouts, fire at cyclic rates of 600 to 1,000 rounds per minute, have barrels ranging from 6 to 10 inches long and are most often chambered for the 9mm Parabellum cartridge.

See also Assault Rifle and Machine Gun.

Swaging The process by which most lead and jacketed bullets are tightly assembled and brought to final form and dimensions. The core and jacket (in the case of a lead bullet, simply a rough slug) are placed in a die of the size and configuration of the finished bullet. Then a punch exerts great pressure on the bullet material, expanding and forcing it to completely fill the die and bringing it to final size and shape. This is generally

Simple swaging press and die set
for making short-jacketed bullets.

called the "expanding-up" principle and results in a very solid assembly of core to jacket.

Lead is relatively stable and does not spring back to any significant degree after being formed under pressure—while the bullet jacket *is* springy, and after being expanded to fill the die, shrinks back towards its original dimensions and clings tightly to the lead core.

Actually swaging is the forming of any cold metal in a die or over a negative form which gives it its final shape and dimensions.

Dies are available for home swaging of all types of bullets in most heavy-duty handloading presses.

Swivel   See SLING SWIVEL.

Takedown A rifle in which the barrel may be easily removed from the action for ease of shipping or carrying.

Tang An extension of the receiver, trigger guard, or other part which seats into the stock to link parts together, spread recoil loads, and provide a more secure assembly. Is also reinforces weak sections of the stock.

Temperature Effect The change in a bullet's velocity produced by the change in propellant temperature. In modern conventional ammunition loaded with nitrocellulose-type propellant, the velocity will vary 1.7 feet per second for each degree Fahrenheit variation in propellant temperature.

Basic performance specifications are established at, or corrected to, 70 degrees F. Thus, a cartridge fired at less than that temperature will produce less than standard velocity, or *vice versa*.

For example, a load listed as producing 3,000 feet per second, if fired when the propellant temperature is 10 degrees F, the 60-degree temperature reduction multiplied by 1.7 reduces the velocity by 102 feet per second, or down to 2,898 feet per second.

Through Bolt In any long gun, a long bolt extending through the center of the buttstock, threaded into the receiver, drawing the stock up tightly. The strongest method of attaching a separate buttstock.

Throat Diameter In a revolver, the diameter of the chamber throat at the front of the cylinder.

Thumbhole Stock A rifle stock with a comb extending full length from the receiver and with a hole for the shooter's thumb.

Thumb Rest Usually on a handgun, a ridge on the thumb-side of the grip which forms a shelf shaped to conform to the natural contour of the shooter's thumb in the one-hand, shooting position. Thumb rests may be adjustable in sophisticated target-type stocks, but they are generally formed integrally with the stock. They may vary in size from only a rudimentary ridge of little value on up through a carefully contoured channel which virtually encloses the thumb. The latter type is generally found only on expensive competition guns.

Raised curved ridge on grip forms rest for shooter's thumb.

On a rifle, thumb rests are generally found only on a few highly specialized target guns, consisting of a shelf on the thumb-side of the grip shaped to provide support for the thumb in a relaxed position.

Top Lever The pivoted lever at the upper rear of the receiver of break-open guns, which disengages the locking system to allow the gun to be opened.

Trajectory The path of a bullet in flight. For all practical purposes, the bullet begins decelerating and falling toward earth the instant it leaves the muzzle, the rates of deceleration and fall continually increasing.

Trajectory is generally measured in two different ways but most often in terms of "midrange trajectory height," which is the distance between the bullet's path and the line of sight from the gun to its aiming point at a specific range. For example, a "200-yard midrange trajectory height" indicates the highest point the bullet's patch reaches above the line of sight when the rifle is zeroed at 200 yards. This point occurs approximately halfway.

Trajectory is also measured in terms of "drop." This is a measurement taken at right angles to the extended centerline of the bore down to the path of the bullet at any given point. Drop at 200 yards would be the distance below the bore's centerline to the bullet's path at the range.

See also Bullet Drop and Midrange Trajectory Height.

Trap A covered recess in the stock for storing cartridges, spare parts, or cleaning gear. Fitted with a hinged or sliding cover, usually of metal, it is most frequently located in the face of the butt. It is sometimes placed in the pistol grip or in the belly of the stock between butt and grip.

Trapdoor The popular name of the so-called "cam-lock" action designed by Allin to convert muzzle-loading rifles to breechloaders, and further developed into the Springfield M1873 single-shot rifle. Likened to a trapdoor, because the breech block is pivoted at one end, and unlatched and opened by lifting the other.

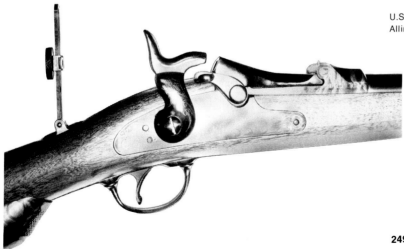

U.S. trapdoor action, derived from Allin patent.

249

Tranquilizer Gun See Capture Gun.

Trap Stock A shotgun buttstock with less than usual drop and greater length of pull to adapt it specifically to trap shooting.

Trigger The part of a gun against which finger pressure is brought directly to fire the gun.

Trigger Guard A loop of metal which protects the trigger and sometimes supports the trigger assembly and magazine.

Trigger Reach In a handgun, the distance from the rear edge of the grip to the trigger in its rest position. If trigger reach is too short, the gun hand will be cramped and unsteady during firing—if too long, proper trigger control will be difficult. In the case of double-action shooting, a too-long trigger reach may actually make it impossible for individuals with small hands or short fingers to fire the gun.

Trigger Shoe A separate and curved piece of steel or aluminum slotted to fit over the front face of a trigger, and secured by small set screws, to either increase the area engaged by the

Trigger shoe on Winchester rifle.

trigger finger, or to move the effective surface of the trigger farther forward. Trigger shoes intended for target use often incorporate an adjustable trigger stop, and are normally serrated to provide a non-slip surface.

Trigger Squeeze   Pulling the trigger to fire a gun while maintaining complete control with minimum disturbance. Proper squeeze consists of gradually applying ever-increasing pressure until the sear is disengaged and the gun fires, while avoiding any tendency to flinch or jerk at the instant of sear release. Follow through is quite important at this point to avoid disturbing the gun by abnormal finger movement.

Trigger Stop   Any mechanical device which halts rearward trigger movement at the precise instant the sear disengages, allowing the gun to fire. Though many forms have been used, the most common is a screw passing through the trigger to contact either trigger guard or frame or receiver. Or the reverse may be true with the screw passing through some part of the gun to contact the trigger. The screw can be turned in or out to adjust trigger travel to the point of sear release.

Try Gun, or Try Stock   A fully adjustable stock, probably of British origin, and widely used by British custom gunmakers. Generally built upon a double-barrelled shotgun, it consists of a stock which is made in several parts and fitted with clamps, screws, and sliding members so that virtually all dimensions may be quickly altered to fit the gun to any individual.

A typical British try gun will allow pivoting the stock both vertically and horizontally at the wrist, raising and lowering the butt, raising and lowering the comb, lengthening and shortening the pull, and changing pitch. Guns of this type are highly specialized items, quite costly, and are seldom encountered in the United States.

There is a much simpler try stock, manufactured here by Reinhart Fajen, which may be assembled to a sample gun and used to make essentially the same adjustments, however, it is limited to changing only the height of buttplate, the height of the comb, the length of pull, the angle of the comb, and pitch.

A try gun is used by very carefully fitting it to an individual after studying his physique and shooting habits and then observing his shooting. Once the proper dimensions are finalized, they are used to fabricate a custom-made stock to precisely fit the shooter.

Tubular Magazine   A tube under the barrel or in the butt of a repeating rifle into which cartridges fit nose-to-tail.

Tumbling   Agitating cases or bullets in a mildly abrasive compound to clean and polish, usually in a rotating "tumbler."

Turn Barrel A form of muzzle-loading gun (usually a rifle) in which two barrels are joined, one above the other, and then pivoted to a common breech. Detents are provided so that 180 degrees of rotation aligns either barrel with the hammer, lock, and breech for firing. Only one lock and hammer are used, and both barrels are fitted with percussion nipples. In addition, each barrel has its own set of sights.

Turn-barrel rifle with barrels between firing positions.

This system offers advantages over the traditional double-barrelled gun in that it has only one firing mechanism, and that the barrels need not be regulated. Still, it provides rapid two-shot capability. Turn-barrel guns were not very common during the muzzle-loading era. Today, though, at least two modern examples are being manufactured.

Twenty Two (.22) Rifle Any rifle chambered for any of the several .22 rimfire cartridges, normally excluding the more powerful .22 Winchester Magnum Rimfire, and the low-power rimfire cartridges of larger caliber. The .22 rimfire is by far the most popular of all rifles throughout the world. The simplest .22 rifles are available at extremely low cost, yet produce excellent accuracy and power. In their most sophisticated forms, they may cost hundreds of dollars and deliver one-hole accuracy.

All types of actions are used: single shot, bolt, lever, pump, and auto—with numerous variations of each.

Magazine systems vary from butt-mounted tubes through under receiver rotary types, conventional box, and underbarrel tubes.

While .22 rifles are used a great deal for hunting small game, they are not recommended for anything larger, and their principal uses are for plinking and target shooting.

Twist The spiral shape of rifling lands and grooves and generally expressed (in small arms) as a ratio, i.e., 1:10 indicating one complete turn of the rifling for every 10 inches of barrel length. Every bullet must be given a high rate of spin to stabilize it about its longitudinal axis in flight, and for any caliber (more correctly, for any cartridge) the standard rate of twist is that which will stabilize the longest and heaviest bullets used. The longer the bullet, the higher the rate of twist required, and therefore a twist suitable for the longest and heaviest bullets will be substantially greater than that desired for the shortest and lightest bullets to be used. So unless a cartridge is to be loaded with only one weight and length of bullet, the rate of twist must always be a compromise in favor of the longest bullet.

For example, twist of the .30/06 cartridge was standardized at 1:10 (one turn in 10 inches) to stabilize the long 220-grain bullets of the heaviest load — yet the most commonly used bullet weighs only 150 grains and can be adequately stabilized to normal hunting ranges with a 1:12 twist, and the lighter bullets can be handled with a 1:14 twist, or even a 1:16 twist if velocities are kept well above 3,000 feet per second.

Upland Game Birds, Guns for The typical upland gun should be relatively short overall, with a short barrel of 26 inches or less, of medium bore, lightweight for fast handling, and bored to throw moderately dense patterns of small shot (No. 6 or smaller) only out to 40 yards or less. It should be lightly stocked, with a fair amount of drop.

While the 12 gauge has always been extremely popular as an upland gun, the tendency is more and more toward using the lighter and handier 20 gauge guns, often with 3-inch magnum ammunition which, with its 1¼-ounce load, duplicates the performance of 12-gauge field loads used 30 years ago.

Upland birds are shot at relatively close ranges, often in medium to thick cover, and are relatively small and easily killed. They are also often shot at extremely close ranges where maximum speed of engagement is required, and where excessively dense shot patterns are too destructive.

Upset (Bullet) Under extreme pressure, all metals become plastic and flow as a fluid. Thus, bullets, being made of soft lead and copper alloy, will yield and flow under relatively low pressures. This is called bullet upset. At the initial buildup of chamber pressure, the forward portion of a bullet tends to remain in place of its own inertia while its base is moved forward by the expanding gases—which results in the bullet expanding radially as far as the bore will allow. In fact, under some circumstances the *barrel* yields slightly under the force of the expanding bullet, producing a very slight egg-shaped bulge

255

in the bore around the bullet. When pressures are high enough, this bulge will actually travel down the bore, the barrel springing back to its original dimensions after the bullet passes.

Upset, on the other hand, can be a valuable aid to the bullet in sealing the bore to prevent the escape of powder gases around it. In the event an undersized bullet is used, such as in high-performance handgun ammunition, upsetting produces a better bore-to-bullet fit than could be obtained otherwise.

Excessively hard or strongly constructed bullets will not produce significant upset at relatively low chamber pressures. Softer bullets, however, may upset so much under very high pressures that they lose their shape and their accuracy is destroyed. If gas pressure is too great (for the particular bullet construction), the instant the bullet leaves the muzzle, its base will upset and enlarge to a substantially greater diameter than the bore. This can be readily demonstrated in a .357 Magnum revolver fired with its barrel removed: The bullet upsets so much as it leaves the chamber mouth that it often scrapes the edges of the barrel seat in the frame.

Variable Choke   See Adjustable Choke.

Varmint   A corruption of the word vermin, any species which is considered detrimental to man and should be reduced in number or destroyed. Any birds or animals classified as varmints and not protected by state of federal laws may normally be shot at any time. But due to vastly different environmental situations and widely varying state and federal laws, species considered varmints in one area may be protected in another. For example, the mountain lion is protected in California, but is still classified as a varmint in some cattle-raising western states.

Varmint hunting requires the maximum in long-range accuracy and flatness of trajectory and, for many areas, minimum report and muzzle blast. Also, highly desirable is bullet design and construction which will reduce ricochet probability to a minimum. Explosive expansion or impact with target is also considered essential.

These characteristics are combined best in high velocity .22 caliber cartridges ranging from the .222 Remington with its 50-grain bullet at 3,100 feet per second, to the .220 Swift and .22/250 with 50–55 grain bullets in the 3,700–4,000 feet-per-second range. Bullets are lightly constructed, superbly accurate, ricochets are very rare, and expansion on target is astounding.

The .22 calibers do not perform well in significant winds, being deflected too much for consistent shooting beyond 250–300 yards on windy days. For such conditions and for ultra-long ranges the 6mm/.243 class of cartridges typified by the .243 Winchester and 6mm Remington with thin-jacketed 80- to 90-grain bullets at 3,400–3,600 feet per second are better choices.

Varmints, Guns for   Since varmints are generally small—ranging from the fist-sized striped gophers of the northwestern plains up through prairie dogs, woodchucks, and the larger rock chuck and coyote—an extremely high degree of accuracy is required in both rifle and cartridge, considering also that even the smallest varmints are often in open country at ranges exceeding 200 yards. Generally speaking, accuracy of at least one minute of angle or better is considered essential for typical varminting—meaning a gun/ammunition combination capable of 2-inch groups of 200 yards, 3-inch groups at 300 yards, etc. This degree of accuracy is usually best obtained with rigid bolt actions and relatively heavy, stiff barrels. It also requires, at least to a moderate degree, hand tuning the rifle to suit the particular load. Since varmints are normally shot from a rest of some sort, a thick, heavy target-style stock dimensioned generally for the prone position, is best.

First-shot hits at extended ranges necessitate as flat a trajectory as possible to offset poor range estimation. Flat trajectory means using relatively light small-caliber bullets driven at the highest practical velocity—and this high velocity also helps nullify the effect of the strong winds so often encountered in good varmint-shooting country.

All things considered, modern high-velocity cartridges in the .22- to .243-(6mm) range are the most effective. The .222, .223, and .222 Remington Magnum are generally considered best on even the smallest varmints, out to 200–250 yards, and to even greater ranges on the larger species, providing no great amount of wind is present.

Given longer ranges and windy conditions, the higher-velocity .22's, such as the .22/250 and .220 Swift, are better choices with their heavier bullets and higher velocities. At extreme ranges and severe wind conditions, the 6mm class, such as the .243 Winchester and 6mm Remington, are superior and will permit sure kills out to 400 yards or more.

A more recent development, the .25/06 Remington, is superior even to the 6mms, but is considered excessively large, powerful, and noisy, for varmint use. In any event, the 6mms proved themselves capable of making consistent kills at 400 to 500 yards under fairly acceptable conditions.

If I were to select a varmint battery, it would consist first of a short-action bolt rifle with a stiff, heavy 20-inch barrel chambered for the .223 Remington, supplemented by a long-range rifle of similar configuration but with a 26-inch barrel and chambered for the 6mm Remington. Weight would run about 8 pounds on the first rifle and 9 on the second.

See also VARMINT.

Vent In a breech-loader, a gas escape route; in a muzzle-loader, the hole through the nipple between the percussion cap and the main propelling charge; in a flintlock the hole through the barrel wall between the flashpan and the main propelling charge.

See also GAS PORT, NIPPLE, and FLINTLOCK.

Ventilated Rib A projection on top of a barrel running its full length, usually square or rectangular in cross section, and with the sights affixed to it.

While generally limited to shotguns, it is found on some recent models of Colt revolvers, and for a short time was standard on the Remington M600 rifle. And, of course, there have been custom installations of such ribs upon virtually all types of firearms.

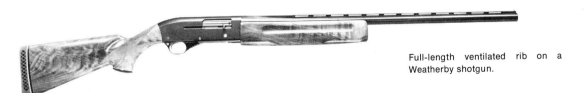

Full-length ventilated rib on a Weatherby shotgun.

The ventilated rib is used principally on shotguns because it offers a uniform, raised sighting plane which is an advantage in shooting where precise aiming is not required. It also acts to dissipate barrel heat during sessions of rapid fire and thus reduce "mirage" or heat waves that would interfere with sighting the target.

Today, ventilated ribs are generally made separately, then brazed, welded or epoxied to the barrel as a separate operation just before blueing.

There are two types of ribs: (1) the older variety in which the narrow posts or supports (which raise the rib above the barrel) are machined as an integral part of the rib; (2) the modern design in which the supports are simply short lengths of steel tubing with male dovetail shapes at their tops, mated and soldered to female dovetails on the rib's underside.

Volcanic Rifle The earliest repeating rifle manufactured in any significant quantity in the United States for use with self-contained ammunition.

Originally called a "volitional repeater," the Volcanic depended upon a so-called "rocket ball," which consisted of a lead bullet with a hollow base filled with a fulminate propelling charge which was covered by a cork disc or other material. Upon firing, the fulminate was ignited by firing-pin impact and the fulminate-enclosing disc was either consumed, or followed the bullet out the bore. Walter Hunt first patented this cartridge in 1848 in a form where the base was closed by a cork disc containing a hole for the admission of the flash from a separate primer. He also patented a tubular magazine under the barrel, and these features were then combined with the toggle-link-breech patent of Louis Jennings.

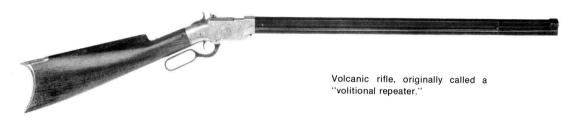

Volcanic rifle, originally called a "volitional repeater."

Horace Smith and Daniel Wesson (Smith & Wesson) purchased the patents (both gun and ammunition), made major improvements, and manufactured a limited number of the type, both as rifles and as repeating pistols.

The Smith & Wesson Volcanic design was relatively weak and the cartridge was low powered and injurious to the bore because of its fulminate propelling charge.

Benjamin Tyler Henry then designed a .44 rimfire metallic cartridge and vastly improved the Jennings Smith & Wesson action to handle it. The resulting rifle was introduced in 1860 as the Henry, and became during the American Civil War the first truly practical breech-loading repeater. It is worth noting that the 1860 Henry was then further improved into the Winchester M1866, then into the M1873, and finally into the M1876.

It's safe to say that the Hunt/Jennings Smith & Wesson Volcanic rifle made possible the rapid development of the American lever-action rifle and was directly responsible for the conception and tremendous growth of the Winchester Repeating Arms Company.

See also HENRY RIFLE and WINCHESTER REPEATING ARMS COMPANY.

V-Ring The inner, tie-breaking scoring ring on big-bore rifle targets. In such targets, the maximum score is five for any hit within the inner scoring ring. As rifles, ammunition, and shooters improved to the point that too many perfect scores and ties were being produced, the V-ring was added. Thus, a ten shot string in which all of the shots fell within the five-ring with four of them inside the V-ring was scored as a 50/4V. This score beats a 50/3V and would be beaten by a 50/6V, and only a perfect score would be a 50/10V. On standard American targets, the V-ring is one-half the diameter of the five-ring.

See also X-Ring.

Waterfowl, Guns for Waterfowl are mainly large, strong, heavily muscled birds and are generally shot at relatively long ranges. Consequently they require shotguns throwing heavy charges of large shot in a dense pattern to the longest range possible. Today, this calls for a 30- to 32-inch barrel, tightly choked 12-gauge gun chambered for the 3-inch magnum shell with loadings of 1⅝ to 1⅞ ounces of shot. It also requires a heavy straight stock to reduce the effect of the very substantial recoil of such loads.

Current federal law prohibits the use of gauges larger than 10 on migratory waterfowl. Since the 10-gauge may be lawfully used, a fair percentage of waterfowlers use such guns, often in 3½-inch magnum chambering with 2 to 2½ ounces of shot.

Wadcutter Bullet A type of bullet—which may be solid lead, full-metal jacketed, or any combination in Wadcutter Bullet between—which presents a rectangular profile. It is cylindrical, varying only to allow lubricating grooves, cannelures, or very slight nose protrusions. In factory loaded ammunition, this type of bullet is generally solid at the nose, but contains a conical cavity in its base, which shifts the center of gravity forward, improving its stability at low velocities. Wadcutter bullets used by handloaders are more often solid, and minus base cavities, because of the difficulty in casting uniform bullets with the one.

The wadcutter's main purpose is relatively short-range target shooting for which it is driven at very low velocities—less than 800 feet per second—and it is found only in the more popular revolver cartridges such as .38 Special and .32 S&W.

The wadcutter design is an inefficient ballistic shape, and thus

Typical wadcutter bullet which may be purely cylindrical.

263

loses velocity at a very rapid rate. This shortcoming is accepted in short-range competitive pistol shooting because of the very high degree of accuracy that has been developed, and because the precise round holes this type bullet cuts in the target are so easily scored.

Wad Pressure   Amount of downward force required on a shotshell wad column to achieve optimum burning of the powder charge.

Pacific Verelite wads come in three lengths to suit a variety of different cases and loads.

Wad, Shotshell   In its most modern form, a plastic structure that fills the space between the powder charge and the shot charge, seals the powder gases behind the shot charge, and provides a cushioning action during initial acceleration. Sometimes a shot cup is used to prevent direct contact between shot pellets and the bore's surface.

In its less sophisticated form, a separate overpowder wad seals the gases in the bore. It's a cup-shaped plastic or resilient-fiber unit placed open side down so that its flange or skirt is spread tightly against the bore by expanding gases. Accompanying this wad is a fiber filler wad which fills the space between powder and shot and offers some cushioning (though less than the one-piece plastic wad) for the shot charge.

In its oldest form, the overpowder wad was simply a stiff cardboard disc which fitted tightly against the bore to seal gases, and supplemented by fiber filler wads of the type already described.

Prior to use of the star-type or folded crimp, shotshells also required an overshot wad which was a thin, stiff, frangible cardboard disc crimped over the shot charge to hold it in place. These combined wads are referred to as a "wad column," whether a one-piece unit or several components.

The better the sealing action of the overpowder portion of the wad, the higher the chamber pressure and velocity will be for a given powder charge. As a result, when today's highly efficient plastic overpowder and single-unit wad columns came into use, it became necessary to reduce the standard powder charges that had been used with the older card-over powder-wad loads.

The cushioning action of the filler wads or the single-unit wad column reduces shot deformation and clumping caused by initial acceleration, resulting in more uniform and denser patterns. In addition, the more efficient the cushioning action, the less violent recoil will be.

The shot cup, which prevents direct contact between the outer layer of shot pellets and the hard steel bore, eliminates the flattening or scrubbing of those pellets which causes them to fly wide of the pattern. Again, the result is denser and more uniform patterns.

Weatherby Rifles The rifle/cartridge combinations designed and produced by Roy Weatherby (and later under his direct supervision by Weatherby, Incorporated).

Following World War II, Weatherby designed his own particular set of wildcat cartridges based upon the belted .300/.375 Holland & Holland case, in various lengths, with its body blown out to minimum taper and using a unique double-radius shoulder and moderate-length neck.

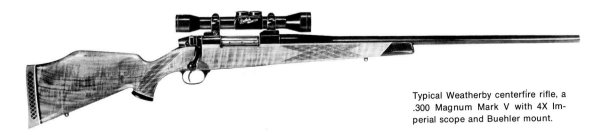

Typical Weatherby centerfire rifle, a .300 Magnum Mark V with 4X Imperial scope and Buehler mount.

Weatherby cartridges were loaded to pressures then considered quite high and to velocities 10 to 15 per cent greater than generally available in factory ammunition.

They were first paired with carefully modified and built rifles based upon the standard Mauser M98 and other suitable actions. Stocks were of unusually flamboyant style for the period.

In the middle to late 1950s, a special Weatherby action, known as the Mark V, was designed and manufactured initially in Germany by the J. P. Sauer Company for exclusive sale by Weatherby.

Since their early development, Weatherby calibers have been available as factory-loaded ammunition whose production Weatherby arranged overseas under his own name, a practice still continued today under the Weatherby headstamp, but including the two most powerful sporting rifle cartridges in the world—the .378 and .460 Weatherby, introduced in the late 1950s.

The Mark V action was originally designed around these abnormally large cartridges based on the old .416 Rigby case with a Holland & Holland style belt added at the rear. Only Weatherby Mark V rifles have been manufactured in these calibers, and no other actions except true magnum-length Mausers are suitable for handling such large rounds.

Weatherby rifles have always been available in highly decorated versions and have generally been a mixture of production and custom gunsmithing, as they are today, premium-priced guns of unusually fine workmanship.

See also Appendix 5, ballistic tables, Weatherby section for precise performance data.

Wesson, Daniel Baird (1825–1906) The American gunsmith who with Horace Smith formed Smith and Wesson, Incorporated in 1855 to market its new breech-loading, rimfire revolver and its .22 Short cartridges. He obtained his early training apprenticed to his brother Edwin, a gunsmith, and later worked for another brother, Frank, also a successful gun maker. He became superintendent of the Leonard Pepperbox plant, and later met Horace Smith at Allen, Brown, Luther, rifle makers. In 1854 Smith & Wesson formed a partnership to produce a lever-action repeating pistol under Henry and S&W patents. In 1855 the Volcanic Repeating Arms Co. was formed, but Wesson left it the next year, reestablishing the partnership with Horace Smith to produce an improved rimfire cartridge and a revolver for it, based on Rollin White patents. This was the beginning of the famed Smith & Wesson Company, which thrives today. Wesson retired in 1883, and his great-grandson is still producing revolvers today through the D. B. Wesson Co., *not* related in any way to the Smith & Wesson Co.

See SMITH, HORACE; SMITH & WESSON; HENRY, TYLER B.; VOLCANIC.

Wheellock An early form of firearm dating from the first quarter of the 16th century, far superior to its matchlock predecessor, and replaced by the flintlock.

Essentially the wheellock ignited a priming charge (which flashed through to fire the propelling charge) by spinning a roughened or serrated wheel against a piece of pyrite or similar spark-producing mineral held in the jaws of a "dog," which somewhat resembled the hammer of a flintlock.

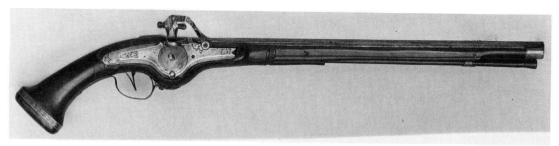

Wheellock pistol, 17th century.
(Metropolitan Museum of Art.)

Prior to firing the wheel had to be wound up, rotating about its axle a short length of chain attached to a strong spring, placing it under a heavy load. The wheel was held by a rudimentary sear connected to the trigger. The dog, containing the pyrites, was then lowered to press the pyrites against the rim of the wheel and in contact with the priming powder. When the sear was released the spring spun the wheel and its rough-

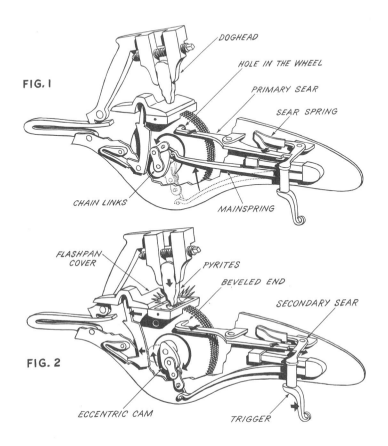

FIG. I

DOGHEAD
HOLE IN THE WHEEL
PRIMARY SEAR
SEAR SPRING
CHAIN LINKS
MAINSPRING

FLASHPAN COVER
PYRITES
BEVELED END
SECONDARY SEAR
FIG. 2
ECCENTRIC CAM
TRIGGER

Wheellock mechanism works as follows: chain links tension mainspring, cocking trigger mechanism *(Fig. 1)*, as bevelled point of primary sear slips into hole in wheel under tension of sear spring. Pulling trigger *(Fig. 2)* releases primary sear from notch in secondary sear, and force of mainspring spins wheel, dislodging bevelled point of the primary sear from hole. Flashpan cover is pushed back by eccentric cam and the doghead is impelled down, causing the pyrite to touch serrated edges of wheel, sending sparks into powder in flashpan.

ened rim rubbed the face of the pyrites producing a shower of sparks which ignited the priming powder.

Though vastly superior in a technical sense to the match lock, the wheellock was costly to manufacture, requiring a high degree of metal-working skill. Consequently, it was not

A wheellock made in 1680 by C. Zelner, well-known gunmaker of Salzberg, Austria.

widely distributed. Though military wheellocks were made, most surviving examples are high-grade sporting arms exhibiting a high degree of artistic skill and ornamentation.

Because of its cost, complexity, and maintenance problems, the wheellock never entirely supplanted the matchlock and both types remained in service side by side until displaced by the flintlock in the late 17th century.

Many wheellocks were painstakingly fashioned and ornately decorated by the finest gunsmiths for the hunting aristocracy.

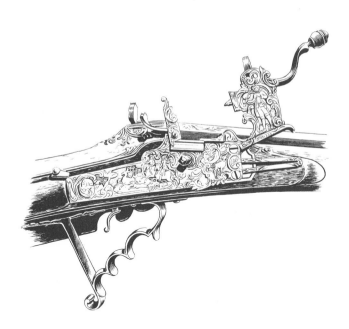

Wildcat Any cartridge not standardized within the shooting industry or not standardized domestically within the Sporting Arms and Ammunition Manufacturers Institute (SAAMI).

A wildcat cartridge is born when a gunsmith or gun enthusiast alters an existing cartridge case to suit his own particular needs. This alteration may consist of nothing more than shortening the case, or necking it down or up to use bullets of a different diameter. Or it may include extensive modification which might taper or lengthen, or reshape the rim or extraction groove, etc. Wildcatters have even gone so far as to convert large-caliber, straight-bodied rimmed cases, such as the .45/70 to small-caliber, rimless, bottleneck cases.

The most common form of wildcatting consists of necking the case down and increasing its powder capacity by fire-forming the shoulder portion to larger diameter and a more acute angle to increase powder capacity and thereby increase velocity and energy.

Though most wildcatters claim quite substantial performance improvements over standard factory loads, they generally tend to be overly optimistic, and proper ballistic tests usually show no great gain.

Winchester, Oliver F. (1810–1880) The New England shirt manufacturer who formed the Winchester Repeating Arms company.

See also Winchester Repeating Arms Company.

Winchester Repeating Arms Company Formed by Oliver Winchester in 1866 to manufacture the Model 1866 rifle from Henry patents, which had produced the successful Henry Repeating Rifle during the Civil War.

The Winchester M1866 was the first commercially successful lever-action repeating rifle and upon its success was founded the Winchester dynasty which survives today as the present Winchester-Western Division of Olin Industries.

Following the M1866, Winchester went on to even further successes with the M1873, M1886, and M1894—the latter of which is still in production with more than 3,000,000 guns having been produced.

See also Henry Rifle and Winchester, Oliver F.

Windage In a muzzle-loading smoothbore using round balls, the clearance between the ball and the bore which allows easy loading and generous barrel- and ball-manufacturing tolerances.

Also the escape of propellant gases through this clearance or gap.

In a sighting system, the lateral adjustment provided to either place line of sight and bullet trajectory in the same vertical plane, or to diverge line of sight and trajectory to compensate for lateral wind. While generally applied only to the rear element of metallic sighting systems, some older guns' front sights were adjustable for windage, and were called "windgauge" sights for that reason.

Wind Rule A formula used to calculate the allowance that must be made to offset the effect of wind blowing at a known velocity and direction. The result is in minutes of angle (MOA) required to compensate for wind blowing at 90 degrees to the bullet's path.

One simply multiplies the range (in hundreds of yards) by the wind velocity (in miles per hour), divided by a constant representing a particular cartridge/load combination. For example, the constant for the .30/06, M2 ball cartridge is ten, that for the .30 M1 carbine with its 110-grain bullet is five. Assuming the cartridge used is the M2 .30/06, shooting at 300 yards with a 9 o'clock wind at 10 miles per hour, the wind rule correction is 3 minutes of angle *into* the wind.

Wundhammer Swell A rifle stock feature attributed to custom gunsmith Louis Wundhammer. It consists of a bulge on the right side of the pistol grip which comfortably fills the palm of the trigger hand. In its original form, it was a relatively small bulge which aided in consistently obtaining the same hand-to-stock relationship. In more recent years it has reappeared in a much exaggerated form as an overly large bulge which actually negates the effect of the original and makes consistent hand placement more difficult.

X-Ring In domestic pistol and smallbore rifle shooting, the tie-breaking ring inside the maximum-value scoring ring of all targets. Its purpose and function is exactly the same as the V-ring in big-bore rifle competition.

See also V-Ring.

Zeroing In The process of aligning any gun sight (either metallic or telescopic) so that its line of sight intersects the trajectory of any bullet at the desired range. Unless the line of sight is known to be reasonably in agreement with the trajectory, bore sighting will simplify the process a great deal. Initial zeroing should also be conducted at a relatively short range, perhaps 25 or 50 yards, so that if gross errors exist, there will be no difficulty in placing the first shot on the target where it can be seen and used as a basis for correction.

See also Bore Sight, Sighting In.

Bibliography

BALLISTICS AND HANDLOADING

Cartridges of the World, by Frank C. Barnes, John T. Amber ed. Digest Books, Inc. Northfield, Ill., 1972. 378pp, illus. Paperbound. $6.95.

Centerfire American Rifle Cartridges, 1892–1963, by Ray Bearse. A. S. Barnes & Co., S. Brunswick, N.J., 1966. 198pp, illus. $6.98. Identification manual covering caliber, introduction date, origin, case type, etc. Self-indexed and cross-referenced. Headstamps and line drawings are included.

Centerfire Pistol and Revolver Cartridges, by H. P. White, B. D. Munhall & Ray Bearse. A. S. Barnes, N.Y., 1967. 85pp plus 170pp, illus. $10.00. A new and revised edition covering the original Volume I, *Centerfire Metric Pistol and Revolver Cartridges* and Volume II, *Centerfire American and British Pistol and Revolver Cartridges,* by White and Munhall, formerly known as *Cartridge Identification.*

Complete Guide to Handloading, by Phil Sharpe, Funk & Wagnalls, N.Y., 1953 (3rd ed. 2nd rev.). 734pp, profusely illus., numerous line and half-tone charts, tables, lists, etc. $10.00. The bible of handloaders ever since its first appearance in 1937, but badly dated now.

Handbook for Shooters and Reloaders, by P. O. Ackley, Salt Lake City, Utah, 1970, Vol I., 567 pp, illus. $9.00. Vol II, a new printing with specific new material. 495pp, illus. $9.00. Both volumes, $17.50.

Handloaders Digest, ed. by John T. Amber, Digest Books, Inc. Northfield, Ill., 1972. 320pp, well illus. Stiff paper covers. $5.95. This 6th edition contains the latest data on ballistics, maximum loads new tools, equipment, reduced loads, etc., plus a fully illus. catalog section current, prices and specifications.

Home Guide to Cartridge Conversions, by Geo. C. Nonte, Jr., Stackpole Books, Harrisburg, Pa., 1967. 404pp, illus. $8.95. A new, revised and enlarged ed. of instructions, charts and tables for making ammunition no longer available, or which has become too expensive on the commercial market.

Make Muzzle Loader Accessories, by R. H. McCrory, R. H. McCrory, Publ., 1972. 46pp. Paper. $2.25. A revised 2nd ed. covering over 20 items from powderhorns to useful tools. Well illus.

Shooter's Bible Black Powder Guide, by George Nonte, Shooter's Bible, Inc., S. Hackensack, N.J., 1969. 214pp, well illus. $3.95. Information on black-powder weapons, ammunition, shooting. etc.

Small Arms Ammunition Identification Guide, An Army Intelligence Document, Paladin Press,

Boulder, Co., 1972. 254pp, illus. Paper. $5.00. An exact reprint of FSTC-CW-7068, 1969 updated. An identification guide for most countries.

COLLECTORS

The Age of Firearms, by Robert Held. Digest Books, Inc., Northfield, Ill., 1970. New, fully rev. and corrected ed. Paper covers. 192pp, fully illus. $.95. A popular review of firearms since 1475 with accent on their effects on social conditions, and the craft of making functional/artistic arms.

Early Loading Tools and Bullet Molds, by R. H. Chamberlain. The Farm Tribune, Porterville, Ga., 1971. 75pp, illus. Paper covers. $3.00. An excellent aid to collectors.

The Firearms Dictionary, by R. A. Steindler, Stackpole Books, Harrisburg, Pa., 1970. 256pp, nearly 200 illus. $7.95. A super single-source reference to more than 1800 English and foreign gun-related words, phrases and nomenclature, etc. Highly useful to all armsmen — collectors, shooters, hunters, etc.

German Mauser Rifle — Model of 1898, by J. E. Coombes and J. L. Aney. A reprint in paper covers by Francis Bannerman Sons, New York, N.Y., of their 1921 publication. 20pp, well illus. $1.50. Data on the subject weapon and its W.W. I development. Bayonets and ammunition are also described and illus.

German Submachine Guns and Assault Rifles. WE, Inc. Old Greenwich, Conn., 1967. 161pp. $5.95. Aberdeen Proving Ground reports on over 50 models of WW II German rapid-fire weapons are reprinted.

The Kentucky Rifle, by J. G. W. Dillin. Geo. Shumway, York, Pa., 1967. 5th ed. 202pp., illus. $20.00. A respected work on the long rifles developed in colonial days and carried by pioneers and soldiers. Much information of value to collectors and historians. Limited ed.

Metallic Cartridges, T. J. Treadwell, compiler. The Armoury, N.Y.C., 1959. Unpaginated. 68 plates. Paper, $2.95; Cloth, $5.95. A reduced-size reproduction of U.S. Ordnance Memoranda No. 14 originally publ. in 1873, on regulation and experimental cartridges manufactured and tested at Frankford Arsenal, Philadelphia, Pa.

The NRA Gun Collector's Guide, by staff members of NRA. National Rifle Assn. Washington, D.C., 1972. 256pp, well illus. $4.50. A wealth of information on collecting and collectors' arms, with 64 major and 41 short articles, selected from the last 18 years of *The American Rifleman.*

The Winchester Book, by Geo. Madis, Art & Reference House, Lancaster, Texas, 1971. 542pp, illus. $20.00.

GENERAL

To All Sportsmen; and Particularly to Farmers and Gamekeepers, by Co. Geo. Hanger, Richmond Publ. Co., Richmond, England, 1971. 226pp. $9.50. Reprint of an 1814 work on hunting, guns, horses, veterinary techniques, etc.

The American B.B. GUN, by A. T. Dunathan, A. S. Barnes, S. Brunswick, N.J., 1971. 154pp, illus. $10.00. Identification reference and a price guide for B.B. guns, plus a brief history and advertising plates.

Americans and Their Guns, compiled by Jas. B. Trefethen, ed. by Jas. E. Serve, Stackpole Books, Harrisburg, Pa., 1967. 320pp, illus. $9.95. The National Rifle Association of America story through nearly a century of service to the nation. More than a history — a chronical of help to novice and expert in the safe and proper use of firearms for defense and recreation, as well as a guide for the collector of arms.

The Anatomy of Firearms, by R. L. Wallack, Simon & Schuster, N.Y., 1965. 320pp, illus. $6.95. Guide to guns of all types, ammunition, ballistics, repairs and adjustments, and related topics.

Arms of The World: The 1911 ALFA Catalogue. Edited by Joseph J. Schroeder, Jr. Digest Books, Northfield, Ill. 701pp. Paper, $5.95.

The Art of Shooting, by C. E. Chapel. A. S. Barnes, N.Y., 1960. 424pp, illus. $3.95. A comprehensive, simplified guide to every aspect of pistol, revolver, and rifle shooting. A history of rifle development is included.

Author and Subject Index to the American Rifleman Magazine 1961-1970, by W.R. Burrell, Galesburg, Miss., 1971. 64pp. $6.50. Alphabetical listing by author, title and subject.

Black Powder Guide, by Geo. Nonte, Jr. Shooter's Bible Publ., S. Hackensack, N.J., 1969. 214pp, fully illus. $3.95.

Black Powder Snapshots, by Herb Sherlock. Standard Publications. Huntington, W. Va. 50pp, illus. $10.00. Deluxe large volume containing 23 major Sherlock drawings and 95 punchy, marginal sketches.

Carbine Handbook, by Paul Wahl. Arco Publ. Co., N.Y., 1964. 80pp, illus. $6.00; Paperbound, $3.95. A manual and guide to the U.S. Carbine, cal. 30, M1, with data on its history, operation, repair, ammunition, and shooting.

The Complete Book of The Air Gun, by G. C. Nonte, Jr. Stackpole Books, Harrisburg, Pa., 1970. 288pp. Illus. $7.95. From plinking to Olympic competition, from BB guns to deluxe rifles, pistols, the air shotgun.

Complete Book of Rifles and Shotguns, by Jack O'Connor, Harper & Bros., N.Y., 1961. 447pp, illus. $6.95. A splendid two-part book of encyclopedic coverage on every detail of rifle and shotgun.

Complete Book of Shooting, by Jack O'Connor et al. Outdoor Life-Harper & Row, N.Y., 1965. 385pp, illus. $5.95. Fundamentals of shooting with rifle, shotgun, and handgun in the hunting field and on target ranges.

The Complete Book of Trick and Fancy Shooting, by Ernie Lind, Winchester Press, N.Y., 1972. 159pp, illus. $5.95. Step-by-step instructions for acquiring the whole range of shooting skills with rifle, pistol and shotgun; includes practical hints on developing your own shooting act.

Encyclopedia of Firearms, ed. by H. L. Peterson, E. P. Dutton, N.Y., 1964. 367pp, 100pp. of illus. incl. color. $13.50. Fine reference work on firearms, with articles by 45 top authorities covering classes of guns, manufacturers, ammunition, nomenclature, and related topics.

Encyclopedia of Modern Firearms, Vol. 1, compiled and publ. by Bob Brownell, Montezuma, Ia., 1959. 1057pp. plus index, illus. $22.50. Dist. by Bob Brownell, Montezuma, Ia. 50171. Massive accumulation of basic information of nearly all modern arms pertaining to "parts and assembly." Replete with arms photographs, exploded drawings, manufacturers' lists of parts, etc.

Firearms, by Walter Buehr. Crowell Co., N.Y., 1967, 186pp, illus. $5.95. From gunpowder to guided missile, an illustrated history of firearms for military and sporting uses.

Firearms Dictionary, by R. A. "Bob" Steindler. Stackpole Books, Harrisburg, Pa. 288pp, illus. $7.95.

The Fireside Book of Guns, by Larry Koller. Simon & Schuster, N.Y., 1959. 284pp, illus. in artistic photography and full-color plates. $12.95. On all counts the most beautiful and colorful production of any arms book of our time, this work adequately tells the story of firearms in America — from the first explorers to today's sportsmen.

Fundamentals of Small Arms, U.S. TM9-2205. Normount Armament Co. Forest Grove, Ore. 236pp, illus. Paperbound. $3.50. Reprint of the U.S. Army technical manual dated 7 May 1952.

Gas, Air and Spring Guns of the World, by W. H. B. Smith. Stackpole Books, Harrisburg, Pa., 1957. 279pp, well illus. $4.98. A detailed, well documented history of the air and gas gun industry throughout the world. It includes ancient and modern arms, and it devotes a chapter to accurate velocity tests of modern arms.

The Golden Guide to Guns, by Larry Koller. Golden Press, N.Y., 1966. 160pp, illus. Paperbound, pocket-size. $1.00. Introduction to rifles, shotguns, and handguns for all uses. Profusely illus., much in color.

Great American Guns and Frontier Fighters, by Will Bryant, Grosset & Dunlap, N.Y., 1961. 160pp, illus. $3.95. Popular account of firearms in U.S. history and of the events in which they played a part.

Gun Digest, 26th ed., ed. by John Amber. Digest Books, Inc. Northfield, Ill., 1972, 480pp, profusely illus, 32pp, in full color. Paper cover. $6.95. Known as the world's greatest gun book because of its factual informative data for shooters, hunters, collectors, reloaders and other enthusiasts. Truly of encyclopedic importance.

Gun Digest Treasury, ed. by John Amber, 4th ed., 1972. Digest Books Inc. Northfield, Ill. 352pp, illus. Paper. $5.95. The best from 25 years of the *Gun Digest,* selected from the annual editions.

The Gun, 1834, by Wm. Greener, with intro. by D. B. McLean. Normount Technical Publ., Forest Grove, Oreg., 1971. 240pp, illus. Paper. $4.50. Reprint of the 1835 British ed. on various small firearms.

The Gunfighter, Man or Myth? by Joseph G. Rosa, Oklahoma Press, Norman, Okla., 1969. 229pp, illus. (including weapons). $5.95. A well-documented work on gunfights and gunfighters of the West and elsewhere. Great treat for all gunfighter buffs.

Guns and Shooting, A Bibliography, by R. Riling. Greenberg, N.Y., 1951. 343pp, illus. $20.00. A selected listing, with pertinent comments and anecdote, of books and printed material on arms and ammunition from 1420 to 1950.

Hatcher's Notebook, by Maj. Gen. J. S. Hatcher. Stackpole Books, Harrisburg, Pa., 1952. 2nd ed. with four new chapters, 1957. 629pp, illus. $11.95. A dependable source of information for gunsmiths, ballisticians, historians, hunters, and collectors.

Instinct Shooting, by Mike Jennings. Dodd, Mead & Co., N.Y., 1959, 157pp, 20 line drawings, illus. $3.95. All about Lucky McDaniel and his surprisingly successful discovery of a new aerial shooting technique, one which will let almost anyone, novices preferred, hit flying targets with only minutes of instruction.

Introduction to Muzzle Loading, by R. O. Ackerman. Publ. by the author, Albuquerque, N.M., 1966. 20pp, illus. with author's sketches. $1.50. This booklet, in paper wrappers, will be Book No. 1 of the projected series. Contains a glossary of muzzle-loading terms, and is aimed at the novice.

Kuhlhoff on Guns, by Pete Kuhlhoff, Winchester Press, N.Y., 1970. 180pp, illus. $5.95. A selection of firearms articles by the late Gun Editor of *Argosy Magazine.*

Modern ABC'S of Guns, by R. A. Steindler. Stackpole Books, Harrisburg, Pa., 1965. 191pp, illus. $4.95. Concise lexicon of today's sporting firearms, their components, ammunition, accessory equipment and use.

Modern Police Firearms, by Duke Roberts and A. P. Bristow. Glencoe Press, Beverly Hills, Cal., 1969. 170pp, illus., in line and halftone. $5.95. An informative work covering all pertinent details, with chapters on safety, ballistics, maintenance, marksmanship, chemical agents, the shotgun, plus legal and ethical aspects.

No Second Place Winner, by Wm. H. Jordan, publ. by the author, Shreveport, La. (Box 4072), 1962. 114pp, illus. $6.00. Guns and gear of the peace officer, ably discussed by a U.S. Border Patrolman for over 30 years, and a first-class shooter with handgun, rifle, etc.

Pageant of the Gun, by Harold L. Peterson. Doubleday & Co., Inc. Garden City, N.Y., 1967. 352pp, profusely illus. $3.95.

The Redbook of Used Gun Values 1972, publ. by Publishers Dev. Corp., Skokie, Ill., 1971. 130pp, illus. Paper covers. $2.50. Lists many types and modifications of rifles, shotguns, and handguns, arranged by makers, with prices estimated according to condition.

Shooting Muzzle Loading Hand Guns, by Charles T. Haven. Guns Inc. M.A. 1947. 132pp, illus. $6.50. A good summary of shooting methods, both contemporary and modern. Dueling with M.L. handguns is also covered.

Small Arms Lexicon and Concise Encyclopedia, by Chester Mueller and John Olson. Stoeger Arms., So. Hackensack, N.J., 1968. 312pp, 500 illus. $14.95. Definitions, explanations, and references on antiques, optics ballistics, etc. from A to Z. Over 3,000 entries plus appendix.

Small Arms of The World, by W. H. B. Smith and J. E. Smith. 9th ed., 1969. Stackpole Books, Harrisburg, Pa. 786pp, profusely illus. $17.95. A most popular firearms classic for easy reference. Covers the small arms of 42 countries, clearly showing operational principles. A timeless volume of proven worth.

Teaching Kids to Shoot, by Henry M. Stebbins. Stackpole Books, Harrisburg, Pa., 1966. 96pp, illus. $2.95. Designed for parents and leaders who want to develop safety conscious firearms users.

Triggernometry, by Eugene Cunningham. Caxton Printers Lt., Caldwell, Id., 1970. 441pp, illus. $7.95. A classic study of famous outlaws and lawmen of the West—their stature as human beings, their exploits and skills in handling firearms. A reprint.

GUNSMITHING

Gunsmith Kinks, by F. R. (Bob) Brownell. F. Brownell & Son, Montezuma, Ia. 1st ed., 1969. 496pp, well illus. $9.95. A widely useful accumulation of shop kinks, short cuts, techniques and pertinent comments by practicing gunsmiths from all over the world.

The Gunsmith's Manual, by J. Stelle and W. Harrison. Rutgers Book Center, Highland Park, N.J., 1972. 276pp, illus. $9.95. Exact reprint of the original. For the American gunsmith in all branches of the trade.

Gunsmithing Simplified, by H. E. Macfarland. Washington, D.C., 1950, A. S. Barnes, N.Y., 1959. 303pp, illus. $6.95. A thorough, dependable, concise work with many helpful shortcuts.

Home Gun Care & Repair, by P. O. Ackley, Stackpole Books, Harrisburg, Pa., 1969. 191pp, illus. $5.95.

The NRA Gunsmithing Guide, National Rifle Association, Wash., D.C., 1971. 336pp, illus. Paper. $5.50. Information of the past 15 years from the *American Rifleman,* ranging from 03A3 Springfields to Model 92 Winchesters.

HANDGUNS

The Handbook of Handgunning, by Paul B. Weston. Crown Pub., N.Y., 1968. 138pp, illus. with photos. $4.95. "New concepts in pistol and revolver shooting," by a noted firearms instructor and writer.

The Handgun, by Geoffrey Boothroyd, Crown Pub., N.Y., 1970. 564pp, profusely illus. plus copious index. $19.95. A massive and impressive work, excellently covering the subject from matchlocks to present-day automatics. Many anecdotes, much comment and pertinent data, including ammunition, etc.

Military Pistols and Revolvers, by I. V. Hogg. Arco Pub. Co., N.Y., 1970. 80pp, illus. $3.50. The handguns of the two World Wars shown in halftone illus. with brief historical and descriptive text.

Modern Pistol Shooting, by P. C. Freeman. Faber & Faber, London, England, 1968. 176pp, illus. $5.00. How to develop accuracy with the pistol. Fine points in technique are covered, with information on competitive target shooting.

Pistol and Revolver Guide, by George Nonte. Stoeger Arms Corp., S. Hackensack. N.J., 1967. 192pp, well illus. Paper wrappers. $3.95. A history of the handgun, its selection, use and care, with a glossary and trade directory.

Pistols, A Modern Encyclopedia, by Stebbins, Shay & Hammond. Stackpole Co., Harrisburg, Pa., 1961. 380pp, illus. $4.98. Comprehensive coverage of handguns for every purpose, with material on selection, ammunition, and marksmanship.

Pistols of the World, by Claude Blair, Viking Press, N.Y., 1968. 206pp, plus plates. $9.98. Authoritative review of handguns since the 16th century, with chapters on major types, manufacture, and decoration. Fine photographic illustrations.

Pistols, Revolvers, and Ammunition, by M. H. Josserand and J. Stevenson, Crown Pub., N.Y., 1972. 341pp, illus. $7.50. Basic information classifying the pistol, revolver, ammunition, ballistics, and rules of safety.

Sixguns by Keith, by Elmer Keith. Stackpole Co., Harrisburg, Pa., 1968 (reprint of 1961 edition). 335pp, illus. $4.95. Long a popular reference on handguns, this work covers all aspects, whether for the shooter, collector or other enthusiasts.

HUNTING

Asian Jungle, African Bush, by Charles Askins. Stackpole Books, Harrisburg, Pa., 1959. 258pp, illus. $4.95.

Complete Book of Hunting, by Clyde Ormond. Outdoor Life-Harper & Row, New York, Rev. Ed., 1972. 432pp. $6.95.

Art of Hunting Big Game in North America, by Jack O'Connor. Outdoor Life-A. Knopf, New York, 1967. 404pp. $8.95.

RIFLES

The Book of Rifles, by W. H. B. Smith, Stackpole Books, Harrisburg, Pa., 1963 (3rd ed.), 656pp, profusely illus. $6.00. An encyclopedic reference work on shoulder arms, recently updated. Includes rifles of all types, arranged by country of origin.

Description of Telescopic Musket Sights, Inco, 1972. 10pp, 4 plates. Paper. $1.00. Reprint of 1917 War Dept. pamphlet No. 1957, first publ. in 1908.

The Rifle Book, by Jack O'Connor. Random House (Knopf), N.Y., 1948. 3rd ed., 1964. 338pp, illus. $10.00.

Rifles, a Modern Encyclopedia, by H. M. Stebbins. Book Sales, New York, N.Y., 1970. A reprint of the original of 1958. 376pp, well illus. $4.98. A comprehensive work covering subject for target and game. A limited number of original, deluxe and numbered full-leather bound copies at $25.00.

Shooter's Bible Gunsight Guide, by George Nonte. Shooter's Bible, Inc., So. Hackensack, N.J., 1968. 224pp, illus. $3.95. Catalog data, descriptions and comment, plus articles on all types of modern gun sights.

Springfield Rifles, M1903, M1903A1, M1903A4, compiled by the publ., Normount Armament Co., Forest Grove, Or., 1968. Over 115pp, illus. Paper wrappers. $2.50. Routine disassembly and maintenance to complete ordnance inspection and repair, bore sighting, trigger adjustment, accessories, etc.

SHOTGUNS

Automatic and Repeating Shotguns, by R. Arnold. Barnes & Co., N.Y., 1960. 173pp, illus. $2.95. Their history and development, with expert professional advice on choosing a gun for clay target shooting, game shooting, etc.

Book of Shotgun Sports, by Sports Illustrated eds. J. B. Lippincott Co., Phila, Pa., 1967. 88pp, illus. $3.50. Introduction to target shooting, game shooting, and gunmanship.

Field, Skeet and Trapshooting, by C. E. Chapel. Revised ed. Barnes & Co., N.Y., 1962. 291pp, illus. $6.95. A useful work on shotgun shooting, including gun types, ammo, accessories, marksmanship, etc.

The Golden Age of Shotgunning, by Bob Hinman, Winchester Press, N.Y., 1971. 175pp, illus, $8.95. The story of American shotgun and wingshooting from 1870 to 1900.

Parker, America's Finest Shotgun, by P. H. Johnson, Outlet Book Co., Inc. N.Y., 1968. 260pp., illus. $3.95. An account of a great sporting arm—from post Civil War until 1947, when it was sold to Remington. Values, models etc.

Shooting for Beginners, by E. N. Barclay. Percival Marshall & Co., London, 1963. 74pp, illus. $1.75. Concise introduction to British techniques and customs in shotgunning for game birds.

The Shotgun Book, by Jack O'Connor. Alfred A. Knopf, N.Y., 1965. 332pp, plus index, illus. with line and photos. $10.00. The definitive, authoritative book with up-to-date chapters on wildfowling, upland gunning, trap and skeet shooting. It includes practical advice on shotgun makes, models and functions, as well as data on actions.

Shotguns by Keith, by Elmer Keith. Stackpole Books, Harrisburg, Pa., 1967. 307pp, plus illus.

A new edition. $2.98. Guns and their accessories from history to ornamentation, their ammunition, and the practical use of American, English, and European arms.

PERIODICAL PUBLICATIONS

Alaska Sportsman, Alaska Northwest Pub. Co., Box 4-EEE, Anchorage, Alaska 99503. $8.00 yr. Hunting & fishing articles.

American Field, 222 W. Adams St., Chicago, Ill. 60606. $9.00 yr. Field dogs & trials, occasional gun & hunting articles.

The American Rifleman, National Rifle Assn., 1600 Rhode Island Ave., N.W., Washington, D.C. 20036. $7.50 yr. Firearms articles of all kinds.

The American West, American West Publ. Co., 599 College Ave., Palo Alto, Ca. 94306. $9.00 yr.

Argosy, Popular Publ., Inc. 205 E. 42nd St., New York, N.Y. 10017. $7.00 yr.

Army, Assn. of the U.S. Army, 1529 18th Ave., N.W. Washington, D.C. 20036. $7.50 yr. Occasional articles on small arms.

Australian Shooters Journal, P.O. Box 90, Stafford, Brisbane, Qld., 4053 Australia. $5.50 yr. locally; $7.00 yr. overseas. Hunting & shooting articles.

Canadian Journal of Arms Collecting, Museums Restoration Service, P.O. Box 2037, Sta. D, Ottawa, Ont. Canada. $4.00 yr.

Deutsches Waffen Journal, Journal-Verlag Schwend GmbH, Postfach 340, D7170 Schwabisch Hall, Germany. $11.50 yr. Antique and modern arms, their history, technical aspects, etc. German test.

Ducks Unlimited, Inc, P.O. Box 66300, Chicago, Ill. 60666.

Enforcement Journal, Natl. Police Officers Assn., Natl. Police Academy Bldg., 1890 S. Tamiami Trail, Venice, Fla. 33595. $6.00 yr.

The Field, The Harmsworth Press Ltd., 8 Stratton St., London W.I., England. $29.50 yr. Hunting & shooting articles.

Field & Stream, Holt, Rinehart & Winston, Inc., 383 Madison Ave., New York, N.Y. 10017. $5.00 yr. Articles on firearms plus hunting & fishing.

Fishing and Hunting Guide, Fishing & Hunting Guide Ltd., P.O. Box 48, Dolton, Ill. 60419. $3.00 yr.

Fur-Fish-Game, A. R. Harding Pub. Co., 2878 E. Main St., Columbus, Ohio 43209. $3.50 yr.

The Gun Report, World Wide Gun Report, Inc., Box 111, Aledo, Ill. 61231. $6.00 yr. For the gun collector.

Gunsport & Gun Collector, The Clark Bldg., Suite 2100, Pittsburgh, Pa. 15222. $5.00 yr.

Gun Week, Sidney Printing & Publishing Co., P.O. Box 150, Sidney, Ohio 45365. $5.00 yr. U.S. & possessions, $6.00 yr; Canada $7.00 yr. Tabloid paper on guns, hunting, shooting.

Gun World, Gallant Publishing Co., 130 Olinda Pl., Brea, Calif. 92621. $7.50 yr. For the hunting, reloading & shooting enthusiast.

Guns & Ammo, Petersen Pub. Co., 8490 Sunset Blvd., Los Angeles, Calif. 90069. $7.50 yr. Guns, shooting, & technical articles.

Guns, Guns Magazine, 8150 N. Central Park Ave., Skokie, Ill. 60076. $7.50 yr. Articles for gun collectors, hunters and shooters.

Guns Review, Revenhill Pub. Co. Ltd., Standard House, Bonhill St., London E.C. 2, England. $10.20 yr. For collectors & shooters.

The Handgunner, U.S. Revolver Assn., 59 Alvin St., Springfield, Mass. 01104. $5.00 yr. General handgun & competition articles.

The Handloader Magazine, Dave Wolfe Pub. Co., Box 3030, Prescott, Ariz. 86301. $7.00 yr.

Hobbies, Lightner Pub. Co., 1006 S. Michigan Ave., Chicago, Ill., 60605. $6.00 yr.; Canada $7.00; foreign $7.50. Collectors departments.

International Shooting Sport, Union Internationale de Tir, 62 Wiesbaden-Klarenthal, Klarenthalerstr., Germany. $6.00 yr., p.p. For the international target shooter.

The Journal of the Arms & Armour Society, F. Wilkinson (Secy.), 40 Great James St., Holborn, London WC1, England. $4.00 yr. Articles for the collector.

Law and Order, Law and Order Magazine, 37 W. 38th St., New York, N.Y. 10018. $7.00 yr. Articles on weapons for law enforcement.

The Luger Journal, Robt. B. Marvin, Publ., P.O. Box 326, Jasper, Fla. 32052. $6.00 yr.

Muzzle Blasts, National Muzzle Loading Rifle Assn., P.O. Box 67, Friendship, Ind. 47021. $6.00 yr. For the black-powder shooter.

National Rifle Assn. Journal (British), Natl. Rifle Assn. (BR), Bisley Camp, Brookwood, Woking, Surrey, England.

National Sportsman's Digest, National Sportsman's Club, Box 2003, Dallas, Texas 75221. $8.00 yr. Subs. includes membership in the club, etc.

New Zealand Wildlife, New Zealand Deerstalkers Assoc. Inc., P.O. Box 263, Wellington, N.Z. $2.00 U.S. & Canada, elsewhere on application. Hunting & shooting articles.

Ordnance, American Ordnance Assn., 819 Union Trust Bldg. Wash., D.C. 20005. $8.00 yr. Occasional articles on small arms and related subjects.

Outdoor Life, Popular Science Pub. Co., 355 Lexington Ave., New York, N.Y. 10017. $6.00 yr. Arms column by Jim Carmichel.

Outdoor World, Country Beautiful Corp, 24198 W. Bluemound Rd. Waukesha, Wis. 53186. $7.95 yr. Conservation and wildlife articles.

Police Times, 1100 N.E. 125th St., N. Miami, Fla. 33161.

Popular Mechanics, Hearst Corp. 224 W. 57th St., New York, N.Y. 10019. $5.00 yr. $5.75 Canada, $7.00 foreign. Hunting & shooting articles.

Precision Shooting, Precision Shooting, Inc., 8 Cline St., Dolgeville, N.Y. 13329. $5.00 yr. Journal of the International Benchrest Shooters.

The Rifle Magazine, Dave Wolfe Publishing Co., Box 3030, Prescott, Ariz. 86301. $9.00 yr. Journal of the NBRSA.

The Rifleman, National Smallbore Rifle Assoc. 113 Southwark St. London, S.E.1, England. $7.00 (5 yrs.). Data on British and International matches, and technical shooting articles.

Rod and Gun in Canada, Rod and Gun Pub. Corp., 1219 Hotel deVille, Montreal 129, P.Q. Canada. $3.00 yr. $5.00 2 yrs., out of Canada, postage $1.00 yr. extra. Regular gun and shooting articles.

Saga, Gambi Publ., 333 Johnson Ave., Brooklyn, N.Y. 11026. $6.00 yr. U.S., $6.50 Canada.

Bibliography

The Shooting Industry, Publisher's Dev. Corp, 8150 N. Central Pk., Skokie, Ill. 60076. $7.00 yr.

The Shooting Times & Country Magazine (England), Cordwallis Estate, Clivemont Rd., Maidenhead, Berksh., England. $20 yr. Game shooting, wildfowling and firearms articles.

Shooting Times, PJS Publications, News Plaza, Peoria, Ill. 61601. $5.85 yr. Gun ads plus articles on every gun activity.

The Shotgun News, Snell Publishing Co., Columbus, Nebr. 68601. $4.00 yr. Sample copy 50¢. Gun ads of all kinds.

The Skeet Shooting Review, National Skeet Shooting Assn., 212 Linwood Bldg., 2608 Inwood Rd., Dallas, Tex. 75235 $9.00 yr. (Assn. membership of $10.00 includes mag.) Scores, averages, skeet articles.

Sporting Goods Business, Gralla Publications, 1501 Broadway, New York, New York 10063. Trade Journal.

The Sporting Goods Dealer, 1212 N. Lindbergh Blvd., St. Louis, Mo. 63166. $4.00 yr. The sporting goods trade journal.

Sports Afield, The Hearst Corp., 250 W. 55th St., New York, N.Y. 10019. $4.00 yr. Pete Brown on firearms plus hunting and fishing articles.

Sports Age Magazine, 3000 France Ave. So., Minneapolis, Minn. 55416. Trade journal.

Sports Illustrated, Time, Inc., 541 N. Fairbanks Court, Chicago, Ill. 60611. $12.00 yr. U.S. Poss. and Canada; $16.00 yr. all other countries. Articles on the current sporting scene.

Trap & Field, 1100 Waterway Blvd., Indianapolis, Ind. 46202. $7.00 yr. Official publ. Amateur Trapshooting Assn. Scores, averages, trapshooting articles.

True, Fawcett Publ., Inc. Fawcett Bldg. Greenwich, Conn. 06830. $7.00 yr. U.S. Poss., and Canada; $10.00 yr. all other countries.

Wildlife Review, Fish & Wildlife Branch. Dep't of Rec. and Conservation Parliament Bldgs., Victoria, B.C., Canada. $1.00 yr.

Appendix

Appendix 1

American and Foreign Arms Associations

UNITED STATES

Alabama

ALABAMA GUN COLLECTORS ASSN., Thomas M. Stewart, 601 Eastwood Pl., Birmingham, Ala. 35216

NORTH ALABAMA GUN COLL. ASSN., P. O. Box 564, Huntsville, Ala. 35802

Arizona

ARIZONA GUN COLLECTORS. Miles S. Vaughn, 1129 S. 6th Ave., Tucson, Ariz. 85701

ARMS COLLECTORS OF THE SOUTHWEST. Robert Kuban, Box 543, Yuma, Ariz. 85364

INTERNATIONAL CARTRIDGE COLL. ASSN., INC. A. D. Amesbury, 4065 Montecito Ave., Tucson, Ariz. 85711

NATIONAL RELOADING MFRS. ASSN., INC. Box 1697, Prescott, Ariz. 86301

Arkansas

ARKANSAS GUN & CARTRIDGE COLL. CLUB. M. Cutrell, 2006 E. 7th Pine Bluff, Ark. 71601

FT. SMITH DEALERS & COLL. ASSN., Tony Smith, 1407 57 Terrace, Ft. Smith, Ark. 72901

California

CALIF. HUNTERS & GUN OWNERS ASSOC., V. H. Wacker, 2309 Cipriani Blvd., Belmont, Cal. 94002

GREATER CALIF. ARMS & COLLECTORS ASSN., Donald L. Bullock, 8291 Carburton St., Long Beach, Cal. 90808

LOS ANGELES GUN & CTG. COLLECTORS ASSN., F. H. Ruffra, 20810 Amie Ave., Torrance, Cal. 90503

NORTHERN CALIFORNIA HISTORICAL ARMS COLL. ASSN., Julia Lundwall, 25 Mizpah St., San Francisco Cal. 94131

SAN BERNARDINO VALLEY ARMS COLLECTORS, INC., F. Schaperkotter, 2697 Acacia Ave., San Bernardino, Cal. 92405

SANTA BARBARA ANTIQUE ARMS COLL. ASSN., INC., Tom McKissack, P. O. Box 6291, Santa Barbara, Cal. 93111

SOUTHERN CALIFORNIA ARMS COLLECTORS ASSN., Frank E. Barnyak, 4204 Elmer Ave., N. Hollywood, Cal. 91602

U.S. INTERNATIONAL TRAP & SKEET ASSN., Box 1437, Huntington Beach, Cal. 92647

Colorado

ARAPAHOE GUN COLLECTORS. Bill Rutherford, 2968 S. Broadway, Englewood, Colo. 80110

COLORADO GUN COLLECTORS ASSN., Arnie Dowd, 5970 Estes Ct., Arvada, Colo. 80002

PIKES PEAK GUN COLLECTORS GUILD. Charles Cell, 406 E. Uintah St., Colorado Springs, Colo. 80903

Connecticut

ANTIQUE ARMS COLL. ASSN. OF CONN., A. Darling, 35 Stanley St., New Haven, Conn. 06511

NATIONAL SHOOTING SPORTS FDTN., INC. Warren Page, Pres. 1075 Post Rd., Riverside, Conn. 06878

STRATFORD GUN COLLECTORS ASSN., INC., P. O. Box 52, Stratford, Conn. 06497

YE CONN. GUN GUILD, INC., Rob. L. Harris, P. O. Box 67, Cornwall Bridge, Conn. 06754

Delaware

DELAWARE ANTIQUE ARMS COLLECTORS, C. Landis, 2408 Duncan Rd., Wilmington, Del. 19808

District of Columbia

AMERICAN MILITARY INST., Box 568, Washington, D.C. 20044

AMERICAN ORDNANCE ASSN., 819 Union Trust Bldg., Washington, D.C. 20005

NATIONAL RIFLE ASSN., 1600 Rhode Island Ave. Washington, D.C. 20036

Florida

AMERICAN POLICE PISTOL & RIFLE ASSN., 1100 N.E. 125th St., No. Miami, Fla. 33161 (law enforcement members only)

FLORIDA GUN COLLECTORS ASSN., Box Marvin, P. O. Box 470, Jasper, Fla. 32052

NATIONAL POLICE OFFICERS ASSN. OF AMERICA, Natl. Police Hall of Fame Bldg., Venice, Fla. 33595

TAMPA BAY GUN COLLECTORS ASSN., Col. Emmet M. Jeffreys, 401 49th St., N. St. Petersburg, Fla. 33710

Georgia

GEORGIA ARMS COLLECTORS, James F. Watterson, 2915 Paces Lake Ct., N.W. Atlanta, Ga. 30339

Illinois

CENTRAL ILLINOIS GUN COLLECTORS ASSN., INC. Donald E. Bryan, R.R. #2, Jacksonville, Ill. 62650

FORT DEARBORN FRONTIERSMEN, Al Normath, 8845 Pleasant Ave., Hickory Hills, Ill. 60457

FOX VALLEY ARMS FELLOWSHIP, INC., Graham Burnside, 203 Oregon Ave., Dundee, Ill. 60118

ILLINOIS STATE RIFLE ASSN., 2800 N. Milwaukee Ave., Chicago, Ill. 60618

ILLINOIS GUN COLLECTORS ASSN., P. E. Pitts, P. O. Box 1524, Chicago, Ill. 60690

LITTLE FORT GUN COLLECTORS ASSN., Ernie Robinson, P. O. Box 194, Gurney, Ill. 60031

MISSISSIPPI VALLEY GUN & CARTRIDGE COLL. ASSN., Mel Sims, Box 426, New Windsor, Ill. 61465

SAUK TRAIL GUN COLLECTORS, L. D. Carlock, Rte. 1, Box 169, Prophetstown, Ill. 61277

WABASH VALLEY GUN COLLECTORS ASSN., INC. Mrs. Betty Baer, 1002 Lincoln Pk. Ave., Danville, Ill. 61832

Indiana

AMERICAN SINGLE SHOT RIFLE ASSN., G. H. Crontz, 11439 Wicker Ave., Cedar Lake, Ind. 46303

CENTRAL INDIANA GUN COLL. ASSN., Paul E. Daughterty, 421 E. Washington St., Hartford City, Ind. 47348

CRAWFORDSVILLE GUN CLUB, INC., Rob. J. K. Edmonds, R.R. 2, Crawfordsville, Ind. 47933

MIDWEST GUN TRADERS, INC., Glen Wittenberger, 4609 Oliver St., Ft. Wayne, Ind. 46806

NATIONAL MUZZLE LOADING RIFLE ASSN., Box 67, Friendship, Ind. 47021

NORTHERN INDIANA GUN COLLECTORS ASSN., Joe Katona, 16150 Ireland Rd., Mishawaka, Ind. 46544

SOUTHERN INDIANA GUN COLLECTORS ASSN., INC., Harold M. McClary, 509 N. 3rd St., Boonville, Ind. 47601

TIPPECANOE GUN & CARTRIDGE COLLECTORS CLUB, Leonard Ledman, R.R. 12, Box 212, Lafayette, Ind.

Iowa

CEDAR VALLEY GUN. COLL., R. L. Harris, 1602 Wenig Rd., N.E. Cedar Rapids, Iowa 52402

CENTRAL STATES GUN COLLECTORS ASSN., Chas. J. Versluls, 701 Broadway, Watterloo, Ia. 50703

EASTERN IOWA GUN & CARTRIDGE COLLECTORS ASSN., F. Fitzpatrick, 305 N. Eliza St., Maquoketa, Ia. 52060

QUAD CITY ARMS COLL. ASSN., A. Squire, 1845 W. 3rd St. Davenport, Ia. 52802

Kansas

CHISHOLM TRAIL ANTIQUE GUN COLL. ASSN., P. O. Box 13093, Wichita, Kans. 67213

FOUR STATE COLLECTORS ASSN., M. G. Wilkinson, 915 E. 10th Pittsburgh, Kans. 66762

KANSAS CARTRIDGE COLL. ASSN., Bob Linder, Box 84, Plainville, Kans. 67663

MISSOURI VALLEY ARMS COLLECTORS ASSN., Chas P. Samuel, Jr., Box 8204, Shawnee Mission, Kans. 66208

SOLOMON VALLEY GUN COLLECTORS, Frank Wheeler, Box 230, Osborne, Kans. 76473

Kentucky

JOHN HUNT MORGAN GUN COLL. INC., P. O. Box 525, Paris, Ky. 40361

KENTUCKIANA ARMS COLL. ASSN., Charles R. Phelps, Box 1776, Louisville, Ky. 40201

KENTUCKY GUN COLLECTORS ASSN., INC., J. A. Smith, Box 64, Owensboro, Ky. 42301

Louisiana

ARK-LA-TEX GUN COLLECTORS ASSN., Ray Franks, 1521 Earl St., Shreveport, La. 71108

BAYOU GUN CLUB, John West, 825 Ida., New Orlena, La.

PELICAN ARMS COLLECTORS, B. Thompson, 9142 Cefalu Dr., Baton Rouge, La. 70811

Maryland

CUMBERLAND VALLEY ARMS COLLECTORS ASSN., Mrs. S. Naylor, Rte. #2, Hagerstown, Md. 21740

MARYLAND ARMS COLL. ASSN., INC. H. R. Moale, 2602 Hillcrest Ave., Baltimore, Md. 21234.

PENN-MAR-VA ANTIQUE ARMS SOC., T. Wibberley, 54 E. Lincoln Ave., Hagerstown, Md. 21740

POTOMAC ARMS COLLECTORS ASSN., Bill Summerfelt, P. O. Box 93, Riverdale, Md. 20840

Massachusetts

BAY COLONY WEAPONS COLLECTORS INC., Ronald B. Santurjian, 47 Homer Rd., Belmont, Mass. 02178

MASSACHUSETTS ARMS COLLECTORS, John J. Callan, Jr., 15 Montague St. Worcester, Mass. 01603

U.S. REVOLVER ASSN., Stanley A. Sprague, 59 Alvin St., Springfield, Mass. 01104

Michigan

MICHIGAN ANTIQUE ARMS COLL., INC., W. H. Heid, 8914 Borgman Ave., Huntington Woods, Mich. 48070

MICHIGAN RIFLE & PISTOL ASSN., John W. Novitch, 124 Moss Ave., Highland Park, Mich. 48203

ROYAL OAK GUN COLLECTORS, Margaret Parket, 13143 Borgmann, Huntington Woods, Mich. 48070

Minnesota

MINNESOTA WEAPONS COLL. ASSN., INC., W. Nemitz, 1069 S. Crestview Dr., St. Paul, Minn. 55119

TWIN PORTS WEAPONS COLLECTORS, Jack Puglisi, 6504 Lexington St., Duluth, Minn. 55807

Mississippi

DIXIE ARMS COLLECTORS, Ruth Creecy, 1509 W. 7th, Hattiesburg, Miss. 39401

MISSISSIPPI GUN COLLECTORS ASSN., Mrs. J. E. Swinney, Box 1332, Hattiesburg, Miss. 39401

Missouri

EDWARDSVILLE, ILL. GUN COLLECTORS, A. W. Stephensmeier, 317 N. Grand Bl., St. Louis, Mo. 63103

MERAMEC VALLEY GUN COLLECTORS, L. W. Olson, Star Route, St. Clair, Mo.

MINERAL BELT GUN COLL. ASSN., G. W. Gunter, 1110 E. Cleveland Ave., Monett, Mo. 65708

Montana

MONTANA ARMS COLLECTORS ASSN., Chris Corensen, 175 6th Ave. N.W., Kalispell, Mont. 59901

NORTH AMERICAN SPORTSMEN'S ASSN., Box 1943-2501 4th Ave. N. Billings, Mont. 59103

Nebraska

NEBRASKA GUN & CARTRIDGE COLLECTORS, E. M. Zalud, 710 West 6th St., North Platte, Neb. 69101

PINE RIDGE GUN COLL. Loren Pickering, 509 Elm St., Crawford, Neb. 69339

New Hampshire

MAPLE TREE GUN COLL. ASSN., E. P. Hector, Meriden Rd., Lebanon, N.H. 03766

NEW HAMPSHIRE ARMS COLLECTORS INC., James Tillinghast, Box 5, Marlow, N.H. 03456

New Jersey

EXPERIMENTAL BALLISTICS ASSOCIATES, Ed Yard, 110 Kensington, Trenton, N.J. 08618

JERSEY SHORE ANTIQUE ARMS COLLECTORS, Bob Holloway, 1755 McGallard Ave., Trenton, N.J. 08610

NEW JERSEY ARMS COLLECTORS CLUB, INC., Joseph Rixon, 122 Bender Ave., Roselle Park, N.J. 07204

New Mexico

NEW MEXICO GUN COLLECTORS ASSN., P. O. Box 14145, Albuquerque, N.M. 87111

SANTA FE GUN COLLEC. ASSN., Ernie Lang, 1085 Nugget, Los Alamos, N.M. 87544.

New York

ARMOR & ARMS CLUB, J. K. Watson, 51 W. 51st St., New York, N.Y. 10019

FORT LEE ARMS COLLECTORS, W. E. Sammis, R.D. 776 Brookridge Dr., Valley Cottage, N.Y. 10898

HUDSON-MOHAWK ARMS COLLECTORS ASSN., INC., Bennie S. Pisarz 108 W. Main St., Frankfort, N.Y. 13340

INTERNATIONAL BENCHREST SHOOTERS, Emory L. Tooly, 8 Cline St. Dolgeville, N.Y. 13329

IROQUOIS ARMS COLLECTORS ASSN., Dennis Freeman, 12144 McNeely Rd., Akron, N.Y. 14001

LONG ISLAND ANTIQUE GUN COLL. ASSN., Frank Davison, 8 Johnson Pl., Baldwin, N.Y. 11510

MID-STATE ARMS COLL. & SHOOTERS CLUB, Bennie S. Pisarz, 108 W. Main St., Frankfort, N.Y. 13340

NEW YORK STATE ARMS COLLECTORS ASSN., INC., Marvin Salls, R.D. 1, Ilion, N.Y. 13357

SPORTING ARMS & AMMUNITION MANUFAC-TURERS' INST., 420 Lexington Ave., New York, N.Y. 10017

WESTCHESTER ARMS COLLECTORS CLUBS, INC., F. E. Falkenbury, Secy., 75 Hillcrest Rd., Hartsdale, N.Y. 10530

North Carolina

CAROLINE GUN COLLECTORS ASSN., N.C., Bill Harvey, P. O. Box 464, Wilson, N.C. 27893

Ohio

AMATEUR TRAP SHOOTING ASSN., P. O. Box 246, Vandalia, O. 45377

AMERICAN SOCIETY OF ARMS COLLECTORS, INC., Rob. F. Rubendunst, 6550 Baywood Ln., Cincinnati, O. 45224

BARBERTON GUN COLLECTORS ASSN., R. N. Watters, 1108 Bevan St., Barberton, O. 44203

MAUMEE VALLEY GUN COLLECTORS ASSN., J. Jennings, 3450 Gallatin Rd., Toledo, O. 43606

NATIONAL BENCH REST SHOOTERS ASSN., INC., Bernice McMullen, 607 W. Line St., Mierva, O. 44657

OHIO GUN COLLECTORS, ASSN., INC., Mrs. C. D. Rickey, 130 S. Main St., Prospect, O. 43342

THE STARK GUN COLLECTORS, INC., Russ E. McNary, 147 Miles Ave., N.W. Canton, O. 44708

TRI-STATE GUN COLLECTORS, Doyt S. Gamble, 1115 N. Main St., Lima, O. 45801

Oklahoma

INDIAN TERRITORY GUN COLLECTORS ASSN., P. O. Box 4491, Tulsa, Okla. 74104

Oregon

JEFFERSON STATE ARMS COLLECTORS, Art Chipman, 2251 Ross Lane, Medford, Ore. 97501

OREGON ARMS COLL. ASSN., INC., Dick Hamilton, P. O. Box 152, Junction City, Ore. 97448

WILLIAMETTE VALLEY ARMS COLL, ASSN., M. Brooks, 2110 W. 20th., Eugene, Ore. 97405

Pennsylvania

BOONE & CROCKETT CLUB, C/O Carnegia Museum, 4400 Forbes Ave., Pittsburgh, Pa. 15213

CENTRAL PENN ANTIQUE ARMS ASSN., Geo. Smithgall, 549 W. Lemon St., Lancaster, Pa. 17603

FORKS OF THE DELAWARE WEAPONS ASSN., INC., John F. Scheid, 348 Bushkill St., Easton, Pa. 18042

LANCASTER MUZZLE LOADING RIFLE ASSN., James H. Frederick Jr. R.D. 1 Box 447, Columbia, Pa. 17512

NORTHERN TIER ANTIQUE GUN COLLECTORS, Cliff Briedinger, Trout Run, Pa. 17771

PENNSYLVANIA ANTIQUE GUN COLLECTORS ASSN., Zenas H. Hoover, 222 Philadelphia St., Indiana, Pa. 15701

PENNSYLVANIA GUN COLLECTORS ASSN., Arch Waugh, R.D. 2, Washington, Pa. 15301

PRESQUE ISLE GUN COLLECTORS ASSN., James Welch, 156 E. 37th St., Erie, Pa. 16506

SOMERSET RIFLE & PISTOL CLUB, J. Richard Ross, 2 Stein Bldg, Somerset, Pa. 15501

TWO LICK VALLEY GUN COLLECTORS, Zenas Hoover, 222 Phila. St., Indiana, Pa. 15701

South Carolina

BELTON GUN CLUB INC., J. K. Phillips, P. O. Box 605, Belton, S.C. 29627

NATL. ARMS COLL. ASSN., INC., Jim McNelley, Box 1462, Columbia, S.C. 29201

SOUTH CAROLINA ARMS COLL. ASSN., J. W. McNelley, 3215 Lincoln, Columbia, S.C. 29201

South Dakota

DAKOTA TERRITORY GUN COLL. ASSN., INC., H. A. Jons, 1711 W. 12th St., Sioux Falls, So. Dak. 57104

Tennessee

MEMPHIS ANTIQUE WEAPONS ASSN. F. Dauser, 3429 Jenkins, Memphis, Tenn. 38118

MEMPHIS GUN COLLECTORS ASSN., R. L. Haley, 3888 S. Lakewood Dr., Memphis, Tenn. 38128

SMOKY MOUNTAIN GUN COLLECTORS ASSN., P. O. Box 22, Oak Ridge, Tenn. 37830

TENNESSEE GUN COLLECTORS ASSN., INC., M. H. Parks, 3556 Pleasant Valley Rd., Hansville, Tenn. 37204

Texas

ALAMO ARMS COLLECTORS, Bill Brookshire, 410 Rector, San Antonio, Texas 78216

HOUSTON GUN COLLECTORS ASSN. C. McKim, 5454 Stillbrooke, Houston, Texas 77035

NATIONAL SKEET SHOOTING ASSN., James M. Leer, Jr., 212 Linwood Bldg. 2608 Inwood Rd., Dallas, Tex. 75235

NATIONAL SPORTSMAN'S CLUB, P. O. Box 2003, Dallas, Tex. 75221

PASO DEL NORTE GUN COLLECTORS INC., Ken Hockett, 1216 Mescalero, El Paso, Tex. 79925

PERMIAN BASIN RIFLE & PISTOL CLUB, INC., E. L. Good, Box 459, Midland, Tex. 79701

PIONEER GUN COLLECTORS ASSN., J. O. Wingate, 4611 Cherokee, Amarillo, Tex. 79109

SABINE GUN COLLECTORS CLUB, Mrs. Irene Vivier, 1042 Iowa, Beaumont, Tex. 77705

TEXAS GUN COLLECTORS ASSN., Mrs. Taska Clerk, 3119 Produce Row, Houston, Tex. 77023

WACO GUN COLLECTORS, C. V. Pruitt, 4021 N. 26th, Waco, Tex. 76708

Utah

UTAH GUN COLLECTORS ASSN., S. Gerald Keogh, 875 20th St., Ogden, Utah 84401

Virginia

NORTH-SOUTH SKIRMISH ASSN., John L. Rawls, P. O. Box 114, McLean, Va. 22101

SHENANDOAH VALLEY GUN COLL. ASSN., Daniel E. Blye, P. O. Box 926, Winchester, Va. 22601

VIRGINIA ARMS COLLECTORS & ASSN., W. H. Bacon, 4601 Sylvan Rd., Richmond, Va. 23225

Washington

WASHINGTON ARMS COLLECTORS, INC., Don Zwicker, 446 Pelly Ave., Renton, Wa. 98055

Wisconsin

CHIPPEWA VALLEY WEAPONS COLLECTORS, J. M. Sullivan, 504 Ferry St., Eau Claire, Wis. 54701

GREAT LAKES WEAPONS COLL. ASSN., INC., E. Warnke, 2249A N. 61 St., Wauwatosa, Wis. 53213

WISCONSIN GUN COLLECTORS ASSN., INC., Rob. Zellmer, W180N8996 Leona Lane, Menomonee Falls, Wis. 53051

Wyoming

WYOMING GUN COLLECTORS, Bob Funk, 224 N. 2W., Riverton, Wyo. 82501

AUSTRALIA

NAT'L SPORTING SHOOTERS ASSN. OF AUSTRALIA, G. O. Nelis, P.O. Box 90, Stafford, Brisbane, Qld., Australia 4053

CANADA

Alberta

CANADIAN HISTORICAL ARMS SOCIETY, P.O. Box 901, Edmonton, Alb. Canada T5J 2L8

Ontario

NIAGARA ARMS COLLECTORS, Box 948, Beamsville, Ont. Canada

ONTARIO ARMS COLLECTORS ASSN., P. Peddle, 174 Ellerslie Ave., Willowdale, Ont. Canada

OSHAWA ANTIQUE GUN COLL., INC., Gordon J. Dignem, 613 Rosmere St., Oshawa, Ont. Canada

Quebec

LOWER CANADA ARMS COLLECTORS ASSN., Secretary, P.O. Box 1162, St. B. Montreal 101, Quebec, Canada.

EUROPE

England

ARMS AND ARMOUR SOCIETY OF LONDON, F. Wilkinson, 40 Great James St., Holborn, London W.C.I.

MUZZLE LOADERS' ASSN. OF GREAT BRITAIN, M. A. Malet, 43 Sandpit Ln. St. Albans, Hertfs, England

NATIONAL RIFLE ASSN. (BRITISH), Bisley Camp, Brookwood, Woking, Surrey, England

France

LES ARQUEBUSIERS DE FRANCE, Mme. Marckmann, 70 Rue des Chantiers, 78-Versailles, France

NEW ZEALAND

NEW ZEALAND DEERSTALKERS ASSN., J. M. Murphy, P.O. Box 263, Wellington, New Zealand

SOUTH AFRICA

HISTORICAL FIREARMS SOC. OF SOUTH AFRICA, "Minden" 11 Buchan Rd., Newlands, Cape Town, South Africa

Directory of Goods and Services

AMMUNITION (Commercial)

Alcan Shells (see Smith & Wesson-Fiocchi, Inc.)

Amron Corp., 525 Progress Ave., Waukesha, Wis. 53186

Cascade Cartridge Inc. (see Omark)

Federal Cartridge Co., 2700 Foshay Tower, Minneapolis, Minn. 55402

Frontier Cartridge Co., Inc., Box 906, Grand Island, Neb. 68801

Omark-CCI, Inc., Box 856, Lewiston, Ida. 83501

Remington Arms Co., Bridgeport, Conn. 06602

Service Armament, 689 Bergen Blvd., Ridgefield, N.J. 07657

Smith & Wesson-Fiocchi, Inc., 3640 Seminary Rd., Alton, Ill. 62002

Speer-DWM, Box 896, Lewiston, Ida. 83501

Super-Vel Cartridge Co., Box 40, Shelbyville, Ind. 46176

Weatherby's, 2781 E. Firestone Blvd., South Gate, Calif. 90280

Winchester-Western, East Alton, Ill. 62024

AMMUNITION (Foreign)

Abercrombie & Fitch, Madison at 45th St., New York, N.Y. 10017

Ammodyne, Box 1859, Los Angeles, Calif. 90053 (RWS)

Canadian Ind., Ltd. (C.I.L.) Box 10, Montreal, Que., Canada

C-I-L Ammunition Inc., P.O. Box 831, Plattsburgh, N.Y. 12901

Centennial Arms Co., 3318 W. Devon Ave., Chicago, Ill. 60645 (Hirtenberg, Austrian)

Colonial Ammunition Co., Box 8511, Auckland, New Zealand

DWM, Speer Prods. Inc., Box 641, Lewiston, Ida. 83501

Gevelot of Canada, Box 1593, Saskatoon, Sask., Canada

Hy-Score Arms Co., 200 Tillary, Brooklyn, N.Y. 11201

Paul Jaeger Inc., 211 Leedom St., Jenkintown, Pa. 19046

S. E. Lazlo, 200 Tillary, Brooklyn, N.Y. 11201

NORMA-Precision, South Lansing, N.Y. 14882

Oregon Ammo Service, Box 19341, Portland, Ore. 97219

Stoeger Arms Corp., 55 Ruta St., S. Hackensack, N.J. 07606

James C. Tillinghast, Box 568, Marlow, N.H. 03456

CHOKE DEVICES AND RECOIL ABSORBERS

A&W Engineering, 6520 Rampart St., Houston, Tex. 77036 (shotgun diverter)

Arms Ingenuity Corp., Box 1, Weatogue, Conn. 06089 (Jet-Away)

Contra-Jet, 7920 49th Ave., S. Seattle, Wash. 98118

Dahl's Gun Shop, Rt. 2, Billings, Mont. 59101

Edwards Recoil Reducer, 269 Herbert St., Alton, Ill. 62002

Emsco Chokes, 101 Second Ave., S. E. Waseca, Minn. 56093

Herter's Inc., Waseca, Minn. 56093 (Vari-Choke)

Lyman Gun Sight Products, Middlefield, Conn. 60455 (Cutts Comp.)

C. R. Pedersen & Son, Ludington, Mich. 49431 (Sha-Cul brake)

Pendleton Dekickers, 1210 S.W. Hailey Ave., Pendleton, Ore. 97801

Poly-Choke Co., Inc., Box 296, Hartford, Conn. 06101

St. Louis Precision Products, 902 Michigan Ave., St. Louis, Mich. 48880 (Gun-Tamer)

GUN CASES, CABINETS AND RACKS

Alco Carrying Cases Inc., 601 W. 26th St., New York, N.Y. 10001

Amer. Safety Gun Case Co., Holland, Mich. 49424

Aremac Co., 101 N. Verity Parkway, Middletown, O. 45042

Artistic Wood Specialties, 923-29 W. Chicago Ave., Chicago, Ill. 60622

Morton Booth Co., Box 123, Joplin, Mo. 64801

Boyt Co., Box 1108, Iowa Falls, Ia. 50126

Brewster Corp., Old Lyme, Conn. 06371

Browning Arms Co., Rt. 4, Box 624-B, Arnold, Mo. 63010

Castle Sptg. Goods, Inc., 498 Nepperhan Ave., Yonkers, N.Y. 10701

Challanger Mfg. Co., 94-28 Merrick Blvd., Jamaica, N.Y. 11433

Cincinnati Ind. Inc. (Cindus), Cincinnati (Lockland), O. 45215

Coladonato Bros., Box 156, Hazleton, Pa. 18201

Dutton's, 7840 Phillips Hwy., Jacksonville, Fla. 32216 (single rack)

Ellwood Epps Sporting Goods, Clinton, Ont., Canada

Farber Bros., Inc., 821 Linden Ave., Memphis, Tenn. 38101 (truck pouch)

Ferrell Co., Rte. 3, Gallatin, Tenn. 37066 (Redi-Rack)

Flambeau Plastics Corp., 801 Lynn, Baraboo, Wis. 53913

Gun-Ho Case Mfg. Co., 110 East 10th St., St. Paul, Minn. 55101

Gun Racks, Inc., P.O. Box 22675, Houston, Tex. 77027

B. E. Hodgdon, Inc., 7710 W. 50 Hiway, Shawnee-Mission, Kans. 66202

Ithaca Gun Co., Terrace Hill, Ithaca, N.Y. 14850

J-K Imports, Box 403, Novato, Cal. 94947 (leg o' mutton case)

Jumbo Sports Prods., P.O. Box 280-Airport Rd., Frederick, Md. 21701

Kolpin Bros. Co., Inc. Box 231, Berlin, Wis. 54923

Marble Arms Corp. 1120 Superior, Gladstone, Mich. 49837

National Sports Div., 19 E. McWilliams St., Fon du Lac, Wis. 54935

Nortex Co., 2821 Main St., Dallas, Tex. 75226 (automobile gun rack)

Paul-Reed, Inc., P.O. Box 227, Charlevoix, Mich. 49720

Penguin Assoc., Inc., Box 97, Parkersburg, Pa. 19365

Precise Imp. Corp., 3 Chestnut, Suffern, N.Y. 10901

Pretto Cabinet Co., 1201 E. Walnut, Oglesby, Ill. 61348

Protecto Plastics, Inc., Box 37, Wind Gap, Pa. 18091

Richland Arms Co., 321 W. Adrian, Blissfield, Mich. 49228

Saf-T-Case, Box 10592, Dallas, Tex. 75207

San Angelo Die Castings, Box 984, San Angelo, Tex. 76901

Buddy Schoellkopf, 4100 Platinum Way, Dallas, Tex. 75237

Sile Distr., 7 Centre Market Pl., New York, N.Y. 10013 (leg o' mutton case)

Stearn Mfg. Co., Div. & 30th St., St. Cloud, Minn. 56301

Sure Shoot'n, Box 195, Jacksonville, Ill. 62650 (leg o' mutton case)

Western Holder Co., Box 33, Menomonee Falls, Wis. 53051

Woodstream Corp., Box 327, Lititz, Pa. 17543

Yield House, Inc. RFD, No. Conway, N.H. 03860

GUNS AND GUN PARTS, REPLICA AND ANTIQUE

Antique Gun Parts, Inc. 569 S. Braddock Ave., Pittsburgh, Pa. 15221 (ML)

Armoury Inc., Rte. 25, New Preston, Conn. 06777

Bannerman, F., Box 126, Blue Point, Long Island, N.Y. 11715

Shelley Braverman, Athens, N.Y. 12015 (obsolete guns)

Philip R. Crouthamel, 817 E. Baltimore, E. Lansdowne, Pa. 19050

Charles E. Duffy, Williams Lane, West Hurley, N.Y. 12491

Federal Ordnance Inc., P.O. Box 36032, Los Angeles, Cal. 90036

Greeley Arms Co., Inc. 223 Little Falls Rd., Fairfield, N.J. 07006

Gunner's Armory, 2 Sonoma, San Francisco, Cal. 94133

H&B Gun Corp., 1228 Fort St., Lincoln Park, Mich. 48166

Hunter's Haven, Zero Prince St., Alexandria, Va. 22314

Bob Lovell, Box 401, Elmhurst, Ill. 60126

Numrich Arms Co., West Hurley, N.Y. 12491

Pacific Intl. Import Co., 2416-16th St. Sacramento, Cal. 95818

Potomac Arms Corp. (see Hunter's Haven)

Reed & Co., Shokan, N.Y. 12481

Martin B. Retting, Inc., 11029 Washington, Culver City, Cal. 90230

Santa Barbara of America, Ltd. 930 N. Beltline Rd., #132, Irving, Tex. 75060 (barrels and barreled actions)

Sarco, Inc. 192 Central, Stirling, N.J. 07980

R. A. Saunders, 3253 Hillcrest Dr., San Antonio, Tex. 78201 (clips)

Schmid & Ladd, 14733 Hwy. 19 S9., Clearwater, Fla. 33516

Sherwood Distr. Inc., 7435 Greenbush Ave., No. Hollywood, Cal. 91605

Clifford L. Smires, R.D., Columbus, N.J. 08022 (Mauser rifles)

Sporting Arms, Inc., 9643 Alpaca St., So. El Monte, Cal. 91733 (M-1 Carb access.)

N. F. Strebe, 4926 Marlboro Pike, S.E. Washington, D.C. 20027

Triple K-Mfg. Co., 568-6th Ave., San Diego, Cal. 92101

GUNS, U.S.-MADE

Agawam Arms Co., 916 Suffield St., Agawam, Mass. 01001

American Firearms Mfg. Co., Inc. 5732 Kenwick Dr., San Antonio, Texas 78238

ArmaLite, 118 E. 16th St., Costa Mesa, Calif. 92627

Auto Mag Corp., 2480 E. Colorado Blvd. Pasadena, Cal. 91107

Caraville Arms, P.O. Box 377, Thousand Oaks, Cal. 91360

Champlin Firearms, Inc., Box 3191, Enid, Okla. 73701

Charter Arms Corp., 265 Asylum, Bridgeport, Conn. 06610

Clerke Recreation Prod., 2040 Broadway, Santa Monica, Cal. 90404 (22 Cal. Rev.)

Colt's, 150 Huyshope Ave., Hartford, Conn. 06102

Commando Arms, Inc., Box 10214, Knoxville, Tenn. 37355

Cumberland Arms, 1222 Oak Dr., Manchester, Tenn. 37355

Day Arms Corp., 7515 Stagecoach Lane, San Antonio, Tex. 78227

Firearms Development, Inc., 218 Austin St., Denton, Tex. 76201

Firearms Intl. Corp. (see Garcia)

Gera Arms, 1535 McKinley, Azusa, Cal. 91702

Golden Age Arms Co., Box 82, Worthington, O. 43085

Gyrojet (see Intercontinental Arms)

Harrington & Richardson, Park Ave., Worcester, Mass. 01610

High Standard Mfg. C9., 1817 Dixwell Ave. Hamden, Conn. 06514

Independent Res. & Development, Inc. (I.R.D.), 6304 Locker Lane, San Antonio, Tex. 78238

Intercontinental Arms, Inc. 2222 Barry Ave., Los Angeles, Cal. 90064

Ithaca Gun Co., Ithaca, N.Y. 14850

Iver Johnson Arms & Cycle Works, Fitchburg, Mass. 01420

Jackson Hole Arms Corp., Box T, Jackson, Wyo. 83001

J & R Carbine (see: PJK Inc.)

Kent Firearms Ltd., Inc. 14 E. Woodland Ave., Springfield, Pa. 19064

MBAssociates (see Intercontinental Arms)

Marlin Firearms Co., 100 Kenna Dr., New Haven, Conn. 06473

Merrill Co., Inc. 209 Howard St., Fonda, Ia. 50540

O. F. Mossberg & Sons, Inc. 7 Grasso St., No. Haven, Conn. 06473

Navy Arms Co., 689 Bergen Blvd., Ridgefield, N.J. 07657

Noble Mfg. Co., Inc. S. Main St., Haydenville, Mass. 01039

Numrich Arms Corp., W. Hurley, N.Y. 12491

PJK Inc., 1527 Royal Oak Dr., Bradbury, Cal. 91010 (J&R Carbine)

Plainfield Machine Co., Inc. Box 447 Dunellen, N.J. 08812

Potomac Arms Corp. P.O. Box 35, Alexandria, Va. 22313 (ML replicas)

Appendix 2.

Ranger Arms Co., Box 704, Gainesville, Tex. 76240 (Texan Mag.)

Rau Arms Corp. 220 Metcalf Rd., El Dorado, Kans. 67042

Remington Arms Co., Bridgeport, Conn. 06602

Savage Arms Corp., Westfield, Mass. 01085

Sears, Roebuck & Co., 825 S. St. Louis, Chicago, Ill. 60607

Seventrees Ltd., 315 W. 39th St., New York, N.Y. 10018

Smith & Wesson, Inc., Springfield, Mass. 01101

Sporting Arms, Inc., 2643 Alpaca St., S. El Monte, Cal. 91733 (M-1 carbine)

Sterling Arms Corp., 2206 Elmwood Ave., Buffalo, N.Y. 14216

Sturm, Ruger & Co., Southport, Conn. 06490

Thompson-Center Arms, Box 2405, Rochester, N.H. 03867 (Contender pistol)

Tingle, 1125 Smithland Pike, Shelbyville, Ind. 46176 (muzzleloader)

Universal Firearms Corp., 3746 E. 10th St., Hialeah, Fla. 33013

Ward's, 619 W. Chicago, Chicago, Ill. 60607 (Western Field brand)

Weatherby's, 2781 E. Firestone Blvd., South Gate, Calif. 90280

Dan Wesson Arms, 293 S. Main St., Monson, Mass. 01057

Western Valley Arms Co., 524 W. Main St., Alhambra, Cal. 91801

Winchester Repeating Arms Co., New Haven, Conn. 06504

Winslow Arms Co., P.O. Box 578, Osprey, Fla. 33595

GUNSMITH SCHOOLS

Colorado School of Trades, 1545 Hoyt, Denver, Colo. 80215

Lassen Junior College, 11100 Main St., Susanville, Cal. 96130

Oregon Technical Institute, Klamath Falls, Ore. 97601

Penn. Gunsmith School, 812 Ohio River Blvd., Ovklon, Pittsburgh, Pa. 15202

Trinidad State Junior College, Trinidad, Colo. 81083

HANDGUN ACCESSORIES

A&R Sales Co., 99163 3/4 Rush St., So. El Monte, Cal. 91733

Barami Corp. 6250 E. 7 Mile Rd., Detroit, Mich. 48234 (Hip-Grip)

B. L. Broadway, 1503 Jasper, Chula Vista, Cal. 92011 (machine rest)

Case Master, 4675 E. 10 Ave. Miami, Fla. 33013

Central Specialties Co., 6030 Northwest Hwy., Chicago, Ill. 60631

John Dangelzer, 3056 Frontier Pl, N.E. Albuquerque, N.M. 87106 (flasks)

Bill Dyer, 503 Midwest Bldg., Oklahoma City, Okla. 73102 (grip caps)

R. S. Frielich, 396 Broome St., New York, N.Y. 10013 (cases)

Hunt Eng., 121-17th St., Yucaipa, Cal. 92399 (Multi-Loader)

R. G. Jensen, 16153½ Parthenia, Sepulveda, Cal. 91343 (auxiliary chambers)

Matich Loader, Box 958, So. Pasadena, Cal. 91030 (Quick Load)

J. McArthur, 1961 Overlook Ave., Youngstown, O. 44509 (sling)

Pachmayr, 1220 S. Grand, Los Angeles, Cal. 90015 (cases)

Platt Luggage, Inc., 2301 S. Prairie, Chicago, Ill. 60616 (cases)

Jules Reiver, 4104 Market St., Wilmington, Del. 19899 (cases)

Roger A. Smith, 19320 Heber St., Glendora, Cal. 91740 (Wrist-Loc)

Sportsmen's Equipment Co., 415 W. Washington, San Diego, Cal. 92103

M. Tyler, 1326 W. Britton, Oklahoma City, Okla. 73114 (grip adaptor)

HANDGUN GRIPS

Beckelhymer's, Hidalgo & San Bernardo, Laredo, Tex. 78040

Caray Sales Co., 2044 Hudson St., Ft. Lee, N.J. 07024

Cloyce's Gun Stocks, Box 1133, Twin Falls, Ida. 83301

Crest Carving Co., 14849 Dillow St., Westminster, Cal. 92683

Custom Combat Grips, 148 Shepherd Ave., Brooklyn, N.Y. 11208

Enforcer Prod. Div., Caray Sales Co., 2044 Hudson St., Ft. Lee, N.J. 07024

J. M. Evans, 5078 Harwood Rd., San Jose, Cal. 95124

Fitz, Box 49797, Los Angeles, Cal. 90049

Herrett's, Box 741, Twin Falls, Ida. 83301

Hogue Custom Grips, Box 1001, Cambria, Cal. 93428

Mershon Co., Inc. 1230 S. Grand Ave., Los Angeles, Cal. 90015

Mustang Pistol Grips, 13830 Hiway 395, Edgemont, Cal. 92508

Safety Grip Corp., Box 456, Riverside, St., Miami, Fla. 33135

Sanderson Custom Pistol Stocks, 17695 Fenton, Detroit, Mich. 48219

Jay Scott, 81 Sherman Place, Garfield, N.J. 07026

Sile Dist., 7 Centre Market Pl., New York, N.Y. 10013

Sports, Inc., 5501 Broadway, Chicago, Ill. 60640 (Franzite)

John W. Womack, 3006 Bibb St., Shreveport, La. 71108

HOLSTERS AND LEATHER GOODS

American Sales & Mfg. Co., P.O. Box 677, Laredo, Tex. 78040

Berns-Martin, Box 335, Elberton, Ga. 30635

Bianchi Holster Co., 212 W. Foothill Blvd., Monrovia, Calif. 91016

Edward H. Bohlin, 931 N. Highland Ave., Hollywood, Calif. 90038

Boyt Co., Box 1108, Iowa Falls, Ia. 51026

E. A. Brandin Saddle Co., Rte. 2, Box 243-A, Monroe, La. 71201

Brauer Bros. Mfg. Co., 817 N. 17th, St. Louis, Mo. 63106

Browning Arms Co., Rt. 4, Box 624-B, Arnold, Mo. 63010

J. M. Bucheimer Co., Airport Rd., Frederick, Md. 21701

Cole's Acku-Rite, Box 25, Kennedy, N.Y. 14747

Colt's, 150 Huyshope Ave., Hartford, Conn. 06102

Daisy Mfg. Co., Rogers, Ark. 72756

Eugene DeMayo & Sons, Inc. 2795 Third Ave., Bronx, N.Y. 10455

Filmat Enterpr., Inc., 200 Market St., East Paterson, N.J. 07407

Flintrop Arms Co., 4034 W. National Ave., Milwaukee, Wis. 53215

Goerg Ent. 3009 S. Laurel, Port Angeles, Wash. 98362

Hoyt Holster Co., P.O. Box 1783, Costa Mesa, Cal. 92626

Don Hume, Box 351, Miami, Okla. 74354

The Hunter Co., 1215 12th St., Denver, Colo. 80204

Jet Sports Corp., 4 Centre Market Pl., New York, N.Y. 10013

Jumbo Sports Prods., P.O. Box 280, Airport Rd., Frederick, Md. 21701

George Lawrence Co., 306 S.W. First Ave., Portland, Ore. 97204

MMGR Corp., 5710 12th Ave., Brooklyn, N.Y. 11219

S. D. Myres Saddle Co., Box 9776, El Paso, Tex. 79988

Pony Express Sport Shop, 17460 Ventura Blvd., Encino, Cal. 91316

Red Head Brand Co., 4100 Platinum Way, Dallas, Tex. 75237

R. E. Roseberry, 810 W. 38th, Anderson, Ind. 46014

Safariland Leather Products, 1946 S. Myrtle Ave., Monrovia, Cal. 91016

Safety Speed Holster, Inc., 910 S. Vail, Montebello, Cal. 90640

San Francisco Gun Exchange, 75 Fourth St., San Francisco, Cal. 91403

Buddy Schoellkopf Products, Inc., 4100 Platinum Way, Dallas, Tex. 75237

Seventrees, Ltd., 315 W. 39 St., New York, N.Y. 10018

Sile Distr., 7 Centre Market Pl., New York, N.Y. 10013

Smith & Wesson Leather Co., 2100 Roosevelt, Springfield, Mass. 01101

Swiss-Craft Co., Inc., 33 Arctic St., Worcester, Mass. 01604

Tandy Leather Co., 1001 Foch, Ft. Worth, Texas 76107

Whitco, Box 1712, Brownsville, Tex. 78520 (Hide-A-Way)

Woodland Sport and Gift Shop, Box 107, Mayfield, N.Y. 12117

METALLIC SIGHTS

B-Square Eng. Co., Box 11281, Ft. Worth, Tex. 76110

Bo-Mar Tool & Mfg. C9., Box 168, Carthage, Tex. 75633

Maynard P. Buehler, Inc., 17 Orinda Highway, Orinda, Cal. 94563

Chicago Gun Center, 3109 W. Armitage, Chicago, Ill. 60647

Christy Gun Works, 875 57th St., Sacramento, Cal. 95819

Clerke Technicorp., 2040 Broadway Ave., Santa Monica, Cal. 90404

Art Cook Supply, Rte. 2, Box 123B, Laurel, Md. 20810 (Illum. gunsight)

Firearms Dev. Lab., Box 278, Scotts Valley, Calif. 95060

Freeland's Scope Stands, Inc., 3734-14th Ave., Rock Island, Ill. 61201

P. W. Gray Co., Fairgrounds Rd., Nantucket, Mass. 02554 (shotgun)

Lyman Gun Sight Products, Middlefield, Conn. 06455

Marble Arms Corp., 1120 Superior, Gladstone, Mich. 49837

Merit Gunsight Co., P.O. Box 995, Sequim, Wash. 98382

Micro Sight Co., 242 Harbor Blvd., Belmont, Calif. 94002

Minature Machine Co., 212 E. Spruce, Deming, N.M. 88030

Oxford Corp., 100 Benbro Dr., Buffalo, N.Y. 14225 (Illum, Sight)

C. R. Pedersen & Son, Ludington, Mich. 49431

Redfield Gun Sight Co., 1315 S. Clarkson St., Denver, Colo. 80210

Schwarz's Gun Shop, 41-15th St., Wellsburg, W.Va. 26070

Simmons Gun Specialties, Inc. 700 Rodgers Rd., Olathe, Kans. 66061

Slug Site Co., 3835 University, Des Moines, Ia. 50311

Williams Gun Sight Co., 7389 Lapeer Rd., Davison, Mich. 48423

W. H. Womack, 2124 Meriwether Rd., Shreveport, La. 71108

MISCELLANEOUS

Accurizing Service, Herbert G. Troester, Cayuago, N.D. 58013

Adhesive Flannel, Forest City Prod., 722 Bolivar, Cleveland, O. 44115

Ammo Pouch, Creed Ent., 13167 E. Garvey Ave., Baldwin Park, Cal. 91706

Arms Books, Normount Technical Publications, Forest Groove, Oreg. 97116

Arms Bookseller, Norm Flayderman, RFD 2, Squash Hollow, New Milford, Conn. 06776

Arms Bookseller, Rutgers, Mark Aziz, 127 Raritan Ave., Highland Park, N.J. 08904

Arms Research, American Arms Co., 1641 Maplecrest Dr., Bloomington, Ind. 47401

Barrel Band Swivels, Phil Judd, 83 E. Park St. Butte, Mont. 59701

Barrel Bedding Device, W. H. Womack, 2124 Meriwether Rd., Shreveport, La. 71108

Bedding Kit, Bisonite Co., Box 84, Buffalo, N.Y. 14217

Bedding Kit, Fenwall, Inc., 400 Main St., Ashland, Mass. 01721

Bench Rest Pedestal, Jim Brobst, 299 Poplar, Hamburg, Pa. 19526

Bench Rest Stands, Suter's, 401 Tejon, Colorado Springs, Colo. 80902

Bore Collimator, Alley Supply Co., Box 458, Sonora, Calif. 95370

Bore Collimator, Collins Co., Box 40, Shepherdsville, Ky. 40165

Bore Lamp, Spacetron, Inc., Box 84, Broadview, Ill. 60155

Borescope, Eder Inst. Co., 2293 N. Clybourn, Chicago, Ill. 60614

Bore Sighter, Rifleman's Bore Sighter Co., P.O. Box 1701, Saginaw, Mich. 48605

Breech Plug Wrench, Swaine Machine, 195 O'Connell, Providence, R.I. 02905

Can Thrower, Trius Prod. Box 25, Cleves, O. 45002

Capper, Muzzle-Loading, Pat Burke, 3339 Farnsworth Rd., Lapeer, Mich. 48446

Cartridge Boxes, Llanerch Gun Shop, 2800 Township Line, Upper Darby, Pa. 19083

Cartridge Boxes, Shooters Supplies, 1589 Payne Ave., St. Paul, Minn. 55101

Cartridge Box Labels, Milton Brynin, Box 162, Fleetwood Sta., Mt. Vernon, N.Y. 10552

Cartridge Box Labels, Jasco, Box 49751, Los Angeles, Cal. 90049

Cartridge Box Labels, Peterson Label Co. P.O. Box 186Z, Redding Ridge, Conn. 06876

Cartridge Carrier, N. H. Schiffman, P.O. Box 7373, Murray, Utah 84107

Case Gauge, Plum City Ballistics Range, Box 128, Plum City, Wis. 54761

Chrome Brl. Lining, Marker Mach. Co., Box 426, Charleston, Ill. 61920

Color Hardening, Alamo Heat Treating Co., Box 55345, Houston, Tex. 77055

Crossbows, Midwest Crossbow Co., 9043 S. Western, Chicago, Ill. 60620

Crow Caller, Wightman Elec. Inc., Bx 989, Easton, Md. 21601

Custom Bluing, J. A. Wingert, 124 W. 2nd St., Waynesboro, Pa. 17268

E-Z Loader, Del Rey Prod., P.O. Box 91561, Los Angeles, Cal. 90009

Ear-Valv, Sigma Eng. Co., 11320 Burbank Blvd., N. Hollywood, Cal. 91601

Flat Springs, Alamo Heat Treating Co., Box 55345, Houston, Tex. 77055

Gas Pistol, Penguin Assoc., Inc., Box 97, Parkesburg, Pa. 19365

Gun Bedding Kit, Resin Div., Fenwal, Inc., 400 Main St., Ashland, Mass. 01601

Gun Jewelry, Sid Bell, Originals, Box 188, Tully, N.Y. 13159

Gun Jewelry, Al Popper, 614 Turnpike St., Stoughton, Mass. 02072

Gun Lock, Bor-Lok Prods., 4200 California St., San Francisco, Cal. 94118

Gun Lock, E&C Enterprises, P.O. Bx 823, S. Pasadena, Cal. 91030

Gun Lock Chain, Lundy Corp., 1123-24 Davenport Bk. Bldg., Davenport, Ia. 52801

Gun Lok, 4780 Old Orchard Trail, Orchard Lake, Mich. 48034

Gun Sling, Trail Guide Prods. Corp. 15407 McGinty Rd., Wayzata, Minn. 55391

Gun Socks Covers, E&C Enterprises, P.O. Box 823, S. Pasadena, Cal. 91030

Gun Socks Covers, East-Tenn Mills, Inc., Box 1030, Johnson City, Tenn. 37601

Hearing Protector, American Optical Corp., Mechanic St., Southbridge, Mass. 01550 (ear valve)

Hearing Protector, Bausch & Lomb, 635 St. Paul St., Rochester, N.Y. 14602

Hearing Protector, David Clark Co., 360 Franklin St. Worcester, Mass. 01601

Hearing Protector, Curtis Safety Prod. Co., Box 61, Webster Sq. Sta., Worcester, Mass. 01603 (ear valve)

Hearing Protector, Hodgdon, 7710 W. 50 Hiway, Shawnee Mission, Kans. 66202

Hearing Protector, Human Acoustics, Inc., 888 E. Williams St. Carson City, Nev. 89701

Hearing Protector, Sigma Eng. Co., 11320 Burbank Blvd., No. Hollywood, Cal. 91601 (Lee-Sinoc ear valve)

Hearing Protector, Willson Prods. Div., P.O. Box 622, Reading, Pa. 19603

Hollow Pointer, Goerg Ent., 3009 S. Laurel St., Port Angeles, Wash. 98362

Hull Bag, D. Titus, 119 Morlyn, Bryn Mawr, Pa. 19010

Insert Barrels (22 RF), H. Owen, P.O. Box 774, Sunnyvale, Cal. 94088

Leather Rest-Bags, B. Tuller, 29 Germania, Galeton, Pa. 16922

Lightnin-Loader, Hunter Mfg. Co., Box 2882, Van Nuys, Cal. 91404

Magazine Clip (Colyer), Great Northern Trading Post, 13001 Hwy. 65 N.E., Rte. 4, Anoka, Minn. 55303

Magazine Clips, Amer. Firearms Mfg. Co., Inc., 5732 Kenwick Dr., San Antonio, Tex. 78238

Miniature Guns, C. H. Stoppler, 1426 Walton Ave., New York, N.Y. 10452

Monte Carlo Pad, Frank A. Hoppe Div., P.O. Box 97, Parkesburg, Pa. 19365

Nipple Wrenches, Chopie Tool & Die Co., 531 Copeland Ave., La Crosse, Wis. 54601

Pell Remover, A. Edw. Terpening, 838 W. Darlington Rd., Tarpon Springs, Fla. 33589

Personal Firearms Record Book, Box 201, Park Ridge, Ill. 60068

Portable Gun Rest, Central Specialties Co., 630 Northwest Hwy., Chicago, Ill. 60631 (Gun-Rak)

Powder Horns, Thos. F. White, 5801 Westchester Ct., Worthington, O. 43085

Pressure Testing Machine, York-Cantrell, Inc., 30241 Rosebriar, St. Clair Shores, Mich. 48082

Recoil Pads, etc. Mershon Co., Inc. 1230 S. Grand, Los Angeles, Cal. 90015

Recoil Reducer, J. B. Edwards, 269 Herbert St. Alton, Ill. 62002

Rifle Rests, Edw. L. Bagrosky, 13451 Philmont Ave., Philadelphia, Pa. 19116

Rifle Rests, E. L. Beecher, 2155 Demington Dr., Cleveland Hgts, O. 44106

Rifle Rests, Cole's Acku-Rite Prod., Box 25, Kennedy, N.Y. 14747

Rifles Rests, E-N Gun Prod., 1015 Van Hoy Ave., Winston-Salem, N.C. 27104

Rifle Rests, Frontier Arms, Inc., Box 2593, Cheyenne, Wyo. 82001

Rifle Rests, The Gun Case, 11035 Maplefield, El Monte, Cal. 91733

Rifle Rests, Harris Engr., Inc., Box 305, Fraser, Mich. 48026 (bipods)

Rifle Rests, Rob. W. Hart & Son, 401 Montgomery St., Nescopeck, Pa. 18635

Rifle Rests, Rec. Prods., Res., Inc. 158 Franklin Ave., Ridgewood N.J. 07450 (Buttspipod)

Rifle Rests, Ten Ring Mfg. Co., Box 157, New City, N.Y. 10956 (Rifle-Mate)

Rifle Rests, Basil Tuller, 29 Germania, Galeton, Pa. 15922 (Protektor sandbags)

Rifle Rests, W. H. Womack, 2124 Meriwether Rd., Shreveport, La. 71108

Rifle Slings, Bianchi, 212 W. Foothill Blvd. Monrovia, Cal. 91016

RIG, NRA Scoring Plug, Rig Prod. Co., Box 279, Oregon, Ill. 60161

Rubber Cheekpiece, W. H. Lodewick, 2816 N.E. Halsey, Portland, Ore. 97232

Rust Bluing/Browning, L. B. Thompson, 568 E. School Ave., Salem, O. 44460

Safeties, Doc Line Co., 18440 John R. St., Detroit, Mich. 48203

Safeties, Williams Gun Sight Co., 7389 Lapeer Rd., Davison, Mich. 48423

Salute Cannons, Naval Co., Rt. 611, Doylestown, Pa. 18901

Scope Safeties, W. H. Lodewick, 2816 N.E. Halsey, Portland, Ore. 97232

Sharpening Stones, Russell's Arkansas Oilstones, P.O. Box 474, Fayetteville, Ark. 72701

Shooting/Testing Glasses, Clear View Sports Shields, P.O. Box 255, Wethersfield, Conn. 06107

Shooting Glasses, Bushnell Optical Corp., 2828 E. Foothill Blvd. Pasadena, Cal. 91107

Shooting Glasses, M. B. Dinsmore, Box 21, Wyomissing, Pa. 19610

Shooting Glasses, Mitchell's Box 539, Waynesville, Mo. 65583

Shooting Ranges, Shooting Equip. Inc., 2001 N. Parkside Ave., Chicago, Ill. 60639

Shotgun Recoil Kit, CHB, 3063 Hiram, Wichita, Kan. 67217

Shotgun Sight, binocular, Trius Prod., Box 25, Cleves, O. 45002

Shotshell Catcher, Old Mill Trap & Skeet, 300 Mill Ridge Rd., Secaucus, N.J. 07094 (Seymour)

Shotshell Pouches, Filmat Enterpr., Inc., 200 Market St., East Paterson, N.J. 07407

Silver Grip Caps, Bill Dyer, P.O. Box 75255, Oklahoma City, Okla. 73107

Slide Safety (Mausers), Doc Line Co., 18440 John R., Detroit, Mich. 43203

Snap Caps, Filmat, 200 Market, East Paterson, N.J. 07407

Springfield Safety Pin, B-Square Co., P.O. Box 11281, Ft. Worth, Tex. 76110

Springs, W. Wolff Co., Box 232, Ardmore, Pa. 19003

Swivels, Michaels, P.O. Box 13010, Portland, Ore. 97213

Swivels, Sile Dist., 7 Centre Market Pl., New York, N.Y. 10013

Swivels, Williams Gun Sight, 7389 Lapeer, Davison, Mich. 48423

Targ-Dots, Peterson Label Co., P.O. Box 186Z, Redding Ridge, Conn. 06876

Teenuts, Dot Products Supply Co., 10544 Lunt Ave. Rosemont, Ill. 60018

Trap, claybird, Deerback Prod. 8239 Hayle Ave. Dallas, Tex. 75227

Trap, claybird, Outers Lab., Inc., Box 37, Onalaska, Wis. 54650

Trap, claybird, Trius Prod. Box 25, Cleves, O. 45002

Triggers, Canjar Rifle Acc., 500 E. 45th St., Denver, Colo. 80216

Trigger Guards, Beesley Mfg. Co., P.O. Box 17075, Salt Lake City, Utah 84117 (Bee-Safe)

Trigger Guards, Michaels, P.O. Box 13010, Portland, Ore. 97213

Trigger Pull Gauge, Ohaus, 29 Hanover Rd., Florham Park, N.J. 07932

Trigger Release, Schwab Gun Shop, 1103 E. Bigelow, Findlay, O. 45840

Trigger Shoe, Flaigs, Babcock Blvd., Millvale, Pa. 15209

Trigger Shoe, Pacific Tool Co., Box 4495, Lincoln, Neb. 68504

Trigger Show, Melvin Tyler, 1326 W. Britton, Oklahoma City, Okla. 73114

Worldhunting Info., Jack Atcheson, 2309 Hancock Ave, Butte, Mont. 59701

MUZZLE-LOADING BARRELS OR EQUIPMENT

Luther Adkins, Box 281, Shelbyville, Ind. 47176 (breech plugs)

Armoury, Inc., Rte. 25, New Preston, Conn. 06777

Henry S. Beverage, New Gloucester, Me. 04260 (brass bullet mold)

John Bivins, Jr., 446 S. Main, Winston-Salem, N.C. 27101

Jesse F. Booher, 2751 Ridge Ave., Dayton, O. 45414

G. S. Bunch, 7735 Garrison, Hyattsville, Md. 20784 (flask repair)

Pat Burke, 3339 Farnsworth Rd., Lapeer, Mich. 48446 (capper)

Challanger Mfg. Co., 94-28 Merrick Blvd., Jamaica, N.Y. 11433 (H&A guns)

Cherry Corners Gun Shop, Rte. 1, 8010 Lafayette Rd., Lodi, O. 44254

Earl T. Cureton, Rt. 6, 7017 Pine Grove Rd., Knoxville, Tenn. 37914 (powder horns)

John N. Dangelzer, 3056 Frontier Pl. N.E., Albuquerque, N.M. 87106 (powder flasks)

Ted Fellowes, 9245 16th Ave., S.W. Seattle, Wash. 98106

Firearms Imp. & Exp. Corp., P.O. Box 691, Biscayne Annex, Miami, Fla. 33152

Golden Age Arms Co., Box 82, Worthington, O. 43085

A. R. Goode, 3306 Sellman Rd., Adelphi, Md. 20783

International M. L. Parts Co., 19453 Forrer, Detroit, Mich. 48235

JJJJ Ranch, Wm. Large, Rte. 1, Ironton, O. 45638

Art LeFeuvre, 1003 Hazel Ave., Deerfield, Ill. 60015 (antique gun restoring)

Kindig's Log Cabin Sport Shop, R.D. 1, Box 275, Lodi, O. 44254

Les' Gun Shop (Les Bauska), Box 511, Kalispell, Mont. 59901

Lever Arms Serv. Ltd., 771 Dunsmuir, Vancouver 1, B.C. Canada

M.C.K.E-Z Load Co., R.R. 1, Pekin, Ill. 61554

Maryland Gun Exchange Inc., Rt. 40 West, RD 5, Frederick, Md. 21701

Jos. W. Mellott, 334 Rockhill Rd., Pittsburgh, Pa. 15243 (barrel blanks)

Miller & Son's Replicas, Rt. 1, Box 260, Marine-on-St. Croix, Minn. 55047

W. L. Mowrey Gun Works, Inc., Box 711, Olney, Tex. 73674

Numrich Corp., W. Hurley, N.Y. 12491 (powder flasks)

Bob Paris, Gettysburg, Pa. 17325 (barrels)

Penna. Rifle Works, 319 E. Main St., Ligonier, Pa. 15658 (ML guns, Parts)

Fred Renard, Rt. 1., Symsonia, Ky. 42082 (ML)

H. M. Schoeller, 569 S. Braddock Ave., Pittsburgh, Pa. 15221

C. E. Siler, 181 Sandhill School, Asheville, N.C. 28806 (flint locks)

Thos. F. White, 5801 Westchester Ct., Worthington, O. 43085 (powder horn)

Lou Williamson, 103 S. Jennings, Ft. Worth, Tex. 76104

PISTOLSMITHS

Alamo Heat Treating, Box 55345, Houston, Tex. 77055

Allen Assoc. 7448 Limekiln Pike, Philadelphia, Pa. 19138 (speed-cock lever for 45 ACP)

Bain & Davis Sporting Goods, 559 W. Las Tunas Dr., San Gabriel, Cal. 91776

Behlert & Freed, Inc. 33 Herning Ave., Cranford, N.J. 07016 (short actions)

R. M. Champlin, Stanyan Hill, Wentworth, N.H. 03282

F. Bob Chow, Gun Shop, 3185 Mission, San Francisco, Cal. 94110

J. E. Clark, 7424 Broadacres Rd., Shreveport, La. 71109

Custom Gunshop, 33 Herning Ave., Cranford, N.J. 07016

Day Arms Corp., 7515 Stagecoach Lane, San Antonio, Tex. 78227

Alton S. Dinan, Jr., P.O. Box 6674, Canaan, Conn. 06018

Dan Dwyer, 915 W. Washington, San Diego, Cal. 92103

Giles' 45 Shop, Rt. 1, Box 47, Odessa, Fla. 33556

H. H. Harris, 1237 S. State, Chicago, Ill. 60605

Gil Hebard Guns, Box 1, Knoxville, Ill. 61448

Macs Accuracy Serv., 3260 Lakewood, So. Seattle, Wash. 98144 (45 ACP)

Rudy Marent, 9711 Tiltree, Houston, Tex. 77034 (Hammerli)

Maryland Gun Exchange, Inc., Rte. 40 W., RD 5, Frederick, Md. 21701

Match Arms Co., 831 Mary St., Springdale, Pa. 15144

Pachmayr Gun Works, 1220 S. Grand Ave., Los Angeles, Cal. 90015

Geo. E. Sheldon, 7 Balsam St., Keene, N.H. 03431

R. L. Chockey Guns, Inc. 1614 S. Choctaw, E. Reno, Okla. 73036

Silver Dollar Guns, 7 Balsam St., Keene, N.H. 03431 (45 auto only)

Sportsmens Equip. Co., 915 W. Washington, San Diego, Cal. 92103

Armand D. Swenson, 3223 W. 145th St., Gardena, Cal. 90249

RIFLE BARREL MAKERS

P. O. Ackley, P.O. Box 17347, Salt Lake City, Utah 84117

Apex Rifle Co., 7628 San Fernando, Sun Valley, Cal. 91352

Christy Gun Works, 875 57th St., Sacramento, Cal. 95819

Clerke Technicorp., 2054 Broadway Ave., Santa Monica, Cal. 90404

Cuthbert Gun Shop, 715 S. 5th Coos Bay, Ore. 97420

J. Dewey Gun Co., Clinton Corners, N.Y. 12514

Douglas Barrels, Inc., 5504 Big Tyler Rd., Charleston, W.Va. 25312

Federal Firearms Co., Inc. Box 145, Oakdale, Pa. 15071 (star bbls., actions)

A. R. Goode, 3306 Sellman Rd., Adelphi, Md. 20783

Hart Rifle Barrels, Inc., RD 2, Lafayette, N.Y. 13084

Wm. H. Hobaugh, Box 657, Phillipsburg, Mont. 59858

Hoffman Rifle Barrel Co., Bucklin, Kans. 67834

Intern'l Casting Co., 19453 Forrer, Detroit, Mich. 48235

Johnson Automatics, Box 306, Hope Valley, R.I. 02832

Les' Gun Shop, Box 511, Kalispell, Mont. 59901

McGowen Rifle Barrels, Rte. 3, St. Anne, Ill. 60964

Nauman Gun Shop, 1048 S. 5th, Douglas, Wyo. 82633

Nu-Line Guns, Inc., 3727 Jennings Rd., St. Louis, Mo. 63121

Numrich Arms., W. Hurley, N.Y. 12491

Bob Parks, Gettysburg, Pa. 17325

Rheinmetall (see John Weir)

SS&D, Inc., Clinton Corners, N.Y. 12514 (cold-formed bbls)

Sanders Cust. Gun Serv., 2358 Tyler Lane, Louisville, Ky. 40205

Sharon Rifle Barrel Co., P.O. Box 106, Kalispell, Mont. 59901

Ed Shilen Rifles, 4510 Harrington Rd., Irving, Tex. 75060

Titus Barrel & Gun Co., Box 151, Heber City, Utah 84032

John E. Weir, 4301 Cottage, Independence, Mo. 64055

Wilson Arms, Box 364, Stony Creek, Branford, Conn. 06405

SCOPES, MOUNTS, ACCESSORIES, OPTICAL EQUIPMENT

Alley Supply Co., P.O. Box 458, Sonora, Cal. 95370 (scope collimator)

American Import Co., 1167 Mission, San Francisco, Cal. 94103

Anderson & Co., 1203 Broadway, Yakima, Wash. 98902 (lens cap)

Bausch & Lomb Inc., 635 St. Paul St., Rochester, N.Y. 14602

Bridge Mount Co., Box 3344, Lubbock, Tex. 79410 (one-piece target mts)

Browning Arms, Rt. 4, Box 624-B Arnold, Mo. 63010

Maynard P. Buehler, Inc., 17 Orinda Hwy., Orinda, Cal. 94563

Bullitco, Box 40 Shepherdsville, Ky. 40165 (scope collimator)

D. P. Bushnell & Co., Inc., 2828 E. Foothill Blvd., Pasadena, Cal. 91107

Kenneth Clark, 18738 Highway 99, Madera, Cal. 93637

Collins Co., Box 40, Shepherdsville, Ky. 40165 (Scope collimator)

Colt's, Hartford, Conn. 06102

Conetrol, Hwy. 123 South, Seguin, Tex. 78155

Continental Arms Corp., 697-5th Ave., New York, N.Y. 10022 (Nickel)

Don's Gun Shop, 128 Ruxton, Manitou Springs, Col. 80829 (claw mtg. 0 rings)

Duo-Gun Prod., 3213 Partridge Ave. Oakland, Cal. 94605 (mount)

Flaig's Babcock Blvd., Millvale, Pa. 15209

Freeland's Scope Stands, Inc., 3734 14th, Rock Island, Ill. 61201

Bert Friedberg & Co., 820 Mission St., San Francisco, Cal. 94103

Griffin & Howe, Inc., 589-8th Ave., New York, N.Y. 10017

E. C. Herkner Co., Box 5007, Boise, Idaho 83702

Herter's Inc., Waseca, Minn. 56093

J. B. Holden Co., Box H-1495, Plymouth, Mich. 48170 (Ironsighter)

The Hutson Corp., P.O. 1127, Arlington, Tex. 76010

Hy-Score Arms Corp., 200 Tillary St., Brooklyn, N.Y. 11201

Paul Jaeger, 211 Leedom St. Jenkintown, Pa. 19046 (Nickel)

Jana Intl. Co., Box 1107, Denver, Colo. 80201

Jason Empire, 1211 Walnut, Kansas City, Mo. 64106

Kesselring Gun Shop, Box 350, Rt. 1, Burlington, Wash. 98283

Kuharsky Bros., 2425 W. 12th St., Erie, Pa. 16500

Kwik-Site, 27367 Michigan, Inkster, Mich. 48141 (rings)

T. K. Lee, Box 2123, Birmingham, Ala. 35201 (reticles)

E. Leitz, Inc., Rockleigh, N.J. 07647

Leupold & Stevens Inc., P.O. Box 688, Beaverton, Ore. 97005

Jake Levin & Son, Inc., 1211 Walnut, Kansas City, Mo. 64106

Lyman Gun Sight Products, Middlefield, Conn. 06455

Marble Arms Co., 1120 Superior St., Gladstone, Mich. 49837

Marlin Firearms Co., 100 Kenna Dr., New Haven, Conn. 06473

Mashburn Arms Co., 112 W. Sheridan, Oklahoma City, Okla. 73102

O. F. Mossberg & Sons, Inc., 7 Grasso Ave., North Haven, Conn. 06473

Normark Corp., 1710 E. 78th St., Minneapolis, Minn. 55423 (Single-point)

Numrich Arms, West Hurley, N.Y. 12491

Nydar Div., Swain Nelson Co., Box 45, Glenview, Ill. 60025 (shotgun sight)

PGS, Peters' Inc., 622 Gratiot Ave., Saginaw, Mich. 48602 (scope shields)

R. J. Enorec Inc., 175 N. 5th St., Saddle Brook, N.J. 07662 (bullet mold)

Pachmayr Gun Works, 1220 S. Grand Ave., Los Angeles, Cal. 90015

Pacific Tool Co., Box 4495, Lincoln, Neb. 68504

Precise Imports Corp., 3 Chestnut, Suffern, N.Y. 10901 (PIC)

Premier Reticles, Ocala, Fla. 32670

Ranging Inc., P.O. Box 9106, Rochester, N.Y. 14625

Realist, Inc., N. 93 W. 16288, Megal Dr., Menomonee Falls, Wis. 53051

Redfield Gun Sight Co., 5800 E. Jewell Ave., Denver, Colo. 80222

S&W Mfg. Co., Box 247, Pittsburgh, Pa. 16340 (Insta-mount)

Savage Arms, Westfield, Mass. 01085

Scope Inst. Co., 25-20 Brooklyn-Queens Expressway West, Woodside, N.Y. 11377

Southern Precision Inst. Co., 710 Augusta St., San Antonio, Tex. 78215

Stoeger Arms Co., 55 Ruta Ct., S. Hackensack, N.J. 07606

Swift Instruments, Inc., 952 Dorchester Ave., Boston, Mass. 02125

Tasco, 1075 N.W. 71st, Miami, Fla. 33138

Thompson-Center Arms, P.O. Box 2405, Rochester, N.H. 03867 (handgun scope)

Tradewinds, Inc., Box 1191, Tacoma, Wash. 98401

John Unertl Optical Co., 3551-5 East St., Pittsburg, Pa. 15215

Universal Firearms Corp., 3746 E. 10th Ct., Hialeah, Fla. 33013

Vissing Co., Box 437 Idaho Falls, Idaho 83401 (lens cap)

Weatherby's, 2781 Firestone, South Gate, Cal. 90280

W. R. Weaver Co., 7125 Industrial Ave., El Paso, Tex. 79915

Williams Gun Sight Co., 7389 Lapeer Rd., Davison, Mich. 48423

Carl Zeiss, Inc., 444 Fifth Ave., New York, N.Y. 10018 (Hensoldt)

SURPLUS GUNS, PARTS AND AMMUNITION

Allied Arms Ltd., 655 Broadway, New York, N.Y. 10012

Century Arms, Inc., 3-5 Federal St., St. Albans, Vt. 05478

W. H. Craig, Box 927, Selma, Ala. 36701

Cummings Intl. Inc., 41 Riverside Ave, Yonkers, N.Y. 10701

Eastern Firearms Co., 790 S. Arroyo Pkwy., Pasadena, Cal. 91105

Fenwick's, P.O. Box 38, Weisburg, Whitehall, Md. 21161

Hunter's Lodge, 200 S. Union, Alexandria, Va. 22313

Lever Arms Serv. Ltd., 771 Dunsmuir St., Vancouver, B.C., Canada

Mars Equipment Corp., 3318 W. Devon, Chicago, Ill. 60645

National Gun Traders, 251-55 W. 22nd, Miami, Fla. 33135

Pacific Intl. Imp. Co., 2416-16th St., Sacramento, Cal. 95818

Plainfield Ordnance Co., Box 447, Dunellen, N.J. 08812

Potomac Arms Corp. Box 35, Alexandria Va. 22313

Ruvel & Co., 3037 N. Clark St., Chicago, Ill. 60614

Service Armament Co., 689 Bergen Blvd., Ridgefield, N.J. 07657

Sherwood Distr. Inc., 9470 Santa Monica Blvd., Beverly Hills, Cal. 90210

Z.M. Military Research Co., 9 Grand Ave., Englewood, N.J. 07631

Cartridge Interchangeability

Caliber	Rimfire	Remarks
.22 LR	5.6mm LFB	.22 BB and CB Cap, .22 Short, .22 Long may be fired in .22 LR chamber.
.22 Magnum Rimfire	.22 Winchester Magnum Rimfire.	.22 WRF may be fired .22 MR chamber

Caliber	Centerfire Pistol and Revolver	Remarks
.22 Rem. Jet	.22 Centerfire Magnum; .22 Jet	
.221 Remington	.221 Fireball; .221 Rem. Fireball	
.256 Win. Magnum	.256 Magnum; .256 Win.	
.25 ACP	6.35mm Browning; DWM 508A; 25ASP, .25 Auto Pistol; .25 Colt Auto; 6.35mm Auto; 6.35mm ACP; 6.35mm Fur Selbstlader Pistole.	

Caliber	Centerfire Pistol and Revolver	Remarks
.30 Luger	7.65mm Luger; 7.65mm Parabellum; 7.65mm Borchardt-Luger; 7.65mm Luger, Swiss, M1900.	
.30 Mauser	7.63mm Mauser, DWM 403; .30 Auto, Mauser and Borchardt; 7.63mm Mauser, M1896; .30/7.63 Mauser	7.62mm Tokarev may be used.
.32ACP	DWM 479A; GR 619; .30 Browning; .32 Browning; 7.65mm Browning; .32 ASP; .32 Colt Auto; .32 Auto; .32 Auto Colt; .32/7.65 Auto; 7.65mm Auto; 7mm-65 Pour Pistolet Automatique; 7.65mm ACP; 7.65mm Browning M1897; 7.65mm Browning M1900; 7.65mm Browning, Mauser, Beretta; 7.65mm Pist. Patronen No. 19; 7.65mm Pist. Patronen 260 (h); 7.65mm for Browning Pistole.	

Caliber	Centerfire Pistol and Revolver	Remarks
7.65 Long Auto Pistol (French)	7.65mm French Long; 7.65mm L Pistolet-Mitrailleur Mod. 1938.	
.32 Colt NP	.32 Colt New Police .32 Police; .32 Colt Police Positive	Interchangeable with .32 S&W Long; .32 Long and Short Colt may be fired but cases will bulge; .32 S&W may be used.
.32 Short Colt	.32 Short CF	
.32 Long Colt	.32 Colt; .32 Long Colt, outside lube.	.32 Short Colt may be used.
.32 S&W Long	.32 Long S&W; .32 S&W Long Revolver	Interchangeable with .32 Colt NP; .32 S&W may be used; also .32 Short and Long Colt, but cases will bulge.
.32 S&W	.32 Smith & Wesson; DWM 202; 8.15x15.80 Smith & Wesson Cal. .32 Revolver.	.32 Short Colt may be used, but case will bulge.
.32/20 Win.	.32/20 WCF; .32 Winchester; 8.33mm (cal. .32) Winchester; 8.0x33.0 Winchester .32.	
7.62mm Russian Nagant	7.62mm Rev. Patr. 2602 (r); 7.5mm Russian Nagant; 7.62mm Nagant; 8mm Russian Nagant; 8x38 GR 684.	
7.62mm Tokarev	7.62mm Russian Tokarev Auto Pistol; 7.62mm Pist. Patr. 2601 (r); 7.62mm Tokarev M30.	7.63mm Mauser may be used.
8mm Nambu	8mm Nambu Auto Pistol 8mm Japanese Nambu	
8mm Lebel Revolver	GR 662; 7.7mm Clair Auto Pistol; 8mm Reglementaire M1892; 8mm Revolver M1892; 8.3x27.5 Lebel Revolver; 8mm French Ord. Rev. M1892.	
9mm Browning Long	9mm Army Browning; 9mm Auto Pistol; 9mm Long; 9mm Long Browning; 9mm Swedish M1907	
9mm Bergman-Bayard	9mm Largo; DWM 456,456B; 9mm Bayard; 9mm Bayard Armee Pistol; 9mm Bergmann Mars #6; 9mm Mars; 9mm Star Auto Pistol	9mm Steyr may be used; .38 ACP and .38 Super will *usually* work.
9mm Japanese Revolver Pattern 26 (M1893)	9mm Nambu	
9mm Mauser	DWM 487; 9mm Mauser, Export Model; 9mm Mauser Selbstlader Pistole; 9.08x25.0 Kal. 9mm Mauser.	

Caliber	Centerfire Pistol and Revolver	Remarks
9mm Luger	9mm Parabellum; DWM 480C,D, 487C; 9mm Beretta M1915; 9mm Glisenti; 9mm Pistolen Patrone 400(b); 9mm Pist. Patr. 08; 9mm Pist. Patr. M1941; 9mm Pour Mi 34 et GP; 9mm Suomi; 9mm Swedish M39; 9mm 40M. Parabellum.	
9mm Steyr	DWM 577; GR 892; 9mm Mannlicher; 9mm M12	9mm Bergman Bayard may be used; .38 ACP & .38 Super may *sometimes* be used.
.357 Magnum	.357 S&W Magnum	.38 Special may be used.
.380 ACP	DWM 540; .38 Colt Auto Hammerless; .380 Auto Hammerless Pistol; .380 Auto Webley; .380 CAPH; .380(9mm) Auto; 9mm Auto Pistol (.380); 9mm Beretta. M1934; 9mm Browning Short; 9mm Corto; 9mm Kurz; 9mm Pist. Patr. 400(h); 9mm Pistolen Patronen No. 21; 9mm Short; 9mm Short Browning.	
.38 ACP	.38 Automatic Pistol; .38 Automatic Colt; .38 Colt Automatic; .38 CAP; .38 Super.	
.38 Colt NP	.38 Colt New Police; .38 Colt Police Positive Revolver; .380 Revolver.	Interchange with .38 S&W.
.38 Special	.38 Colt Special; .38 S&W Special; .38/44; .38/44 Special.	
.38 S&W	.38 Smith & Wesson; DWM 261; .38 S&W Revolver; .38 S&W Short; .38 Super Police; 9.2x19.8 Smith & Wesson Kal. .38 Revolver; .380 Revolver.	Interchange with .38 Colt NP.
.38/40 Win.	.38/40 WCF; .38 WCF; .38 Win. M73	
.41 Long Colt	.41 L.DA; .41 Long Colt Double Action; .410 Extra Long Colt.	.41 Short Colt may be used.
.41 Short Colt	.41 S.D.A.; .41 Short CF; .41 Short Colt Double Action.	
.41 Magnum	.41 Remington; .41 Remington Magnum; .41 S&W Magnum.	
.44 Special	.44 S&W Special; .44 Smith & Wesson Spcl.	.44 Russian may be used.
.44 Magnum	.44 S&W Magnum; .44 Remington Magnum.	.44 Russian & .44 Spcl. may be used.
.44/40	.44 WCF; .44/40 Win.	
.45 ACP	.45 Colt Auto; .45 Automatic Colt; .45 Automatic Colt, Govt. Model; 11.25mm Auto Pistol.	

Caliber	Centerfire Pistol and Revolver	Remarks
.45 Auto-Rim	.45 AR	.45 ACP may be used.
.45 Colt	.45 Colt U.S.A.; .45 Colt Army & Double Action; .45 Colt DA; .45 Colt M1909.	
.455 Webley	.455 Enfield; .455 Enfield MKI, MKII; .455 Govt. Pattern 1881; DWM 228; .455 Eley; .455 Colt; 11.7x22.0 RN .455.	

Caliber	Centerfire Rifle	Remarks
.22 Hornet	5.6x35R	
.223 Remington	5.56mm U.S.; 5.56x45mm; .223/5.56mm Military	
.243 Winchester	6x51mm Winchester	
.25/35 Winchester	.25/35 WCF; 6.5x52R	
6.5mm Italian	6.5mm Mannlicher-Carcano; 6.5x52mm Italian M1891	
6.5mm Japanese	6.5mm Arisaka; 6.5x50mm Japanese Arisaka.	
6.5mm Swedish	6.5x55mm; 6.5x55mm Mauser; 6.5mm Swedish Mauser 6.5x55 Norwegian Krag.	
.270 Winchester	.270 WCF	
7mm Mauser	7x57mm; 7x57mm Mauser	
7mm Remington Magnum	7mm Magnum	
7.35mm Italian	7.35mm Carcano; 7.35mm Terni; 7.35mm M38.	
.30/30 Winchester	.30/30; .30/30 WCF; .30 WCF; 7.62x51R.	
.308 Winchester	7.62mm NATO; 7.62mm U.S.; 7.62x51mm; 7.62mm M59.	
.30/06	.30/1906 U.S.; .300 U.S.; Cartridge .30,M2; Cartridge .30,M1; 7.62x63mm; .30 U.S. Gov't.	
.300 H&H Magnum	Holland's Super .300; .300 H&H; .30 Super; .300 Belted Rimless Magnum	
7.7mm Japanese	7.7x58mm; 7.7mm Arisaka	
.303 British	.303 Enfield; 7.7x57R	
7.65mm Mauser	.30 Mauser; 7.65x53mm; 7.65mm Argentine Mauser; 7.65mm M1889	
8mm Mauser	8x57mm Mauser; 7.92x57mm	
.358 Winchester	8.8mm Winchester; .358 (8.8mm) Winchester	
.375 Magnum	.375 Holland & Holland; .375 Belted Rimless Magnum Nitro Express; .375 H&H Magnum	

Note: The above listing contains only those cartridges for which generally-recognized synonyms exist and/or where some degree of interchangeability occurs.

Table of Bullet Energies

This table of energies has been worked out by application of the existing formula for computing energy and gives the foot-pounds of striking energy for one grain of bullet weight. The formula for using this table is simple: multiply the foot-pounds opposite the desired velocity by the weight of your bullet. Velocities have been carefully worked out for each increasing ten foot-seconds. For example, to obtain the energy of a 145-grain bullet at 2835 f.s. locate 2830 f.s. in the proper column and you find the energy to be 17.78 foot-pounds. The next figure is for 2840 f.s. and runs 17.91. Difference, .13 foot-pounds. Halve this and get .06, which, added to 17.78, gives 17.84. To get bullet energy, multiply 17.84 by 145 grains, and the figure is 2586.8 or 2587 foot-pounds. Use of this table saves much time in figuring muzzle or remaining energy of bullets.

Velocity in fps	Energy	Velocity in fps	Energy	Velocity in fps	Energy	Velocity in fps	Energy	Velocity in fps	Energy
600	.80	820	1.49	1040	2.40	1260	3.52	1480	4.86
610	.82	830	1.53	1050	2.45	1270	3.58	1490	4.93
620	.85	840	1.56	1060	2.49	1280	3.63	1500	5.00
630	.88	850	1.60	1070	2.54	1290	3.69	1510	5.06
640	.91	860	1.64	1080	2.59	1300	3.75	1520	5.13
650	.94	870	1.68	1090	2.63	1310	3.81	1530	5.19
660	.96	880	1.72	1100	2.68	1320	3.86	1540	5.26
670	.99	890	1.76	1110	2.73	1330	3.92	1550	5.33
680	1.02	900	1.79	1120	2.78	1340	3.98	1560	5.40
690	1.05	910	1.83	1130	2.83	1350	4.04	1570	5.47
700	1.08	920	1.87	1140	2.88	1360	4.10	1580	5.54
710	1.11	930	1.92	1150	2.93	1370	4.16	1590	5.61
720	1.15	940	1.96	1160	2.99	1380	4.22	1600	5.68
730	1.18	950	2.00	1170	3.04	1390	4.29	1610	5.75
740	1.21	960	2.04	1180	3.09	1400	4.35	1620	5.82
750	1.24	970	2.08	1190	3.14	1410	4.41	1630	5.90
760	1.28	980	2.13	1200	3.19	1420	4.47	1640	5.97
770	1.31	990	2.17	1210	3.25	1430	4.54	1650	6.04
780	1.34	1000	2.22	1220	3.30	1440	4.60	1660	6.12
790	1.38	1010	2.26	1230	3.36	1450	4.66	1670	6.19
800	1.42	1020	2.31	1240	3.41	1460	4.73	1680	6.26
810	1.45	1030	2.35	1250	3.47	1470	4.79	1690	6.34

Appendix 4

Velocity in fps	Energy	Velocity in fps	Energy	Velocity in fps	Energy	Velocity in fps	Energy	Velocity in fps	Energy
1700	6.41	2280	11.54	2860	18.16	3440	26.23	4020	35.89
1710	6.49	2290	11.64	2870	18.29	3450	26.38	4030	36.07
1720	6.57	2300	11.74	2880	18.42	3460	26.54	4040	36.25
1730	6.64	2310	11.83	2890	18.55	3470	26.69	4050	36.43
1740	6.72	2320	11.95	2900	18.67	3480	26.85	4060	36.61
1750	6.80	2330	12.05	2910	18.80	3490	27.00	4070	36.79
1760	6.88	2340	12.16	2920	18.93	3500	27.16	4080	36.97
1770	6.95	2350	12.26	2930	19.06	3510	27.31	4090	37.15
1780	7.03	2360	12.37	2940	19.19	3520	27.47	4100	37.33
1790	7.11	2370	12.47	2950	19.32	3530	27.62	4110	37.51
1800	7.19	2380	12.58	2960	19.45	3540	27.78	4120	37.70
1810	7.27	2390	12.68	2970	19.59	3550	27.94	4130	37.88
1820	7.35	2400	12.78	2980	19.72	3560	28.10	4140	38.06
1830	7.43	2410	12.90	2990	19.85	3570	28.25	4150	38.25
1840	7.51	2420	13.00	3000	20.00	3580	28.41	4160	38.43
1850	7.60	2430	13.11	3010	20.12	3590	28.57	4170	38.62
1860	7.68	2440	13.22	3020	20.25	3600	28.73	4180	38.80
1870	7.76	2450	13.33	3030	20.39	3610	28.94	4190	38.99
1880	7.84	2460	13.44	3040	20.52	3620	29.10	4200	39.18
1890	7.94	2470	13.55	3050	20.66	3630	29.26	4210	39.36
1900	8.01	2480	13.66	3060	20.79	3640	29.42	4220	39.55
1910	8.10	2490	13.77	3070	20.93	3650	29.58	4230	39.74
1920	8.18	2500	13.88	3080	21.07	3660	29.75	4240	39.92
1930	8.37	2510	13.99	3090	21.16	3670	29.91	4250	40.11
1940	8.35	2520	14.10	3100	21.29	3680	30.07	4260	40.30
1950	8.44	2530	14.20	3110	21.43	3690	30.24	4270	40.49
1960	8.53	2540	14.32	3120	21.57	3700	30.40	4280	40.68
1970	8.61	2550	14.44	3130	21.71	3710	30.56	4290	40.87
1980	8.70	2560	14.55	3140	21.85	3720	30.73	4300	41.06
1990	8.79	2570	14.67	3150	21.99	3730	30.90	4310	41.25
2000	8.88	2580	14.78	3160	22.12	3740	31.06	4320	41.45
2010	8.97	2590	14.89	3170	22.26	3750	31.23	4330	41.64
2020	9.06	2600	15.01	3180	22.41	3760	31.40	4340	41.83
2030	9.15	2610	15.13	3190	22.55	3770	31.56	4350	42.02
2040	9.24	2620	15.24	3200	22.69	3780	31.73	4360	42.22
2050	9.33	2630	15.36	3210	22.83	3790	31.90	4370	42.41
2060	9.42	2640	15.48	3220	22.97	3800	32.07	4380	42.61
2070	9.50	2650	15.59	3230	23.12	3810	32.24	4390	42.80
2080	9.60	2660	15.71	3240	23.26	3820	32.41	4400	43.00
2090	9.70	2670	15.83	3250	23.41	3830	32.58	4410	43.19
2100	9.80	2680	15.96	3260	23.55	3840	32.75	4420	43.39
2110	9.90	2690	16.07	3270	23.70	3850	32.92	4430	43.58
2120	9.98	2700	16.19	3280	23.84	3860	33.09	4440	43.78
2130	10.07	2710	16.31	3290	23.99	3870	33.26	4450	43.98
2140	10.17	2720	16.43	3300	24.14	3880	33.45	4460	44.18
2150	10.26	2730	16.55	3310	24.28	3890	33.62	4470	44.38
2160	10.36	2740	16.67	3320	24.43	3900	33.78	4480	44.58
2170	10.45	2750	16.79	3330	24.58	3910	33.95	4490	44.77
2180	10.55	2760	16.91	3340	24.73	3920	34.12	4500	44.97
2190	10.65	2770	17.04	3350	24.87	3930	34.30	4510	45.17
2200	10.74	2780	17.16	3360	25.02	3940	34.48	4520	45.37
2210	10.84	2790	17.28	3370	25.17	3950	34.65	4530	45.58
2220	10.94	2800	17.41	3380	25.32	3960	34.82	4540	45.78
2230	11.04	2810	17.53	3390	25.47	3970	35.00	4550	45.98
2240	11.14	2820	17.66	3400	25.62	3980	35.18	4560	46.18
2250	11.24	2830	17.78	3410	25.77	3990	35.36	4570	46.38
2260	11.34	2840	17.91	3420	25.93	4000	35.53	4580	46.59
2270	11.44	2850	18.04	3430	26.08	4010	35.71	4590	46.79

Ballistics Charts

Ballistics for Standard Pistol and Revolver Centerfire Ammunition Produced by the Major U. S. Manufacturers

Cartridge	Bullet Grs.	Bullet Style	Muzzle Velocity	Muzzle Energy	Barrel Inches
22 Jet	40	SP	2100	390	8³/₈
221 Fireball	50	SP	2650	780	10¹/₂
25 (6.35mm) Auto	50	MC	810	73	2
256 Winchester Magnum	60	HP	2350	735	8¹/₂
30 (7.65mm) Luger Auto	93	MC	1220	307	4¹/₂
30 (7.63mm) Mauser Auto	85	MC	1410	375	5¹/₂
32 S&W Blank	No bullet		—	—	—
32 S&W Blank, BP	No bullet		—	—	—
32 Short Colt	80	Lead	745	100	4
32 Long Colt, IL	82	Lub.	755	104	4
32 Colt New Police	100	Lead	680	100	4
32 (7.65mm) Auto	71	MC	960	145	4
32 (7.65mm) Auto Pistol	77	MC	900	162	4
32 S&W	88	Lead	680	90	3
32 S&W Long	98	Lead	705	115	4
7.5 Nagant	104	Lead	722	120	4¹/₂
32-20 Winchester	100	Lead	1030	271	6
32-20 Winchester	100	SP	1030	271	6
357 Magnum	158	SP	1550	845	8³/₈
357 Magnum	158	MP	1410	695	8³/₈
357 Magnum	158	Lead	1410	696	8³/₈
357 Magnum	158	JSP	1450	735	8³/₈
9mm Luger	116	MC	1165	349	4
9mm Luger Auto	124	MC	1120	345	4
38 S&W Blank	No bullet		—	—	—
38 Smith & Wesson	146	Lead	685	150	4
38 S&W	146	Lead	730	172	4
380 MK II	180	MC	620	153	5

IL-Inside Lubricated; JSP-Jacketed Soft Point; WC-Wadcutter; Rh-Round Nose; Hp-Hollow Point; Lub-Lubricated; MC-Metal Case; SP-Soft Point; MP-Metal Point; LGC-Lead Gas Check; JHP-Jacketed Hollow Point

Ballistics for Standard Pistol and Revolver Centerfire Ammunition (continued)

Cartridge	Bullet Grs.	Bullet Style	Muzzle Velocity	Muzzle Energy	Barrel Inches
38 Special Blank	No bullet		—	—	—
38 Special, IL	150	Lub.	1060	375	6
38 Special, IL	150	MC	1060	375	6
38 Special	158	Lead	855	256	6
38 Special	200	Lead	730	236	6
38 Special	158	MP	855	256	6
38 Special	125	SJHP		Not available	
38 Special	158	SJHP		Not available	
38 Special WC	148	Lead	770	195	6
38 Special Match, IL	148	Lead	770	195	6
38 Special Match, IL	158	Lead	855	256	6
38 Special Hi-Speed	158	Lead	1090	425	6
38 Special	158	RN	900	320	6
38 Colt New Police	150	Lead	680	154	4
38 Short Colt	128	Lead	730	150	6
38 Short Colt, Greased	130	Lub.	730	155	6
38 Long Colt	150	Lead	730	175	6
38 Super Auto	130	MC	1280	475	5
38 Auto, for Colt 38 Super	130	MC	1280	475	5
38 Auto	130	MC	1040	312	4½
380 Auto	95	MC	955	192	3¾
38-40 Winchester	180	SP	975	380	5
41 Long Colt, IL	200	Lub.	730	230	6
41 Remington Magnum	210	Lead	1050	515	8¾
41 Remington Magnum	210	SP	1500	1050	8¾
44 S&W Special	246	Lead	755	311	6½
44 Remington Magnum	240	SP	1470	1150	6½
44 Remington Magnum	240	Lead	1470	1150	6½
44-40 Winchester	200	SP	975	420	7½
45 Colt	250	Lead	860	410	5½
45 Colt, IL	255	Lub., L	860	410	5½
45 Auto	230	MC	850	369	5
45 ACP	230	JHP	850	370	5
45 Auto WC	185	MC	775	245	5
45 Auto MC	230	MC	850	369	5
45 Auto Match	185	MC	775	247	5
45 Auto Match, IL	210	Lead	710	235	5
45 Auto Rim	230	Lead	810	335	5½

IL-Inside Lubricated; JSP-Jacketed Soft Point; WC-Wadcutter; Rh-Round Nose; HP-Hollow Point; Lub-Lubricated; MC-Metal Case; SP-Soft Point; MP-Metal Point; LGC-Lead Gas Check; JHP-Jacketed Hollow Point

Ballistics of Super Vel Cartridge Corporation Handgun Ammunition

Cartridge	Bullet Gr. Style	Bullet Style (a)	Muzzle Velocity	Muzzle Energy	Barrel Inches
380 ACP	80	JHP	1026	188	5
9mm Luger	90	JHP	1422	402	5
9mm Luger	110	SP	1325	428	5
38 Special	110	JHP/SP	1370	458	6
38 Special	147	HBWC	775	196	6
38 Special Int.	158	Lead	1110	439	6
357 Magnum	110	JHP/SP	1690	697	6
44 Magnum	180	JHP/SP	2005	1607	6
45 Auto	190	JHP	1060	743	5

(a) JHP-Jacketed Hollow Point; JSP-Jacketed Soft Point; HBWC-Hollow Base Wad Cutter.

Ballistics of Standard Shotshell Ammunition
Loaded by the Major U. S. Manufacturers

Gauge	Length Shell Ins.	Powder Equiv. Drams	Shot Ozs.	Shot Size
MAGNUM LOADS				
10	$3^1/_2$	5	2	2, 4
12	3	$4^1/_2$	$1^7/_8$	BB, 2, 4
12	3	$4^1/_4$	$1^5/_8$	2, 4, 6
12	$2^3/_4$	4	$1^1/_2$	2, 4, 5, 6
16	$2^3/_4$	$3^1/_2$	$1^1/_4$	2, 4, 6
20	3	$3^1/_4$	$1^1/_4$	2, 4, 6, $7^1/_2$
20	3	Max	$1^3/_{16}$	4
20	$2^3/_4$	3	$1^1/_8$	2, 4, 6, $7^1/_2$
28	$2^3/_4$	Max	1	6, $7^1/_2$, 8, 9
LONG RANGE LOADS				
10	$2^7/_8$	$4^3/_4$	$1^5/_8$	4
12	$2^3/_4$	$3^3/_4$	$1^1/_4$	BB, 2, 4, 5, 6, $7^1/_2$, 9
16	$2^3/_4$	$3^1/_4$	$1^1/_8$	4, 5, 6, $7^1/_2$, 9
16	$2^3/_4$	3	$1^1/_8$	4, 5, 6, $7^1/_2$, 9
20	$2^3/_4$	$2^3/_4$	1	4, 5, 6, $7^1/_2$, 9
28	$2^3/_4$	$2^1/_4$	$3/_4$	4, 6, $7^1/_2$, 9
FIELD LOADS				
12	$2^3/_4$	$3^1/_4$	$1^1/_4$	$7^1/_2$, 8, 9
12	$2^3/_4$	$3^1/_4$	$1^1/_8$	4, 5, 6, $7^1/_2$, 8, 9
12	$2^3/_4$	3	$1^1/_8$	4, 5, 6, 8, 9
12	$2^3/_4$	3	1	4, 5, 6, 8
16	$2^3/_4$	$2^3/_4$	$1^1/_8$	4, 5, 6, $7^1/_2$, 8, 9
16	$2^3/_4$	$2^1/_2$	1	4, 5, 6, 8, 9
20	$2^3/_4$	$2^1/_2$	1	4, 5, 6, $7^1/_2$, 8, 9
20	$2^3/_4$	$2^1/_4$	$7/_8$	4, 5, 6, 8, 9
SCATTER LOADS				
12	$2^3/_4$	3	$1^1/_8$	8
16	$2^3/_4$	$2^1/_2$	1	8
20	$2^3/_4$	$2^1/_4$	$7/_8$	8
TARGET LOADS				
12	$2^3/_4$	3	$1^1/_8$	$7^1/_2$, 8, 9
12	$2^3/_4$	$2^3/_4$	$1^1/_8$	$7^1/_2$, 8, 9
16	$2^3/_4$	$2^1/_2$	1	8, 9
20	$2^3/_4$	$2^1/_4$	$7/_8$	8, 9
28	$2^3/_4$	$2^1/_4$	$3/_4$	9
410	3	Max	$3/_4$	4, 5, 6, $7^1/_2$, 9
410	$2^1/_2$	Max	$1/_2$	4, 5, 6, $7^1/_2$, 9
SKEET & TRAP				
12	$2^3/_4$	3	$1^1/_8$	$7^1/_2$, 8, 9
12	$2^3/_4$	$2^3/_4$	$1^1/_8$	$7^1/_2$, 8, 9
16	$2^3/_4$	$2^1/_2$	1	8, 9
20	$2^3/_4$	$2^1/_4$	$7/_8$	8, 9
BUCKSHOT				
12	3 Mag	$4^1/_2$	—	00 Buck — 15 pellets
12	3 Mag	$4^1/_2$	—	4 Buck — 41 pellets
12	$2^3/_4$ Mag	4	—	2 Buck — 20 pellets
12	$2^3/_4$ Mag	4	—	00 Buck — 12 pellets
12	$2^3/_4$	$3^3/_4$	—	00 Buck — 9 pellets
12	$2^3/_4$	$3^3/_4$	—	0 Buck — 12 pellets
12	$2^3/_4$	$3^3/_4$	—	1 Buck — 16 pellets
12	$2^3/_4$	$3^3/_4$	—	4 Buck — 27 pellets
16	$2^3/_4$	3	—	1 Buck — 12 pellets
20	$2^3/_4$	$2^3/_4$	—	3 Buck — 20 pellets
RIFLED SLUGS				
12	$2^3/_4$	$3^3/_4$	1	Slug
16	$2^3/_4$	3	$1^7/_8$	Slug
20	$2^3/_4$	$2^3/_4$	$5/_8$	Slug
410	$2^1/_2$	Max	$1/_5$	Slug

Ballistics for Standard Centerfire Rifle Ammunition Produced by the Major U. S. Manufacturers

Cartridge	Bullet Wt. Grs.	Bullet Type(g)	Velocity (fps) Muzzle	100 yds.	200 yds.	300 yds.	Energy (ft. lbs.) Muzzle	100 yds.	200 yds.	300 yds.	Mid-Range Trajectory 100 yds.	200 yds.	300 yds.
218 Bee	46	HP	2860	2160	1610	1200	835	475	265	145	0.7	3.8	11.6
22 Hornet	45	SP	2690	2030	1510	1150	720	410	230	130	0.8	4.3	13.0
22 Hornet (c. d)	45	HP	2690	2030	1510	1150	720	410	230	130	0.8	4.3	13.0
22 Hornet	46	HP	2690	2030	1510	1150	740	420	235	135	0.8	4.3	13.0
222 Remington (e)	50	PSP, MC, PL	3200	2660	2170	1750	1140	785	520	340	0.5	2.5	7.0
222 Remington Magnum (c, d)	55	SP, PL	3300	2800	2340	1930	1330	955	670	455	0.5	2.3	6.1
223 Remington (c, d, e)	55	SP, PL	3300	2800	2340	1930	1330	955	670	455	0.5	2.1	5.4
22-250 Remington (a, c, d)	55	PSP, PL	3760	3230	2745	2305	1730	1275	920	650	0.4	1.7	4.5
225 Winchester (a, b)	55	PSP	3650	3140	2680	2270	1630	1200	875	630	0.4	1.8	4.8
243 Winchester (e)	80	PSP, PL	3500	3080	2720	2410	2180	1690	1320	1030	0.4	1.8	4.7
243 Winchester (e)	100	PP, CL, PSP	3070	2790	2540	2320	2090	1730	1430	1190	0.5	2.2	5.5
6mm Remington (c, d)	80	PSP, HP, PL	3450	3130	2750	2400	2220	1740	1340	1018	0.4	1.8	4.7
6mm Remington (c, d)	100	PCL	3190	2920	2660	2420	2260	1890	1570	1300	0.5	2.1	5.1
244 Remington (c, d)	90	PSP	3200	2850	2530	2230	2050	1630	1280	995	0.5	2.1	5.5
25-06 Remington (c, d)	87	HP	3500	3070	2680	2310	2370	1820	1390	1030	0.5	2.1	5.5
25-06 Remington (c, d)	120	PSP	Not Available				Not Available				Not Available		
25-20 Winchester	86	L, Lu	1460	1180	1030	940	405	265	200	170	2.6	12.5	32.0
25-20 Winchester	86	SP	1460	1180	1030	940	405	265	200	170	2.6	12.5	32.0
25-35 Winchester	117	SP, CL	2300	1910	1600	1340	1370	945	665	465	1.0	4.6	12.5
250 Savage	87	PSP, SP	3030	2660	2330	2060	1770	1370	1050	820	0.6	2.5	6.4
250 Savage	100	ST, CL, PSP	2820	2460	2140	1870	1760	1340	1020	775	0.6	2.9	7.4
256 Winchester Magnum (b)	60	OPE	2800	2070	1570	1220	1040	570	330	200	0.8	4.0	12.0
257 Roberts (a, b)	87	PSP	3200	2840	2500	2190	1980	1560	1210	925	0.5	2.2	5.7
257 Roberts	100	ST, CL	2900	2540	2210	1920	1870	1430	1080	820	0.6	2.7	7.0
257 Roberts	117	PP, CL	2650	2280	1950	1690	1820	1350	985	740	0.7	3.4	8.8
6.5 Remington Magnum (c)	100	PSPCL	3450	3070	2690	2320	2640	2090	1610	1190	Not Available		
6.5mm Remington Magnum (c)	120	PSPCL	3030	2750	2480	2230	2450	2010	1640	1330	0.6	2.3	5.7
264 Winchester Magnum	100	PSP, CL	3700	3260	2880	2550	3040	2360	1840	1440	0.4	1.6	4.2
264 Winchester Magnum	140	PP, CL	3200	2940	2700	2480	3180	2690	2270	1910	0.5	2.0	4.9
270 Winchester	100	PSP	3480	3070	2690	2340	2690	2090	1600	1215	0.4	1.8	4.8
270 Winchester (e)	130	PP, PSP	3140	2880	2630	2400	2850	2390	2000	1660	0.5	2.1	5.3
270 Winchester	130	ST, CL, BP, PP	3140	2850	2580	2320	2840	2340	1920	1550	0.5	2.1	5.3
270 Winchester (c, d)	150	CL	2800	2440	2140	1870	2610	1980	1520	1160	0.6	2.9	7.6
270 Winchester (a, b, e)	150	PP	2900	2620	2380	2160	2800	2290	1890	1550	0.6	2.5	6.3
280 Remington (c, d)	125	PCL	3190	2880	2590	2320	2820	2300	1860	1490	0.5	2.1	5.3
280 Remington (c, d)	150	PCL	2900	2670	2450	2220	2800	2370	2000	1640	0.6	2.5	6.1
280 Remington (c, d)	165	CL	2820	2510	2220	1970	2910	2310	1810	1420	0.6	2.8	7.2
284 Winchester (a, b)	125	PP	3200	2880	2590	2310	2840	2300	1860	1480	0.5	2.1	5.3
284 Winchester (a, b)	150	PP	2900	2630	2380	2160	2800	2300	1890	1550	0.6	2.5	6.3
7mm Mauser (e)	175	SP	2490	2170	1900	1680	2410	1830	1400	1100	0.8	3.7	9.5

Ballistics for Standard Centerfire Rifle Ammunition Produced by the Major U. S. Manufacturers

Cartridge	Wt. Grs.	Bullet Type(g)	Velocity (fps)				Energy (ft. lbs.)				Mid-Range Trajectory		
			Muzzle	100 yds.	200 yds.	300 yds.	Muzzle	100 yds.	200 yds.	300 yds.	100 yds.	200 yds.	300 yds.
7mm Remington Magnum	125	CL	3430	3080	2750	2450	3260	2630	2100	1660	0.6	1.8	4.7
7mm Remington Magnum (e)	150	PP, CL	3260	2970	2700	2450	3540	2940	2430	1990	0.4	2.0	4.9
7mm Remington Magnum (e)	175	PP	3070	2720	2400	2120	3660	2870	2240	1750	0.5	2.4	6.1
7mm Remington Magnum (c, d)	175	PCL	3070	2860	2660	2460	3660	3170	2740	2350	0.5	2.1	5.2
30 Carbine (e)	110	HSP, SP	1980	1540	1230	1040	950	575	370	260	1.4	7.5	21.7
30-30 Winchester (c, d)	150	CL	2410	1960	1620	1360	1930	1280	875	616	0.9	4.5	12.5
30-30 Winchester (e)	150	HP	2410	2020	1700	1430	1930	1360	960	680	0.9	4.2	11.0
30-30 Winchester (a, b)	150	PP, ST, OPE	2410	2020	1700	1430	1930	1360	960	680	0.9	4.2	11.0
30-30 Winchester (a)	170	PP, HP, CL, ST, MC	2220	1890	1630	1410	1860	1350	1000	750	1.2	4.6	12.5
30 Remington	170	ST, CL	2120	1820	1560	1350	1700	1250	920	690	1.1	5.3	14.0
30-06 Springfield	110	PSP	3370	2830	2350	1920	2770	1960	1350	900	0.5	2.2	6.0
30-06 Springfield	125	PSP	3200	2810	2480	2200	2840	2190	1710	1340	0.5	2.2	5.6
30-06 Springfield (c, d)	150	BP	2970	2710	2470	2240	2930	2440	2030	1670	0.5	2.4	6.0
30-06 Springfield (e)	150	PP	2970	2620	2300	2010	2930	2280	1760	1340	0.6	2.5	6.5
30-06 Springfield	150	ST, PCL, PSP	2970	2670	2330	2130	2930	2370	1920	1510	0.6	2.4	6.1
30-06 Springfield	180	PP, CL, PSP	2700	2330	2010	1740	2910	2170	1610	1210	0.7	3.1	8.3
30-06 Springfield (e)	180	ST, BP, PCL	2700	2470	2250	2040	2910	2440	2020	1660	0.7	2.9	7.0
30-06 Springfield	180	MCBT, MAT	2700	2520	2350	2190	2910	2540	2200	1900	0.6	2.8	6.7
30-06 Springfield	220	PP, CL	2410	2120	1870	1670	2830	2190	1710	1360	0.8	3.9	9.8
30-06 Springfield (a, b)	220	ST	2410	2180	1980	1790	2830	2320	1910	1560	0.8	3.7	9.2
30-40 Krag	180	PP, CL	2470	2120	1830	1590	2440	1790	1340	1010	0.8	3.8	9.9
30-40 Krag	180	ST, PCL	2470	2250	2040	1850	2440	2020	1660	1370	0.8	3.5	8.5
30-40 Krag	220	ST	2200	1990	1800	1630	2360	1930	1580	1300	1.0	4.4	11.0
300 Winchester Magnum	150	PP, PCL	3400	3050	2730	2430	3850	3100	2480	1970	0.4	1.9	4.8
300 Winchester Magnum	180	PP, PCL	3070	2850	2640	2440	3770	3250	2790	2380	0.5	2.1	5.3
300 Winchester Magnum (a, b)	220	ST	2720	2490	2270	2060	3620	3030	2520	2070	0.6	2.9	6.9
300 H & H Magnum	150	ST	3190	2870	2580	2300	3390	2740	2220	1760	0.5	2.1	5.2
300 H & H Magnum	180	ST, PCL	2920	2670	2440	2220	3400	2850	2380	1970	0.6	2.4	5.8
300 H & H Magnum	220	ST, CL	2620	2370	2150	1940	3350	2740	2260	1840	0.7	3.1	7.7
300 Savage (e)	150	PP	2670	2350	2060	1800	2370	1840	1410	1080	0.7	3.2	8.0
300 Savage	150	ST, PCL	2670	2390	2130	1890	2370	1900	1510	1190	0.7	3.0	7.6
300 Savage (c, d)	150	CL	2670	2270	1930	1660	2370	1710	1240	916	0.7	3.3	9.3
300 Savage (e)	180	PP, CL	2370	2040	1760	1520	2240	1660	1240	920	0.9	4.1	10.5
300 Savage	180	ST, PCL	2370	2160	1960	1770	2240	1860	1530	1250	0.9	3.7	9.2
303 Savage (c, d)	180	CL	2140	1810	1550	1340	1830	1310	960	715	1.1	5.4	14.0
303 Savage (a, b)	190	ST	1980	1680	1440	1250	1650	1190	875	660	1.3	6.2	15.5
303 British (e)	180	PP, CL	2540	2300	2090	1900	2580	2120	1750	1440	0.7	3.3	8.2

(a) — Winchester only; (b) — Remington only; (c) — Peters only; (d) — Speer DWM; (e) — Cartridges also available from Federal; (f) — Not safe in Winchester 1873 rifle or handguns; (g) — HP-Hollow Point; SP-Soft Point; PSP-Pointed Soft Point; PP-Winchester Power Point; L-Lead; Lu-Lubaloy; ST-Silvertip; HSP-Hollow Soft Point; MC-Metal Case; BT-Boat Tail; MAT-Match; BP-Bronze Point; CL-Core Lokt; PCL-Pointed Core Lokt; OPE-Open Point Expanding; PL-Power-Lokt.

Ballistics for Standard Centerfire Rifle Ammunition Produced by the Major U. S. Manufacturers (continued)

Cartridge	Bullet Wt. Grs.	Type	Velocity (fps) Muzzle	100 yds.	200 yds.	300 yds.	Energy (ft. lbs.) Muzzle	100 yds.	200 yds.	300 yds.	Mid-Range Trajectory 100 yds.	200 yds.	300 yds.
303 British (c, d)	215	SP	2180	1900	1660	1460	2270	1720	1310	1020	1.1	4.9	12.5
308 Winchester	110	PSP	3340	2810	2340	1920	2730	1930	1349	900	0.5	2.2	6.0
308 Winchester (a, b)	125	PSP	3100	2740	2430	2160	2670	2060	1640	1300	0.5	2.3	5.9
308 Winchester (e)	150	PP	2860	2520	2210	1930	2730	2120	1630	1240	0.6	2.7	7.0
308 Winchester	150	ST, PCL	2860	2570	2300	2050	2730	2200	1760	1400	0.6	2.6	6.5
308 Winchester (e)	180	PP, CL	2610	2250	1940	1680	2720	2020	1500	1130	0.7	3.4	8.9
308 Winchester	180	ST, PCL	2610	2390	2170	1970	2720	2280	1870	1540	0.8	3.1	7.4
308 Winchester (a, b)	200	ST	2450	2210	1980	1770	2670	2170	1750	1400	0.8	3.6	9.0
32 Winchester Special (c, d, e)	170	HP, CL	2280	1920	1630	1410	1960	1390	1000	750	1.0	4.8	12.5
32 Winchester Special (a, b)	170	PP, ST	2280	1870	1560	1330	1960	1320	920	665	1.0	4.8	13.0
32 Remington (c, d)	170	CL	2120	1800	1540	1340	1700	1220	895	680	1.0	4.9	13.0
32 Remington (a, b)	170	ST	2120	1760	1460	1220	1700	1170	805	560	1.1	5.3	14.5
32-20 Winchester HV (f)	80	OPE, HP	2100	1430	1090	950	780	365	210	160	1.5	8.5	24.5
32-20 Winchester	100	SP, L, Lu	1290	1060	940	840	370	250	195	155	3.3	15.5	38.0
8mm Mauser (e)	170	PP, CL	2570	2140	1790	1520	2490	1730	1210	870	0.8	3.9	10.5
338 Winchester Magnum (a, b)	200	PP	3000	2690	2410	2170	4000	3210	2580	2090	0.5	2.4	6.0
338 Winchester Magnum (a, b)	250	ST	2700	2430	2180	1940	4050	3280	2640	2090	0.7	3.0	7.4
338 Winchester Magnum (a, b)	300	PP	2450	2160	1910	1690	4000	3110	2430	1900	0.8	3.7	9.5
348 Winchester (a)	200	ST	2530	2220	1940	1680	2840	2190	1670	1250	0.4	1.7	4.7
348 Winchester (c, d)	200	CL	2530	2140	1820	1570	2840	2030	1470	1090	0.8	3.8	10.0
35 Remington (c, d)	150	CL	2400	1960	1580	1280	1920	1280	835	545	0.9	4.6	13.0
35 Remington (e)	200	PP, ST, CL	2100	1710	1390	1160	1950	1300	860	605	1.2	6.0	16.5
350 Remington Magnum (c, d)	200	PCL	2710	2410	2130	1870	3260	2570	2000	1550	Not Available		
350 Remington Magnum (c, d)	250	PCL	2410	2190	1980	1790	3220	2660	2180	1780	Not Available		
351 Winchester Self-Loading	180	SP, MC	1850	1560	1310	1140	1370	975	685	520	1.5	7.8	21.5
358 Winchester (a, b)	200	ST	2530	2210	1910	1640	2840	2160	1610	1190	0.8	3.6	9.4
358 Winchester (a, b)	250	ST	2250	2010	1780	1570	2810	2230	1760	1370	1.0	4.4	11.0
375 H&H Magnum	270	PP, SP	2740	2460	2210	1990	4500	3620	2920	2370	0.7	2.9	7.1
375 H&H Magnum	300	ST	2550	2280	2040	1830	4330	3460	2770	2230	0.7	3.3	8.3
375 H&H Magnum	300	MC	2550	2180	1860	1590	4330	3160	2300	1680	0.7	3.6	9.3
38-40 Winchester	180	SP	1330	1070	960	850	705	455	370	290	3.2	15.0	36.5
44 Magnum (c, d)	240	SP	1750	1360	1110	980	1630	985	655	510	1.6	8.4	—
44 Magnum (b)	240	HSP	1750	1350	1090	950	1630	970	635	480	1.8	9.4	26.0
444 Marlin (c)	240	SP	2400	1845	1410	1125	3070	1815	1060	675	Not Available		
44-40 Winchester	200	SP	1310	1050	940	830	760	490	390	305	3.3	15.0	36.5
45-70 Government	405	SP	1320	1160	1050	990	1570	1210	990	880	2.9	13.0	32.5
458 Winchester Magnum	500	MC	2130	1910	1700	1520	5040	4050	3210	2570	1.1	4.8	12.0
458 Winchester Magnum	510	SP	2130	1840	1600	1400	5140	3830	2900	2220	1.1	5.1	13.5

(a)—Winchester only; (b)—Remington only; (c)—Peters only; (d)—Speer DWM; (e)—Cartridges also available from Federal; (f)—Not safe in Winchester 1873 rifle or handguns; (g)—HP-Hollow Point; SP-Soft Point; PSP-Pointed Soft Point; PP-Winchester Power Point; L-Lead; Lu-Lubaloy; ST-Silvertip; HSP-Hollow Soft Point; MC-Metal Case; BT-Boat Tail; MAT-Match; BP-Bronze Point; CL-Core Lokt; PCL-Pointed Core Lokt; OPE-Open Point Expanding; PL-Power-Lokt.

Speer/DWM Ballistics
Ammunition Manufactured by DWM in Germany and Distributed Through Speer Outlets in This Country

Cartridge	Wt. Grs.	Bullet Type (a)	Velocity (fps)				Energy (ft. lbs.)				Mid-Range Trajectory		
			Muzzle	100 yds.	200 yds.	300 yds.	Muzzle	100 yds.	200 yds.	300 yds.	100 yds.	200 yds.	300 yds.
5.6 × 35 R Vierling	46	SP	2030	1500	1140		418	224	130		1.2	7.5	Not Available
5.6 × 50 R (Rimmed) Mag.	50	PSP	Not Available				Not Available				Not Available		
5.6 × 52 R (Savage H.P.)	71	PSP	2850	2460	2320	2200	1280	947	846	766	.3	2.3	6.5
5.6 × 61 SE	77	PSP	3700	3360	3060	2790	2350	1920	1605	1345	.1	1.1	3.4
5.6 × 61 R	77	PSP	3480	3140	2840	2560	2070	1690	1370	1120	.1	1.3	4.0
6.5 × 54 MS	159	SP	2170	1925	1705	1485	1660	1300	1025	810	.5	4.1	11.5
6.5 × 57 Mauser	93	PSP	3350	2930	2570	2260	2300	1760	1350	1040	.1	1.7	4.8
6.5 × 57 R	93	PSP	3350	2930	2570	2260	2300	1760	1350	1040	.1	1.7	4.8
7 × 57 Mauser	103	PSP	3330	2865	2450	2060	2550	1890	1380	977	.1	1.7	5.2
	162	TIG	2785	2480	2250	2060	2780	2200	1820	1520	.3	2.4	6.7
7 × 57 R	103	PSP	3260	2810	2390	2000	2430	1820	1320	920	.1	1.8	5.3
	139	SP	2550	2240	1960	1720	2000	1540	1190	910	.3	2.9	8.6
	162	TIG	2710	2420	2210	2020	2640	2120	1750	1460	.3	2.4	6.9
7 × 64	103	PSP	3572	3110	2685	2283	2930	2230	1670	1190	.1	1.4	4.4
	139	SP	3000	2570	2260	1980	2780	2040	1570	1200	.2	2.2	6.4
	162	TIG	2960	2603	2375	2200	3150	2440	2030	1740	.2	2.0	6.0
	177	TIG	2880	2665	2490	2325	3270	2820	2440	2130	.2	2.0	5.6
7 × 65 R	103	PSP	3480	3010	2590	2200	2770	2100	1540	1120	.1	1.5	4.7
	139	SP	3000	2570	2260	1980	2780	2040	1570	1200	.2	2.2	6.4
	162	TIG	2887	2540	2320	2140	3000	2320	1930	1650	.2	2.2	6.3
	177	TIG	2820	2600	2420	2255	3120	2660	2300	2000	.2	2.1	5.9
7mm SE	169	ToSto	3300	3045	2825	2620	4090	3480	3010	2600	.1	1.4	3.9
7 × 75 R SE	169	ToSto	3070	2840	2630	2430	3550	3050	2620	2240	.1	1.6	4.5
30-06	180	TUG	2854	2562	2306	2077	3261	2632	2133	1726	.2	2.2	6.3
8 × 57 JS	123	SP	2968	2339	1805	1318	2415	1497	897	477	.2	2.7	8.8
	198	TIG	2732	2415	2181	1985	3276	2560	2083	1736	.3	2.5	7.1
8 × 57 JR	196	SP	2391	1991	1742	1565	2488	1736	1316	1056	.5	3.9	11.2
8 × 57 JRS	123	SP	2970	2340	1805	1318	2415	1497	897	477	.2	2.7	8.8
	196	SP	2480	2140	1870	1640	2680	2000	1510	1165	.4	3.3	9.4
	198	TIG	2600	2320	2105	1930	2970	2350	1950	1620	.3	2.7	7.6
8 × 60 S	196	SP	2585	2162	1890	1690	2905	2030	1560	1245	.4	3.2	9.2
	198	TIG	2780	2450	2205	2010	3390	2625	2130	1770	.3	2.4	6.9
9.3 × 62	293	TUG	2515	2310	2150	2020	4110	3480	3010	2634	.3	2.8	7.5
9.3 × 64	293	TUG	2640	2450	2290	2145	4550	3900	3410	3000	.3	2.4	6.6
9.3 × 72 R	193	FP	1925	1600	1400	1245	1590	1090	835	666	.5	5.7	16.6
9.3 × 74 R	293	TUG	2360	2160	1998	1870	3580	3000	2560	2250	.3	3.1	8.7

(a) FP–flat point; SP–soft point; PSP–pointed soft point; TIG–Brenneke Torpedo Ideal; TUG–Brenneke Torpedo Universal; ToSto–Vom Hofe Torpedo Stop Ring; SM–Stark Mantel (strong jacket).

Ballistics for Standard Rimfire Ammunition Produced by the Major U. S. Manufacturers

Cartridge	Bullet Wt. Grs.	Bullet Type(a)	Velocity (fps) Muzzle	Velocity (fps) 100 yds.	Energy (ft. lbs.) Muzzle	Energy (ft. lbs.) 100 yds.	Mid-Range Trajectory 100 yds.	Handgun Barrel Length	Ballistics M.V. fps	Ballistics M.E. ft. lbs.	
22 Short	29	C, L*	1045	810	70	42	5.6	6"	865	48	
22 Short Hi-Vel.	29	C, L	1125	920	81	54	4.3	6"	1035	69	
22 Short HP Hi-Vel.	27	C, L	1155	920	80	51	4.2	–	–	–	(per 500)
22 Short	29	D	1045	–	70	–	–	–	–	–	(per 500)
22 Short	15	D	1710	–	97	–	–	–	–	–	
22 Long Hi-Vel.	29	C, L	1240	965	99	60	3.8	6"	1095	77	
22 Long Rifle	40	L*	1145	975	116	84	4.0	6"	950	80	
22 Long Rifle	40	L*	1120	950	111	80	4.2	–	–	–	
22 Long Rifle	40	L*	–	–	–	–	–	6¾"	1060	100	
22 Long Rifle	40	C	1165	980	121	84	4.0	–	–	–	
22 Long Rifle Hi-Vel.	40	C, L	1335	1045	158	97	3.3	6"	1125	112	
22 Long Rifle HP (Hi-Vel.)	37	C, L	1365	1040	149	86	3.4	–	–	–	
22 Long Rifle HP (Hi-Vel.)	36	C	1365	1040	149	86	3.4	–	–	–	
22 Long Rifle	No	12 Shot	–	–	–	–	–	–	–	–	
22 WRF (Rem. Spl.)	45	C, L	1450	1110	210	123	2.7	–	–	–	
22 WRF Mag.	40	JHP	2000	1390	355	170	1.6	6½"	1550	213	
22 WRF Mag.	40	MC	2000	1390	355	170	1.6	6½"	1550	213	
22 Win. Auto Inside lub.	45	C, L	1055	930	111	86	4.6	–	–	–	
5mm Rem. RFM	38	PLHP	2100	1605	372	217	Not Available				

(a) C-Copper Plated; L-Lead (wax coated); D-Disintegrating; L-Lead Lubricated; MC-Metal Case; HP-Hollow Point; JHP-Jacketed Hollow Point

Ballistics of Norma-Precision Centerfire Rifle Ammunition Manufactured in Sweden

Cartridge	Wt. Grs.	Bullet Type (a)	Velocity (fps) Muzzle	100 yds.	200 yds.	300 yds.	Energy (ft. lbs.) Muzzle	100 yds.	200 yds.	300 yds.	Max. Height of Trajectory (in.) 100 yds.	200 yds.	300 yds.
22 Hornet	45	SPS	2690	2030	1510	1150	720	410	230	130	Not Available		
220 Swift	50	PSP	4111	3611	3133	2681	1877	1448	1090	799	.2	.9	3.0
222 Remington	50	PSP	3200	2660	2170	1750	1137	786	523	340	.0	2.0	6.2
223	50	SPP	3300	2900	2520	2160	1330	1027	776	570	.4	2.4	6.8
22-250	50	SPS	3800	3300	2810	2350	1600	1209	885	613	Not Available		
	55	SPS	3650	3200	2780	2400	1637	1251	944	704	Not Available		
243 Winchester	75	HP	3500	3070	2660	2290	2041	1570	1179	873	.0	1.4	4.1
	100	PSP	3070	2790	2540	2320	2093	1729	1433	1195	.1	1.8	5.0
6mm Remington	100	SPS	3190	2920	2660	2420	2260	1890	1570	1300	.4	2.1	5.3
250 Savage	87	PSP	3032	2685	2357	2054	1776	1393	1074	815	.0	1.9	5.8
	100	PSP	2822	2514	2223	1956	1769	1404	1098	850	.1	2.2	6.6
257 Roberts	100	PSP	2900	2588	2291	2020	1868	1488	1166	906	.1	2.1	6.2
	120	PSP	2645	2405	2177	1964	1865	1542	1263	1028	.2	2.5	7.0
6.5 Carcano	156	SPRN	2000	1810	1640	1485	1386	1135	932	764	Not Available		

Appendix 5.

Ballistics of Norma-Precision Centerfire Rifle Ammunition (continued)

Cartridge	Wt. Grs.	Bullet Type (a)	Velocity (fps) Muzzle	100 yds.	200 yds.	300 yds.	Energy (ft. lbs.) Muzzle	100 yds.	200 yds.	300 yds.	Max. Height of Trajectory (in.) 100 yds.	200 yds.	300 yds.
6.5 Japanese	139	PSPBT	2428	2280	2130	1990	1820	1605	1401	1223	.3	2.8	7.7
6.5 × 54 MS	156	SPRN	2067	1871	1692	1529	1481	1213	992	810	.6	4.4	11.9
	139	PSPBT	2580	2420	2270	2120	2056	1808	1591	1388	.2	2.4	6.5
6.5 × 55	156	SPRN	2461	2240	2033	1840	2098	1738	1432	1173	.3	3.0	8.2
	139	PSPBT	2789	2630	2470	2320	2402	2136	1883	1662	.1	2.0	5.6
	156	SPRN	2493	2271	2062	1867	2153	1787	1473	1208	.3	2.9	7.9
270 Winchester	110	PSP	3248	2966	2694	2435	2578	2150	1773	1448	.1	1.4	4.3
	130	PSPBT	3140	2884	2639	2404	2847	2401	2011	1669	.1	1.6	4.7
	150	PSPBT	2802	2616	2436	2262	2616	2280	1977	1705	.0	2.0	5.7
7 × 57	110	PSP	3068	2792	2528	2277	2300	1904	1561	1267	.1	1.6	5.0
	150	PSPBT	2756	2539	2331	2133	2530	2148	1810	1516	.1	2.2	6.2
	175	SPRN	2490	2170	1900	1680	2410	1830	1403	1097	.4	3.3	9.0
7mm Remington Magnum	150	PSPSBT	3260	2970	2700	2450	3540	2945	2435	1990	.4	2.0	4.9
	175	SPRN	3070	2720	2400	2120	3660	2870	2240	1590	.5	2.4	6.1
7 × 61 S & H (26 in.)	160	PSPBT	3100	2927	2757	2595	3416	3045	2701	2393	.0	1.5	4.3
30 U.S. Carbine	110	SPRN	1970	1595	1300	1090	948	622	413	290	.8	6.4	19.0
30-30 Winchester	150	SPFP	2410	2075	1790	1550	1934	1433	1066	799	.9	4.2	11.0
	170	SPFP	2220	1890	1630	1410	1861	1349	1003	750	.7	4.1	11.9
308 Winchester	130	PSPBT	2900	2590	2300	2030	2428	1937	1527	1190	.1	2.1	6.2
	150	PSPBT	2860	2570	2300	2050	2725	2200	1762	1400	.1	2.0	5.9
	180	PSPBT	2610	2400	2210	2020	2725	2303	1952	1631	.2	2.5	6.6
	180	SPDC	2610	2400	2210	2020	2725	2303	1952	1631	.7	3.4	8.9
7.62 Russian	180	PSPBT	2624	2415	2222	2030	2749	2326	1970	1644	.2	2.5	6.6
308 Norma Magnum	180	DC	3100	2881	2668	2464	3842	3318	2846	2427	.0	1.6	4.6
30-06	130	PSPBT	3281	2951	2636	2338	3108	2514	2006	1578	.1	1.5	4.6
	150	PS	2972	2680	2402	2141	2943	2393	1922	1527	.1	1.9	5.7
	180	PSPBT, SPDC	2700	2494	2296	2109	2914	2487	2107	1778	.1	2.3	6.4
	220	SPRN	2411	2197	1996	1809	2840	2358	1947	1599	.3	3.1	8.5
300 H & H	180	PSPBT	2920	2706	2500	2297	3409	2927	2499	2109	.0	1.9	5.3
	220	SPRN	2625	2400	2170	1986	3367	2814	2301	1927	.2	2.5	7.0
7.65 Argentine	150	PSP	2920	2630	2355	2105	2841	2304	1848	1476	.1	2.0	5.8
303 British	130	PSP	2789	2483	2195	1929	2246	1780	1391	1075	.1	2.3	6.7
	150	PSP	2720	2440	2170	1930	2465	1983	1569	1241	.1	2.2	6.5
	180	PSPBT	2540	2340	2147	1965	2579	2189	1843	1544	.2	2.7	7.3
7.7 Japanese	130	PSP	2950	2635	2340	2065	2513	2004	1581	1231	.1	2.0	5.9
	180	PSPBT	2493	2292	2101	1922	2484	2100	1765	1477	.3	2.8	7.7
8 × 57 JR	196	SPRN	2362	2045	1761	1513	2428	1820	1530	996	.4	3.7	10.6
8 × 57 JS	123	PSP	2887	2515	2170	1857	2277	1728	1286	942	.1	2.3	6.8
	159	SPRN	2723	2362	2030	1734	2618	1970	1455	1062	.2	2.6	7.9
	196	SPRN	2526	2195	1894	1627	2778	2097	1562	1152	.3	3.1	9.1
358 Winchester	200	SPS	2530	2210	1910	1640	2843	2170	1621	1195	.4	3.1	8.8
	250	SPS	2250	2010	1780	1570	2811	2243	1759	1369	.6	3.9	10.4
358 Norma Magnum	250	SPS	2790	2493	2231	2001	4322	3451	2764	2223	.2	2.4	6.6
375 H & H Magnum	300	SPS	2550	2280	2040	1830	4333	3464	2773	2231	.3	2.8	7.6
44 Magnum	240	SPFP	1750				1640		Not Available				

(a) P-Pointed; SP-Soft Point; HP-Hollow Point; FP-Flat Point; RN-Round Nose; BT-Boat Tail; MC-Metal Case; DC-Dual Core; SPS-Semi-pointed Soft Point.

Appendix 5

Ballistics for Weatherby Magnum Ammunition
Supplied by Weatherby's Inc. for use in Weatherby Rifles

Cartridge	Wt. Grs.	Bullet Type (a)	Velocity (fps)				Energy (ft. lbs.)				Mid-Range Trajectory		
			Muzzle	100 yds.	200 yds.	300 yds.	Muzzle	100 yds.	200 yds.	300 yds.	100 yds.	200 yds.	300 yds.
224 Weatherby Varmintmaster	50	PE	3750	3160	2625	2140	1562	1109	765	508	0.7	3.6	9.0
224 Weatherby Varmintmaster	55	PE	3650	3150	2685	2270	1627	1212	881	629	0.4	1.7	4.5
240 Weatherby	70	PE	3850	3395	2975	2585	2304	1788	1376	1038	0.3	1.5	3.9
240 Weatherby	90	PE	3500	3135	2795	2475	2444	1960	1559	1222	0.4	1.8	4.5
240 Weatherby	100	PE	3395	3115	2850	2595	2554	2150	1804	1495	0.4	1.8	4.4
257 Weatherby	87	PE	3825	3290	2835	2450	2828	2087	1553	1160	0.3	1.6	4.4
257 Weatherby	100	PE	3555	3150	2815	2500	2802	2199	1760	1338	0.4	1.7	4.4
257 Weatherby	117	SPE	3300	2900	2550	2250	2824	2184	1689	1315	0.4	2.4	6.8
270 Weatherby	100	PE	3760	3265	2825	2435	3140	2363	1773	1317	0.4	1.6	4.3
270 Weatherby	130	PE	3375	3050	2750	2480	3283	2685	2183	1776	0.4	1.8	4.5
270 Weatherby	150	PE	3245	2955	2675	2430	3501	2909	2385	1967	0.5	2.0	5.0
7mm Weatherby	139	PE	3300	2995	2715	2465	3355	2770	2275	1877	0.4	1.9	4.9
7mm Weatherby	154	PE	3160	2885	2640	2415	3406	2874	2384	1994	0.5	2.0	5.0
300 Weatherby	150	PE	3545	3195	2890	2615	4179	3393	2783	2279	0.4	1.5	3.9
300 Weatherby	180	PE	3245	2960	2705	2475	4201	3501	2925	2448	0.4	1.9	5.2
300 Weatherby	220	SPE	2905	2610	2385	2150	4123	3329	2757	2257	0.6	2.5	6.7
340 Weatherby	200	PE	3210	2905	2615	2345	4566	3748	3038	2442	0.5	2.1	5.3
340 Weatherby	210	Nosler	3165	2910	2665	2435	4660	3948	3312	2766	0.5	2.1	5.0
340 Weatherby	250	SPE	2850	2580	2325	2090	4510	3695	3000	2425	0.6	2.7	6.7
378 Weatherby	270	SPE	3180	2850	2600	2315	6051	4871	4053	3210	0.5	2.0	5.2
378 Weatherby	300	SPE	2925	2610	2380	2125	5700	4539	3774	3009	0.6	2.5	6.2
460 Weatherby	500	RN	2700	2330	2005	1730	8095	6025	4465	3320	0.7	3.3	10.0

(a) PE-Pointed Expanding; SPE-Semi-Pointed Expanding; RN-Round Nose; Nosler-Nosler Partition Controlled Expansion Bullet. All velocities taken from 26-inch barrels.

Useful Firearms Data

Capacities of Popular Calibers

Here are capacities of popular calibers. Capacities are measured to the base of a normally seated bullet in the instance of straight cases, and to the junction of neck and shoulder in bottle neck cases. Cubic capacity is determined by weighing amount of water case will hold, and calculating from that the volume in both cubic inches and cubic centimeters.

Case	Grains Water	Cubic Inches	Cubic Cm.	Case	Grains Water	Cubic Inches	Cubic Cm.
.22 Hornet (late)	11.4	.045	.739	.270 Winchester	62.9	.250	4.07
.22 K-Hornet	13.4	.053	.870	.280 Remington	61.9	.245	4.00
.218 Bee	14.8	.059	.960	.284 Winchester	62.4	.247	4.04
.222 Remington	23.8	.094	1.54	7mm Mauser	53.2	.211	3.45
.22 Rem. Mag.	28.8	.094	1.87	7mm Rem. Mag.	79.9	.317	5.17
.223 Remington	28.3	.112	1.84	.30 Carbine	15.0	.059	.972
.219 Wasp	27.0	.107	1.76	.30/30 Winchester	35.8	.142	2.32
.219 Zipper	33.0	.131	2.14	.30 Remington	37.0	.147	2.39
.224 Weatherby	35.8	.142	2.32	.300 Savage	46.3	.184	3.00
.225 Winchester	38.0	.151	2.46	.30/40 Krag	47.5	.188	3.08
.22/250 Remington	42.1	.167	2.73	.308 Winchester	49.8	.198	3.23
.220 Swift	44.6	.177	2.89	.30/06 Springfield	61.3	.242	3.98
.243 Winchester	50.6	.200	3.28	.300 H & H Mag.	80.0	.318	5.18
6mm Remington	51.5	.204	3.33	.308 Norma Mag.	81.2	.322	5.27
.25/20 Winchester	14.6	.058	.946	.300 Win. Mag.	83.6	.332	5.42
.25/35 Winchester	33.7	.134	2.18	.300 Weatherby	91.7	.364	5.91
.25 Remington	35.3	.140	2.28	.303 Savage	34.3	.136	2.22
.250 Savage	42.0	.166	2.72	.303 British	45.9	.182	2.97
257 Roberts	53.7	.213	3.46	7.65mm Arg.	52.4	.208	3.39
6.5mm Jap.	44.0	.174	2.85	.32/40	33.4	.132	2.16
6.5mm M-S	45.0	.179	2.91	.32 Win. Special	35.8	.142	2.32
6.5x55mm	51.9	.206	3.36	.32 Remington	37.0	.147	2.39
6.5mm Rem. Mag.	66.1	.260	4.27	8x57mm Mauser	53.6	.212	3.46
.264 Win. Mag.	79.8	.318	5.17	.338 Win. Mag.	78.6	.313	5.09

The weight of water capacity given is simply a convenience of measurement—under no circumstances should this be interpreted as loading data or a charge recommendation for *any* powder. It is only a basis for comparison of case volume and bears no practical relationship to the amount of any particular powder that might constitute a safe load.

Capacities of Popular Calibers (continued)

Case	Grains Water	Cubic Inches	Cubic	Case	Grains Water	Cubic Inches	Cubic Cm.
.348 Winchester	66.4	.263	4.30	.32 S & W Long	9.5	.037	.615
.358 Winchester	45.7	.182	2.96	.32/20 Winchester	15.3	.061	.992
.35 Remington	40.2	.159	2.60	.38 S & W	7.0	.028	.454
.350 Rem. Mag.	62.2	.246	4.03	.380 Auto	6.0	.024	.388
.375 H & H Mag.	85.7	.340	5.53	9mm Luger	8.7	.035	.562
.38/40 Winchester	33.8	.134	2.19	.38 Super Auto	10.7	.043	.691
.38/55	37.5	.149	2.43	.38 Special	11.7	.047	.758
.444 Marlin	54.0	.214	3.50	.357 Magnum	15.2	.060	.984
.45/70	48.7	.194	4.16	.41 Rem. Mag.	21.0	.083	1.36
.458 Winchester	68.0	.270	4.40	.44 S & W Russian	18.8	.075	1.22
				.44 S & W Special	20.5	.081	1.33
HANDGUNS				.44 Rem. Mag.	25.2	.100	1.63
.22 Remington Jet	16.9	.067	1.09	.44/40 Winchester	32.6	.129	2.11
.221 Rem. Fireball	20.8	.083	1.35	.45 Auto Rim	13.8	.053	.862
.256 Winchester	19.0	.075	1.23	.45 A.C.P.	13.9	.055	.900
.32 S & W	3.3	.012	.214	.45 Colt	30.3	.119	1.96

Sectional Densities of Bullets

Following are *sectional densities of bullets* of popular weights in standard calibers.

Bullet	Sectional Density	Bullet	Sectional Density
22 CALIBER (.222″)		6.5mm (.264″)	
40 Gr.	.114	100 Gr.	.206
22 CALIBER (.223″)		129 Gr.	.266
45 Gr.	.128	140 Gr.	.288
22 CALIBER (.224″)		160 Gr.	.330
45 Gr.	.128	270 CALIBER (.277″)	
50 Gr.	.143	100 Gr.	.186
53 Gr.	.151	130 Gr.	.242
55 Gr.	.157	150 Gr.	.279
60 Gr.	.171	7mm(.284″)	
6mm (.243″)		120 Gr.	.212
70 Gr.	.169	139 Gr.	.246
75 Gr.	.181	154 Gr.	.273
87 Gr.	.210	175 Gr.	.310
100 Gr.	.241	7.35mm (.300″)	
25 CALIBER (.257″)		128 Gr.	.202
60 Gr.	.130	30 CALIBER (.308″)	
75 Gr.	.162	100 Gr.	.151
87 Gr.	.188	110 Gr.	.166
100 Gr.	.216	130 Gr.	.196
117 Gr.	.253	150 Gr.	.227

Sectional Densities of Bullets (continued)

Bullet	Sectional Density	Bullet	Sectional Density
165 Gr.	.247	158 Gr.	.177
168 Gr.	.253	35 CALIBER (.358″)	
170 Gr.	.257	200 Gr.	.224
180 Gr.	.272	250 Gr.	.280
190 Gr.	.286	275 Gr.	.308
220 Gr.	.332	375 CALIBER (.375″)	
303 CALIBER (.312″)		270 Gr.	.275
150 Gr.	.218	300 Gr.	.306
174 Gr.	.252	44 CALIBER (.429″)	
32 CALIBER (.321″)		240 Gr.	.186
170 Gr.	.234		
8mm (.323″)		44 CALIBER (.430″)	
150 Gr.	.206	265 Gr.	.204
170 Gr.	.233	45 CALIBER (.452″)	
338 CALIBER (.338″)		185 Gr.	.127
200 Gr.	.250	45 CALIBER (.454″)	
225 Gr.	.281	250 Gr.	.173
250 Gr.	.312	45 CALIBER (.458″)	
348 CALIBER (.348″)		300 Gr.	.206
200 Gr.	.236	350 Gr.	.243
35 CALIBER (.357″)		500 Gr.	.347

Weights and Measures

Following are tables of weights and measures that are frequently required in hand-loading problems that arise.

"Metric" and "U.S." Constants—Conversion Factors

Millimeters	×	.03937	Inches
"	×	25.4	"
Centimeters	×	.3937	"
"	×	2.54	"
Meters	×	39.37	" (Act of Congress)
"	×	3.281	Feet
"	×	1.094	Yard
Square mm.	×	.0155	Square Inches
" "	×	645.1	" "
Square cm.	×	.155	" "
" "	×	6.451	" "
Cubic cm.	×	16.383	Cubic inches
" "	×	3.69	Fluid drachms
" "	×	29.57	Fluid ounces
Grams	×	15.4324	Grains (Act of Congress)
" (water)	×	29.57	Fluid ounces
Grams	×	28.35	Ounces avoirdupois
Kilograms	×	2.2046	Pounds
"	×	35.3	Ounces avoirdupois
Kilograms per sq. cm. (Atmosphere)	×	14.223	Pounds per sq. in.
Kilogrammeters	×	7.233	Foot-pounds

Measures of Weight

AVOIRDUPOIS OR COMMERCIAL WEIGHT

1 gross or long ton equals 2240 pounds.
1 net or short ton equals 2000 pounds.
1 pound equals 16 ounces equals 7000 grains.
1 ounce equals 16 drachms equals 437.5 grains.

The following measures for weight are now seldom used in the United States:

1 hundredweight equals 4 quarters equals 112 pounds (1 gross or long ton equals 20 hundredweights); 1 quarter equals 28 pounds; 1 stone equals 14 pounds; 1 quintal equals 100 pounds.

TROY WEIGHT, USED FOR WEIGHING GOLD AND SILVER

1 pound equals 12 ounces equals 5760 grains.
1 ounce equals 20 pennyweights equals 480 grains.
1 pennyweight equals 24 grains.
1 carat (used in weighing diamonds) equals 3.168 grains.
1 grain Troy equals 1 grain avoirdupois equals 1 grain apothecaries' weight.

APOTHECARIES' WEIGHT

1 pound equals 12 ounces equals 5760 grains.
1 ounce equals 8 drachms equals 480 grains.
1 drachm equals 3 scriples equals 60 grains.
1 scruple equals 20 grains.

Weight of Square and Round Steel Bars in Pounds
Per Linear Foot

Based on 489.6 lbs. per cubic foot. For wrought iron deduct 2 per cent. For high-speed steel add 11 per cent.

Thickness or Diameter Inches	Weight of Sq. Bar 1 Ft. Long	Weight of Round Bar 1 Ft. Long	Thickness or Diameter Inches	Weight of Sq. Bar 1 Ft. Long	Weight of Round Bar 1 Ft. Long
			$7/8$	2.603	2.044
			$15/16$	2.989	2.347
			1	3.400	2.670
			$1^1/16$	3.838	3.014
			$1^1/8$	4.303	3.379
$1/32$	.0033	.0026	$1^3/16$	4.795	3.766
$1/16$	.0133	.0104	$1^1/4$	5.312	4.173
$1/8$	.0531	.0417	$1^5/16$	5.857	4.600
$3/16$	.1195	.0938	$1^3/8$	6.428	5.019
$1/4$	.2123	.1669	$1^7/16$	7.026	5.518
$5/16$	.3333	.2608	$1^1/2$	7.650	6.008
$3/8$	.4782	.3756	$1^9/16$	8.301	6.520
$7/16$	.6508	.5111	$1^5/8$	8.978	7.051
$1/2$	.8500	.6676	$1^{11}/16$	9.682	7.604
$9/16$	1.076	.8449	$1^3/4$	10.41	8.178
$5/8$	1.328	1.043	$1^{13}/16$	11.17	8.773
$11/16$	1.608	1.262	$1^7/8$	11.95	9.388
$3/4$	1.913	1.502	$1^{15}/16$	12.76	10.02
$13/16$	2.245	1.763	2	13.60	10.68

Conversion Table: Millimeters to Inches

MM	.0	.1	.2	.3	.4	.5	.6	.7	.8	.9
0	—	.003937	.007874	.01181	.015748	.019685	.023622	.027559	.031496	.035433
1	.03937	.043307	.047244	.051181	.055118	.059055	.062992	.066929	.070866	.074803
2	.07874	.082677	.086614	.090551	.094488	.098425	.102362	.106299	.110236	.114173
3	.11811	.122047	.125984	.129921	.133858	.137795	.141732	.145669	.149606	.153543
4	.157480	.161417	.165354	.169291	.173228	.177165	.181102	.185039	.188976	.192913
5	.196850	.200787	.204724	.208661	.212598	.216535	.220472	.224409	.228346	.232283
6	.236220	.240157	.244094	.248031	.251968	.255905	.259842	.263779	.267716	.271653
7	.275590	.279527	.283464	.287401	.291338	.295275	.299212	.303149	.307086	.311023
8	.314960	.318897	.322834	.326771	.330708	.334645	.338582	.342519	.346456	.350393
9	.354330	.358267	.362204	.366141	.370078	.374015	.377952	.381889	.385826	.389763
10	.393700	.397637	.401574	.405511	.409448	.413385	.417322	.421259	.425196	.429133
11	.433070	.437007	.440944	.444881	.448818	.452755	.456692	.460629	.464566	.468503
12	.472440	.476377	.480314	.484251	.488188	.492125	.496062	.499999	.503936	.507873
13	.511810	.515747	.519684	.523621	.527558	.531495	.535432	.539369	.543306	.547243
14	.551180	.555117	.559054	.562991	.566928	.570865	.574902	.578739	.582676	.586613
15	.590550	.594487	.598424	.602361	.606298	.610235	.614172	.618109	.622046	.625983
16	.629920	.633857	.637794	.641731	.645668	.649605	.653542	.657479	.661416	.665353
17	.669290	.673227	.677164	.681101	.685038	.688975	.692912	.696849	.700786	.704723
18	.708660	.712597	.716534	.720471	.724408	.728345	.732282	.736219	.740156	.744093
19	.748030	.751967	.755904	.759841	.763778	.767715	.771652	.775589	.779526	.783463
20	.787400	.791337	.795274	.799211	.803148	.807085	.811022	.814959	.818896	.822833
21	.826770	.830707	.834644	.838581	.842518	.846455	.850392	.854329	.858266	.862203
22	.866140	.870077	.874014	.877951	.881888	.885825	.889762	.893699	.897636	.901573
23	.905510	.909447	.913384	.917321	.921258	.925195	.929132	.933069	.937006	.940943
24	.944880	.948817	.952754	.956691	.960628	.964565	.968502	.972439	.976376	.980313
25	.984250	.988187	.992124	.996061	.999998	1.003935	1.007872	1.011809	1.015746	1.019683
26	1.023620	1.027557	1.031494	1.035431	1.039368	1.043305	1.047242	1.051179	1.055116	1.059053
27	1.062990	1.066927	1.070864	1.074801	1.078738	1.082675	1.086612	1.090549	1.094486	1.098423
28	1.102360	1.106797	1.110234	1.114171	1.118108	1.122045	1.125982	1.129919	1.133856	1.137793
29	1.141730	1.145667	1.149604	1.153541	1.157478	1.161415	1.165352	1.169289	1.173226	1.177163
30	1.181100	—	—	—	—	—	—	—	—	—

Decimal Equivalents of Fractions of an Inch

$1/64$	0.015625	$17/64$	0.265625	$33/64$	0.515625
$1/32$	0.03125	$9/32$	0.28125	$17/32$	0.53125
$3/64$	0.046875	$19/64$	0.296875	$35/64$	0.546875
$1/16$	0.0625	$5/16$	0.3125	$9/16$	0.5625
$5/64$	0.078125	$21/64$	0.328125	$37/64$	0.578125
$3/32$	0.09375	$11/32$	0.34375	$19/32$	0.59375
$7/64$	0.109375	$32/64$	0.359375	$39/64$	0.609375
$1/8$	0.125	$3/8$	0.375	$5/8$	0.625
$9/64$	0.140625	$25/64$	0.390625	$41/64$	0.640625
$5/32$	0.15625	$13/32$	0.40625	$21/32$	0.65625
$11/64$	0.171875	$27/64$	0.421875	$43/64$	0.671875
$3/16$	0.1875	$7/16$	0.4375	$11/16$	0.6875
$13/64$	0.203125	$29/64$	0.453125	$45/64$	0.703125
$7/32$	0.21875	$15/32$	0.46875	$23/32$	0.71875
$15/64$	0.23475	$31/64$	0.484375	$47/64$	0.734375
$1/4$	0.250	$1/2$	0.500	$3/4$	0.750
$49/64$	0.765625	$27/32$	0.84375	$59/64$	0.921875
$25/32$	0.78125	$55/64$	0.859375	$15/16$	0.9375
$51/64$	0.796875	$7/8$	0.875	$61/64$	0.953125
$13/16$	0.8125	$57/64$	0.890625	$31/32$	0.96875
$53/64$	0.828125	$29/32$	0.90625	$63/64$	0.984375

Appendix 7

Abbreviations

AE: Automatic Ejectors
AP: Armor Piercing in reference to bullets.
API: Armor Piercing Incendiary in reference to bullets.
AR: Automatic Rifle
AS: Automatic Safety

BB: Bevel Base in reference to bullets.
BC: Ballistic Coefficient in reference to bullets.
BC: Battery Cup primer.
BN: Bottle Neck in reference to a cartridge case.
BP: Black Powder
BPE: Black Powder Express in a cartridge designation.
BT: Boat Tail in reference to bullets; Beaver Tail in reference to stocks.

CF: Centerfire
CI: Center of Impact
CT: Copper Tube in a bullet designation.

DA: Double action in a handgun.
DB: Double Barrel in reference to a gun; Double Base in reference to powder.
Den: Headstamp for Denver Ordnance Plant.
DST: Double Set Trigger
DT: Double Trigger
DWM: Deutsche Waffenundmunitions Fabrik, used as a headstamp and as a prefix to numerical cartridge designations.

EC: Headstamp for Evansville/Chrysler Ammunition plant.
Ex: Excellent in NRA condition standards.
ECS: Headstamp for Evansville/Chrysler/Sunbeam Ammunition plant.

F: Fair in NRA condition standards.
F: Fire, in reference to a gun safety.
FA: Headstamp for Frankford Arsenal.
FB: Flat Base in reference to bullets.
FC: Full Choke in reference to shotguns; Full Charge in reference to ammunition.
FC or **FCC:** Federal Cartridge Corporation headstamp.
FP: Foot-Pounds in reference to energy.
FPS: Feet per Second in reference to velocity.
FP: Full Patch (FMJ) in reference to bullets.
FMJ: Full Metal Jacket in reference to bullets.
FS: Full Stock.
FW: Featherweight.

G (Gew.): *Gewehr,* German word for rifle.
G: Good in NRA condition standards.
GC: Gas Check in reference to bullets.
GR: G. Roth, used as a headstamp and as a prefix to numerical cartridge designations.

H: Hodgdon (B.E.) as a prefix in a powder designation.
HB: Hollow Base in reference to bullets; Heavy Barrel in reference to barrels.

HE: Hand Ejector (ejection) in reference to a revolver.

H&H: Holland & Holland, old-line British gun-making firm sometimes called "Holland's."

HJ: Half Jacket in reference to bullets.

HP: Hollow Point in reference to bullets; High Power in reference to cartridge or gun designations.

Hy: Hornady Manufacturing Company.

IC: Improved Cylinder Choke.

IL: Inside Lubricated in reference to bullets.

Imp: Improved in a cartridge designation.

IMR: Improved Military Powder as a prefix in a powder designation.

JHP: Jacketed Hollow Point in reference to Super Vel bullets.

JSP: Jacketed Soft Point in reference to Super Vel bullets.

K (Kar.): Karabine, German word for carbine.

L: Lead in reference to bullets.

LC: Headstamp for Lake City Arsenal.

LC: Long Colt, in reference to handgun cartridges.

LE: Lee Enfield rifle.

LGS: Lyman Gun Sight Co.

LMG: Light Machine Gun

LP: Large Pistol primer

LR: Large Rifle primer

LW: Light Weight

M: Model, as M-16 rifle.

Mag: Magazine

MC: Metal Case in reference to bullets; Monte-Carlo style comb in reference to stocks.

MC or Mod.: Modified Choke

ME: Muzzle Energy of a bullet in foot pounds.

MH: Martini-Henry rifle or Merwin Hulbert revolver.

MK: Mark, sometimes used instead of M or Model, as in Revolver, .455, MKVI.

MOA: Minute of Angle

MP: Metal Point or Metal Piercing in reference to bullets.

MR: Mean Radius, average shot distance from center of impact.

MRT: Mid-Range Trajectory height

MS: Mannlicher-Schoenauer rifle

MV: Muzzle Velocity of a bullet in feet per second.

N: Norma Projectilfabrik as a prefix in a powder designation.

NC: Non-Corrosive in reference to primers.

NE: Nitro Express in a cartridge designation.

NE: Non-Ejector

NM: National Match, in reference to guns, equipment, or ammunition manufactured or selected specifically for the U.S. National Rifle & Pistol Matches.

NMNC: Non-Mercuric, Non-Corrosive in reference to primers.

NSE: Non-Selective Ejectors

OL: Outside lubricated in reference to bullets.

OP: Over Powder wad; Open Point in reference to bullets.

OU: Over-under, barrels place one above the other. Sometimes indicates "Superposed."

OS: Over Shot wad

PB: Plain Base in reference to bullets.

PC or PCC: Peters Cartridge Co., in reference to a headstamp or ammunition label.

PG: Pistol Grip

PP: Paper Patch in reference to bullets.

PP: Power-Point (Winchester) or protected point, in reference to bullets; Police Positive in reference to Colt Revolvers; Pistole Polizei (Police Pistol) in reference to Walther pistols.

PPC: Police Pistol Course, a course of fire used in training police in handgun marksmanship.

PSP: Pointed Soft Point in reference to bullets.

QD: Quick Detachable

R: Sturm, Ruger, Inc.

RB: Rolling Block (Remington) rifle or pistol

RE: Recoil Energy

Rem-UMC: Remington-Union Metallic Cartridge Co.

RF: Rapid Fire in reference to target shooting.

RF: Rim Fire in reference to ammunition.

RGS: Redfield Gun Sight Co.

R-P: Remington-Peters

RPM: Rounds per Minute in reference to cyclic rate of fire of an automatic weapon.

RV: Recoil Velocity

S: Safe, in reference to a gun safety.

SA: Savage Arms

SA: Single Action in a handgun; also Springfield Armory.

SAA: Single Action Army, a Colt revolver.

SBS: Side-By-Side in reference to double barrel guns.

SA: Sierra Products

SB: Single Base Powder

SD: Sectional Density in reference to bullets.

SF: Slow Fire

SL: Headstamp for St. Louis Ordnance Plant.

SMG: Submachine Gun

SMLE: Short Magazine Lee Enfield rifle

SO: Secant Ogive, a term used by Hornady to describe a particular form of bullet ogive.

SP: Small Pistol primer

Sp.: Speer Products

SP: Spire Point or Soft Point in reference to bullets.

Spcl: Special, as in .44 Special, in a cartridge designation

Spitz: Spitzer (pointed) bullet

SR: Small Rifle primer

SR: Semi-Rimmed in reference to a cartridge case.

SRC: Saddle Ring Carbine

SS: Single Shot

SST: Single Selective Trigger; also single set trigger.

ST: Set Trigger or Single Trigger

ST: Silvertip (Winchester-Western) in reference to bullets.

S&W: Smith & Wesson

SWC: Semi Wadcutter in reference to bullets.

S&W/F: Smith & Wesson Fiocci

SV: Super Vel Cartridge Corp.

SX: Super X (Winchester-Western) in cartridge designations; also designates a form of varmint bullet by Hornady.

TD: Take Down

TW: Headstamp for Twin Cities Arsenal.

TF: Timed Fire

Tr: Tracer in reference to bullets.

UMC: Union Metallic Cartridge Co.

Var: Variable, indicating variable magnification in a scope sight.

VG: Very Good in NRA condition standards.

VR: Ventilated Rib

WC: Wad Cutter in reference to bullets.

WCC: Headstamp for Western Cartridge Co.

WRA: Winchester Repeating Arms Co.

W-W: Winchester-Western

X: Single-diameter magnification, ie, 3X is magnification of 3 diameters.

Foreign Gun Terms

ENGLISH	FRENCH	GERMAN	SPANISH
action	*fonctionnement*	*Arbeitsspiel*	*acción*
ammunition	*munition*	*Munition*	*munición*
army	*armée*	*Armee*	*ejército*
arsenal	*arsenal*	*Arsenal*	*arsenal*
ballistics	*balistique*	*Schießlehre, Ballistik*	*balística*
band	*grenadière*	*Ring*	*anillo del cañon*
barrel	*canon*	*Lauf*	*cañon*
barrel length	*longueur de canon*	*Lauflänge*	*largo de cañon*
bayonet	*baionnette*	*Seitengewehr*	*bayonetta*
bipod	*bipied*	*Zweibein*	*bípode*
blowback	*recul*	*Rückstoß*	*retrocéso*
bolt (or breech)	*culasse mobile*	*Verschlußstück*	*suporte del cierre*
bore	*âme*	*Laufinneres*	*ánima*
bore diameter			*diámetro de ánima*
box magazine	*boîte-chargeur*	*Stangenmagazin*	*cargador en barra*
bullet	*balle*	*Geschoß*	*balla*
butt	*crosse*	*Kolben*	*culata*
caliber	*calibre*	*Kaliber*	*calibre*
carbine	*carabine*	*Karabiner*	*carabina*
cartridge	*cartouche*	*Patrone*	*cartucho*
cartridge case	*douille*	*Patronenhülse*	*vaina*
cartridge case rim		*Hülsenrand*	*reborde de vaina*
centerfire	*cartouche à amorce centre*		*cartucho de percusión central*
chamber	*chambre*	*Patronenlager*	*la recámera*
clip (charger)	*lame-chargeur*	*Patronenrahmen, Ladestreifen*	*cargador*
cocking handle	*poignée d'armement*	*Spannhebel oder-griff*	*palanca de cargar*
compensator	*armortisseur de recul*	*Mündungsbremse oder Rückstoßbremse*	*freno de boca*

ENGLISH	FRENCH	GERMAN	SPANISH
corrosion	corrosion	Feuergeschwindigkeit/Kadenz	corrosivo
cyclic rate of fire	cadence de tir	Zylinder	cadencia
cylinder	barillet	Unterbrecher	cilindro
disconnector	disjoncteur	Auswerfer	interruptor
ejector	éjecteur		expulsor
ejection port	fenêtre d'éjection	Auswurföffnung	ventana de expulsión
elevation	hausse	Erhöhung	elevación
energy	énergie	Energie	energía
erosion	érosion	Rohrabnutzung, Ausbrennung	erosión; degaste
extractor	extracteur	Auszieher	extractor
feet per second	pied par seconde	Fuß/sec.	f/sec.
firing pin	percuteur	Nadel	percutor
front sight	guidon	Korn	punto de mira
fore stock	sous-garde	Vorderschaft	culata delantera
full automatic	automatique	Vollautomatisch	automático
gas	gaz	Gas	gas
gas operated	fonctionnat par ratour de gaz	Gasdrucklader	arma de carga por toma de gases
grip	poignée	Griffstück	empuñadura
grip safety	sûreté de poignée	Griffsicherung	serguro de empuñadura
groove	rayure	Nute, Zug	raya
hammer	chien (revolver); percuteur (automatic weapon)	Hammer oder Schlagstück	martillo
handguard	guarde-main	Handschutz	guardamano
head		Reibfläche, Patronenboden	culote
headspace	feuillure	Verschlußabstand	holgura de culote
holdopen device	arretoir de culasse	Verschlußfang	palanca de agarre del cierre
housing	carcasse	Gehäuse	cajón de mecanismo
integral firing pin	percuteur fixe	Fester Schlagbolzen	percutor fijo
left-hand twist	raya à gauche	Linksdrall	rayado de paso izquierdo
line of sight	ligne de visée	Visierlinie (ballistics); Schußlinie (gunnery)	línea de mira
lock	culasse verrouillée	Verriegelter Verschluß	cierre
locked breech	mitrailleuse	Maschinengewhr	cierre blogueado
machine gun	chargeur	Magazin, Munitionslager; Kasten (rifle)	ametralladora
magazine		Magazin-Kapazität	cargador
magazine capacity	capacité du chargeur	Magazin-Halter	capacidad de cargador
magazine catch	arretoir du chargeur		palanca de enganchar del cargador

ENGLISH	FRENCH	GERMAN	SPANISH
magazine follower	transporteur	Zubringer	transportador
magazine housing	gaine de chargeur	Magazingehäuse	cajón del cargador
magazine spring	ressort de chargeur	Magazin-Feder	muelle del cargador
magazine-type feed	mechanisme d'alimentation	Art der Patronenzuführung	modo de guía del cartucho
mechanism	mechanisme	Mechanismus	mecanismo
metallic sight	appareil de visée	Visier	mira abierta
military	militaire	Militärisch	de modo militar
model	type	Modell	modelo
muzzle	bouche, gueule	Mündung	boca
muzzle energy		Mündungsarbeit, Mündungsenergie	energía inicial
muzzle loader			pieza de avancarga
muzzle velocity	vitesse initiale	Mündungs-Geschwindigkeit	velocidad inicial
nipple	mamelon	Nippel	pezón
number of lands and grooves	nombre de rayures	Anzahl de Felder und Züge	numero del rayado
open U notch	cran de mire	Offene U Kimme	alza en forma del U
peep sight	hausse oeilleton	Lochkimme	alza de mirilla
pin	goupille	Stift	pasador
pistol	pistolet	Pistole	pistola
pressure	pression	Druck	presión
primer	amorce, étoupille	Zündhütchen	cápsula fulminante
projectile	projectile	Geschoß	proyectil
propellant	poudre	Treibmittel	carga de proyección
range	distance	Entfernung	distancia
receiver	boîte de culasse	Hülse (pistol & rifle); Griffstück (pistol)	cajón de los mecanismos
receiver housing	carcasse	Verschluß-Gehäuse	cajón del cierre
rear sight	hausse	Visier	puntería
recoil	recul	Rücklauf, Rückstoß	retroceso
revolver	revolver	Revolver	revolver
rifle	fusil	Gewehr	fusil
rifling	rayure, rainure	Drall	rayado
right-hand twist	raye a droite	Rechtsdrall	rayado de paso derecho
rim fire	cartouche à amorce périphérique		cartucho de percusión excéntrica

ENGLISH	FRENCH	GERMAN	SPANISH
rounds	coups	Schuß	tiros
rounds per minute	coups minute	Schuß per Minute	tiros por minuto (cadencia)
safety	mécanisme de sécurité	Sicherung	seguro
safety catch (or lever)	levier de sécurité	Sicherungs-Flügel	palanca de seguro
screw	écrou	Schraube	tornillo
sear	gâchette	Abzugsstollen (rifle); Abzugsstange (pistol)	fiador
selective fire	semi automatique ou automatique	Wahlweises Feuer	tiro elegible
selector	selecteur	Umschalthebel	palanca de cambiar
self-loading	a chargement automatique	Selbstladepistole (pistol); Selbstladegewehr (rifle)	autocarga
semi-automatic	semi automatique	Halbautomatisch	semiautomático
separate firing pin	percuteur mobile	Loser Schlagbolzen	percutor aparte
service	service	Dienst	servisio
shotgun	fusil de chasse	Flinte, Schrotgewehr	escopeta
shotshell		Schrotpatrone	cartucho de escopeta
sights	système de visée	Visierung	puntería
sling	bretelle	Riemen	correa
sling swivel	battant de grenadière	Riemenbügel	hebillo de la correa
spring	ressort	Feder	muelle
stock	fut	Schaft	culata
submachine gun	pistolet-mitrailleur	Maschinenpistole	pistola ametralladora
telescopic sights	hausse télescopique	Zielfernrohr, Richtfernrohr, Optik	anteojo de puntería
trajectory	trajectoire	Flugbahn	trayectoria
trigger	detende	Abzug	gatillo
trigger guard	pontet	Abzugsbügel	guardamonte
type	type	Typ	tipo
velocity	vélocité	Geschwindigkeit	velocidad
weight, loaded	poids-chargé	Gewicht, geladen	peso cargado
weight of loaded magazine	poids du chargeur	Gewicht des geladenen Magazins	peso del cargador lleno
weight, unloaded	poids non chargé	Gewicht, ungeladen	peso del cargador vacío
wooden stock	fut en bois	Holzschaft	culata de madera

Index

Index